Democracy, Security, Peace

Series Editor Prof Dr Michael Brzoska

DSP Volume 217

A publication of the Institute for Peace Research
and Security Policy at the University of Hamburg

Mayeul Hiéramente/Patricia Schneider (Eds.)

The Defence in International Criminal Trials

Observations on the Role of the Defence at the ICTY, ICTR and ICC

Nomos

Die Deutsche Nationalbibliothek lists this publication in the Deutsche Nationalbibliografie; detailed bibliographic data is available in the Internet at http://dnb.d-nb.de

ISBN 978-3-8487-3137-4 (Print)
978-3-8452-7510-9 (ePDF)

British Library Cataloguing-in-Publication Data
A catalogue record for this book is available from the British Library.

ISBN 978-3-8487-3137-4 (Print)
978-3-8452-7510-9 (ePDF)

Library of Congress Cataloging-in-Publication Data
Hiéramente, Mayeul / Schneider, Patricia
The Defence in International Criminal Trials
Observations on the Role of the Defence at the ICTY, ICTR and ICC
Mayeul Hiéramente / Patricia Schneider (Eds.)
279 p.

ISBN 978-3-8487-3137-4 (Print)
978-3-8452-7510-9 (ePDF)

1. Edition 2016

Inhalt

Abkürzungsverzeichnis 7

Benjamin Ferencz
Preface 11

Heiko Ahlbrecht
Vorwort 15

Colleen Rohan
The Defence in International Criminal Trials:
Important Actor or Necessary Evil? 17

Mayeul Hiéramente
Die Deutungshoheit im Gerichtssaal oder
„Die Bändigung des Ungeheuers"
Anmerkungen zum sich selbst verteidigenden Angeklagten 29

Philipp Graebke
Die Verteidigung im Verfahren gegen Adolf Eichmann 51

Julia Gebhard
Arguing Human Rights from the Bench?
How Judges in International Criminal Courts
Perceive International Human Rights Law 72

Marie O'Leary
Compelling Fair Trials: The Necessity of Effective
Court Powers to Ensure a Defendant's Right "to examine,
or have examined, the witnesses against him or her" 93

Masha Fedorova
Disclosure of Information as an Instrument Ensuring Equality
of Arms in International Criminal Proceedings 115

Eleni Chaitidou and Elisa Hoven
The Person's Liberty at Stake –
A Tour d'Horizon on the Rights of the Arrested Person
under the Rome Statute 149

Sally Alexandra Longworth
Sentencing at the International Criminal Court 200

Isabel Düsterhöft and Dominic Kennedy
How to Manage the Defence – Experiences from the ADC-ICTY 227

Philipp Müller
Promoting Justice between Independence and Institutional Constraints: The Role of the Office of the Public Counsel of the Defence at the ICC 245

Mayeul Hiéramente und Patricia Schneider
Kein faires Verfahren ohne effektive Verteidigung – Zusammenfassende Bemerkungen zu einem vergessenen Akteur der internationalen Strafjustiz und Ausblick 269

Abkürzungsverzeichnis

ACHR	African Charter on Human and Peoples' Rights
A. Ch.	Appeals Chamber
Abs.	Absatz
ADAD	Association des Avocats de la Défense
ADC-ICTY	Association of Defence Counsel - The International Criminal Tribunal for the former Yugoslavia
Art	Article/Artikel
ASP	The Assembly of States Parties
CAT	Convention against Torture
CICC	Coalition for the International Criminal Court
CSS	Counsel Support Section
DCC	Decision on the Confirmation of Charge
DM	Deutsche Mark
DRC	Democratic Republic of the Congo
e.g.	for example, zum Beispiel (exempli gratia)
ECCC	Extraordinary Chambers in the Courts of Cambodia
ECHR	European Court of Human Rights
ECOSOC	United Nations Economic and Social Council
ECtHR	European Court of Human Rights
EDS	Electronic Disclosure System
EGMR	Europäischer Gerichtshof für Menschenrechte
EMRK	Europäische Menschenrechtskonvention
ESCOR	Economic and Social Council Official Records
ETS	European Treaty Series
EU	European Union / Europäische Union
FPLC	Forces Patriotiques pour la Libération du Congo
GAOR	General Assembly Official Records
HRC	Human Rights Committee
HRL	Human Rights Law
IACtHR	Inter-American Court of Human Rights
IAGMR	Interamerikanischer Gerichtshof für Menschenrechte
IBA	The International Bar Association
IPbpR	Internationaler Pakt über bürgerliche und politische Rechte
ICC	International Criminal Court
ICCPR	International Covenant on Civil and Political Rights

ICJ	International Court of Justice
ICL	International Criminal Law
ICLB	International Criminal Law Bureau
ICRC	International Committee of the Red Cross
ICTR	International Criminal Tribunal for Rwanda / Internationales Straftribunal für Ruanda
ICTY	International Criminal Tribunal for the Former Yugoslavia
IFOR	Implementation Force
IFSH	Institut für Friedensforschung und Sicherheitspolitik an der Universität Hamburg
IGH	Internationaler Gerichtshof
ILC	International Law Commission
IStGH	Internationaler Strafgerichtshof
IT	Information and Technology Informationen und Technologie
LAS	Legal Advisory Section
MICT	Mechanism for International Criminal Tribunals
Mio.	Million(en)
NMT / IMT	Nuremberg Military Tribunal / International Military Tribunal
NNG	Nazis and Nazi Collaborators (Punishment) Law
NS	Nationalsozialistisch
NSDAP	Nationalsozialistische Deutsche Arbeiterpartei
ODIHR	Office for Democratic Institutions and Human Rights
OLA	Office of Legal Affairs
OLAD	The Office of Legal Aid and Defence
OPCD	Office of the Public Counsel for the Defence (ICC)
OSCE	Organization for Security and Co-operation in Europe
OSZE	Organisation für Sicherheit und Zusammenarbeit in Europa
OTP	Office of the Prosecutor
PIDS	Public Information and Documentation Section
PIU	Public Information Unit
PTC	Pre-Trial Chamber
Res.	Resolution
RPE	Rules of Procedure and Evidence
RSHA	Reichssicherheitshauptamt
RUF	Revolutionary United Front

SCOR	Security Council Official Records
SCSL	Special Court for Sierra Leone
SD	Sicherheitsdienst des Reichsführers SS
SS	Schutzstaffel der NSDAP
StIGH	Ständiger Internationaler Gerichtshof
STL	Special Tribunal for Lebanon
StPO	Strafprozessordnung
T. Ch.	Trial Chamber
UN	United Nations
UNGA	United Nations General Assembly
UNHCR	United Nations High Commissioner for Refugees
UNICRI	United Nations Interregional Crime and Justice Research Institute
UNSC	United Nations Security Council
UNTS	United Nations Treaty Series
UPC (RP)	Union des Patriotes Congolais (Réconciliation et Paix)
VPRS	Victims Participation and Reparations Unit
VWU	Victims and Witnesses Unit

Benjamin Ferencz[*]

Preface

This is being written on November 20, 2015, which is exactly 70 years after the trial against Nazi war criminals began before the International Military Tribunal at Nuremberg. Since that time many new international courts have been created and international trials are now in process trying defendants from many lands for the most atrocious crimes committed against other human beings. Despite current shortcomings there can be no doubt that the progress toward applying the rule of law has been very impressive particularly if one recognizes that the newborn institutions are prototypes that will be improved with time.

I am now in my 96th year. I have tried only two criminal cases in my life. The first was in one of the subsequent Nuremberg proceedings (the *Einsatzgruppen* case), in which 22 defendants were convicted of the calculated murder of over 1 million people, including thousands of children killed one shot at a time. I was assisted by a staff of three other prosecutors and each defendant was entitled to counsel of his choice and an assistant. We were thus outnumbered by at least 10:1. I was then 27 years old. The second case was when I was invited to make the closing remarks in the first prosecution by the new International Criminal Court in The Hague, for the creation of which I had labored for half a century. I was then 92 years old.

My determination to pursue the rule of law was driven to large extent by my personal experiences as a combat soldier in World War II. I participated in every major battle of the war in Europe. As a sergeant in General Patton's army I joined the liberating forces entering several Nazi concentration camps to gather evidence for future war crimes trials. The horrors I personally witnessed are incomprehensible to any rational mind.

The law has never been static but has always evolved to meet the needs of the society it was designed to protect. The evolution of international criminal law has been an ongoing process. The fair trial for adversaries defeated in war is a relatively modern invention. Indeed, the notion of humane treatment for all combatants is a principle still being espoused in many quarters but practiced by very few. "The Defence in International Criminal Trials" gives rise to many questions and problems which deserve consideration. It is not merely a matter of protecting the rights of an accused criminal suspect. The social interest of the public should always be a primary consideration. Punishment of convicted offenders should always have, as its principal objective, the deterrence of criminal behavior by others. In order for the de-

---

* Benjamin B. Ferencz, J. D. Harvard Law School 1943. All of his writings and lectures are available free on his website, www.benferencz.org.

terrent effect to have a lasting impact it is vital that the trials are open to public scrutiny and to be so conducted that the fairness will never be challenged despite the gravity of the offense. We owe that much to ourselves as well as to the accused.

If the rule of law is to be effective criminal trials must be able to reveal the truth. If the public feels that truth has been distorted the outcome will lose all credibility. On the contrary, acquittals based on false testimony or evidence will serve only to enhance more crime. It is not the primary responsibility of the defense counsel to obtain the freedom of the client by illegal or impermissible means.

Unfortunately, we have not yet developed an effective international criminal system which can ensure justice through judicial process everywhere. Humanitarian interventions are frequently a subterfuge for nations to obtain their own political or economic goals. The statutes for the International Criminal Court as well as other tribunals require both judges and prosecutors to take all facts and circumstances into account. Where it is clear that humanitarian intervention imposes a legitimate responsibility (R2P) it will be up to the court and the prosecutor, and not the protagonists, to determine whether force is permissible. Morality may determine whether a trial is justified or sentences should be mitigated. These dilemmas remain a gray zone which should be clarified as international criminal law is further developed. All persons, regardless of the magnitude of the crime, are entitled to a fair trial and an opportunity to explain their motivation and deeds. Unfortunately, our current world order still lacks unbiased and competent judicial tribunals to judge the legality or acceptability of many deeds which large numbers of the population hold to be contemptible crimes. It is not up to the parties or their allies to decide which side is right and which side is wrong. That requires an independent judgment, which is recognized and acceptable to the world community. As long as that instrument is lacking or lacks enforcement capability the protagonists will continue to slaughter each other as they have always done and continue to do now.

The Nuremberg Tribunals recognized that illegal warfare is the supreme international crime because all of the other crimes are committed when groups or nations consider themselves to be at war. Crimes are committed by individuals and those who are responsible for the massive cruelties should not be able to obtain asylum by politically organized amnesties.

When the United Nations Charter was accepted it was anticipated that the work of the Nuremberg Tribunals would be continued by establishing a permanent International Criminal Court which would be governed by a code of punishable international crimes. Defining aggression was assigned to a stream of different committees. By 1974, the General Assembly approved "a consensus definition of aggression" reached by the appropriate Special Committee. However, major powers were not prepared to entrust any independent tribunal with authority to determine whether their use of armed force was legal or criminal. Seventy years after the Nuremberg trials and years of debate by learned jurists, it is pathetic to argue that the supreme international crime – the one word "aggression" – could not be properly defined. The political will remains absent and the world remains in increasing peril.

It is a pity that, despite almost 70 years of effort by many learned lawyers, the Kampala amended definition of aggression of June 2010 remains full of loopholes and ambiguities . Calling the illegal use of force in violation of the UN Charter a punishable "crime against humanity" under ICC, domestic, and universal jurisdiction serves as a clearer warning to perpetrators everywhere that there will be no place to hide. It is high time to stop playing deceptive games with the future of humankind.

Layers who are interested in peace and a more humane world order should denounce the illegal use of force as a crime against humanity. The ICC Statute condemns as crimes against humanity, such acts as murder, apartheid, torture, rape, and similar abominations. It allows the punishment of "other inhumane acts." Similar provisions exist in many national criminal codes. The UN Charter prohibits the use of armed force except in self-defense against an armed attack or if mandated by the Security Council. Those individuals who are responsible for violating that fundamental principle should be brought before a court to explain and try to justify their action. The public will be able to decide whether the killing of innocent civilians can be justified or whether it is a punishable crime despite the arguments of the defense counsel and their clients and friends. The court of public opinion will be the final arbiter of what actions are justifiable or worthy of punishment adequate to deter such behavior in the future.

We have yet to learn that you cannot kill an ideology with a gun. What is needed is an ideology better suited to meet the needs of society. We have got to place less faith on military armaments that now have the capacity in cyberspace to cut off the electrical grid on planet Earth. Instead we must be willing to teach tolerance, compassion and a willingness to compromise. Prosecutors, defense counsel, judges, and the public must conclude that law is better than war. Transgressors should know they can be tried by any court that apprehends the perpetrator at anytime and anywhere under principles of universal jurisdiction which are already recognized in many countries. Those individual leaders who use armed force that is not in self-defense and not approved by the Security Council and knowing that it will inevitably kill large numbers of innocent civilians, should be held to criminal account. It is also important for the victims to be given an increased status in the search for justice. It is an old principle of tort law that he who causes unjustified harm is under a duty to compensate the victim and seek to minimize the damage. The victims of armed conflict with its devastating effect should be able to seek their remedies in a civil court of law in addition to the punishment of the perpetrators in criminal proceedings.

*Heiko Ahlbrecht**

Vorwort

Mit Verabschiedung des Statuts des Internationalen Strafgerichtshofs am 17. Juli 1998 gelang der zentrale Durchbruch zu einem international verankerten Völkerstrafrecht und einem Ständigen Internationalen Strafgerichtshof (ICC), zuständig für die schwersten Menschheitsverbrechen. Zu diesem Zeitpunkt blickte man bereits auf die ersten Verfahren des Internationalen Strafgerichtshofs für das ehemalige Jugoslawien (ICTY) und des Internationalen Strafgerichtshofs für Ruanda (ICTR) zurück, deren grundlegende Rechtsnormen durch das ICC-Statut völkerstrafrechtlich in fortgeschriebener Form kodifiziert wurde. Zentrales und zugleich besonderes Merkmal dieser völkerstrafrechtlichen Entwicklung ist die Kodifikation eines allgemeinen und eines besonderen Teils des materiellen Völkerstrafrechts einerseits, zugleich aber auch die Entwicklung eines völkerrechtlichen Strafprozessrechts mit angloamerikanischen Grundsätzen im Schwerpunkt, in vielen Bereichen aber durch das kontinentaleuropäische Strafprozessverständnis modifiziert. Verkürzt gesagt: Es handelt sich um eine Mischung aus dem US-amerikanischen Parteienprozess (common law) und dem kontinentaleuropäischen Strafprozess (civil law) mit einem die materielle Wahrheit ermittelnden und über diese letztlich judizidierendem Gerichtskörper in einem Strafprozess, der von adversarischen Elementen bestimmt ist. Sowohl der ICTY wie auch der ICC haben ihren Sitz in Den Haag, im Herzen Europas, was das Erstaunen darüber erhöht, dass die Mitgliedstaaten der EU und erst recht nicht die Mitglieder des Europarates in der Lage sind, sich auf einen gemeinsames europäisches Straf- und Strafprozessrecht zu einigen. Vor allen Dingen die Fortschrittlichkeit der Hauptverhandlungsdokumentation (komplette Video- und Audiodokumentationen nebst Wortprotokoll der Hauptverhandlung, die jeweils am Ende des Verhandlungstages elektronisch zur Verfügung gestellt werden) in den Verfahren vor den Internationalen Strafgerichtshöfen ist eine Benchmark, die für die Verteidigung in jedem europäischen Mitgliedstaat in deren nationalen Strafprozessen überaus wünschenswert wäre – sie dient im Übrigen der Objektivierung der Suche nach der Wahrheitsfindung und der Qualität der Beweismittel.

Die besondere Herausforderung an eine Verteidigertätigkeit vor den Internationalen Strafgerichtshöfen liegt neben der intensiven zeitlichen Inanspruchnahme jedoch an anderer Stelle. Es ist das Verdienst dieses Sammelbandes, zentrale und in der Praxis wichtige Themen oder auch Streitfelder der Verteidigung darzustellen und im Detail anhand der vorliegenden Recht-

---

* Rechtsanwalt Prof. Dr. Heiko Ahlbrecht, zugelassener Verteidiger am ICTY, Mitglied der ADC-ICTY.

sprechung der verschiedenen Strafgerichtshöfe wissenschaftlich zu kommentieren und praktisch zu unterlegen. Dies beginnt bei der Durchsetzung der Verteidigungsrechte und führt über die Spannungsfelder des eigenen Verteidigungsrechts des Angeklagten, das Konfrontationsrecht oder auch die dem deutschen Strafprozess nicht bekannte Handhabung der Offenlegung von Beweismaterialien aus dem Ermittlungsverfahren (disclosure) bis hin zur Organisation und (strategischen) Planung der Verteidigung der üblicherweise inhaftierten Mandanten. In diesem Kontext nehmen die operativen Unterstützungsmöglichkeiten durch das Office of Public Counsel for the Defence, aber auch durch die in Den Haag ansässige Verteidigervereinigung ADC-ICTY einen Unterschwerpunkt der Beschreibung ein. In der Praxis betrifft dies vielfältigste Fragestellungen wie beispielsweise die Bildung von Verteidigungsteams, den Umgangs mit den teilweise mehr als voluminösen Beweismitteln, Verteidigungskosten sowie Kosten für Sachverständige und eigene Ermittlungen oder sonstige Aktivitäten der Verteidigung.

Nur eine echte, gehaltvolle Verteidigung kann ein faires Verfahren und die Einhaltung des Grundsatzes der Waffengleichheit zwischen Ermittlungsbehörde und Verteidigung gewährleisten. Nur eine Verteidigung auf prozessualer Augenhöhe unter Ausübung aller Verteidigungsmöglichkeiten eröffnet die Möglichkeit einer Annäherung an ein gerechtes Urteil und ein "fair trial". Dies ist die zentrale Botschaft und zugleich das wichtige Leitmotiv, dem sich die Herausgeber und Autoren dieses Werkes verschrieben haben.

Colleen Rohan[*]

The Defence in international criminal trials: important actor or necessary evil?

> *"If you are determined to execute a man in any case, there is no occasion for a trial. The world yields no respect to courts that are merely organized to convict."*
>
> Justice Robert Jackson[1]

When initially considering how to go about approaching the topic of this article my first instinct was to write only about the importance of the Defence as an institution and the importance of the Defence function within the international courts in assuring fair trials and the fair and balanced development of international law as a whole. After all, what kind of legal system would develop if only one side of a complex set of facts was heard as a means of determining whether an individual or group of individuals was culpable for war crimes. No one would want to live with an international legal system that was that skewed; certainly not Lady Justice whose scales would be necessarily well out of balance.

I then considered outlining the historical list of difficulties which have plagued the defence side of the courtroom in international criminal cases: insufficient funding, inadequate or no access to important witnesses; limitations on cross-examination due to increasing use of written statements; undermining of the right to a public trial by the overuse of closed, private sessions; lack of cooperation from relevant government and police agencies, late disclosure from prosecutors or the failure to disclose exculpatory evidence. These are topics which have been addressed before[2] and which will remain subjects of inquiry and controversy in the international courts.

---

* Colleen Rohan has served as counsel and legal consultant on a number of cases at the ICTY since 2006 and is currently representing individuals in the EULEX war crimes courts in Kosovo. She served as President of the ADC-ICTY and as a member of the ICTY Disciplinary Panel. She organized and edited the „ADC-ICTY Manual on Criminal Defence: ADC-ICTY Developed Practices." She is a founding member of the International Criminal Law Bureau and is a member of 9 Bedford Row Chambers International Section. She maintains law offices in The Hague, Netherlands and Pristina, Kosovo.

1 Rule of Law Among Nations Speech, 13 April 1945, https://www.roberthjackson.org/wp-content/uploads/2015/01/Rule_of_Law_Among_Nations.pdf ; presented prior to the opening of the Nuremberg trials.

2 See, e.g. Ellis, M. S. „The Evolution of Defense Counsel Appearing Before the International Criminal Tribunal for the Former Yugoslavia". *New England Law Review* vol. 37:4. , K Gibson, C Lussiaa-Berdou, „Disclosure of Evidence," in Principles of Evidence in International Criminal Justice, K. Kahn, C Buisman, C Gosnell, eds (Oxford Press, 2010); K. S. Gallant, „Politics, Theory and Institutions: Three Reasons Why International Criminal Defence is Hard, and What Might Be Done about One of Them". Kluwer Academic

The more intriguing issue, though, became why the public and even members of the legal profession believe or express the attitude that the defence in a criminal case is ever unnecessary or irrelevant. That attitude essentially equates with the view that it is improper for the accused in criminal cases to have rights since they are guilty and the presumption of innocence is just a fiction.[3]

However that is not the case under international law nor, for that matter, in most domestic courts. Every person charged with a crime is entitled to a defence. The fact that acquittals are returned after trial demonstrates that all indictments are not founded on solid evidence. The existence of Innocence Projects now flourishing in various countries reflects that not all verdicts are well informed or reliable. Human beings make mistakes. Initial perceptions can be wrong.

Unfortunately, the tendency for the public to pre-judge an accused or to view the Defence function as unnecessary or even unethical because of the presumed character of the accused or the nature of the charged crimes is, as one commentator put it: "cognitive dissonance at its worst." Defence lawyers who represent people accused of crime honor the rule of law which requires "a stringent process before taking away a citizens' freedom ... ."[4]

I. The defence function in the international criminal courts

Since 1993 when the International Criminal Tribunal for the Former Yugoslavia (ICTY) was first established by the United Nations Security Council[5] a number of international courts have been created to prosecute war crimes, crimes against humanity, and genocide arising from various regional conflicts, including the International Criminal Tribunal for Rwanda (ICTR), the Special Tribunal for Lebanon (STL), the Special Court for Sierra Leone (SCSL), and the Extraordinary Criminal Chambers in Cambodia (ECCC).[6] As of the writing of this article, a Special Court for Kosovo is in the making,

---

Publishers, 2004; Tolbert, David. "The ICTY and Defense Counsel: A Troubled Relationship". *New England Law Review* vol. 37:4; Tuinstra, Jarinde Temminck. "Defence Counsel in International Criminal Law". University of Amsterdam, 2009; Tuinstra, Jarinde Temminck. "Defending the Defenders: The Role of Defence Counsel in International Criminal Trials". *Journal of International Criminal Justice*, 2010; The Ashgate Research Companion, W. Schabas, Y. McDermott, N Hayes eds, C Chernor Jalloh, A BiBella, "Equality of Arms in International Criminal Law: Continuing Challenges."

3 An ICTY judge (who is no longer sitting at that institution) once famously gave a public speech in which he stated his view that there is no such thing as the presumption of innocence as the mere existence of the (unproved) allegations in the Indictment is sufficient to negate that presumption.

4 See discussion at: http://ethicsalarms.com/2013/08/15/yes-the-best-criminal-defense-lawyers-represent-the-worst-people-or-you/ .

5 See UNSC Res 827 (25 May 1993).

6 The ECCC is not an international court. It is a domestic court which functions with significant international financial and professional assistance.

reportedly to address war crimes committed by ethnic Albanians during the conflict in Kosovo.[7] The International Criminal Court also came into being upon passage and enforcement of the Rome Statute in 2002.[8]

With the exception of the ECCC, which utilizes a civil law system based on French law, all of these courts employ a hybrid mix of the civil or continental legal system and the adversarial legal system. In general the trial process itself, however, is, at least in theory, adversarial in structure. That is, each party to the case is able to conduct its own factual investigation of the case and during trial each party (prosecution, defence and, at the ICC and STL, victim's counsel) is entitled to present witnesses as part of its case and to cross-examine witnesses presented by the opposing party or parties.

This process presumes the inclusion of an active defence presence before, during and after trial. International instruments that address the subject of the rights of the accused who are brought before these criminal courts clearly delineate that the accused is presumed to be innocent[9], is entitled to a fair and public trial,[10] without undue delay[11], is entitled to the assistance of legal counsel,[12] has the right to confront and cross-examine witnesses called against him or her at trial[13], and has the right to "adequate" time and facilities to prepare a defence.[14]

Additionally, the prosecution bears the burden of proof at trial; to prove the underlying charges and the accused's factual and legal responsibility for them beyond a reasonable doubt. This is a burden which *never* shifts to the accused. Hence, the accused has *no* burden to prove he or she is not guilty, although in practice most accused have put on some form of affirmative defence to the charges.[15]

---

7 See BBC News, "Kosovo Parliament Approves Special War Crimes Court", 4 August 2015 http://www.bbc.com/news/world-europe-33770897 . Two prosecutions of Kosovar Albanians were already brought at the ICTY during its mandate*; Prosecutor v Limaj et al*, ICTY Case No IT-03-66-T *and Prosecutor v Hardinaj et al*, ICTY Case No IT-04-84-T and IT-04-84*bis*-T. The proposed new Special Court for Kosovo is intended to pursue additional prosecutions.

8 ICC Statute of the International Criminal Court, 2187 UNTS 90 (17 July 1998, entered into force 1 July 2002).

9 See, e.g. ICTY Statute, Art. 21 (3); ICTR Statute, Art 20(3); ICC Statute, Art 66; International Covenant for Civil and Political Rights (ICCPR), Art 14(2); European Convention for the Protection of Human Rights and Fundamental Freedoms, Art 6(2).

10 ICTY Statute, Art 21(2); ICTR Statute, Art 20(2); ICC Statute, Art 67(1); ICCPR, Art 14(1); ECHR, Art 6(1).

11 ICTY Statute, Art 21(4); ICTR Statute Art 20(4); ICC Statute, Art 67(1); ICCPTR, Art 14(3)(c); ECHR, Art 6(1) [trial must be "within a reasonable time"].

12 ICTY Statute, Art 21(4)(b); ICTR Statute, Art 20(4)(b); ICC Statute, Art 67(1)(b); ICCPR, Art 14(3)(b); ECHR, Art 6(3)(c).

13 ICTY Statute, Art 21(4)(e); ICTR Statute, Art 20(4)(e); ICC Statute, Art 67(1)(e); ICCPR, Art 14(3)(e); ECHR, Art 6(3)(d).

14 ICTY Statute, Art 21(4)(b); ICTR Statute, Art 20(4)(b); ICC Statute, Art 67(1)(b); ICCPR, Art 14(3)(b); ECHR, Art 6(3)(b).

15 See, e.g. *Prosecutor v Limaj et al* (Trial Judgement) ICTY Case No. IT-03-66-T (30 November 2005), para 10; *Prosecutor v Naletilic and Martinovic* (Trial Judgement) ICTY Case No. IT-98-34-T (31 March 2003).

Given that all accused are presumed innocent unless and until the prosecution meets its burden to prove guilt beyond a reasonable doubt, the accused's right to "adequate" time and facilities to prepare a defence refers not just to the preparation of an affirmative defence case but also to adequate time and facilities with which to investigate the credibility of and to prepare to meet the prosecution's evidence at trial.[16]

Despite the existence of these rights and all that they imply – including the indispensable role and function of the defence to ensure fair trials in international criminal proceedings – the international criminal courts, including the ICC, do not recognize the Defence as one of the pillars or organs of the court.[17] There is usually very little communication between victims' rights groups, NGO's and even journalists regarding the Defence view of proceedings in any given case; even cases in which acquittals have occurred in whole or in part. The Defence has been, for the most part, historically excluded from official outreach events and official legacy conferences put on by the various international courts. As a result the public at large is generally ill-informed about the role and function of the defence. This gap in knowledge has potentially far-reaching consequences for the continuing development of a fair and balanced system of law in the international courts.

A few months ago, for example, I was interviewed by an individual who was writing a Ph.D thesis intended to include an analysis of the defence function in the international criminal courts. The individual is not an attorney nor did he have any particular interest in "defending the defence". After he became immersed in his topic, however, he developed some concerns. As he put it: "An anonymous reviewer of a paper I submitted last year to a peer-reviewed political science journal commented, in a critique of my argument, that fairness for defendants is a poor source of legitimacy for trials because it's the victims that really matter. Two audience members at a presentation of a paper on defence rights in international trials at a West Coast political science conference this year made the same comment more forcefully: 'we shouldn't concentrate on fairness for perpetrators of mass atrocities – increasing defendant rights just weakens the legitimacy of trials'".[18]

It is understandable that these kinds of attitudes exist among those who have suffered through armed conflicts and/or been the victims of war crimes. It would be difficult, if not impossible for such victims and witnesses to maintain a neutral or detached view about subsequent legal proceedings re-

16 See general discussion of this right in "The Ashgate Research Companion to International Law, eds W Schabas, Y. McDermott, N. Hayes (Ashgate Publishing Ltd. 2013), C. Rohan, "Protecting the Rights of the Accused in International Criminal Proceedings: Lip Service or Affirmative Action:", p. 290.

17 The sole exception to this is the STL which has a defence office that is considered to be an organ of that court.

18 Interview with the author in November 2015 by Martin Burke, Research Fellow, Ralph Bunche Institute for International Studies, New York, and PhD Candidate in International Politics, the City University of New York Graduate Center.

lated to these events in their own lives. It is also understandable, though regrettable, that the public at large may develop similar views. The cases brought in the international courts invariably involve horrendous crimes committed against vulnerable civilians during war. News coverage of such crimes is usually widespread in the international press. More often than not the identity of the perpetrators is widely assumed and discussed well before any arrest or legal proceedings take place.

It is inexcusable, however, that such attitudes are expressed among those who are actively involved in observing and assessing the work of the international courts and therefore, individuals who present themselves as reasonably well informed about the underlying legal process. Indeed, if the international legal community is to maintain and continue to develop a legitimate, reliable system of law then courts, activists, academics, politicians, and other commentators must accept that international criminal trials are held "not to convict those presumed to be guilty in a theater piece designed to assuage an outraged public" but to dispassionately evaluate the actual evidence regarding the specific accused. Any other approach simply fails to respect and enforce the rule of law. An accused, in accordance with democratic principles and international law must be tried in a setting which recognizes the presumption of innocence and is designed to promote fair and "legitimate" verdicts. That will occur only when the rights of all parties, including the human rights of the accused, are valued and enforced.

Any other position reflects a wholesale misunderstanding of international law, the defence function in the international courts, the reasons for the courts themselves, and rests on situational attitudes which serve to violate, not enforce, the rule of law.

As Justice Jackson also remarked in his famous speech on the Rule of Law Among Nations:

> *"The ultimate principle is that you must put no man on trial under the form of judicial proceedings if you are not willing to see him freed if not proven guilty."*[19]

The international courts have on occasion unwittingly reinforced misguided attitudes and beliefs, in particular regarding the notion that the Defence is somehow irrelevant to or a minor player in international criminal proceedings.

The ICTY, to provide only one example, put together its "ICTY Manual on Developed Practices"[20] which was published in May of 2009. The Manual, as described on the ICTY website, is "part of a broader project to promote and preserve the Tribunal's legacy."[21] The ICTY Manual is an impor-

19 Rule of Law Among Nations Speech, 13 April 1945, https://www.roberthjackson.org/wp-content/uploads/2015/01/Rule_of_Law_Among_Nations.pdf.

20 The Manual is available electronically at: http://www.icty.org/x/file/About/Reports%20and%20Publications/ICTY_Manual_on_Developed_Practices.pdf.

21 See http://www.icty.org/en/node/8127.

tant publication. It explains the history of the institution, its internal structure and many of the basic legal principles at work in the day-to-day functioning of the ICTY; a Tribunal which is considered by most, including this author, to be a successful example of the fair, reliable and efficient imposition of international criminal law.

At the time the ICTY Manual was produced the Defence at the ICTY was asked to contribute to it by writing a chapter on the Defence role, function and experience at the Tribunal. The Defence chapter was excluded however when objections were raised by the Prosecution, and the institution acceded to them. The Defence never learned of the existence of the objection by the Prosecution to inclusion of the Defence legacy nor was it given any opportunity to discuss or respond to it until the final decision to exclude the Defence was *a fait accompli*. Hence the official ICTY Manual contains no contribution from the Defence at all, despite the fact that the Manual represents itself as preserving the legacy of that court.

This particular set-back for the Defence in being excluded from the official ICTY Manual turned out to be a cloud with a silver lining. The United Nations Interregional Crime and Justice Research Institute, which had sponsored the ICTY Manual, thereafter agreed, on its own initiative and that of the Association of Defence Counsel Practicing Before the ICTY (ADC-ICTY), to sponsor a separate Manual for the Defence. Hence, a practice oriented manual written by experienced ICTY Defence counsel, the "Manual on International Criminal Defence: ADC-ICTY Developed Practices," was published in 2011, as part of the War Crimes Justice Project involving the ADC-ICTY, UNICRI, and the O.S.C.E. Office for Democratic Institutions and Human Rights (ODIHR).[22] Since the independent publication of the Defence Manual the ICTY has included it on its new official website.[23]

In this instance, then, the initial exclusion of the Defence was ultimately rectified; a step forward for the Defence, not to mention an illustration of the need for defence counsel associations, like the ADC-ICTY, at the international courts.[24] The subsequent inclusion of the Defence Manual on the official ICTY website is also a positive comment on the ICTY's evolution as an institution; specifically its ultimate recognition of the Defence function and legacy as an important contributor to the legacy of the institution as a whole.

---

22 This Manual is available electronically on the ADC-ICTY website: http://adc-icty.org/ The Manual has been translated into Serbian/Croatian/Bosnian and Albanian. It is currently being translated into Spanish.

23 http://www.icty.org/en/node/8127.

24 The ADC-ICTY is the only association of Defence counsel which has been official recognized by an international court. It was just recently officially recognized as the association of defence counsel for the Mechanism for International Criminal Tribunals (MICT); the institution created to carry out essential functions of the ICTY and ICTR now that both institutions have completed their mandates. A movement is in progress to create an official association of defence counsel at the ICC, however as of the date of this writing such an association has not yet been formed.

Public comments made by officials in the international courts have unfortunately also served the opposite end: to directly and improperly promote ideas which undermine and misconstrue the Defence function as well as the rights of the accused. These comments, which have not been corrected in the public press or otherwise rectified, may continue to mislead the public and, in doing so, undermine the rule of law.

At the ICTY, for example, there are general regulations[25] which provide that prosecutors must "avoid outside the courtroom, making public comments or speaking to the media about the merits of particular cases or the guilt or innocence of specific accused while judgment in such matters is pending before a Chamber of the Tribunal."[26] Despite these regulations, in 2007 Carla Del Ponte, then the Prosecutor at the ICTY, told a *Der Spiegel* reporter, in an article subsequently published by that magazine, that the *Haradinaj et al.,* case, on trial at the ICTY at the time, should result in a conviction because she had "the evidence to prove" it.[27] It is difficult to conceive of a clearer and more improper comment on the merits of a pending case.

The Trial Chamber refused to grant a Defence request for a hearing on Ms. Del Ponte's inappropriate comments finding that there was no evidence that Ms. Del Ponte's comments affected the fairness or expeditiousness of the trial.[28] While that finding may have been true in this specific case, it is impossible to know whether public comments such as those uttered by Ms. Del Ponte affected the willingness of witnesses to come forward and honestly testify concerning matters that contradicted her claims. The Chamber also did not address other troubling aspects of the prosecutor's comments; their improper, indeed misleading influence on public perceptions and understanding not only of the *Haradinaj et al.* case but of the presumption of innocence to which all accused are entitled under international law.[29]

In *Lubanga,* the first case to go to trial at the ICC, a member of the office of the Prosecutor opined in a public press interview that certain intermediaries used by their office to select witnesses for potential testimony against Mr. Lubanga were "carefully chosen" and "much admired" by the office,[30]

---

25 There is no enforcible, internal Code of Conduct for prosecutors at the ICTY; only "guidelines." See "The ICTY and Defense Counsel: A Troubled Relationship," D. Tolbert, 37 New Eng. L. Rev 975 (2003), 982.

26 ICTY Prosecution Regulations, regulation 2(k).

27 See *Prosecutor v Haradinaj et al*, ICTY Case No. IT-04-84-T, Idriz Balaj's Citation of Prosecutorial Violation of Ethical Code of Conduct and Request for Evidentiary Hearing Regarding Interview of Carla del Ponte, 30 October 2007.

28 *Haradinaj et al*, ICTY Case No. IT-04-84-T, Decision on Idriz Balaj's Request for Evidentiary Hearing Regarding Interview of Carla Del Ponte, 29 January 2008, para 8.

29 Two of the three accused in *Haradinaj et al* were subsequently acquitted of all 37 counts alleged in the Indictment. The third was convicted of 3 of 37 counts. *Prosecutor v Haradinaj et al*, ICTY Case No. IT-04-84-T, Trial Judgement, 3 April 2008.

30 See *Lubanga*, ICC Case No. ICC-01/04-01/06, Decision on Press Interview with Ms. Le Fraper du Hellen, 12 May 2010, paras 3-4 [*Lubanga* Press Decision]; and see the comprehensive discussion of these events in M. Markovic, "The ICC Prosecutor's Missing Code of Conduct," 47 Texas Int'l L. Rev 201, 209 (2011), pp 238-241.

that the prosecution witnesses were "very credible,"[31] that there was no abuse of process regarding disclosure in the case as the Prosecutor was "very experienced," that all exculpatory evidence had been disclosed, and that any contention to the contrary was "just talk" from the Defence.[32] She told the press that Mr. Lubanga would be "going away for a long time."[33] These comments were made before any trial verdict had been returned and *after* the Trial Chamber had previously and specifically admonished the prosecution not to make statements to the press about the merits of the case.[34]

The Trial Chamber, in a court filing, severely criticized the prosecution spokesperson,[35] found the statements "seriously intruded" on the role of the Trial Chamber, were misleading, and were unfair to the accused.[36] No other action was taken however. The offending statements, at least as to those who do not know of or know how to navigate the website of the ICC so as to find the specific court filing, presumably remain entirely uncorrected.

Two months later, despite the events in *Lubanga*, the then ICC Prosecutor wrote a piece for the *Guardian* newspaper in which he misleadingly implied that President Omar Al-Bashir of Sudan, then under warrant of arrest, had already been found guilty by the ICC.[37] No action was taken by the court in response to that public misinformation.

It is not surprising, given these kinds of events, and the historical exclusion of the Defence as an organ of the international courts, that the general public remains largely unaware of the rights of the accused in international criminal proceedings, including the presumption of innocence and the prosecutor's duty to meet its burden to prove the case beyond a reasonable doubt.

The Defence does not have a similar public platform as the official organs of the courts. In addition, ethical codes regulating the conduct of defence counsel were enacted at all the international courts, including the ICC. Defence ethical codes have been historically enforced.

Contrary to the relative inaction taken as to court personnel in the instances mentioned above,[38] a defence lawyer was affirmatively disciplined for engaging in the most general public comment about the international

---

31 *Lubanga* Press Decision, para 6.

32 *Lubanga* Press Decision, para 8.

33 *Lubanga* Press Decision, para 8.

34 *Lubanga* Press Decision, para 15. The comments were also made after the Trial Chamber had previously stayed all proceedings due to the failure of the prosecution to disclose exculpatory evidence.

35 *Lubanga* Press Decision, paras 41-49.

36 *Lubanga* Press Decision, para 49.

37 "Now End This Darfur Denial," Luis-Moreno Ocampo, *Guardian*, 15 July 2010.

38 Ethical Codes of Conduct which regular the professional conduct of defence counsel exist at all the international courts and include detailed procedures for discipline when the codes are violated. The same is not true for the Prosecution at the ICTY and ICTR. The ICC first enacted a Code of Conduct for Prosecutors in September 2013, almost twelve years after it came into existence. There are no enforceable ethical codes for judges at any of the international courts.

courts. In the *Fila* case at the ICTY,[39] a defence attorney who also served in various advisory capacities to the Serbian government and hence was a public figure there, was charged with misconduct for stating in the Serbian press that "the main aim has been achieved, Serbia has been demonized."[40] The statement was held by the majority of the ICTY Disciplinary Panel[41] to violate Article 3(v) of the ICTY Code of Conduct for Defence Counsel. That article states that defence counsel "shall take all necessary steps to ensure that their actions do not bring proceedings before the Tribunal into disrepute". The majority of the Disciplinary Board in *Fila* held that Mr. Fila's comment, even though it did not refer to the ICTY or to any specific case or individual at the ICTY, violated Article 3(v). In fact, it went on to hold that Article 3(v) imposed "a positive obligation on all counsel to protect the reputation of the Tribunal."[42]

There was no evidence in *Fila* that Mr. Fila's comment brought "proceedings before the Tribunal into disrepute." To the contrary, Mr. Fila's opinion, whether one agrees with it or not, was precisely that and nothing more. He did not refer to any pending cases and the statement was not an attempt to influence judicial authorities in any pending cases. He named no names. He made no factually false assertions. He did not vouch for the credibility or reliability of anyone. He merely stated his opinion.

The Tribunal, and other international courts, are public international institutions. Healthy debate about the effect of their work is important to the positive development of international law as well as the continued development of a democratic society. The interest in encouraging freedom of expression in a democratic society certainly outweighs any theoretical and unproven benefit of censorship. Open and honest discussion of the mistakes and successes of the international courts should take place without the potential – for defence counsel – of facing ethical proceedings for expressions of opinion.

Again, small wonder that the public, including members of victim's rights groups, NGO's and journalists, are at times misinformed as to the rights of the accused, the responsibilities of the international criminal courts to enforce those rights, the Defence function as an institution, and the primary purpose of the trials.

I have been asked over the years, as have many attorneys who practice in the international courts, to give lectures to law students and new lawyers interested in international criminal law. One of the first questions I will usu-

---

39 *In the Matter of Mr. Toma Fila*, ICTY Disciplinary Board Case No. IT-13-93-Misc-1; IT-05-87-A, 3 July 2013 [hereinafter "*Fila* Decision"].

40 *Fila* Decision, paras 81-90.

41 The *Fila* Decision was a split decision of the ICTY Disciplinary Board, with a majority of three and two dissents.

42 *Fila* Decision", para 70] The Majority, in interpreting this ethical code which applies only to defence counsel, did not find that a similar, positive obligation to protect the reputation of the Tribunal applies to any other actors at the Tribunal such as prosecutors, judges or other staff.

ally ask these groups is what they view as the purpose of an international criminal trial. The answers are interesting. The students respond by explaining that international criminal trials will end impunity for political and military leaders; deter future war crimes; establish an historical record of the conflict at issue; result in reconciliation among the people in the conflict or post-conflict region; provide reparations for the victims of war crimes, crimes against humanity and genocide; give victims a voice in court, and develop and strengthen international criminal law by imposing the rule of law throughout the world.

There is nothing wrong with these answers. These goals are laudable. Most are listed on the websites of the international courts as among their aspirations and sometime achievements.[43] What is distressing are the many times that students fail to mention that an international criminal trial is also about determining the guilt or innocence of the particular accused on trial; the fundamental and primary reason for the trial.

By its very nature a criminal trial, domestic or international, concerns itself, first and foremost, with the culpability of the accused. Students and young lawyers who are not taught or who fail to understand the importance of that fundamental fact may find themselves participating in the building of international courts that give only lip service to the presumption of innocence, the proper burden of proof of crime, and due process of law. As a society we should do everything we can to avoid this kind of development; not to perpetuate it because it may be seen as difficult or distasteful to openly discuss the necessity to enforce the rights of accused charged with horrific war crimes.

This final point leads back to the comment about fairness for defendants in international trials being "a poor source of legitimacy for trials because it's the victims that really matter."

The international criminal trial process provides victims with a forum in which to tell what happened to them and to testify as to who they believe is culpable. Understandably, not all victims wish to testify in an international court; but many do. At the ECCC, the STL and at the ICC, victims participate in the trials through counsel and are permitted to put questions to witnesses through counsel, under circumstances specified by the rules of evidence and procedure which apply to each of those courts. All international courts also provide significant support systems for victims and witnesses in criminal cases, including financial assistance, medical and psychological support, and protective measures for victims and witnesses and their families when appropriate. Victims are also entitled to seek reparations.

At the ICC, a fund for victim reparations was put in place at the time the Rome Statute was enacted: The Trust Fund for Victims. As described on the ICC website:

---

43 See e.g. http://www.icty.org/en/about/tribunal/achievements and see e.g. https://www.icc-cpi.int/en_menus/icc/about%20the%20court/Pages/about%20the%20court.aspx.

"The Rome Statute created two independent institutions: the International Criminal Court and the Trust Fund for Victims.
While it is impossible to fully undo the harm caused by genocide, war crimes, crimes against humanity and the crime of aggression, it is possible to help survivors, in particular, the most vulnerable among them, rebuild their lives and regain their dignity and status as fully-functioning members of their societies.
The Trust Fund for Victims advocates for victims and mobilises individuals, institutions with resources, and the goodwill of those in power for the benefit of victims and their communities. It funds or sets up innovative projects to meet victims' physical, material, or psychological needs. It may also directly undertake activities as and when requested by the Court.
The Trust Fund for Victims can act for the benefit of victims of crimes, regardless of whether there is a conviction by the ICC. It cooperates with the Court to avoid any interference with ongoing legal proceedings."[44]

To the author's knowledge no reparations have been paid to date to any individual victim or collective group at the ICC. The ICC Appeal Court decision on victims' reparations in *Lubanga* held that Mr. Lubanga, even though presently indigent, will remain individually responsible for reparations[45] It ordered that reparations from The Trust Fund for Victims were to be paid on a collective basis and that the group eligible to receive such reparations could include victims of the crimes which were proven, even if those individuals did not participate in the trial or file requests for reparations.[46] In the only other completed case at the ICC, *Katanga*, no appeal was brought from Mr. Katanga's conviction. His sentence will be completed as of 18 January 2016. The court has not yet returned any decision in that case on victims' reparations.[47]

There is no reason whatever, given the obvious sensitivity to victims in the international courts, for any informed individual to juxtapose the rights of victims against the rights of the accused. Both matter in a democratic system of law. Each is entitled to different rights under international law and under the statutes of the various courts and tribunals. Enforcing the rights of one group does not preclude enforcing the rights of the other.

None of these circumstances change the inherent nature of a criminal trial. The verdicts ultimately returned after trial arise from the factual find-

---

44 https://www.icc-cpi.int/en_menus/icc/about%20the%20court/frequently%20asked%20questions/Pages/27.aspx.

45 See https://www.icc-cpi.int/en_menus/icc/press%20and%20media/press%20releases/Pages/pr1092.aspx, and see *Prosecutor v Thomas Lubanga Dyilo*, ICC Case No. ICC-01/04-01/06-3129, "Judgement on the appeals against the 'Decision establishing the principles and procedures to be applied to reparations' of 7 August 2012 with AMENDED order for reparations (Annex A) and public annexes 1 and 2", 3 March 2015.

46 See summary of judgement: https://www.icc-cpi.int/en_menus/icc/press%20and%20media/press%20releases/Pages/pr1092.aspx

47 *Prosecutor v Katanga*, ICC Case No. ICC-01/04-01/07, summary at https://www.icc-cpi.int/en_menus/icc/situations%20and%20cases/situations/situation%20icc%200104/related%20cases/icc%200104%200107/Pages/democratic%20republic%20of%20the%20congo.aspx [noting decision on victims' reparations will be returned on a later date].

ings made on the issue of the individual guilt or innocence of the accused. No individual and no organization should advocate for an international criminal process which serves to lessen or impede the ability to provide the accused with his or her internationally recognized human rights.

II. Conclusion

The underlying value in conducting a criminal trial is, ultimately, to preserve civilized behavior. When prosecutors, as representatives of society, assert that someone has deviated from acceptable societal norms, it is critical that the system which reviews the evidence of that assertion is both dispassionate and fair to all parties, most particularly to the object of the proceedings: the accused. Otherwise society becomes what it seeks to avoid; an entity which does not honor the rule of law.

The critical role of the defence is self-evident. It must be recognized by all actors in the international community as a fundamental means of ensuring the legitimacy of the trial verdicts. To paraphrase the Registrar at the ICTY and MICT: "Far from weakening the integrity of the proceedings ..., a zealous and professional defence only augments the Tribunal's credibility as an independent and impartial judicial organ."[48]

Or, as Judge Patricia Wald, a former judge at the ICTY emphasized: "A vigorous, un-intimidated, knowledgeable defense is the *sine qua non* of a fair trial."[49]

---

48 Address of Mr. John Hocking, Registrar, at the Meeting of Registrars of Final/Appellate, Regional and International Courts, Ottawa, Canada, 14-16 April 2010. "Legal aid and defence support at the ICTY".

49 See PM Wald, "The International Criminal Tribunal for the Former Yugoslavia Comes of Age: Some Observations on Day-to-Day Dilemmas of an International Court," (2001) 5 Journal of Law and Policy 87, 102.

Mayeul Hiéramente[*]

Die Deutungshoheit im Gerichtssaal oder „Die Bändigung des Ungeheuers"

Anmerkungen zum sich selbst verteidigenden Angeklagten

I. Einleitung

Internationale Strafverfahren sind (welt-) politische Ereignisse. Wenn Präsidenten, Regierungschefs oder Generäle vor Gericht gestellt werden, ist die Aufmerksamkeit der Medien gewiss. Dies ist in der Natur der Strafprozesse vor dem Internationalen Strafgerichtshof (ICC) und seiner *ad-hoc* eingerichteten Vorgängern (ICTY, ICTR, ECCC, SCSL, STL) angelegt. Ohne Publizität und mediale Begleitung könnten internationale Strafgerichte die an sie gestellten Erwartungen kaum erfüllen. Der Grund: Die internationalisierte Strafjustiz soll der Aufklärung der Bevölkerung, der Genugtuung der Opfer sowie der Abschreckung tatgeneigter Potentaten dienen und auf diese Weise friedensstiftende Wirkung entfalten und „Geschichte" schreiben. Die ambitionierte Zielsetzung dieser Tribunale manifestiert sich in der Präambel des Römischen Statuts des ICC, in der es heißt:

> „in der Erkenntnis, dass solche schweren Verbrechen den Frieden, die Sicherheit und das Wohl der Welt bedrohen,
> bekräftigend, dass die schwersten Verbrechen, welche die Internationale Gemeinschaft als Ganzes berühren, nicht unbestraft bleiben dürfen [...]
> entschlossen der Straflosigkeit der Täter ein Ende zu setzen und so zur Verhütung solcher Verbrechen beizutragen"

Die Anforderungen an internationale Strafgerichte gehen weit über das hinaus, was auf nationaler Ebene von Polizei, Staatsanwaltschaft und Strafgerichten erwartet wird.[1] Auf nationaler Ebene werden die Fragen, „warum" eine strafrechtliche Aufarbeitung notwendig ist und ob die Verfahren einen positiven Einfluss auf das gesellschaftliche Zusammenleben zeitigen, von Seiten der Politik und Öffentlichkeit nur äußerst selten gestellt. Anders im Falle der Weltstrafjustiz. Internationale Strafgerichte werden durch die explizite Benennung der obigen Zielsetzungen einem Legitimationszwang unterworfen, der in der alltäglichen Praxis kaum ausgeblendet werden kann. Dies

---

* Dr. Mayeul Hiéramente ist Rechtsanwalt in der Kanzlei Wessing & Partner Rechtsanwälte mbB in Düsseldorf sowie Alumnus der International Max Planck Research School on Retaliation, Mediation and Punishment (IMPRS-REMEP) in Freiburg. Er lehrt Völkerstrafrecht im Masterprogramm „Peace and Security Studies" der Universität Hamburg.

1 M. Damaška, *Assignment of Counsel and Perceptions of Fairness*, Journal of International Criminal Justice (2005), 3.

stellt den ICC ebenso wie seine Vorgänger vor ständige Herausforderungen. Sie müssen die entscheidungsrelevanten Beweise erheben, einordnen und juristisch bewerten. Dies ist für sich genommen bereits eine Mammutaufgabe angesichts des Umfangs der Verfahren und des fehlenden eigenen Polizeiapparats. Gleichzeitig wird – obwohl dies *stricto sensu* nicht zur Aufgabe einer strafverfolgenden Institution gehört – von den (das Gericht finanzierenden) Mitgliedstaaten, den Medien und den betroffenen Bevölkerungen ein politischer Mehrwert abverlangt. Der ICC muss sich eben nicht nur an der juristischen Einordnung von Sachverhalten messen lassen. Es ist daher kaum verwunderlich, dass eine Institution wie der ICC neben den Richtern und der Anklagebehörde über zahlreiche Angestellte verfügt, die z.B. im Rahmen des „Outreachs" oder über den Trust Fund for Victims die Botschaft der internationalen Strafjustiz in die Welt tragen. Der ICC ist mehr als ein Gericht. Eine strikte Arbeitsteilung zwischen der „gerichtlichen" und der „edukativen" Tätigkeit findet – geradezu zwangsläufig – nicht statt, weshalb auch die Ermittlungen und Hauptverhandlungen von einem teils messianischen Eifer geprägt sind.[2] Eine rhetorische Überhöhung – auch in der Darstellung des Angeklagten – ist keine Seltenheit.[3]

Insbesondere in den Verfahren gegen Führungspersonen (z.B. Milošević am ICTY) gerät die Suche nach strafrechtlicher Schuld oder Unschuld allzu oft in den Hintergrund der (medialen) Wahrnehmung und wird durch den Wettstreit um die geschichtliche und weltpolitische Deutungshoheit überlagert. Dies hat Auswirkungen auf die Art und Weise wie das Verfahren im Allgemeinen und der Angeklagte im Besonderen wahrgenommen werden. Damit nicht genug: Die Wahrnehmung des Verfahrens durch die Bevölkerung prägt auch den Umgang mit den dort erhobenen Fakten. Ob die Sachverhaltsdarstellungen (insbesondere die historischen Ausführungen[4]) im Urteil als „Wahrheit" akzeptiert werden, hängt maßgeblich davon ab, wie die Adressaten der Botschaft aus Den Haag den Prozessverlauf einordnen. Internationale Strafgerichte stehen aufgrund historisch bedingter (Fehl-)Wahrnehmungen, langjähriger Propaganda sowie – teilweise vernachlässigt – den sozialpsychologischen Rahmenbedingungen einer Vergangenheitsaufarbeitung[5] vor gravierenden Herausforderungen, der von den Straftaten betroffe-

---

2 I. Tallgren, *The Sensibility and Sense of International Criminal Justice,* European Journal of International Law (2002), 561, 593: „*International Criminal Law carries a kind of religious exercise of hope that is stronger than the desire to face everyday life.*" Siehe auch C. Prittwitz, *Internationales Strafrecht: Die Zukunft einer Illusion?*, JRE 2003, 469, 473.

3 Dazu allgemein F. Mégret, *Practices of Stigmatization*, Law & Contemporary Probl. (2013), 287.

4 Zur Geschichtsschreibung in internationalen Strafverfahren siehe die ausführliche Analyse bei U. Ewald, *Reason and Truth in International Criminal Justice*, in: A. Smeulers und R. Haveman (Hrsg.), *Supranational Criminology* (2000), 399, 407 m.w.N.

5 Dazu ausführlich S. Ford, *A Social Psychology Model of the Perceived Legitimacy of International Criminal Courts*, Vanderbilt Journal of Transnational Law (2012), 405; L. Fletcher und H. Weinstein, *Violence and Social Repair: Rethinking the Contribution of Justice to Reconciliation*, Human Rights Quarterly (2002), 573.

nen Bevölkerung ihre Botschaft näher zu bringen und die ihr auferlegte Rolle als Instrument der Friedensschaffung zu erfüllen. Nicht selten werden Personen, die als Kriegsverbrecher durch die internationale Strafjustiz zur Rechenschaft gezogen werden, in der Heimat als Kriegshelden, als einer „von uns" verehrt.[6] Die psychologischen Implikationen der Aufarbeitung von Kollektivunrecht erschweren es internationalen Gerichten und Tribunalen, die Bevölkerung zu erreichen. Widerstreitende Diskurse sind unvermeidbar, die Justiz ist nur eine der vielen zu vernehmenden Stimmen. Der Wettstreit um die Deutungshoheit über die geschichtliche „Wahrheit" wird auf verschiedenen Ebenen ausgetragen. Historiker, Journalisten und politisch motivierte Propagandisten streiten mit der internationalen Strafjustiz um (inter-) nationale Aufmerksamkeit. Nichtregierungsorganisationen unterstützen – in teils unkritischer Weise – die „Outreach"-Bemühungen der Gerichte bei der Vermittlung ihrer Erkenntnisse oder nehmen diese in ihren zahlreichen Reports, Presseerklärungen und Kampagnen sogar vorweg. Dass Entscheidungen internationaler Strafgerichte (Anklage, Haftbefehle, Urteile) auch Gegenstand der politischen Diskussion und Instrumentalisierung sind, versteht sich demgemäß von selbst. Auch wenn seitens der Justiz Wert auf eine neutrale Aufarbeitung von Konflikten – die häufig sogar noch andauern – gelegt wird, ist es kaum zu vermeiden, dass die Strafverfahren in Den Haag auch als Argument im politischen Streit genutzt werden.[7] Kurzum: Der Wettstreit um die politisch-historische Deutungshoheit findet stets nicht nur innerhalb, sondern auch außerhalb des Gerichtssaals statt.

Exemplarisch für diesen Wettstreit stehen die Bemühungen einiger Angeklagter sich vor internationalen Strafgerichten *in persona* zu verteidigen sowie die korrespondieren Anstrengungen der Anklagebehörde, eine „Selbst"-Verteidigung des Angeklagten weitestgehend zu unterbinden und diesem einen professionellen Strafverteidiger zur Seite zu stellen beziehungsweise – aus der Perspektive des Angeklagten – diesem „aufzuzwingen". Ob und inwieweit ein Angeklagter in einem internationalen Strafprozess das Recht hat, sich selbst zu verteidigen, ist seit je her juristisch und rechtspolitisch umstritten; zu unterschiedlich sind die nationalen Rechtstraditionen, zu sehr divergieren die Interessenlagen der beteiligten Akteure. Die Möglichkeit aktiver Teilhabe des Angeklagten im Rahmen des Strafprozesses wird daher juristisch kontrovers diskutiert. Es ist kaum verwunderlich, dass diese – primär strafprozessuale – Meinungsstreitigkeit im Prozess gegen den

6 Siehe J. Clark, *Courting Controversy: The ICTY's Acquittal of Croatian Generals Gotovina and Markač*, Journal of International Criminal Justice (2013), 399.

7 Zur Instrumentalisierung des ICC durch den ugandischen Präsidenten Museveni und der nicht unproblematischen Kooperationswilligkeit der Anklagebehörde siehe S.M.H. Nouwen und W. Werner, *Doing Justice to the Political: The International Criminal Court in Uganda and Sudan*, European Journal of International Law (2010), 941, 946 ; A. Tiemessen, *The International Criminal Court and the politics of prosecutions*, The International Journal of Human Rights (2014), 444, 447. Siehe auch M. Hiéramente, *Wahlen in Zeiten der Strafverfolgung. Die Situation in Kenia und der Internationale Strafgerichtshof, Die* Friedens-Warte (2013), 187, 194-198.

ehemaligen serbischen Präsidenten Slobodan Milošević mit besonderer Verve ausgetragen wurde.[8] Es lohnt sich, die in diesem Zusammenhang geführten Diskussionen einer genaueren Betrachtung zu unterziehen. Dabei soll es vorliegend nicht das Ziel sein, die juristische Debatte fortzuführen oder die vermeintlich „richtige" Interpretation der relevanten Normen zu finden. Im Rahmen der folgenden schlaglichtartigen Betrachtung soll vielmehr illustriert werden, wie der Angeklagte von den beteiligten Praktikern sowie den wissenschaftlichen Beobachtern porträtiert wird und wie sich die Interpretation verfahrensrechtlicher Normen auf die Tätigkeit und Wahrnehmung eines internationalen Strafgerichts auswirken kann. Interessant sind die Diskussionen zum Recht auf „Selbst"-Verteidigung, weil sie eine fundamentale Frage betreffen: Inwieweit ist es dem Angeklagten erlaubt, neben einer Verteidigung gegen den konkreten Tatvorwurf auch seine geschichtliche „Wahrheit" zu verteidigen?

II. Die grundlegende rechtliche Diskussion

An Prominenz gewann die Frage nach einem Recht auf „Selbst"-Verteidigung im Milošević-Verfahren vor dem ICTY. Das dortige Regelwerk sieht im englischen Original in Art. 21 (4) d) folgende Garantie vor:

> „to be tried in his presence, *and to defend himself in person or through legal assistance of his own choosing*; to be informed, if he does not have legal assistance, of this right; and *to have legal assistance assigned to him, in any case where the interests of justice so require,* and without payment by him in any such case if he does not have sufficient means to pay for it;" (Hervorhebung des Autors)

Diese Formulierung, die sich heute auch in Art. 67 (1) des Rom-Statuts des ICC wiederfindet, geht zurück auf Art. 14 (3) d) des Internationalen Pakts über bürgerliche und politische Rechte (IPbpR)[9] sowie eine ähnliche Formulierung in Art. 6 (3) c) der Europäischen Menschenrechtskonvention (EMRK).[10] Trotz dieser vermeintlich weiten Garantie ist es auf nationalstaatlicher Ebene anerkannt, dass ein absolutes Recht auf „Selbst"-Verteidigung

8 Einen guten Überblick über das Verfahren liefern J. Williams, *Slobodan Milošević and the Guarantee of Self-Representation*, Brooklyn Journal of International Law (2007), 553, 559 ff. und G. Boas, *The Right to Self-Representation in International and Domestic Criminal Law – Limitations and Qualifications of that Right*, in: H. Abtahi und G. Boas (Hrsg.), *The Dynamics of International Criminal Justice*, 39, 67 ff.

9 Dazu N. Jorgensen, *The Right of the Accused to Self-Representation Before International Criminal Tribunals*, American Journal of International Law (2004), 711, 713 f.; M. Scharf, *Self-Representation versus Assignment of Defence Counsel before International Criminal Tribunals*, Journal of International Criminal Justice (2006), 31, 33 ff.; P. Ambach, *Selbstvertretung im international Strafprozess*, Zeitschrift für Internationale Strafrechtsdogmatik (2009), 286, 287 ff.

10 Zur Rechtsprechung siehe N. Croquet, *The right to self-representation under the European Convention on Human Rights: what role for the limitation analysis?,* European Human Rights Law Review (2012), 292-308; Jorgensen, Fn. 9, 715 f.; Boas, Fn. 8, 52 ff.

durch einen Angeklagten nicht besteht, das Recht auf „Selbst"-Verteidigung demnach Einschränkungen durch Gesetzgeber und/oder Richter unterliegt.

1. Civil Law v. Common Law

Die Vorgaben von IPbpR und EMRK sind in den Nationalstaaten in fundamental unterschiedlicher Weise umgesetzt worden. Während die Staaten des *Civil Law* grundsätzlich eine Verteidigung durch den Beschuldigten selbst nur unter äußerst restriktiven Bedingungen zulassen, zeigen die durch das *Common Law* geprägten Staaten wie die USA eine deutliche Zurückhaltung bei der Beschränkung der Privatautonomie des durch die Staatsmacht beschuldigten Individuums.[11] Zum Zwecke der Vereinfachung sollen die verschiedenen Rechtstraditionen hier nur in groben Zügen und beispielhaft dargestellt werden.

Exemplarisch[12] für den kontinentaleuropäischen Umgang mit dem Recht auf „Selbst"-Verteidigung ist die ausführliche Normierung im deutschen Strafprozessrecht. In § 140 StPO heißt es auszugsweise:

> „(1) Die Mitwirkung eines Verteidigers ist notwendig wenn,
> 1. die Hauptverhandlung im ersten Rechtszug vor dem Oberlandesgericht oder dem Landgericht stattfindet;
> 2. dem Beschuldigten ein Verbrechen zur Last gelegt wird; [...]
> 4. gegen einen Beschuldigten Untersuchungshaft [...] vollstreckt wird; [...]
> (2) In anderen Fällen bestellt der Vorsitzende auf Antrag oder von Amts wegen einen Verteidiger, wenn wegen der Schwere der Tat oder wegen der Schwierigkeit der Sach- oder Rechtslage die Mitwirkung eines Verteidigers geboten erscheint, oder wenn ersichtlich ist, dass sich der Beschuldigte nicht selbst verteidigen kann [...]."

Ein Verfahren wegen Völkermord, Verbrechen gegen die Menschlichkeit oder Kriegsverbrechen erfordert nach den Vorgaben des deutschen Rechts zwingend die Anwesenheit eines Verteidigers – dies auch dann, wenn der Angeklagte selbst als Jurist geschult ist. Die Zielsetzung der deutschen Legislative erschließt sich bereits aus dem Wortlaut der Norm: die Unterstützung des und Fürsorge für den Angeklagten angesichts der Komplexität der Materie, der faktischen und psychologischen Hindernisse einer Selbstverteidigung sowie der drohenden Konsequenzen (hohe Straferwartung). Die deutsche Regelung hat zweifelsohne bevormundende Züge, da der Staat dem Bürger besonderen Schutz angedeihen lässt, ohne dass dieser besagten Schutz ablehnen kann. Die ausführliche Normierung führt zudem zu einer gesetzgeberisch gewollten Verallgemeinerung: Ein Strafverteidiger wird selbst dann beige-

---

11 Zur Historie siehe Überblick bei E. Cerruti, *Self-Representation in the International Arena: Removing a False Right of Spectacle*, Georgetown Journal of International Law (2009), 919, 920 ff.

12 Überblick bei Williams, Fn. 8, 558 (dort Fußnote 34) sowie Boas, Fn. 8, 50 ff., der auch darauf hinweist, dass in Serbien und Montenegro kein Recht zur „Selbst"-Verteidigung besteht.

ordnet, wenn der Beschuldigte intellektuell und emotional in der Lage ist, sich selbst zu verteidigen. Die abstrakt-generelle Regelung erleichtert jedoch die Rechtsanwendung, da eine Abwägung im konkreten Fall entbehrlich wird. Wer eines Verbrechens beschuldigt wird, wird ist als hilfsbedürftig einzustufen. Diese Verallgemeinerung hat Auswirkungen auf das Verhältnis zwischen Gericht und Angeklagtem. Der mit dem Fall befasste Richter hat das Verhalten oder den Charakter des Angeklagten nicht zu bewerten, sondern stützt seine Beiordnungsentscheidung auf abstrakte, objektive Kriterien: Welche Straftaten sind in der Anklageschrift genannt, befindet sich der Angeklagte in Untersuchungshaft, ist der Sachverhalt rechtlich und tatsächlich komplex? Konflikte sind bei einer Normierung der notwendigen Verteidigung nicht ausgeschlossen (siehe z.B. den NSU-Prozess mit einer Hauptangeklagten, welche die Kooperation mit ihren Anwälten *de facto* aufgekündigt hat) jedoch eher die Ausnahme.

Die Herangehensweise im US-amerikanischen Recht als einer prägenden Rechtsordnung des *Common-Law*-Systems ist fundamental entgegengesetzt. Aufbauend auf dem Urteil des US Supreme Courts in der Rechtssache *Faretta*[13] ist im Grundsatz auch in komplexen Verfahren mit schwerwiegendem Tatvorwurf von einem Recht auf Autonomie[14] und damit auf „Selbst"-Verteidigung auszugehen. Zwar kann der Angeklagte auf dieses Recht verzichten. Auch kann er dieses Rechts – aufgrund bestimmten Verhaltens – verlustig werden. Eine abstrakte Beschränkung des Rechts ist für erstinstanzliche Verhandlungen verfassungsrechtlich jedoch nicht akzeptiert. Es obliegt daher der Einschätzung des Richters, ob in der Person des Angeklagten ein Grund für eine – ausnahmsweise – Beschränkung des Rechts auf „Selbst"-Verteidigung vorliegt. Damit hat das Gericht das Verhalten des konkreten Angeklagten einer Einzelfallbewertung zu unterziehen. Die *Common-Law*-Herangehensweise vermeidet die dem kontinentaleuropäischem Recht innewohnende Tendenz zur verallgemeinernden Bevormundung, eröffnet allerdings Konfliktpotenzial in sensiblen Einzelfällen.

2. Anmerkung zur rechtsvergleichenden Diskussion

Die Bezugnahme auf Regelungen und Argumentationsmuster des nationalen Rechts ist ein wiederkehrendes Element der Rechtsdebatten im internationalen Strafrecht. Derartige Bezugnahmen bergen indes stets das Risiko von Missverständnissen und Simplifizierungen. Rechtsvergleichende Betrachtungen einzelner Normen sind ohne die Berücksichtigung des gesamten Regelungskonstrukts nur bedingt aussagekräftig. Dies zeigt auch die hiesige Diskussion: Besonders Kritiker eines Rechts auf „Selbst"-Verteidigung führen die deutsche Regelung – als Beispiel für die Herangehensweise des *Civil Law*

13 Dazu ausführlich Cerruti, Fn. 11, 924 f., 940 ff.; Jorgensen, Fn. 9, 717f.; Boas, Fn. 8, 41ff.

14 Dazu Williams, Fn. 8, 557. Kritisch Cerruti, Fn. 11, 925, 948, der die Gewährleistung der Autonomie als unzureichenden Grund ansieht.

– ins Feld, obwohl die deutsche Strafprozessordnung im Allgemeinen nicht so restriktiv ist, wie es der § 140 StPO auf den ersten Blick erscheinen lässt. So betont etwa Scharf:

> „It is also important to recognize that while most common law countries recognize a right of self-representation, civil-law countries, including France, Germany and Belgium, among others, do not feel compelled to permit a defendant to represent himself."[15]

Eine Bewertung einer Verfahrensordnung kann nicht bei § 140 StPO – oder den vergleichbaren Beiordnungsvorschriften anderer *Civil-Law*-Rechtsordnungen – enden. So bedeutet z.B. die Beiordnung eines Verteidigers im deutschen Recht gerade nicht, dass dem Angeklagten damit das Heft aus der Hand genommen wird. Dem Angeklagten stehen diverse prozessuale Handlungsrechte neben dem ihm beigeordneten Verteidiger zu, die Beiordnung nimmt ihm diese Mitwirkungsmöglichkeiten nicht. Er hat Antrags- und Rederechte und wirkt an der Beweisaufnahme und insbesondere an der Vernehmung von Zeugen mit. Damit kann er aktiv auf das Verhandlungsgeschehen einwirken.[16] Als Beispiel: § 240 Abs. 2 StPO sieht zur Befragung von Zeugen und Sachverständigen explizit vor:

> „Dasselbe [Fragerecht] hat der Vorsitzende der Staatsanwaltschaft, dem *Angeklagten und dem Verteidiger* sowie den Schöffen zu gestatten." (Hervorhebung des Autors)

Dementsprechend hat die Beiordnung nach deutschem Recht nicht derart schwerwiegende Auswirkungen, wie sie von einigen internationalen Beobachtern suggeriert und wohl auch gewünscht werden. Elementare Beteiligungsrechte bleiben erhalten und erlauben dem Angeklagten, die im amerikanischen Recht so betonte Privatautonomie neben dem gewählten Verteidiger weiter auszuüben. Sie sind nicht zum Schweigen in der zweiten Reihe verdammt.

Betrachtet man die internationale Diskussion, zeigt sich, dass es im Kern um die Mitwirkung des Angeklagten im Prozess und der dortigen Wahrheitsfindung geht. Vielfach geäußerte Forderungen nach einer Beschränkung des Rechts auf „Selbst"-Verteidigung zielen nicht primär auf die Fürsorgefunktion der notwendigen Verteidigung ab, sondern betonen die Gefahren eines „unkontrollierten" Angeklagten. In der wissenschaftlichen Diskussion wird der Angeklagte dementsprechend nicht selten als „Störenfried" portraitiert, dessen Ausführungen es einzuhegen gilt. Deutlich wird dies etwa in den Worten von Cerruti, der die Befürchtungen gegenüber sich selbst verteidigenden Angeklagten generell wie folgt darstellt:

---

15 Scharf, Fn. 9, 35. See also Cerruti, Fn. 11, 920, 972.

16 In internationalen Strafverfahren sind die Mitwirkungsrechte hingegen eingeschränkt, vgl. Ambach, Fn. 9, 286 f.; 302 f. Zum Akayesu-Verfahren vor dem ICTR siehe Jorgensen, Fn. 9, 724.

> „The defendant as self-advocate in an adversarial proceeding tends to abuse all of the other participants at trial, particularly his victims and accusers. He also becomes and abuser of the system itself."[17]

Zu den Angeklagten vor internationalen Strafgerichten ergänzt er:

> „[…] the narrow spectrum of defendants subject to a war crimes prosecution are precisely those politically engaged individuals who are most likely to view a criminal trial, like diplomacy, as merely a continuation of hostilities by other means."[18]

Scharf und Rassi gehen in ihrer Kritik noch deutlich weiter. Deren Ausführungen sind aufschlussreich, weil die zahlreichen Facetten ihrer Kritik unterschwellig in Literatur und Rechtsprechung wiederzufinden sind und Aufschluss über das Verständnis vieler internationaler Akteure gegenüber den Angeklagten in internationalen Strafprozessen liefern. So unterstellen sie – mit Blick auf Milošević[19] und Šešelj, nicht aber z.B. Karadžić[20], möglicherweise nachvollziehbar – eine Tendenz sich selbst verteidigender Angeklagter zu störendem Verhalten:

> „[…] a defendant will act in disruptive manner. Such seems to be inherent in certain types of defendants, in particular former rogue leaders who publicly challenge the court's authority to try them, thereby warranting appointment of counsel." [21]

Scharf und Rassi begründen hier das Aufzwingen eines Verteidigers mit der mangelnden Anerkennung, die der Angeklagte dem Gericht entgegenbringt. Unausgesprochen bleibt, warum ein Angeklagter gezwungen werden sollte, die Legitimität eines Gerichts anzuerkennen und im Falle der Verweigerung einer solchen Anerkennung eine prozessuale Konsequenz folgen soll. Die Erwartung, ein Angeklagter müsse sich nicht nur der Strafgewalt, sondern auch der Deutungshoheit des Gerichts unterwerfen, zieht sich wie ein roter Faden durch die Ausführungen von Scharf und Rassi und spiegelt ein wiederkehrendes Interpretationsmuster im internationalen Strafrecht wieder.[22]

---

17 Cerruti, Fn. 11, 959.

18 Cerruti, Fn. 11, 970.

19 Williams, Fn. 8, 580 ff. betont, dass Milošević – was vom Gericht anerkannt wurde – nicht als „obstructionist" bezeichnet werden könne, obwohl dieser die „Selbst"-Verteidigung für politische Stellungnahmen nutzte.

20 Siehe Z. Juska, *Emerging Voices: The Role of Standby Counsel to a Self-Represented Accused – Lessons Learned from the Karadžić Case*, Opinio Juris, 12.8.2013 (abrufbar unter: http://opiniojuris.org/2013/08/12/emerging-voices-the-role-of-standby-counsel-to-a-self-represented-accused-lessons-learned-from-the-Karadžić-case/; letzter Zugriff: 25.10.2015).

21 M. Scharf und C. Rassi, *Do Former Leaders Have an International Right to Self-Representation in War Crimes Trials?*, Ohio State Journal on Dispute Resolution (2005), 3, 8. Ähnlich Scharf, Fn. 9, 32.

22 Anklänge einer Kritik einer „politischen" Verteidigung findet man auch bei Jorgensen, Fn. 9, 712; I. Bonomy, *The Reality of Conducting a War Crimes Trial*, Journal of International Criminal Justice (2007), 348, 356; Ambach, Fn. 9, 292; G. Sluiter, *Karadžić in Tri-*

Sie monieren zudem die historischen Ausführungen des Angeklagten Milošević:

> „By acting as his own counsel, Milošević has been able to begin each stage of the trial with hours of opening arguments, which have included Hollywood-quality video and slide-show presentations showing the destruction wrought by the 1999 NATO bombing campaign."[23]

Auch die Darstellung des folgenden Szenarios zeigt das nicht seltene Unbehagen gegenüber einer Verteidigung, welche die Grenzen der reinen Rechtsverteidigung gegen den durch die internationale Strafjustiz festgelegten Tatvorwurf überschreitet:

> „If, in contrast, Saddam Hussein were to be permitted to take advantage of the tactics of Slobodan Milošević and portray his trial as ‚victor's justice' at the hands of a ‚puppet court', this *would seriously undermine the goal of fostering reconciliation* between the Iraqi Kurds, Shi'ites, and Sunnis. The *historic record* developed by such a trial *would forever be questioned.*"[24] (Hervorhebungen des Autors)

Die hervorgehobenen Passagen illustrieren, welche Bedenken es – nicht nur von Seiten der Wissenschaft – gegen die aktive Mitwirkung der Angeklagten im Prozess gibt. Diese Bedenken sind grundsätzlich nachvollziehbar, schließlich werden große Hoffnungen in die Errichtung und Aufrechterhaltung internationaler Straftribunale und -gerichte gelegt und beträchtliche Finanzmittel investiert. Es ist jedoch Vorsicht geboten, wenn generelle Erwartungen an die Wirkmöglichkeiten der internationalen Strafjustiz zur Interpretation konkreter Verfahrensnormen herangezogen werden. Boas warnt daher zu Recht vor einer Politisierung internationaler Strafanwendung, wenn er feststellt:

> „The concerns pondered by Scharf and Rassi are legitimate sociological and political concerns. However, they are not appropriate legal concerns. An international criminal tribunal or court must resist the inevitable pressures of politics that impinge upon their work."[25]

Diese Grenzziehung ist in der Praxis ein diffiziles Unterfangen. Dies hat sich auch in den Verfahren vor dem ICTY und anderer internationaler Strafgerichte gezeigt. Die Einzelheiten der Entscheidungsfindung sollen an dieser Stelle nicht erneut rekapituliert werden. Das Augenmerk soll stattdessen auf die Schwierigkeiten einer fallgerechten Begründung gelegt werden.

---

al, Two Procedural Problems, The Hague Justice Portal (2008), 2 (abrufbar unter www.haguejusticeportal.net).

23 Scharf/Rassi, Fn. 21, 4.

24 Scharf/Rassi, Fn. 21, 7. Ähnlich bereits Scharf, Fn. 9, 46.

25 Boas, Fn. 8, 92.

III. Das Recht auf „Selbst"-Verteidigung in Verfahren vor dem ICTY

Das Jugoslawientribunal hat ein grundsätzliches Recht auf „Selbst"-Verteidigung anerkannt. Die Berufungskammer hat in ihrer Entscheidung im Milošević-Verfahren vom 1. November 2004 der Verfahrenskammer dem Grunde nach zugestimmt und deutlich betont:

> „Defendants before this Tribunal, then, have the *presumptive right to represent themselves* notwithstanding a Trial Chamber's judgment that they would be better off if represented by counsel. While this *right to self-representation* is indisputable, jurisdictions around the world recognize that it is *not categorically inviolable*."[26] (Hervorhebung des Autors)

Da das ICTY-Statut, ebenso wie das Rom-Statut des ICC, die Ausnahmekonstellationen nicht explizit normiert,[27] sehen sich die das Recht anwendenden Richter wiederholt vor die Entscheidung gestellt, ob sie die Konfrontation mit einem Angeklagten suchen wollen und ob sie diesem eine Verteidiger beiordnen. Die Berufungskammer hat deutlich gemacht, dass die Berufungsrichter die Begründung einer solchen Ausnahmekonstellation zu überprüfen gedenken.

1. Klassische Begründungsansätze für eine Verweigerung

Die Richter der internationalen Straftribunale haben sich in diversen Verfahren mit Anträgen des Angeklagten, sich selbst zu verteidigen, auseinandergesetzt. Dabei haben die Richter auf einen Fundus aus Argumenten zurückgegriffen, die ihren Ursprung in den nationalstaatlichen Rechtsordnungen und der nationalen Rechtsprechung haben und die für das internationale Strafverfahren adaptiert wurden. Da die normativen Vorgaben des Statuts keine definierten Fallgruppen vorsehen, fällt auch die Interpretation der Argumentation schwer.[28] Nicht selten wurde seitens der entscheidenden Verfahrenskammern eine Vielzahl von Argumenten vorgebracht, die im Zusammenspiel die jeweilige Entscheidung tragen. Einige Argumentationsmuster lassen sich jedoch herauskristallisieren.

---

26 *Prosecutor v. Milošević*, IT-02-54-AR73, Berufungskammer, Entscheidung v. 1.11.2004, para. 11, 12.

27 Zur allgemeinen Regelung der Regel 45*quater*, siehe Jorgensen, Fn. 9, 713. Zur Frage der Existenz einer ausreichenden Rechtsgrundlage siehe C. Hotis, *A ‚Fair and Expeditous' Trial: A Reappraisal of Slobodan Milošević's Right to Self-Representation before the International Criminal Tribunal for the Former Yugoslavia*, Chicago Journal of International Law (2006), 775, 783. Allgemeine Kritik hinsichtlich der unzureichenden Normierung von objektiven Kriterien üben Sluiter, Fn. 22, 3; P. Bassett, *The right to self-representation before International Criminal Tribunals, while not absolute, should only be denied in limited circumstances*, Northern Ireland Legal Quaterly (2011), 235, 236 f. Boas, Fn. 8, 77, plädiert für den flexiblen Rückgriff auf allgemeine Fairnesserwägungen.

28 Williams, Fn. 8, 555 spricht nicht zu Unrecht von einer Improvisation. Auch Hotis, Fn. 27, 776 hält die bisherigen Begründungen für unzureichend.

Das grundsätzliche Problem eines sich selbst verteidigenden Angeklagten sind die regelmäßig zu befürchtenden Verzögerungen des Verfahrens, welche angesichts der begrenzten Ressourcen der internationalen Strafjustiz grundsätzlich zu vermeiden sind.[29] Die Berufungskammer hat im Šešelj-Verfahren vor Verzögerungen und der daraus resultierenden Verschwendung von Ressourcen explizit gewarnt.[30] Die Richter des SCSL haben im Norman-Verfahren[31] zudem darauf hingewiesen, dass die Richter eine zeitnahe Aufarbeitung zu gewährleisten haben und betonen:

> „[There is an] obligation imposed on the Chamber to ensure that a trial is fair and expeditious and that even though this right is conditioned on a „full respect of the rights of the accused", we consider and so hold, that these rights would not include an absolute right of self-representation."[32]

Die Gründe für drohende Beeinträchtigungen des Verfahrens sind mannigfaltig:[33] Strafverfahren dieser Größenordnung erfordern eine Sichtung, Auswertung und Kategorisierung zahlreicher Dokumente. Ohne genaue Kenntnis der Beweislage ist eine effektive Verteidigung schlichtweg nicht möglich. Auch wenn der Angeklagte Unterstützung bei der Auswertung erfährt, sind Verzögerungen zu erwarten. Hinzukommt, dass eine Bewertung der Beweismittel stets im Hinblick auf die rechtliche Relevanz zu erfolgen hat. Internationale Strafverfahren sind – auch aufgrund der Einflüsse verschiedener Rechtstraditionen sowie internationaler Menschenrechtsverträge[34] – juristisch komplexe Verfahren.[35] Die Verteidigung im Verfahren setzt Kenntnis der Abläufe und Gepflogenheiten eines internationalen Prozesses voraus (z.B. Geheimhaltungsvorschriften, Vorgaben an die Befragung von Zeugen,[36] Fristen, Umfangsbegrenzungen für Schriftsätze[37]), die selbst für den juristisch vorgebildeten Angeklagten nicht einfach zu durchschauen sind.[38] Dabei kann auch nicht ausgeblendet werden, dass internationale Strafverfahren grundsätzlich in den Amtssprachen Englisch und Französisch geführt werden. Um als Verteidiger vor den Gerichten zugelassen zu werden, muss eine der Amtsspra-

---

29 Zum Zeit- und Kostendruck siehe Williams, Fn. 8, 567 f. Ob ein derartiger Zeitdruck auch bei einem auf Dauer eingerichteten Tribunal wie dem ICC besteht, bleibt abzuwarten.

30 *Prosecutor v. Šešelj,* IT-03-67- AR 73.3, Berufungskammer, Entscheidung v. 20.10.2006, para. 29. Zur Notwendigkeit einer Verfahrensbeschleunigung siehe auch Williams, Fn. 8, 571 ff.

31 Dazu ausführlich auch Boas, Fn. 8, 57 ff.

32 *Prosecutor v. Norman et al.*, SCSL-04-14-T-125, Verfahrenskammer, Entscheidung v. 8.6.2004, para. 11.

33 Siehe auch Überblick bei Scharf, Fn. 9, 38 ff.

34 Siehe dazu den Beitrag von Gebhard in diesem Band.

35 Dazu Ambach, Fn. 9, 291.

36 Siehe auch Auflistung in *Prosecutor v. Šešelj*, IT-03-67- AR 73.3, Berufungskammer, Entscheidung v. 20.10.2006, para. 29.

37 *Ibid*, para. 10.

38 Ambach, Fn. 9, 291, weist auf die hohen Anforderungen an die Verteidiger hin. Zur Thematik siehe auch C. Buisman u.a., *Trial and Error – How Effective is Legal Representation in International Criminal Proceedings*, International Criminal Law Review (2005), 1-82.

chen beherrscht werden.[39] Dies kann naturgemäß von dem Angeklagten nicht eingefordert werden. Verteidigt sich der Angeklagte selbst, besteht das Risiko sprachlicher Hürden und Missverständnisse sowie gegebenenfalls die Notwendigkeit zeit- und kostenintensiver Übersetzungen.[40] Daher gilt: Entscheidet sich ein Angeklagter, sein Recht auf „Selbst"-Verteidigung geltend zu machen, ist im Regelfall[41] eine unterdurchschnittlich effektive Verhandlungsführung zu erwarten, die zu Verzögerungen führt.

Allein die Möglichkeit von Effektivitätseinbußen kann indes nicht ausreichend für die Bestellung eines Pflichtverteidigers sein. So ist es grundsätzlich problematisch eine Einschränkung von Verfahrensgrundrechten mit mangelnden Ressourcen zu begründen.[42] Die „Effektivität der Strafverfolgung" gebietet auch die Bereitstellung der dafür erforderlichen Mittel. Ein (internationales) Gericht würde sich mit dem Verweis auf mangelnde Ressourcen angreifbar machen. Die Erklärung, man könne für die Ausübung eines prozessualen Rechts die Mehrkosten nicht tragen, würde das Gericht zudem einem Begründungszwang für die Mittelallokation unterwerfen. Die Verteidigung würde eine solche Argumentation sicherlich zum Anlass nehmen einzelne Budgetpositionen in Frage zu stellen, zumal auch die Anklage und die Opferbeteiligung zur Verlängerung des Verfahrens beitragen. Damaška formuliert dies treffend:

> „ [...] the length and undwieldly nature of this procès monstre is, to an extent, of the Tribunal's own making. Speeding it up at the accused's expense [...] seems unfair."[43]

Die Dauer und Komplexität der Verfahren kann auch aus einem anderen Grund nur schwerlich dem „Selbst"-Verteidigungsrecht entgegengehalten werden. Geht man im Einklang mit der ständigen internationalen Rechtsprechung (s.o.) von einem grundsätzlichen Recht des Angeklagten aus, sich selbst zu verteidigen, kann dieses Recht nicht im gleichen Atemzug mit Verweis auf allgemeine Schwierigkeiten der Ausübung dieses Rechts eingeschränkt werden. Eine Beschränkung erfordert eine – im Einzelfall zu begründende – Ausnahmekonstellation. Mit derartigen Sonderfällen haben sich die diversen Gerichte verschiedentlich befasst. Ein klassisches Problem ist der Umgang mit Opferzeugen und deren Identität. In Janković und Stankonvic betont die Verfahrenskammer des ICTY:

> „The Chamber further notes that the accused is restricted from having contacts with any persons other than his family, legal counsel and diplomatic or consular representatives because he threatened to reveal the identities and whereabouts of

39 Für den ICC siehe Regel 21 (1) der Verfahrens- und Beweisanordnung (diese ergänzt das Rom-Statut).

40 Dazu und konkret zum *Šešelj*-Verfahren siehe Jorgensen, Fn. 9, 723.

41 Juzka, Fn. 20, weist auf die besondere Effektivität der Verteidigung durch *Karadžić* hin. Dies dürfte indes der Ausnahmefall sein.

42 Kritik auch bei Hotis, Fn. 27, 776 f.

43 Damaška, Fn. 1, 7.

> protected Prosecutions's witnesses. The disrespect for protective measures ordered by the Chamber does not only disqualify the Accused from representing himself [...]"[44]

Außerdem sieht sie es als unangemessen an, dem Angeklagten das Recht zur Zeugenbefragung zuzubilligen:

> „The Accused is also charged with crimes of a sexual nature [...] The Chamber doubts that it would be appropriate for the Accused to cross-examine at trial witnesses who are also alleged victims of those crimes [...] Yet, the imposition of standby counsel in order to cross-examine those witnesses may be an appropriate measure which would not touch upon the right of the Accused to defend himself in person."[45]

Im bereits erwähnten Norman-Verfahren hatten die Richter des SCSL zu berücksichtigen, dass das bereits laufende Verfahren nicht nur gegen den eine „Selbst"-Verteidigung anstrebenden Angeklagten, sondern zwei weitere Angeklagte geführt wurde. Die Richter der Verfahrenskammer konstatierten daher:

> „If the application [...] were granted, this would have the potential to negatively impact on the fairness and expeditiousness of the trial of these co-accused persons [...]"[46]

Diese Entscheidung berücksichtigt zu Recht, dass ein Angeklagter durchaus auf sein Recht auf ein zügiges Verfahren verzichten,[47] diese Entscheidung aber nicht seinen Mitangeklagten aufzwingen kann. Eine Abwägung der widerstreitenden Interessen der Angeklagten kann mithin in legitimer Weise zur Einschränkung der – nicht absoluten – Rechtsposition des einen Angeklagten führen. Ob eine Verbindung von Verfahren zulässig ist, wenn einer der betroffenen Angeklagten von Anfang an seine Intention, sich selbst zu verteidigen, mitgeteilt hat, ist noch ungeklärt.[48] Nachvollziehbar ist, dass jedenfalls bei einer nachträglichen Geltendmachung des Rechts auf „Selbst"-Verteidigung eine Einschränkung erfolgen kann. Im ICTY-Verfahren gegen

---

44 *Prosecutor v. Janković u. Stanković*, IT-96-23/2-PT, Verfahrenskammer I, Entscheidung v. 19.8.2005, para. 25. Siehe auch *Prosecutor v. Krajišnik*, IT-00-39-T, Verfahrenskammer I, Entscheidung v. 18.8.2005, para. 34. Zu ähnlichen Problemen auf nationaler Ebene siehe Cerruti, Fn. 11, 955.

45 *Prosecutor v. Janković u. Stanković*, IT-96-23/2-PT, Verfahrenskammer I, Entscheidung v. 19.8.2005, para. 21. Zu vergleichbaren Ansätzen im nationalen Recht siehe Boas, Fn. 8, 47 ff.; Hotis, Fn. 27, 783, weist darauf hin, dass dieses Argument einer Einzelfallprüfung bedürfe.

46 *Prosecutor v. Norman et al.*, SCSL-04-14-T-125, Verfahrenskammer, Entscheidung v. 8.6.2004, para. 13.

47 Zu diesem Aspekt siehe auch Williams, Fn. 8, 574 f.; G. Sluiter, *Fairness and the Interests of Justice*, Journal of International Criminal Justice (2005), 9, 11 f..

48 Die Tatsache, dass der Antrag erst relativ spät erfolgte, wird durch die Kammer deutlich hervorgehoben, *Prosecutor v. Norman et al.*, SCSL-04-14-T-125, Verfahrenskammer, Entscheidung v. 8.6.2004, para. 17.19.

Krajišnik hat die Verfahrenskammer diesem Punkt – zu Recht – eine große Bedeutung beigemessen:

> „In sum, a defendant who asserts the right to self-representation prior to the commencement of trial has a strong case. When, however, the request is made during trial, the discretion of the trial judge to dismiss the request is much broader because a new factual assessment enters the calculation, namely the extent to which the requested change in status will disrupt trial proceedings."[49]

Ein kategorisches Ablehnungsrecht haben die Richter indes auch in einer derartigen Fallkonstellation nicht für angemessen erachtet. Es bedarf auch hier einer Einzelfallbetrachtung. Es ist, je nach Verfahrensstadium und bisherigen Kooperation zwischen dem Angeklagten und seinem Verteidiger, nicht zwingend, dass durch die Übernahme der Verteidigung durch den Angeklagten eine signifikante Verzögerung des Verfahrens zu erwarten ist. Es ist für eine effektive Verteidigung oftmals ohnehin dringend notwendig und gängige Praxis, dass der Angeklagte in die Verteidigungsarbeit eng eingebunden wird. Sein Wissen über die Situation vor Ort, die Kenntnisse der Konfliktbeteiligten und -abläufe sind für die Vorbereitung und Durchführung einer Verteidigungsstrategie regelmäßig zwingend erforderlich. Dementsprechend ist es keine Seltenheit, dass der Angeklagte über die Details des Verfahrens umfassend informiert ist. Eine nachträgliche Forderung des Angeklagten, die Verteidigung in seine Hände zu legen, muss daher nicht *ipso facto* zu einer Verfahrensverzögerung führen. Dennoch bestehen keine durchgreifenden Bedenken, einem Angeklagten, der über einen längeren Zeitraum bewusst auf sein Recht auf „Selbst"-Verteidigung verzichtet hat, an dieser Entscheidung festzuhalten.[50]

Die Idee, dass ein Angeklagter durch ein bewusstes Verhalten seines Rechts verlustig werden kann, ist in der *Common-Law*-Rechtsprechung tief verwurzelt und hat auch die internationale Rechtsprechung geprägt. Es ist – da es sich bei dem Recht auf „Selbst"-Verteidigung um ein grundsätzlich abdingbares Recht handelt – nicht zu beanstanden, wenn Verzichtshandlungen – wie im Fall Krajišnik – im Rahmen der Abwägung zu Lasten des Angeklagten berücksichtigt werden. Anerkannt ist ebenfalls, dass Angeklagte durch unbotmäßiges Verhalten das Recht auf „Selbst"-Verteidigung verwirken können. Wiederholte Beleidigungen der Prozessbeteiligten oder verbale Behinderungen des Ablaufs des Prozesses werden regelmäßig zu Lasten des Angeklagten zu berücksichtigen sein.[51] Ein Ausschluss des Rechts auf „Selbst"-Verteidigung in derartigen Extremfällen ist in den Verfahrensregeln angelegt. So heißt es in Art. 63 (2) des Rom Statuts – vergleichbar mit Regelungen anderer Tribunale – für das Recht auf Anwesenheit im Gerichtssaal:

---

49 *Prosecutor v. Krajišnik*, IT-00-39-T, Verfahrenskammer I, Entscheidung v. 18.8.2005, para. 33.

50 Ambach, Fn. 9,. 297.

51 Siehe exemplarisch die Beschreibungen in *Prosecutor v. Janković u. Stanković*, IT-96-23/2-PT, Verfahrenskammer I, Entscheidung v. 19.8.2005, para. 22 ff.

„If the accused, being present before the Court, *continues to disrupt the trial,* the Trial Chamber may remove the accused and shall make provision for him or her to observe the trial and instruct counsel from outside the courtroom, through the use of technology, if required. Such measures shall be taken only *in exceptional circumstances* after reasonable alternatives have proved inadequate, and only for such duration as is strictly required."

Wenn das Regelwerk sogar einen vollständigen Ausschluss des Angeklagten vorsieht, lässt sich für diese Ausnahmefälle grundsätzlich auch die Beiordnung eines Pflichtverteidigers begründen. So hatte auch die Verfahrenskammer im Milošević-Verfahren mit Blick auf die dortige Regel 80 (B) argumentiert:

„Clearly, an accused whose behaviour has resulted in his removal from the courtroom pursuant to Rule 80 (B) of the Rules, has also relinquished his right to defend himself in person."[52]

Dies darf jedoch nicht zur Annahme verleiten, dass eine derartige Entscheidung im Falle eines ausfallend agierenden Angekalgten einfach getroffen werden kann. Ein derartiges Fehlverhalten ist primär als Ordnungswidrigkeit anzusehen und sollte daher eher als „contempt of court" beziehungsweise heute nach Art. 71 (1) des Rom-Statuts geahndet werden.[53] Die Beiordnung eines Pflichtverteidigers ist hingegen keine Sanktion und erfordert als reine Präventivmaßnahme eine Prognoseentscheidung, die der besonderen Bedeutung des Rechts auf „Selbst"-Verteidigung Rechnung trägt.[54] Nur bei einer dauerhaft zu erwartenden Störung des Verfahrensablaufs erscheint eine derart schwerwiegende Maßnahme angezeigt. Die Berufungskammer des ICTY hat es daher für erforderlich erachtet, dass eine vorherige Warnung ausgesprochen wird, um den Angeklagten die Gelegenheit zu geben, sein Verhalten anzupassen.[55] Ebenso wird zu berücksichtigen sein, ob das Verhalten des Angeklagten über den despektierlichen Inhalt hinaus auch signifikante Auswirkungen auf die Dauer des Verfahrens hat und somit zusätzlich auch als Verzögerungstaktik gewertet werden kann.

Eine anders gelagerte Ausnahmekonstellation hatten die Richter des ICTY im Milošević-Verfahren zu bewerten. Milošević mag vielen Beobachtern als politischer Agitator in Erinnerung geblieben sein, der das Jugoslawien-Tribunal als politische Bühne genutzt hat. Ursächlich für die schlussendlich erfolgte Auferlegung eines Pflichtverteidigers war indes dessen Erkrankung, die zu wiederholten Verzögerungen des Verfahrens geführt hatte.[56]

---

52 *Prosecutor v. Milošević,* IT-02-54, Verfahrenskammer, Entscheidung v. 4.4.2003, para. 40.

53 Vgl. dazu O. Triffterer, *Art. 71*, in: O. Triffterer (Hrsg.), *Commentary on the Rome Statute of the International Criminal Court,* 2. Aufl. 2008, Rn. 13.

54 *Prosecutor v. Krajišnik,* IT-00-39-A, Berufungskammer, Entscheidung v. 11.5.2007, Sondervotum von Richter Schomburg, para 4. Siehe auch Bassett, Fn. 27, 243.

55 *Prosecutor v. Šešelj*, IT-03-67-AR 73.3, Berufungskammer, Entscheidung v. 20.10.2006, paras. 22 ff.

56 Sluiter, Fn. 47, 10.

Diffizil war die Entscheidung, weil eine Einschränkung des Rechts auf „Selbst"-Verteidigung für gewöhnlich mit einer bewussten Verhaltensweise des Angeklagten begründet wurde (Verzicht, bewusster Verstoß gegen Vorgaben) und die schwerwiegende Erkrankung dem Angeklagten nicht zum Vorwurf gemacht werden kann.[57] Dennoch haben sich Verfahrens- und Berufungskammer dem Grunde nach für eine Gleichbehandlung bewusster und unbewusster Verfahrensbehinderungen entschieden:

> „There is no difference in principle between deliberate misconduct which disrupts the proceedings and any other circumstances which so disrupts the proceedings as to threaten the integrity of the trial. These are simply examples of circumstances in which the right to represent oneself must yield to the overarching right to a fair trial."[58]

Die Berufungskammer hat sich dem angeschlossen:

> „But it cannot be that the only kind of disruption legitimately cognizable by a Trial Chamber is the intentional variety. How should the Tribunal treat a defendant whose health, while good enough to engage in the ordinary and nonstrenuous activities of everyday life, is not sufficiently robust to withstand all the rigors of trial work – the late nights, the stressful cross-examinations, the courtroom confrontations – unless the hearing schedule is reduced to one day a week, or even one day a month? *Must the Trial Chamber be forced to choose between setting the defendant free and allowing the case to grind to an effective halt? In the Appeals Chamber's view, to ask that question is to answer it.*"[59] (Hervorhebungen des Autors)

Ob diese Argumentationsweise angesichts des historischen Argumentationsansatzes und der wiederholten Betonung der Privatautonomie überzeugt, sei dahingestellt. Im Interesse einer praktischen Handhabbarkeit ist eine verallgemeinernde Gleichbehandlung in jedem Falle nachvollziehbar und zu begrüßen. Dies erlaubt es den Richtern in sensiblen Fällen im Übrigen auch von der Feststellung eines Fehlverhaltens des Angeklagten abzusehen und eine dialogische Lösung zu suchen. Dass dies keinesfalls ein einfaches Unterfangen ist, dürfte sich von selbst verstehen. In der Praxis – insbesondere im Fall Milošević – hat sich gezeigt, dass die Richter bei unverschuldeten Verzögerungen durchaus die Bereitschaft zu Kompromissen gezeigt haben und weitestgehend von einem Aufoktroyieren abgesehen haben. Dem Angeklagten wurde stattdessen weitreichende Unterstützung zuteil.[60] Trotz einiger Forde-

---

57 Kritisch daher Williams, Fn. 8, 576 ff.; 587 ff.; Sluiter, Fn. 47, 13; Damaška, Fn. 1, 6.

58 *Prosecutor v. Milošević*, IT-02-54-T, Verfahrenskammer III, Entscheidung v. 22.9.2004, para. 33.

59 *Prosecutor v. Milošević*, IT-02-54-AR73, Berufungskammer, Entscheidung v. 1.11.2004, para. 14. Siehe auch *Prosecutor v. Šešelj*, IT-03-67-AR 73.3, Berufungskammer, Entscheidung v. 20.10.2006, para. 8.

60 Siehe z. B. *Prosecutor v. Milošević*, IT-02-54-T, Verfahrenskammer III, Entscheidung v. 22.9.2004, para. 84 (siehe auch die dortige Fußnote 143). Siehe auch Ausführungen bei J.T. Tuinstra, Assisting an Accused to Represent Himself, Journal of International Criminal Justice (2006), 47, 50.

rungen aus Politik und Wissenschaft haben die Richter der internationalen Straftribunale den sich selbst verteidigenden Angeklagten einen vergleichsweise weiten Spielraum belassen. Die gefundenen Ergebnisse sind – insbesondere im Lichte der international divergierenden Rechtslagen – nicht zu beanstanden und zeugen häufig von einem feinen Gespür für die Realitäten internationaler Strafverfahren.

2. Politisch heikle Argumentationsmuster

Neben den die Entscheidung tragenden Begründungen lohnt sich ein weiterer Blick auf die Argumentationsmuster der internationalen Strafjustiz.[61] Sie liefern kleine Einblicke in die Entscheidungsfindung der internationalen Richterschaft und veranschaulichen, welche Rolle dem Angeklagten in der Praxis zugeschrieben wird. Ein erstes Beispiel liefert die Verfahrenskammer im Milošević-Verfahren. In ihrer Entscheidung vom 5. November 2009 hatten sich die Richter mit der Frage auseinanderzusetzen, wie auf eine Gerichtssaalabwesenheit des Angeklagten reagiert werden sollte. Zunächst wies das Gericht darauf hin, dass der Angeklagte grundsätzlich ein Recht habe sich selbst zu vertreten. Sollte er jedoch auf sein Anwesenheitsrecht verzichten, solle ein Verteidiger beigeordnet werden, um die Fortführung des Verfahrens zu gewährleisten. Interessieren soll hier nur die Begründung, warum eine aktive Verteidigung in der Sache als erforderlich angesehen wird:

> „In the first place, the *truth-seeking function* of the trial process would be deprived of evidence which may go to challenge the evidence adduced by the Prosecution. Secondly, an important function of the trial, as originally envisaged by the Security Council of the United Nations in the very creation of the Tribunal, was to *seek further peace and reconciliation* among and between the various factions involved in the conflict in the former Yugoslavia. *To allow the Trial Chamber to hear and assess only half of the evidence [...] would be to deny the opportunity the trail process may have to engender such peace and reconciliation* [...].“[62] (Hervorhebung des Autors)

Die Rolle, die dem Angeklagten hier zugesprochen wird, ist für ein Strafverfahren eher ungewöhnlich. Der Angeklagte wird durch das Gericht in die Pflicht genommen, sich aktiv gegen die konkret erhobenen Tatvorwürfe zur Wehr zu setzen, damit die mit der Strafverfolgung angestrebten Ziele verwirklicht werden können.[63] Wahrlich keine Selbstverständlichkeit. In der gleichen Entscheidung wird ihm zudem sogar deutlich zur Kenntnis gebracht, er möge Zeit und Ressourcen zur Verteidigung der konkreten Tatvorwürfe

---

61 Die Betrachtung erhebt weder Anspruch auf Vollständigkeit noch Repräsentativität; sie soll Anreiz zur Reflektion geben.

62 *Prosecutor v. Milošević,* IT-95-5/18-T, Verfahrenskammer, Entscheidung v. 5.11.2009, para. 20. Siehe auch Cerruti, Fn. 11, 978.

63 Kritik an der Berücksichtigung politischer Implikationen im Rahmen der Rechtsanwendung auch bei Boas, Fn. 8, 93.

aufwenden und die historischen Hintergründe weitestgehend ausblenden.[64] Es ist sicherlich eine Besonderheit internationaler Strafverfahren, dass die Verwirklichung der angestrebten Straf- und Strafprozesszwecke[65] in der Rechtsanwendung und Argumentation der beteiligten Akteure eine derart prominente Rolle spielt. Unproblematisch ist ein solches Hineinwirken der sehr allgemein gehaltenen und eher weltpolitischen Zielsetzungen der Präambel in die Verfahrenswirklichkeit nicht. Das strafrechtliche Verfahren dient nicht dazu, den „Politiker“ oder „General“, kurzum die Person des Angeklagten zu richten, sondern konkret nachweisbare Handlungen einer strafrechtlichen Sanktionierung zuzuführen. Die Zwänge des Strafverfahrens muss der Angeklagte tolerieren. Ihm kann indes nicht abverlangt werden, sich mit den Zielen und Bestrebungen des Gerichts zu identifizieren oder diese gar aktiv zu unterstützen. Dennoch werden Angeklagte, die sich dem Verfahren durch demonstratives Schweigen zu entziehen versuchen, kritisch beäugt. Die Forderung, der Angeklagte habe aktiv am Verfahren mitzuwirken findet sich auch in einer Entscheidung des ICTR im Barayagwiza-Verfahren, in dem der Angeklagte die Kooperation mit dem Tribunal und den beigeordneten Anwälten verweigerte:

> „In the present case, Mr. Barayagwiza is actually boycotting the United Nations Tribunal. He has *chosen both to be absent in the trial and to give no instructions as how his legal representation should proceed* in the trial or as to the specifics of his strategy. In such a situation, his lawyers cannot simply abide with his 'instruction' not to defend him. Such instructions, in the opinion of the Chamber, should rather be seen as *an attempt to obstruct judicial proceedings*."[66] (Hervorhebung des Autors)

Dass die Richter der internationalen Straftribunale den politischen Zielsetzungen der Tribunale besondere Rechnung tragen und dies in die Entscheidung konkreter prozessualer Fragen einfließen lassen, zeigt sich auch deutlich in der Entscheidung der Verfahrenskammer des ICTY in der Sache Krajišnik, der eine „Selbst“-Verteidigung beantragt hatte:

> „If his request were honoured, he would end up receiving a very poor defence, which *would only serve to bring the international criminal justice process into disrepute*.“[67] (Hervorhebung des Autors)

---

64 *Prosecutor v. Milošević,* IT-95-5/18-T, Verfahrenskammer, Entscheidung v. 5.11.2009, para. 23.

65 Dazu ausführlich M. Hiéramente, *Internationale Haftbefehle in noch andauernden Konflikten*, 2013, S. 142 ff. m.w.N.

66 *Prosecutor v. Barayagwiza*, ICTR-97-19-T, Verfahrenskammer I, Entscheidung v. 2.11.2000, para. 24. Zustimmung bei Boas, Fn. 8, 62; N. Jorgensen, *The Problem of Self-Representation at International Criminal Tribunals*, Journal of International Criminal Justice (2006), 64, 72.

67 *Prosecutor v. Krajišnik*, IT-00-39-T, Verfahrenskammer I, Entscheidung v. 18.8.2005, para. 34.

Im Seseslj-Verfahren deutet die Berufungskammer des ICTY an, dass sie politische Aktivitäten des Angeklagten – auch wenn sich diese nicht unmittelbar auf die ordnungsgemäße Durchführung des Verfahrens selbst auswirken – als Argument für die Entziehung des Rechts auf „Selbst“-Verteidigung in Erwägung zieht. So werden seitens der Berufungsrichter auch Verstöße gegen die Haftordnung als Argument gegen dessen Recht sich selbst vor Gericht zu vertreten angeführt:

> „Furthermore, in November and December 2003, Šešelj used communications facilities in the United Nations Detention Unit ('UNDU') to make statements to the press concerning the upcoming Serbian parliamentary elections in breach of the Rules of Detention […]“

Die Vermeidung (nicht *per se* illegaler) politischer Agitation wird auch seitens der Anklagebehörde als Argument für eine Beschränkung des Rechts auf „Selbst“-Verteidigung ins Feld geführt. Die Kammer resümiert den Vortrag der Anklage diesbezüglich wie folgt:

> „The Prosecution seeks an order from the Trial Chamber directing that legal counsel be appointed to assist the accused with his defence. In the view of the Prosecution, the interests of justice require such action due to the complexity of the case; *the Accused's express intention to cause harm to the Tribunal and to use the proceedings as a forum for Serb national interests*; the consequent possibility of a disorderly trial; *the necessity to safeguard the administration of justice; and the public interest in the restoration of peace in the former Yugoslavia.*"[68] (Hervorhebung des Autors)

Ein geordnetes, und auf das juristisch Wesentliche beschränkte Verfahren mag für den Praktiker wünschenswert sein, ist indes weitgehend realitätsfremd. Pathos und Emotionen sind aufgrund der Natur der angeklagten Taten ständige Begleiter internationaler Strafverfahren. Dass im Kampf um die prozessuale Wahrheit und die Deutungshoheit auch Ausschweifungen und medienwirksame Statements zu erwarten sind, ist Teil der Lebenswirklichkeit von Kriegsverbrecherprozessen. Halten sich derartige Ausführungen – durch Anklage[69] wie durch die Verteidigung – in einem vertretbaren Rahmen, ist dies zu tolerieren; bei Exzessen hingegen ist gegenzusteuern. Dementsprechend sind Forderungen der Anklagebehörde, verfahrensfremden Vortrag des sich selbst verteidigenden Angeklagten nach Möglichkeit zu unterbinden nachvollziehbar. Das Recht auf „Selbst“-Verteidigung ist richtigerweise Beschränkungen unterworfen. In einen Graubereich der juristischen Argumentation begibt sich die Anklage jedoch, wenn sie zulasten des Angeklagten dessen politische Gesinnung und Aktivitäten mit der Begründung ins Feld führt, dies sei zum Zwecke der Friedensschaffung erforderlich. Der – unter-

68 *Prosecutor v. Šešelj*, IT-03-67-PT, Verfahrenskammer II, Entscheidung v. 9.5.2003, para. 3.

69 Sluiter, Fn. 47, 10, kritisiert daher den Fokus auf das Element der Verfahrensverzögerung. Damaška, Fn. 1, 3 weist darauf hin, dass auch die Anklage nicht nur verfahrensnotwendige Beweisaufnahmen durchführt. Siehe auch Bonomy, Fn. 22, 350.

stellt unschuldige – Angeklagte verwirkt mit der Anklage nicht das Recht, persönlich zu politischen und gesellschaftlichen Themen Stellung zu nehmen.[70] Dies selbst dann nicht, wenn die Äußerungen den erklärten Zielen der internationalen Strafgerichtsbarkeit zuwider laufen mögen. Besagte Argumentationsmuster sollten dementsprechend nicht zulasten des Angeklagten Berücksichtigung finden.

3. Die Pflichtverteidigung in internationalen Strafverfahren

Entscheidet das Gericht, dass der Angeklagte sein Recht, sich selbst zu verteidigen, verwirkt hat oder nicht ordnungsgemäß auszuüben vermag, hat es aktiv zu werden. Die rechtlichen Konsequenzen im Einzelfall sind dabei genau abzuwägen, da im Falle eines Aufzwingens eines Verteidigers weitere zeit- und ressourcenintensive Konfrontation zu erwarten ist[71] und eine Beschränkung des Rechts auf „Selbst"-Verteidigung stets verhältnismäßig sein muss.[72] Braucht der Angeklagte aufgrund von Krankheit oder fehlender rechtlicher Expertise Unterstützung, kann ihm das Recht auf juristische Mitarbeiter zugesprochen oder ein anwaltlicher Ansprechpartner zur Seite gestellt werden.[73] Verweigert sich der Angeklagte einer konstruktiven Verfahrensführung kann ein Verteidiger zur Verfahrensführung oder einigen Rechtshandlungen ermächtigt werden. Sieht das Gericht ein Bedürfnis für eine „neutrale" Stellungnahme zu abstrakten Rechtsfragen, können *amici curiae* (Freunde des Gerichts) mit der neutralen Wahrnehmung von Rechtsinteressen betraut werden.[74] Befürchten die Richter, dass im Laufe des erwartungsgemäß mehrjährigen Verfahrens die Notwendigkeit einer anwaltlichen Begleitung entstehen könnte, werden gegebenenfalls Verteidigungsteams „auf Abruf" durch das Gericht ernannt.[75] Diese können teils mehrere Jahre ein Schattendasein neben dem aktiv sich verteidigenden Angeklagten führen, um im Fall der Fälle einzuspringen.[76] Die Bandbreite situationsbedingter Lösungsansätze ist groß[77] und auf den ersten Blick verwirrend. Die Lösungsansätze sind jedoch Ausdruck der Grundentscheidung internationaler Straftribunale, die Entscheidung des Angeklagten zur „Selbst"-Verteidigung so weit

70 Hotis, Fn. 27, 777, sieht die Wahrung des Rechts auf „Selbst"-Verteidigung sogar als förderlich an. Ähnlich auch Bassett, Fn. 27, 239.

71 Sluiter, Fn. 22, 2; Jorgensen, Fn. 9, 724. Zu den ethischen und standesrechtlichen Schwierigkeiten der Verteidigung eines unkooperativen Angeklagten siehe Jorgensen, Fn. 66, 73 ff.; D. Nsereko, *Ethical Obligations of Counsel in Criminal Proceedings: Representing an Unwilling Client*, Criminal Law Forum (2001), 487-507.

72 Williams, Fn. 8, 594 ff. Dazu auch Hotis, Fn. 27, 780 m.w.N.; Bassett, Fn. 27, 236; Jorgensen, Fn. 66, 66; Ambach, Fn. 9, 298.

73 Siehe dazu Tuinstra, Fn. 60, 50 f. m.w.N.

74 Jorgensen, Fn. 9, 718 ff.; Bassett, Fn. 27, 240 ff.; Tuinstra, Fn. 60, 52ff..

75 Zum Standby counsel siehe Jorgensen, Fn. 9, 720 ff.; Tuinstra, Fn. 60, 55ff.; Boas, Fn. 8, 65 ff. mit Verweis auf die praktischen Probleme.

76 Dazu Tuinstra, Fn. 60, 58ff.

77 Dazu Jorgensen, Fn. 66, 71ff.; Ambach, Fn. 9, 298ff.

wie möglich Geltung zu verschaffen. Die Autonomie des Angeklagten soll so auch in der Praxis respektiert werden. Er ist nicht nur Objekt des Verfahrens, sondern darf und kann dieses mitgestalten.

IV. Der Angeklagte vor dem ICC: ein Ausblick

Anders als seine Vorgänger zielt der ICC nicht auf eine strafrechtliche Aufarbeitung in der Breite ab. Während vor dem ICTY gegen 161 Personen wegen Verbrechen im Zusammenhang mit dem Jugoslawienkonflikt ermittelt wurde, konzentrieren sich die Verfahren vor dem ICC nur auf wenige Führungspersonen. Im Kenia-Verfahren wurden der amtierende Präsident Kenyatta sowie dessen Vize von der Anklagebehörde unter der Führung der Chefanklägerin Bensouda ins Visier genommen; im Verfahren hinsichtlich der Elfenbeinküste wartet der Ex-Präsident Gbagbo auf sein Verfahren; im Verfahren zur Zentralafrikanischen Republik muss sich der ehemalige Präsidentschaftskandidat der Demokratischen Republik Kongo, Bemba, vor Gericht verantworten und im wohl prominentesten Verfahren hat der ICC einen Haftbefehl gegen den sudanesischen Präsidenten al-Bashir verabschiedet.[78] Der Fokus auf Rebellenführer, Politiker und andere Mitglieder der staatlichen bzw. para-staatlichen Leitungsebene hat sich jedoch noch nicht in – durchaus erwarteten beziehungsweise befürchteten[79] – Forderungen nach „Selbst"-Verteidigung niedergeschlagen.[80]

Die Möglichkeit, sich als Angeklagter selbst vor dem ICC zu verteidigen liefert das Rom Statut durchaus.[81] Artikel 67 (1) des Statuts ist den Vorgängerregelungen der Straftribunale nachempfunden und bietet – obwohl der ICC eine deutlich stärkere Prägung durch die kontinentaleuropäischen *Civil-Law*-Staaten erfahren hat – ein rechtliches Einfallstor für einen den Konflikt suchenden Angeklagten. Die Tatsache, dass auch vor dem ICC ein Recht sich selbst zu verteidigen im Grundsatz anerkannt ist, zeigt auch Regel 21 (4) der Verfahrens- und Beweisanordnung, die im englischen Original lautet:

> „A person choosing to represent himself or herself shall so notify the Registrar in writing at the first opportunity."

Die internen Regelungen der Kanzlei greifen diesen Punkt in Regel 119 (2) ebenfalls auf:

---

78 Ob in sämtlichen Verfahren stets die schwersten Verbrechen und wichtigsten Führungspersonen Gegenstand sind, darf trotz der prominenten Riege an Beschuldigten bezweifelt werden.

79 Cerruti, Fn. 11, 925.

80 Kurze Erwähnung fand die Thematik in *Prosecutor v. Lubanga*, ICC-01/04-01/06-915, Vorverfahrenskammer I, Entscheidung v. 24.5.2007, paras. 17, 18.

81 Gut u.a., *Defence Issues*, in: Sluiter u.a. (Hrsg.), *International Criminal Procedure* (2013), 1216.

> „The Registrar shall also provide appropriate assistance to a person who has chosen to represent himself or herself.“[82]

In der Praxis spielen diese Regelungen bisher jedoch keine Rolle. Nicht einmal in einem derzeit laufenden Verfahren wegen Zeugenbestechung[83] gegen ehemalige Mitglieder des Verteidigungsteams des Angeklagten Bemba haben sich die zweifelsohne fachkompetenten Angeklagten auf ihr Recht auf „Selbst“-Verteidigung berufen. Über die Gründe einer diesbezüglichen Zurückhaltung der Angeklagten vor dem ICC kann nur spekuliert werden. Eine Ursache mag die (angestrebte) Universalität des Gerichtshofs sein. Anders als die *ad hoc* und im Hinblick auf einen spezifischen Konflikt eingesetzten Tribunale, beansprucht der ICC universelle und permanente Geltung. Der Vorwurf der selektiven Siegerjustiz ist gegenüber dem ICC schwerer zu erheben,[84] sodass es an einem besonderen Anreiz für eine „politische“ Verteidigung fehlen könnte. Möglicherweise haben auch die Erfahrungen der Vergangenheit Eindruck hinterlassen. Die „Selbst“-Verteidigung hat sich – kaum überraschend – bisher in keinem Fall als juristische Erfolgsstrategie erwiesen.[85] Die Entscheidung, nicht auf professionelle rechtliche Beratung zu vertrauen, beinhaltet mithin stets das Risiko des juristischen Märtyrertods. Dieses Wagnis sind die bisherigen Angeklagten am ICC offenbar nicht gewillt gewesen einzugehen. Dies ist nachvollziehbar. So besteht die realistische Option einer Bestrafung durch das Gericht zu entgehen.

In der vergleichsweise kurzen Schaffenszeit des ICC konnten die Verteidigungsteams zudem bereits einige, sicherlich nicht unbemerkt gebliebene Erfolge erzielen. Mehrere Verfahren wurden eingestellt (siehe etwa die Verfahren gegen Mbarushimana, Kenyatta, Muthaura, Abu Garda) und ein Angeklagter wurde durch die Berufungskammer rechtskräftig freigesprochen (Ngudjolo). Auch wenn diese Verfahren medial oft als Scheitern der Anklage oder gar des ganzen Gerichts gewertet werden, erscheint es vorzugswürdig, diese als Erfolg für die internationale Strafjustiz anzusehen. Es ist eine fundamentale Errungenschaft der völkerstrafrechtlichen Entwicklung, dass mutmaßliche (Völker-) Straftäter vor Gericht gestellt werden und die Unschuldsvermutung gewahrt wird. Der Angeklagte betritt den Gerichtssaal als Unschuldiger. Für nachweisbare Taten ist er zur Verantwortung zu ziehen. Gegen die Vorwürfe darf er sich selbst oder mittels eines Verteidigers mit dem Mitteln der Prozessordnung zur Wehr setzen. Gelingt dies, ist er freizusprechen. Ein Prozess hingegen, in dem ein Freispruch nur eine theoretische Option ist, kommt dem Schauprozess gefährlich nahe.

---

82 Siehe dazu auch Bassett, Fn. 27, 239.

83 Dazu M. Hiéramente, *In the Case Prosecutor v. Defence*, Zeitschrift für Internationale Strafrechtsdogmatik (2014), 123.

84 Zum Vorwurf der Afrikazentriertheit siehe z.B. Resolution der Afrikanischen Union v. 12. Oktober 2013, Ext/Assembly/AU/Dec.1(Oct.2013).

85 Jorgensen, Fn. 9, 711: „*Conventional wisdom holds that a lawyer who represents himself has a fool for a client.*“

Philipp Graebke[*]

Die Verteidigung im Verfahren gegen Adolf Eichmann

Einleitung

Sowohl in der Vergangenheit als auch heute hebt sich Strafverteidigung in völkerstrafrechtlichen Verfahren stets vom „Normalfall" der Verteidigung ab. Auch wenn die Umstände differieren, lassen sich doch Gemeinsamkeiten ausmachen. Verfahren wegen internationaler Verbrechen zeichnen sich häufig durch ein großes Interesse der Politik an ihrem Ablauf und Ausgang, wenn nicht gar durch ihre versuchte oder erreichte Politisierung aus. Ebenso stehen die Verhandlungen regelmäßig unter besonderer Beobachtung von Öffentlichkeit und Medien. Grundsätzlich umstritten war in historischen Verfahren zudem oftmals das anzuwendende – nationale wie internationale – Recht. All dies lässt sich insbesondere am Verfahren gegen Adolf Eichmann vor dem Bezirksgericht in Jerusalem verdeutlichen, welches Gegenstand der folgenden Ausführungen ist.[1]

Adolf Eichmann wurde am 11.05.1960 in Buenos Aires von israelischen Nachrichtendiensten ergriffen und am 22.05.1960 nach Israel verbracht. Am 23.05.1960 wurde Haftbefehl erlassen und die polizeiliche Untersuchung eingeleitet. Die Anklage wurde am 21.02.1961 erhoben. Eichmann wurde in 15 Punkten beschuldigt, Verbrechen nach dem *Nazis and Nazi Collaborators (Punishment) Law 5710-1950*[2] (im Folgenden NNG) begangen zu haben. In der Sache lauteten die Beschuldigungen: Verbrechen gegen das jüdische Volk,[3] Verbrechen gegen die Menschlichkeit, Kriegsverbrechen und Mitgliedschaft in feindlichen Organisationen.[4]

Die Suche nach einem Strafverteidiger für Eichmann begann praktisch mit der Bekanntgabe seiner Ergreifung.[5]

---

* Der Verfasser ist wissenschaftlicher Mitarbeiter bei der Unabhängigen Wissenschaftlichen Kommission beim Bundesministerium der Justiz zur Aufarbeitung der NS-Vergangenheit und Mitglied im Direktorium des Internationalen Forschungs- und Dokumentationszentrums Kriegsverbrecherprozesse an der Philipps-Universität Marburg (ICWC).

1 Vgl. für einen Überblick über die historische Entwicklung mit speziellem Fokus auf die Verteidigung Wilson, A History of the Role of Defense Counsel in International Criminal and War Crimes Tribunals, in: Bohlander u.a. (Hrsg.), Defense in International Criminal Procedings. Cases, Materials and Commentary, Ardsley 2006,, S. 31 ff.

2 Veröffentlicht in Sefer Ha'khukim, der Gesetzessammlung Israels, Nr. 57 v. 09.08.1950, zitiert nach Servatius, Verteidigung Adolf Eichmann. Plädoyer, Bad Kreuznach 1961, S. 81.

3 Ein Tatbestand, der dem des Völkermordes nachgebildet ist.

4 Feindliche Organisationen sollten vor allem diejenigen sein, die das Internationale Militärtribunal in Nürnberg zu verbrecherischen Organisationen erklärt hat. Im Falle Eichmanns ging es um SS, SD und Gestapo.

5 Yablonka, The State of Israel vs. Adolf Eichmann, New York 2004, S. 123.

Hierzu brauchte es aber überhaupt jemanden, der bereit war, diese Aufgabe zu übernehmen. Am 25.05.1960 erschien in der israelischen Tageszeitung *Yedioth Ahronoth* das Ergebnis einer Umfrage unter Anwälten aus Tel Aviv, die deren prinzipielle Einstellung zum Verfahren in Erfahrung bringen wollte.[6] Die befragten Anwälte waren sich natürlich einig, dass Eichmann einen Verteidiger brauche, wer sich aber überhaupt bereit erklärte, die Verteidigung zu übernehmen, tat dies unter ausdrücklichem Verweis auf die berufsständische Pflicht, jederzeit für ein faires Verfahren einzustehen.[7] Israel Hayk, der als erster Verteidiger in einem Verfahren wegen Anschuldigungen nach dem NNG aufgetreten war, erklärte sogar, Eichmann werde er keinesfalls vertreten. Bei seinem damaligen Klienten, einem Kapo, habe es sich immer noch um ein Opfer der Nazis gehandelt. Man könne aber Eichmann keinen Anwalt stellen, der im Grunde seines Herzens lieber als Ankläger gegen seinen eigenen Mandanten aufträte.[8] Die klare Tendenz ging sehr früh zu einem Anwalt aus dem Ausland, allein schon um jeglichen Verdacht einer schlechten Vertretung zu vermeiden.[9] Das sah man auch im Justizministerium so, dessen erste Wahl wohl ein Schweizer Anwalt gewesen wäre. Nun meldeten sich Strafverteidiger aus aller Welt, die man allesamt vom Mossad überprüfen ließ.[10] Unter denen, die in Frage kamen, stach Robert Servatius sehr bald heraus. Während Gideon Hausner nur schreibt, Servatius habe den Nachweis erbringen können, nie der NSDAP angehört zu haben,[11] geht Hanna Yablonka genauer auf die umfangreiche Überprüfung des Kandidaten durch den Mossad ein, die sogar die Überwachung von Auslandsreisen umfasste:[12] Zwar habe Servatius offenbar rechte und militaristische Einstellungen, sei jedoch kein Nationalsozialist. Im Unterschied zu seiner Frau sei er nicht reich,[13] insgesamt erschien er den Agenten als sehr mittelmäßig. Ein anderer Grund für die Wahl war, dass Servatius das Vertrauen des Beschuldigten und seiner Familie genoss. Der Anwalt hatte zunächst Robert Eichmann, den Bruder seines späteren Mandanten, in Linz kontaktiert und sich erst an das israelische Ministerium gewandt, nachdem die Familie dem zugestimmt hatte.[14] Letztere hatte zunächst Alfred Seidl im Sinn gehabt, der im Nürnber-

6 Yablonka, State (o. Fn. 5), S. 123 und Fn. 8.

7 Yablonka, State (o. Fn. 5), S. 123.

8 Yablonka, State (o. Fn. 5), S. 123.

9 Yablonka, State (o. Fn. 5), S. 123 f.

10 Yablonka, State (o. Fn. 5), S. 124.

11 Hausner, Gerechtigkeit in Jerusalem, München 1967, S. 461.

12 Yablonka, State (o. Fn. 5), S. 124 ff; vgl. auch Winkler, Adolf Eichmann und seine Unterstützer. Ein kleiner Nachtrag zu einem bekannten Rechtsfall, in: Renz (Hrsg.), Interessen um Eichmann, Frankfurt am Main 2012, S. 289 ff., S. 307 f.

13 Was für den Mossad vielleicht interessant war, weil die Regierung befürchtete, Servatius' Arbeit könne von Alt-Nazis finanziert werden, Yablonka, State (o. Fn. 5), S. 127; möglicherweise gehörte die Erhebung aber auch nur zur üblichen Vorgehensweise.

14 Servatius, Verteidigung (o. Fn. 2), S. 5; Yablonka, State (o. Fn. 5), S. 124.

ger Hauptkriegsverbrecherprozess Rudolf Hess und Hans Frank verteidigt hatte.[15] Allerdings sei, noch während die Brüder berieten, ein Anruf aus Köln eingegangen, so Robert Eichmann, mit dem Servatius sein Interesse bekundet habe. Nach einem Briefwechsel wurden sich Familie und Anwalt einig.[16] Als Gabriel Bach, *Assistant State Attorney* und einer der Stellvertreter Hausners im Verfahren, Eichmann am 14.06.1960 die Schreiben dreier Anwälte übergab, die sich für seine Verteidigung interessierten, wählte der Beschuldigte sogleich – der Empfehlung seines Bruders folgend – Servatius aus.[17]

Das Verhältnis zwischen beiden gestaltete sich dann zunächst schwierig. Eichmann, der einen überzeugten Nazi erwartet hatte, ging von einer Verteidigungsstrategie aus, die unter Behauptung einer großen Weltverschwörung schlicht den gesamten Holocaust leugnen würde. Offenbar genügte es aber, dass Servatius deutlich wurde und seinem Mandanten klarmachte, dass das Geschehene nicht zu leugnen sei. Sofort schwenkte Eichmann auf die von da ab konstant verfolgte Strategie seines Verteidigers um und äußerte sich gegenüber Dritten über diesen nur im besten Sinne.[18] Avner Less, dem Polizeioffizier, der Eichmann vor Beginn der Hauptverhandlung verhörte, erzählte er, er sei seit seiner ersten Begegnung begeistert von seinem Anwalt, der einen sehr kompetenten Eindruck mache und aus Nürnberg über einschlägige Erfahrung verfüge. Ja, er sehe sogar so aus wie er ihn sich vorgestellt habe.[19]

Ob man aus solcher Außendarstellung auf ein vertrauensvolles Verhältnis schließen kann, bleibt natürlich offen. Jedenfalls wird ihr Umgang miteinander im weiteren Verlauf des Verfahrens vertrauter, was sich an der Art und Weise der Zusammenarbeit zeigt: Beide entwickeln Strategien gemeinsam fort und sehen sich als Team.[20] Bei der Erarbeitung seiner Fragen für das Hauptverhör seines Mandanten griff Dr. Servatius auf eine große Zahl von Notizen zurück, in denen Eichmann die Themen angab, über die er sprechen wollte.[21] Auch während andere Zeugen gehört wurden, machte er immer wieder Vorschläge für Fragen im Kreuzverhör.[22] Hannah Arendt meinte, der Angeklagte habe sich nicht nur viel besser in der Materie ausgekannt als sein Verteidiger,[23] sondern sei auch dessen wichtigster Assistent gewesen.[24]

---

15 Vgl. zu Seidl und seinem Wirken in Nürnberg Safferling/Graebke, Strafverteidigung im Nürnberger Hauptkriegsverbrecherprozess: Strategien und Wirkung, in: Zeitschrift für die gesamte Strafrechtswissenschaft 123 (2011), S. 47 ff.

16 Der Spiegel 1960, Nr. 43, S. 41.

17 Pendorf, Der Verteidiger Eichmanns, in: Die Zeit v. 05.05.1961.

18 Stangneth, »Offenes Visier ist bei mir ein geflügeltes Wort«. Bekenntnisse des Täuschers Adolf Eichmann, in: Renz (Hrsg.), Interessen um Eichmann, Frankfurt am Main 2012, S. 181 ff., S. 195.

19 Less, Nachwort, in: von Lang, Das Eichmann-Protokoll, Berlin 1982, S. 265, S. 275 f.

20 Théofilakis, Der Eichmann-Prozess, aus dem Glaskäfig betrachtet, in: Renz (Hrsg.), Interessen um Eichmann, Frankfurt am Main 2012, S. 147 ff., S. 160.

21 Théofilakis, Glaskäfig (o. Fn. 20), S. 174.

22 Théofilakis, Glaskäfig (o. Fn. 20), S. 159.

23 Arendt, Eichmann in Jerusalem. Ein Bericht von der Banalität des Bösen, München 2011, S. 334.

Die Bezahlung des Anwalts trug mit 20.000 $ zum größten Teil Israel. Zusammen mit 16.000 DM, die Eichmanns Familie aufgebracht hatte, ergab das die 100.000 DM, die Servatius anfangs gefordert hatte.[25] Der Verteidiger lieferte sich nicht nur einen langwierigen Rechtsstreit mit der BRD, die sich beharrlich weigerte die Kosten zu übernehmen,[26] sondern versuchte auch, die ihm von Eichmann übertragenen Verwertungsrechte an seinen Schriften zu Geld zu machen.[27] Dass er dabei mit Alt-Nazis zu tun hatte, schien ihn nicht zu stören; dass einer von ihnen für den Bundesnachrichtendienst arbeitete, wusste er wohl nicht.[28]

Gesetzesänderungen im Vorfeld des Verfahrens

Es blieb aber noch ein Problem: Nach geltendem Recht konnte ein nicht in Israel zugelassener Anwalt nicht als Strafverteidiger auftreten.[29] Die Regierung beschäftigte sich also Anfang Juli 1960 (die Knesset befand sich zu dieser Zeit in der Sommerpause) mit der Möglichkeit einer entsprechenden Gesetzesänderung, wobei zu Beginn noch sechs Minister deutsche Anwälte von der Möglichkeit, Eichmann zu vertreten, ausschließen wollten; lediglich fünf traten auch hierfür ein. Als aber, wie oben beschrieben, alles immer stärker auf Servatius hinauslief, beugte man sich dem Verlauf der Dinge.[30] Am 07.11.1960 beriet der Rechtsausschuss des Parlaments den eingebrachten Gesetzesentwurf. Einige der diskutierten Probleme waren eher politischer Natur, andere wiederum waren Bedenken, welche die Berufsvertretung vorgebracht hatte. Im Ergebnis entschied man sich dafür, dem Justizminister die Befugnis einzuräumen, einen nicht zugelassenen Verteidiger zu ernennen und auch wieder zu entlassen. Außerdem würde Servatius ein israelischer Anwalt zur Seite gestellt, um Rat bezüglich des israelischen Rechts zu geben, jedoch nicht mehr als das und auch nicht im Rahmen der Verhandlungen.[31]

Schon vor seiner offiziellen Ernennung war dem Verteidiger der Kontakt zu Eichmann ermöglicht worden, wenn er auch auf besondere Sicherungsmaßnahmen hinweist.[32]

Und es kam noch zu einer weiteren Gesetzesänderung. Nach geltendem israelischen Recht war es Aufgabe des Präsidenten des Bezirksgerichts, die

---

24 Arendt, Eichmann (o. Fn. 23), S. 360.

25 Vgl. Winkler, Eichmann und seine Unterstützer (o. Fn. 12), S. 305; tatsächlich scheint die Summe aber nicht ausreichend gewesen zu sein, ebda, S. 106.

26 Vgl. insoweit Große, Der Eichmann-Prozess zwischen Recht und Politik, Frankfurt am Main 1995, S. 50 ff.

27 Vgl. Winkler, Eichmann und seine Unterstützer (o. Fn. 12), S. 289 ff.

28 Vgl. Winkler, Eichmann und seine Unterstützer (o. Fn. 12), S. 312 ff.

29 Cohen, Rechtliche Gesichtspunkte zum Eichmann-Prozess, Frankfurt am Main 1963, S. 46; Renz, NS-Verbrechen und Justiz. Eine Einführung, in: Renz (Hrsg.), Interessen um Eichmann, Frankfurt am Main 2012, S. 13 ff., S. 27 f.

30 Yablonka, State (o. Fn. 5), S. 124 f.

31 Yablonka, State (o. Fn. 5), S. 127.

32 Servatius, Verteidigung (o. Fn. 2), S. 5.

Richter in den Spruchkörper zu berufen.[33] Präsident des Bezirksgerichts Jerusalem war Benjamin Halevi, der somit auch die Möglichkeit hatte, sich selbst zu ernennen oder zum Vorsitzenden zu machen. Das allerdings löste heftige innenpolitische Diskussionen aus, denn Halevi hatte einige Jahre zuvor als Richter in einem Verleumdungsprozess amtiert, den Rudolf Kasztner gegen Malkiel Grünwald angestrengt hatte, nachdem dieser jenen der Kollaboration beschuldigt hatte. Kasztner wurde der Versuch vorgeworfen im Rahmen der Aktion „Blut gegen Ware" in Ungarn den Deutschen jüdische Leben durch Lieferung von Material abzukaufen. Hierzu hatte er unter anderem mit Adolf Eichmann verhandelt. In diesem Zusammenhang hatte Halevi Kasztner vorgeworfen, seine Seele an den Satan verkauft zu haben, was nun die Befürchtung schürte, Halevi könnte wegen Befangenheit abgelehnt werden.[34] Da Halevi trotz – oder gerade wegen[35] – der Intervention sowohl des Justizministers als auch des Obersten Gerichtshofs den Vorsitz für sich beanspruchen wollte,[36] diskutierte man auch diesbezüglich eine Änderung des Gesetzes. Eine Rolle könnte insoweit auch gespielt haben, dass sein klageabweisendes Urteil in jenem Verfahren weithin als moralische Verurteilung des Klägers und Bloßstellung der regierenden Mapai-Partei David Ben-Gurions gesehen wurde, der Kasztner angehörte.[37] Erwogen wurden verschiedene Möglichkeiten, u.a. einen Spruchkörper nur aus Richtern des Obersten Gerichts zu bilden. Am Ende stand das *Courts Law (Crimes Punishable by Death)*, ein Kompromiss, den die israelische Presse *The Halevi Bill* nannte.[38] Er nahm Benjamin Halevi zwar den Vorsitz, machte es ihm aber nicht unmöglich, sich selbst zu einem der beiden Beisitzer zu ernennen. In Verfahren, in denen dem Angeklagten die Todesstrafe drohte (die in Israel freilich bereits 1954 außer für internationale Verbrechen oder Verrat abgeschafft und auch in diesen Fällen nie vollstreckt worden war), wurde von nun an der Vorsitzende vom Präsidenten des obersten Gerichts ernannt, die beiden Beisitzer aber weiterhin vom Präsidenten des Bezirksgerichts.[39] Der Vorwurf des Einzelfallgeset-

33 Cohen, Gesichtspunkte (o. Fn. 29), S. 10.

34 Hauff, Die Richter im Eichmann-Prozess, in: Renz (Hrsg.), Interessen um Eichmann, Frankfurt am Main 2012, S. 119 ff., S. 124; Yablonka, State (o. Fn. 5), S. 133 f.

35 Hanna Yablonka erzählte er, er habe sich anfangs nicht selbst ernennen wollen und das erst getan, nachdem Justizminister Rosen öffentlich Druck auf ihn auszuüben versucht habe, Yablonka, State (o. Fn. 5), S. 132.

36 Renz, NS-Verbrechen und Justiz (o. Fn. 29), S. 28 f.

37 Renz, NS-Verbrechen und Justiz (o. Fn. 29), S. 29; auch Yablonka, State (o. Fn. 5), S. 133 f. hält einen solchen politischen Hintergrund für möglich, aber auch für im Ergebnis eher unwahrscheinlich.

38 Yablonka, State (o. Fn. 5), S. 132.

39 Cohen, Gesichtspunkte (o. Fn. 29), S. 67 und S. 9, fehlerhaft eine Passage auf S. 36, wo es heißt, das Plenum des Obersten Gerichtshofs wähle den Vorsitzenden; das Gesetz wurde am 31.01.1961 von der Knesset verabschiedet und am 06.02.1961 in Sefer Ha'khukim veröffentlicht, Nr. 325 v. 06.02.1961, S. 24, zitiert nach Zertal, Israel's Holocaust and the Politics of Nationhood, Cambridge 2010, S. 107 Fn. 46; vgl. ebda für eine weitere (hebräische) Fundstelle des Textes in einer Sammlung von Gesetzesentwürfen.

zes lässt folglich nicht lange auf sich warten,[40] zumindest der Form nach handelte es sich jedoch um ein allgemeines Gesetz, das abstrakt auf eine unbestimmte Vielzahl von Fällen anwendbar war.[41] Dazu allerdings kam es nicht, denn bereits 1965 wurde die Änderung rückgängig gemacht.[42]

Der Beginn der Hauptverhandlung

Die Ablehnung Halevis blieb natürlich trotzdem möglich und nicht zuletzt dieser selbst rechnete fest mit ihr.[43] Robert Servatius allerdings wählte einen anderen Weg.[44] Am 11.04.1961[45] hatte er, unmittelbar nach Verlesung der Anklageschrift, Gelegenheit prozesshindernde Einwendungen vorzutragen. Über diese war dann sofort zu verhandeln, so dass im Falle ihres Durchschlagens eine Erwiderung auf die Anklageschrift entbehrlich gewesen wäre.[46]

Der Verteidiger erklärte, er habe nichts finden können, was die Unparteilichkeit eines einzelnen Richters besorgen ließe.[47] Solche Besorgnis bestehe vielmehr gegenüber allen Mitgliedern des Gerichts, da zu vermuten sei, dass sie selbst oder ihre Angehörigen durch die angeklagte Tat verletzt seien.[48] Überhaupt bestehe an der Tat ein politisches Verfolgungsinteresse des jüdischen Volkes sowie des israelischen Staates. Dieser Staat dürfe im Namen seines Volkes parteiisch sein, er könne somit auch den parteiischen Ankläger stellen, jedoch nicht die Richter.[49]

Servatius entschied sich somit für einen ungewöhnlich verpackten Fundamentaleinwand gegen ein Verfahren in Israel, anstatt die eher erfolgversprechende Ablehnung eines einzelnen Richters zu betreiben. Und in der Tat scheint es doch in Ansehung seines Mandanten unwahrscheinlich, dass bei

---

40 So etwa Renz, NS-Verbrechen und Justiz (o. Fn. 29), S. 28; Yablonka, State (o. Fn. 5), S. 126 f.

41 Worauf zu Recht Cohen hinweist, Cohen, Gesichtspunkte (o. Fn. 29), S. 36.

42 Zertal, Holocaust and Politics (o. Fn. 39), S. 107 Fn 47.

43 Yablonka, State (o. Fn. 5), S. 133.

44 Auch wenn im „Spiegel“, Nr. 16/1961, S. 24 behauptet wird, Servatius habe aus diesem Grund gegen Halevi protestiert, findet sich ein solcher Einwand nicht in den Protokollen.

45 Servatius, Verteidigung (o. Fn. 2), S. 22 spricht vom 10.04.1960.

46 Cohen, Gesichtspunkte (o. Fn. 29), S. 11.

47 Sitzungsprotokoll, Sitzung 1, Teil 2; soweit hier die Protokolle der Verhandlung zitiert werden, beziehen sich die Angaben von Fundstellen auf die online verfügbare Veröffentlichung der Protokolle unter http://www.nizkor.org/hweb/people/e/eichmann-adolf/transcripts/Sessions/ (zuletzt abgerufen am 05.04.2015). Diese Protokolle werden vom israelischen Justizministerium auch in Buchform herausgegeben, State of Israel, Ministry of Justice, Trust for the Publication of the Proceedings of the Eichmann Trial, in cooperation with the Israel State Archives and Yad Vashem - the Holocaust Martyrs' and Heroes' Remembrance Authority (Hrsg.), The trial of Adolf Eichmann: Record of proceedings in the District Court of Jerusalem, Jerusalem 1992. Die Sitzungsprotokolle sind in die englische Sprache übertragen. Robert Servatius hat sein Plädoyer sowie seine Ausführungen zu Beginn der Hauptverhandlung 1961 in deutscher Sprache veröffentlicht in Servatius, Verteidigung (o. Fn. 2); dort sind natürlich nicht die Nachfragen der Richter u.ä. enthalten.

48 Sitzungsprotokoll, Sitzung 1, Teil 2.

49 Sitzungsprotokoll, Sitzung 1, Teil 2.

Ablehnung Halevis jemand nachgerückt wäre, der vorab mehr von Eichmann gehalten hätte, sondern eben nur jemand, der seine Meinung noch nicht öffentlich kundgetan hätte. Gleichzeitig konnte er so auch die internationale öffentliche Diskussion aufgreifen, ob Israel der geeignete Ort sei, das Verfahren durchzuführen.[50] Er verwies sogar auf ein Zitat Yitzhak Olshans, des Präsidenten des Obersten Gerichts, der in einer Entscheidung zur Befangenheit deutlich gemacht habe, dass es für den Ausschluss eines Richters auch genügen könne, wenn die Öffentlichkeit in begründeter Weise dessen Befangenheit besorge.[51]

Zum anderen behauptete Dr. Servatius bei dieser Gelegenheit die Unzuständigkeit des Gerichts. Diese stützte er zum einen auf die Unvereinbarkeit des NNG mit höheren Rechtsgrundsätzen, zum anderen auf die Entführung Eichmanns aus Argentinien.

Zunächst gebe es keinen strafanwendungsrechtlichen Anknüpfungspunkt, der die Gerichtsbarkeit eines israelischen Gerichts legitimieren könne. Für das Territorialitätsprinzip sowie für das passive Personalitätsprinzip ergebe sich das bereits daraus, dass der Staat Israel im Zeitpunkt der Begehung der Tat noch gar nicht bestand. So könne völkerrechtlich ein Zugriff auf die Tat gemäß diesen Prinzipien nicht gerechtfertigt sein.[52] Seine Ausführungen zum Universalitätsprinzip holen dann etwas weiter aus. Das NNG fülle kein völkerrechtliches Vakuum,[53] so wie auch schon das Londoner Statut[54] ein solches Vakuum nicht gefüllt habe. Dieses sei vielmehr reines Besatzungsrecht ohne universelle Geltung gewesen.[55] Auch die spätere Entwicklung zeige, dass gerade keine universelle Rechtsentwicklung in Gang gekommen sei, sondern, dass sich die alten Sitten der internationalen Politik eben doch erhalten hätten.[56] So habe sich auch Art. 6 der Völkermordkonvention für das

---

50 Sitzungsprotokoll, Sitzung 1, Teil 2; so hatte etwa Telford Taylor, stellvertretender amerikanischer Ankläger im Nürnberger Hauptkriegsverbrecherprozess und Hauptankläger in den Nachfolgeprozessen, sich vehement gegen Jerusalem als Verfahrensort ausgesprochen, Taylor, Large Questions in the Eichmann Case, in: New York Times Magazine v. 22.01.1961, S. 11, zitiert nach Bilsky, Der Eichmann-Prozess und die Frage der gerichtlichen Zuständigkeit, in: Renz (Hrsg.), Interessen um Eichmann, Frankfurt am Main 2012, S. 51 ff., S. 61 Fn. 30.

51 Sitzungsprotokoll, Sitzung 1, Teil 2; Servatius verspricht, das vom Vorsitzenden geforderte Aktenzeichen später mitzuteilen, was jedoch zumindest in den Protokollen keinen Niederschlag mehr findet.

52 Sitzungsprotokoll, Sitzung 1, Teil 3.

53 So argumentierte im Sinne einer Ausformulierung naturrechtlicher Prinzipien Generalstaatsanwalt Hausner in seiner Replik, Sitzungsprotokoll, Sitzung 2, Teil 3, auf die Servatius so antwortete, Sitzungsprotokoll, Sitzung 5, Teil 2.

54 Sitzungsprotokoll, Sitzung 1, Teil 3. Das zusammen mit dem sog. Londoner Viermächteabkommen am 08.08.1945 in London verabschiedete Statut für den Internationalen Militärgerichtshof enthielt in 30 Artikeln einige Regeln über das materielle Recht, das Verfahren und die Gerichtsverfassung des Internationalen Militärgerichtshofs in Nürnberg. Verabschiedet von den alliierten Siegermächten sind dem Statut später 19 weitere Staaten beigetreten.

55 Sitzungsprotokoll, Sitzung 5, Teil 2.

56 Sitzungsprotokoll, Sitzung 5, Teil 2.

Territorialitätsprinzip entschieden.[57] Es stehe im Übrigen auch Nationalstaaten nicht zu, ein solches vermutetes Vakuum ohne tauglichen Anknüpfungspunkt an den Täter auszufüllen, könnten andernfalls doch auch die gerade neu entstehenden Staaten die alten Kolonialherren vor ihre Gerichte bringen.[58] Nur soweit Staaten im Krieg von Deutschland besetzt waren, könnten sie, quasi als Ausführungsgesetze zum Londoner Statut, solche Normen erlassen.[59] Der Grundidee des Universalitätsprinzips, Feinde der Menschheit könnten und müssten von jedem Staat verfolgt werden können, hält Servatius entgegen, der Angeklagte sei keine Gefahr mehr für die Menschheit, er bezeichnet ihn gar als friedlichen Bürger.[60]

So zeige sich, dass das NNG – wie das Londoner Statut – ein Ausnahmegesetz sei.[61] Ein solches sei allein legitim, wenn es einen gerechten Zweck verfolge. Ein Strafgesetz verfolge zunächst präventive Zwecke, die in diesem Fall nicht gefördert werden könnten, so dass nur noch der Sühnegedanke verbleibe, der wiederum ein Ausnahmegesetz nicht rechtfertigen könne, weil hierfür zuständige Richter bereits in Deutschland und in den ehemals von Deutschland besetzten Gebieten bereitstünden.[62] Der Umstand, dass das IMT[63] auf dem Londoner Statut beruht habe, sei insofern anders zu bewerten, als es hier unmittelbar nach dem Krieg allein um die Führungsriege der Nazis gegangen sei, zu welcher man den Angeklagten nicht rechnen könne.[64]

Und natürlich sei das Gericht schon deshalb unzuständig, weil das NNG als rückwirkendes Strafgesetz nicht angewandt werden dürfe.[65] Servatius möchte auf dieses – in Verfahren wegen NS-Verbrechen inzwischen unvermeidliche – Argument[66] selbst nicht lange eingehen und übergibt den Verfahrensbeteiligten stattdessen eine schriftliche Ausarbeitung.[67]

57 Sitzungsprotokoll, Sitzung 5, Teil 2; dort heißt es, zuständig seien die Gerichte des Staates, auf dessen Gebiet die Handlung begangen wurde oder ein von den Staaten anerkanntes internationales Gericht.

58 Sitzungsprotokoll, Sitzung 5, Teil 2; die politische Dimension dieses Arguments hätte vor einem Gericht eines Staates mit „Kolonialherren-Geschichte“ wohl stärker verfangen.

59 Sitzungsprotokoll, Sitzung 5, Teil 2.

60 Sitzungsprotokoll, Sitzung 5, Teil 3.

61 Sitzungsprotokoll, Sitzung 1, Teil 3.

62 Sitzungsprotokoll, Sitzung 1, Teil 3. Er verweist insoweit darauf, dass sowohl die Verteidigung als auch der Generalstaatsanwalt von Hessen, Fritz Bauer, die Bundesregierung bereits aufgefordert hatten, ein Auslieferungsersuchen an Israel zu stellen. Diese freilich hatte politisch äußerst wenig Interesse hieran und stellte auch nie einen entsprechenden Antrag, vgl. zum ganzen Große, Eichmann-Prozess (o. Fn. 26), S. 100 ff. und Winkler, Eichmann und seine Unterstützer (o. Fn. 12), S. 290 f.

63 International Military Tribunal.

64 Sitzungsprotokoll, Sitzung 1, Teil 3.

65 Sitzungsprotokoll, Sitzung 1, Teil 3.

66 Vgl. schon die Eingabe der Gesamtverteidigung in Nürnberg, IMT-Sitzungsprotokoll, Bd. 1, S. 186 ff. Das Argument taucht in NS-Verfahren immer wieder auf.

67 Diese Ausarbeitung befindet sich als Annex zu Band I in den Sitzungsprotokollen, zum *nullum crimen* Satz vgl. ab S. 77 bzw. unter http://www.nizkor.org/hweb/people/e/ eichmann-adolf/transcripts/Sessions/Defence-Submission-02-01.html (zuletzt abgerufen am 05.04.2015).

Sodann ging die Verteidigung auf die Entführung Eichmanns aus Argentinien ein, die als Verfahrensfehler ebenfalls zur Unzuständigkeit des Gerichts führe. In verschiedenen Präzedenzfällen, auf die er später auch noch näher einging,[68] hätten Gerichte jeweils den Umstand einer Entführung des Angeklagten ausgeblendet und sich darauf berufen, dass das gerichtliche Verfahren fehlerfrei sei, sie selbst aber mit der vorausgegangenen Ergreifung nichts zu tun gehabt hätten.[69] Das aber sei dem Bezirksgericht nicht möglich, denn die Ergreifung Eichmanns sei auf staatliche Anordnung hin geschehen, wodurch es sich bei ihr um einen schweren Verstoß gegen das Völkerrecht handele, so dass der Staat Israel auf ihr kein Verfahren aufbauen könne.[70] Das habe auch der UN-Sicherheitsrat so gesehen, der eine angemessene Aburteilung[71] des Angeklagten gefordert habe. Damit habe er gerade ein israelisches Gericht ausschließen wollen.[72] Dieser Völkerrechtsverstoß bleibe auch bestehen, nachdem Argentinien und Israel in einer gemeinsamen Erklärung den Streit beigelegt hätten, denn diese enthalte keine Zurücknahme des Vorwurfs des Rechtsbruchs.[73] Ein weiterer völkerrechtlicher Konflikt könne für Israel im Verhältnis zu Deutschland entstehen, denn die Bundesrepublik könne jederzeit intervenieren. Hierauf habe der Angeklagte auch einen Anspruch, dessen Erfüllung er notfalls durch verwaltungsgerichtliche Klage erzwingen werde.[74] Er legte Wert darauf, dass sein Argument hauptsächlich auf der staatlichen Anordnung und Durchführung der Entführung fuße, und beantragte zum Beweis über diese Behauptung zwei Zeugen zu hören, von denen er meinte, sie seien unmittelbar an der Entführung beteiligt gewesen.[75]

Am sechsten Prozesstag verkündete das Gericht seinen Beschluss, dessen Begründung im Urteil[76] enthalten ist. Die Argumente der Verteidigung verfingen nicht, unter Hinweis auf ihre Professionalität erklärten die Richter ihre Unbefangenheit und sie hielten sich auch für zuständig. Unter Heranziehung der Nürnberger Prozesse und umfangreicher Literatur leitet das Gericht die Anwendbarkeit des Universalitätsprinzips für die angeklagten Taten her und beruft sich zudem auf Territorialitäts- und passives Personalitätsprinzip, wobei es insoweit die jüdische Gemeinde im britischen Mandatsgebiet Palästina quasi als Rechtsvorgänger Israels betrachtet. Das NNG sei ausdrücklich retroaktiv, was dem Völkerrecht nicht widerspreche, denn der Normbefehl

68 Sitzungsprotokoll, Sitzung 5, Teil 2.
69 Sitzungsprotokoll, Sitzung 1, Teil 3.
70 Sitzungsprotokoll, Sitzung 1, Teil 3 und Sitzung 5 Teil 2.
71 Die Wortwahl folgt hier Servatius, Verteidigung (o. Fn. 2), S. 33. In der Verhandlung entspann sich ein kurzes Gespräch über die exakte Formulierung, Sitzungsprotokoll, Sitzung 5, Teil 3. Diese hieß „should be brought to appropriate justice", vgl. UN-SC Res. 138 vom 23.06.1960.
72 Sitzungsprotokoll, Sitzung 5, Teil 2.
73 Sitzungsprotokoll, Sitzung 5, Teil 3.
74 Sitzungsprotokoll, Sitzung 5, Teil 3.
75 Sitzungsprotokoll, Sitzung 1, Teil 3.
76 Absatz Nr. 4 ff. des Urteils. District Court of Jerusalem, Az. 40/61, das Urteil befindet sich in den Sitzungsprotokollen.

als solcher habe schon im Tatzeitpunkt bestanden. Die Entführung sei durchaus ein Völkerrechtsbruch gewesen, der jedoch durch die gemeinsame Erklärung beider Staaten geheilt sei, so dass auch die beantragten Zeugen nicht gehört zu werden bräuchten.

Die Beweismittel

Damit ging das Verfahren über zur Erörterung der Schuldfrage. Eichmann bekannte sich in allen Punkten „im Sinne der Anklage, nicht schuldig,[77] der Ankläger hielt sein *opening statement*[78] und legte seine Beweise vor. Sodann war die Verteidigung an der Reihe[79] bevor beide Seiten plädierten[80] und das Gericht sein Urteil über die Schuldfrage verkündete.[81]

Unter den vorgelegten Beweismitteln hatten Augenscheinsbeweise, auch aus Sicht der Verteidigung, die geringste Bedeutung. So beantragte etwa die Anklage in der 66. Sitzung die Vorführung von Dokumentarfilmen über die Geschehnisse in den Konzentrations- und Vernichtungslagern vor und während der Befreiung.[82] Der einzige Einwand, den Dr. Servatius vorbrachte, ging dahin, dass die Filme kein Material enthalten dürften, das erst nach dem Krieg zu Informationszwecken hergestellt wurde.[83] Er bekam die Filme vorab von der Anklage gezeigt und machte im Vorfeld der Vorführung das Gericht auf solche Szenen aufmerksam, in denen er dies für möglich hielt.[84]

Von größerer Bedeutung waren Zeugen. Unter diesen fällt zunächst die große Zahl von Opferzeugen auf, welche die Anklage aufbot. Hier ging es weniger darum einen konkreten Tatnachweis zu führen als vor der nationalen und internationalen Öffentlichkeit die Geschichte der Schoah zu erzählen.[85] Tatsächlich zeichneten diese Zeugen mit ihren Aussagen ein eindrucksvolles Bild vom grausigen Geschehen in den von Deutschland beherrschten Gebieten, in den Ghettos und den Lagern, eine konkrete Beziehung zwischen dem Geschehen und dem Angeklagten konnten sie jedoch häufig nicht herstellen. Insofern verwundert es nicht, dass Servatius in diesen Fällen zumeist von der Möglichkeit des Kreuzverhörs gar keinen Gebrauch machte. Lediglich in

77 Sitzungsprotokoll, Sitzung 6, Teil 1.

78 Sitzungsprotokoll, Sitzung 6, Teil 1.

79 Sitzungsprotokoll, Sitzung 75, Teil 5.

80 Sitzungsprotokoll, Sitzung 110, Teil 1 und Sitzung 114, Teil 1.

81 Sitzungsprotokoll, Sitzung 115-119.

82 Sitzungsprotokoll, Sitzung 66, Teil 1; schon zuvor hatte die Anklage erfragt, ob das Gericht prinzipiell mit der Vorführung einverstanden sei. Servatius sagte, er müsse die Filme sehen bevor er über Einwände entscheiden könne, Sitzungsprotokoll, Sitzung 54, Teil 6.

83 Sitzungsprotokoll, Sitzung 66, Teil 1; die Entscheidung des Gerichts, die Filme vorführen zu lassen, erging in der 68. Sitzung (Entscheidung Nr. 72). Später wurden die Filme vom Gericht auch als Beweisstücke akzeptiert, Sitzungsprotokoll, Sitzung 73, Teil 1.

84 Sitzungsprotokoll, Sitzung 70, Teil 6.

85 Renz, NS-Verbrechen und Justiz (o. Fn. 29), S. 31 und S. 47; Yablonka, Der Eichmann-Prozess – ein jüdisches Nürnberg?, in: Renz (Hrsg.), Interessen um Eichmann, Frankfurt am Main 2012, S. 79 ff., S. 81.

seinem Plädoyer wies er darauf hin, dass er Widersprüche in diesen Aussagen hätte nachweisen können. Da die geschilderten Sachverhalte aber im Wesentlichen feststünden, habe er diese Zeugen aus Rücksicht auf ihr Leid nicht kleinlich angreifen wollen.[86] Er kam auch nicht mehr auf die Einwände zurück, die er zu Beginn des Verfahrens gegen die Filmaufnahmen im Gerichtssaal erhoben hatte. Dort hatte er unter anderem argumentiert, Zeugen könnten in dem Wissen, dass sie gefilmt werden, ihre Aussagen übertreiben, um die Außenwelt zu beeindrucken.[87] Sofern er doch nachfragte, beschränkte er sich meist auf wenige Erkundigungen zu wichtigen Details, so etwa wenn er nach der genauen Fundstelle eines Fotos in einem Bildband fragt, auf dem ein Zeuge Eichmann in Himmlers Gefolge erkannt haben will.[88] Nach Durchsicht verschiedener Ausgaben des Bandes und der Suche in polnischen Archiven musste der Ankläger schließlich einräumen, dass man das Foto nicht habe finden können.[89] Natürlich kann man im Kreuzverhör auch unerwünschte Antworten bekommen. Der Zeuge Grüber, der zuvor gesagt hatte, er habe das Gefühl gehabt, dass Eichmann ihn hasse, gab auf die Frage, was dieser denn genau gesagt habe, zurück, das habe sich aus seinem gesamten Verhalten ergeben. Er fügte allerdings auch gleich an, dass seine Frau das ebenfalls so erlebt und Eichmanns Büro unter Tränen verlassen habe.[90] Der Angeklagte hatte bei der polizeilichen Vernehmung noch ausgesagt, er hätte der Frau nur zu gern geholfen, aber es sei nichts zu machen gewesen.[91]

Vehement bekämpfte der Verteidiger dagegen die Zulassung zweier Dokumente, die als *Affidavits*, also eidesstattliche Versicherungen, angesehen wurden. Dieter Wisliceny, SS-Hauptsturmführer und zeitweise Eichmanns Untergebener, hatte sie im Gefängnis von Bratislava verfasst.[92] Die dort erhobenen Beschuldigungen verfolgten einzig den Zweck, so der Verteidiger, Schuld von Wisliceny auf den Angeklagten abzuwälzen, der so seine eigene Haut habe retten wollen. Neue Tatsachen enthielten die Dokumente hingegen nicht.[93] Das Gericht ließ die beiden Schriftstücke zu,[94] so dass Servatius am

---

86 Eher störten sich an diesen Aussagen die Richter, die auch immer wieder versuchten, sie abzukürzen, etwa Sitzungsprotokoll, Sitzung 27, Teil 8 und die auch im Urteil darauf hinwiesen, dass, was nicht zur Erhellung der Tatvorwürfe, zur Schuld des Angeklagten oder zur Bemessung seiner Strafe beitrage, in ein Verfahren keinen Eingang finden dürfe, Urteil, Abs. Nr. 2; vgl. insoweit auch Hauff, Richter (o. Fn. 34), S. 144 f.

87 Vgl. Decision: Recording of the Proceedings, in Sitzungsprotokoll, Bd I. Das Gericht folgte dem nicht, so dass zum ersten mal in der Geschichte Israels ein Gerichtsverfahren abgefilmt wurde. Vgl. zum ganzen Yablonka, State (o. Fn. 5), S. 56 f.

88 Sitzungsprotokoll, Sitzung 65, Teil 2; auch die Richter interessieren sich sofort hierfür.

89 Sitzungsprotokoll, Sitzung 73, Teil 5; bei Gericht sah der Zeuge, Moshe Bahir, zwei Ausgaben durch, die aber das von ihm beschriebene Foto nicht enthielten, Sitzungsprotokoll, Sitzung 66, Teil 4 und Sitzung 66, Teil 9.

90 Sitzungsprotokoll, Sitzung 41, Teil 5.

91 Vom Vernehmungsoffizier Avner Less in der Hauptverhandlung vorgelesen, Sitzungsprotokoll, Sitzung 11, Teil 3.

92 Wisliceny hatte bereits als Zeuge im Nürnberger Hauptkriegsverbrecherprozess Eichmann schwer belastet, vgl. IMT-Sitzungsprotokoll, Bd. IV, S. 396 ff.

93 Sitzungsprotokoll, Sitzung 14, Teil 3.

94 Sitzungsprotokoll, Sitzung 16, Teil 1 (Entscheidung Nr. 7).

Ende nur der erneute Hinweis in seinem Plädoyer übrig blieb, dass Wisliceny nicht zu trauen sei.[95] Ähnlich energisch wandte sich Servatius gegen die Vernehmung Michael Musmannos, des Vorsitzenden Richters im Einsatzgruppenprozess des NMT[96] und Beisitzers in zwei weiteren Verfahren, sollte dieser doch unter anderem Aussagen über die Möglichkeiten der Befehlsverweigerung im Nazi-Reich machen.[97] Der Verteidiger stellte sich vor allem auf den Standpunkt, der Zeuge könne nur vom Hörensagen berichten und dem Gericht stünden insoweit jeweils bessere Beweismittel zu Gebote.[98] Was die Möglichkeiten der Befehlsverweigerung anbelange könne der Zeuge bestenfalls sagen, ob jemand ohne Konsequenzen einen Befehl habe verweigern können, nicht jedoch warum und wie.[99] Das Gericht ließ die Aussage zu soweit der Zeuge vom Hörensagen über Dinge berichte, die er von inzwischen verstorbenen Personen erfahren habe. Das gleiche galt für Aussagen über die tatsächlichen Möglichkeiten zur Befehlsverweigerung.[100] Diese Entscheidungen hatten für die Verteidigung durchaus über den konkreten Zeugen hinausgehende Bedeutung, denn unter Berufung auf sie ließ das Gericht Beweise auch in ähnlichen Fällen zu. Das war beispielsweise der Fall als Gustave Gilbert, der Gerichtspsychologe im Nürnberger Gerichtsgefängnis, gehört wurde zu Äußerungen, die inzwischen verstorbene Personen ihm gegenüber in Nürnberg gemacht hatten.[101] So fand Eingang ins Verfahren, dass nach Görings Auffassung Eichmann ein größerer Schweinehund als Wisliceny war[102] und dass Rudolf Höß, der Kommandant des Lagers Auschwitz, das Vernichtungsprogramm überhaupt nicht habe erörtern können, ohne andauernd Eichmann zu erwähnen.[103]

Zum Nachweis seiner Schuld bediente sich die Anklage außerdem ca. 1.600[104] verschiedener Dokumente, die oft Eichmann ausgestellt und gezeichnet hatte oder die ihn sonst klar und unmittelbar belasteten. Insbesondere hielt man sie ihm vor, wenn er einzelne Vorwürfe abstritt oder angab, sich nicht zu erinnern. Diese Dokumente sprachen nur allzu oft eine eindeutige Sprache, brachten den Angeklagten etwa direkt in Verbindung mit der Einweisung von Juden in Ghettos und Lager,[105] der Planung der sog. Endlö-

---

95 Sitzungsprotokoll, Sitzung 114, Teil 4.

96 Nuremberg Military Tribunal; vgl. Band IV der sog. Grünen Serie, Trials of War Criminals before the Nuremberg Military Tribunals under Control Council Law No. 10, Washington 1950.

97 Sitzungsprotokoll, Sitzung 39, Teil 1.

98 Sitzungsprotokoll, Sitzung 39, Teil 1.

99 Sitzungsprotokoll, Sitzung 39, Teil 2.

100 Sitzungsprotokoll, Sitzung 39, Teil 3 (Entscheidung Nr. 29).

101 Sitzungsprotokoll, Sitzung 55, Teil 1 (Entscheidung Nr. 58); die Vernehmung Gilberts beginnt ebda.

102 Sitzungsprotokoll, Sitzung 55, Teil 2.

103 Sitzungsprotokoll, Sitzung 55, Teil 2.

104 Renz, NS-Verbrechen und Justiz (o. Fn. 29), S. 32; Servatius, Verteidigung (o. Fn. 2), S. 6.

105 Vgl. etwa Sitzungsprotokoll, Sitzung 91, Teil 6 und Sitzung 98 Teil 5.

sung[106] und ihrer Umsetzung durch Ermordung mittels Gas.[107] Sein Verteidiger konnte am Ende nur noch grundsätzliche Probleme des Dokumentenbeweises behaupten: Es handele sich bei den vorgelegten Schriftstücken ja nur um solche, die zufallsbedingt den Krieg überstanden hätten. Sie müssten folglich aus dem Zusammenhang gerissen sein und zeichneten häufig ein missverständliches Bild vom Geschehen.[108] Dass sein Mandant sich an dieses Geschehen bisweilen erst nach Vorlage von Dokumenten erinnert habe, sei allein dem Zeitablauf geschuldet. Ohne die Dokumente erinnere man sich eben nicht an alle Details.[109]

Auf zwei Dokumente soll hier noch gesondert eingegangen werden. Zum einen unterzeichnete Eichmann in Argentinien eine Erklärung, in der er sich der israelischen Gerichtsbarkeit unterwarf. Servatius trug vor, *prima facie* sei davon auszugehen, dass Zwang angewandt wurde, daher sei die Erklärung nichtig.[110] Generalstaatsanwalt Hausner erklärte auch sogleich, er halte die Erklärung für völlig irrelevant.[111]

Sehr viel mehr Sprengkraft barg das sog. Sassen-Interview. Es handelte sich dabei um Protokolle von Gesprächen, die Eichmann 1957 mit dem ehemaligen SS-Mann Willem Sassen in Buenos Aires geführt hatte und in denen er freimütig seine Funktion im Vernichtungsapparat der SS diskutierte.[112] Nachdem Auszüge hiervon 1960 im „Stern" und in „Time/LIFE" erschienen waren, hat Servatius angeblich gar erwogen, das Mandat niederzulegen, falls sich die dort aufgestellten Behauptungen bewahrheiten sollten. Er habe davon aber wieder Abstand genommen, nachdem Eichmann glaubhaft gemacht habe, seine Aussagen seien von dem Publizisten überzeichnet worden.[113] Weite Teile der Protokolle gelangten in den Besitz der Anklage,[114] die sie als

106 Vgl. etwa Sitzungsprotokoll, Sitzung 20, Teil 4 und Sitzung 106 Teil 3.
107 Vgl. etwa Sitzungsprotokoll, Sitzung 30, Teil 4.
108 Sitzungsprotokoll, Sitzung 114, Teil 4.
109 Sitzungsprotokoll, Sitzung 114, Teil 4.
110 Sitzungsprotokoll, Sitzung 1, Teil 3.
111 Sitzungsprotokoll, Sitzung 1, Teil 4. In der Folge entspann sich eine kleine Diskussion, weil Servatius sich auf dieses Schriftstück berufen hatte, als er die Erstattung seiner Kosten beim Staat Israel beantragte. Auf die Anmerkung Hausners, er könne sich kaum darauf berufen und es gleichzeitig für völlig wertlos halten, entgegnete er, nur die Aussage Eichmanns darin sei wertlos. Darüber hinaus sei aber auch die Zusicherung einer offiziellen Stelle enthalten, dass Eichmann einen Verteidiger bekomme und auf die wolle er sich weiterhin berufen.
112 Vgl. zu Entstehung und Inhalt des Sassen-Interviews Wojak, Eichmanns Memoiren. Ein kritischer Essay, Frankfurt am Main 2004, S. 48 ff.
113 Große, Eichmann-Prozess (o. Fn. 26), S. 51; vgl. auch Yablonka, State (o. Fn. 5), S. 129, die bei Servatius zumindest eine verzweifelte Stimmung ausmacht.
114 Wojak, Eichmanns Memoiren (o. Fn. 112), S. 55 schreibt, Hausner habe auf die Frage des Vorsitzenden, woher er das Material habe, nicht antworten wollen. Der dortige Nachweis in Fn. 51 verweist auf das Protokoll der 72. Sitzung, wo sich ein solches Zwiegespräch allerdings nicht findet. Wojak a.a.O. schreibt auch, sie habe die Zitate der deutschsprachigen Simultanübersetzung entnommen, welche sich in der *Yad Vashem Library* befindet. Möglicherweise wurden diese Passagen bei der Anfertigung des Gerichtsprotokolls entfernt. Während des Verfahrens wurde neben der Simultanübersetzung noch eine genauere

Beweisstück in das Verfahren einführen wollte.[115] Servatius wandte sich vor allem mit dem Argument hiergegen, es gebe mit Sassen, den man als Zeugen hören müsse, ein sehr viel besseres Beweismittel. Bei einer Befragung könne er, Servatius, nachweisen, dass Sassen die Aussagen Eichmanns verfälscht habe, um eine spektakuläre Veröffentlichung zu produzieren.[116] Das Gericht entschied, nur einen sehr kleinen Teil zuzulassen, nämlich diejenigen Seiten, auf denen der Angeklagte handschriftliche Notizen und Korrekturen gemacht hatte.[117] Auch wenn damit der Großteil des Materials der Anklage nicht in das Verfahren eingeführt werden konnte, musste Dr. Servatius im Plädoyer einräumen, dass das Sassen-Interview seinen Mandanten schwer belaste. Man dürfe es jedoch nicht ernst nehmen, es handle sich um das Ergebnis von Provokation, ausgeschmückt durch Sassen und von Eichmann unter Alkoholeinfluss ausgesprochen.[118]

Die Verteidigung auf der anderen Seite legte nur wenige Dokumente vor.[119] Servatius verwies denn auch auf das strukturelle Ungleichgewicht im Verhältnis zur Anklage. Es sei ihm unmöglich gewesen, eigene Entlastungsdokumente herbeizuschaffen, denn weder die Archive der Welt noch die Machtmittel der Regierungen hätten ihm zur Verfügung gestanden.[120]

Auch die Zahl der von der Verteidigung aufgebotenen Zeugen war eher gering. Er sei schließlich nicht in der Lage, das Erscheinen von Zeugen vor Gericht zu erzwingen, so Dr. Servatius.[121] Sachverständige hätten aus Angst vor der Presse zugunsten der Verteidigung nicht Stellung nehmen wollen und die von ihm beantragten Zeugen hätten bei Einreise nach Israel um ihre Freiheit fürchten müssen.[122] Tatsächlich hatte Generalstaatsanwalt Hausner angekündigt, die Zeugen der Verteidigung – mit zwei Ausnahmen – bei ihrer Einreise festzunehmen und nach dem NNG anzuklagen.[123] Die beiden Ausnahmen waren Wilhelm Hoettl und Walter Huppenkothen, denen der Ankläger Immunität zusicherte, da ihm keine Hinweise vorlägen, dass diese beiden Verbrechen gegen das jüdische Volk begangen hätten.[124] Grund hierfür sei

Konsekutivübersetzung für das Protokoll gefertigt, vgl. Servatius, Verteidigung (o. Fn. 2), S. 6.

115 Sitzungsprotokoll, Sitzung 72, Teil 7.

116 Sitzungsprotokoll, Sitzung 72, Teil 8.

117 Sitzungsprotokoll, Sitzung 74, Teil 1 (Entscheidung Nr. 79).

118 Sitzungsprotokoll, Sitzung 114, Teil 4.

119 Arendt, Eichmann (o. Fn. 23), S. 332 spricht von 110 Dokumenten, die die Verteidigung vorgelegt habe. Davon seien allerdings die weitaus meisten aus dem Bestand der Anklage entnommen, 17 seien Skizzen Eichmanns gewesen und nur zwölf habe der Verteidiger selbst beschafft, von denen wiederum die meisten Auszüge aus Büchern gewesen seien.

120 Sitzungsprotokoll, Sitzung 114, Teil 4; vgl. zum ganz ähnlichen Vortrag der Verteidigung im Nürnberger Hauptkriegsverbrecherprozess Safferling/Graebke, Verteidigung in Nürnberg (o. Fn. 14), S. 73 f.

121 Sitzungsprotokoll, Sitzung 1, Teil 3.

122 Sitzungsprotokoll, Sitzung 114, Teil 4.

123 Vgl. bspw. Sitzungsprotokoll, Sitzung 17, Teil 2; das Gericht stellte diesbezüglich auch fest, dass es keine Kompetenz habe, der Exekutive insoweit Vorschriften zu machen, Sitzungsprotokoll, Sitzung 20, Teil 1 (Entscheidung Nr. 11).

124 Sitzungsprotokoll, Sitzung 30, Teil 1.

auch, dass Servatius Hoettl als seinen wichtigsten Zeugen bezeichnet hatte.[125] Beiden erwähnten Zeugen wurden Visa und Immunität zugesichert,[126] was sie jedoch nicht zu einer Reise nach Israel bewegen konnte.[127]

Somit mussten sämtliche Zeugen der Verteidigung sowie einige der Anklage im Rahmen von Rechtshilfeersuchen im Ausland vernommen werden und ihre Aussagen als *Affidavits* in das Verfahren eingeführt werden.[128] Auf diesem Wege wurden zwölf Zeugen in Deutschland, drei in Österreich und einer in Italien vernommen.[129] Servatius betonte, dies sei ein schlechter Ersatz einer echten Vernehmung gewesen, hätten doch die ersuchten Richter schon den umfassenden Stoff nicht beherrschen können.[130] Außerdem wären bei einer Aussage vor Ort richtige Haupt- und Kreuzverhöre möglich gewesen, in denen die Zeugen, Auge in Auge mit dem Angeklagten, einige ihrer diesen schwer belastenden Aussagen hätten zurücknehmen müssen.[131] Bei den Vernehmungen in Deutschland war für die Verteidigung Servatius' Assistent, RA Dr. Dieter Wechtenbruch, anwesend,[132] in Österreich waren Vertreter von Anklage und Verteidigung nicht zugelassen[133] und in Italien durften solche Vertreter nur dort zugelassene Rechtsanwälte sein. Zwar war Shimron im Gegensatz zu Wechtenbruch erlaubt worden, zugegen zu sein, jedoch mussten sich sowohl Anklage als auch Verteidigung italienischer Rechtsanwälte zu ihrer Vertretung bedienen.[134] Echten Nutzen konnte die Verteidigung aus ihren Zeugen nicht ziehen. Diesen ging es zumeist allein darum, sich auf Kosten Eichmanns vom Geschehen zu distanzieren und möglichst alle Schuld bei ihm abzuladen.[135] So wurde Eichmann von seinen eigenen Zeugen als jemand beschrieben, der seine Macht zügellos ausübte und

---

125 Sitzungsprotokoll, Sitzung 30, Teil 1; ebenso, dass nach Aussage des Gerichts das Erscheinen von Zeugen in der Verhandlung nach Möglichkeit anderen Varianten ihrer Aussage vorzuziehen sei, vgl. Sitzungsprotokoll, Sitzung 20, Teil 1 (Entscheidung Nr. 11).

126 Sitzungsprotokoll, Sitzung 30, Teil 1.

127 Vgl. die Bemühungen Dr. Servatius', die immer wieder zur Sprache kamen, Sitzungsprotokoll, Sitzung 41, Teil 2 und Sitzung 56 Teil 4.

128 Sitzungsprotokoll, Sitzung 20, Teil 1 (Entscheidung Nr. 11). Dies beschloss das Gericht, nachdem der Ankläger ein solches Vorgehen schon früh vorgeschlagen hatte, Sitzungsprotokoll, Sitzung 1, Teil 4. Das missversteht Hannah Arendt, die meint, der Ankläger gestehe diesen Zeugen freies Geleit zu, Arendt, Eichmann (o. Fn. 23), S. 331.

129 Zu diesem Zeitpunkt bestand noch kein Rechtshilfeabkommen zwischen Israel und der BRD. Das Europäische Übereinkommen über Rechtshilfe in Strafsachen ist für Israel 1967, für die Bundesrepublik erst 1977 in Kraft getreten, vgl. Bundesgesetzblatt Teil II 1964, S. 1369, 1386 und 1976, S. 1799. Allerdings waren zuvor schon von israelischen Behörden und Gerichten Zeugen für NS-Prozesse in Deutschland vernommen worden. Zwischen Italien und Israel bestand bereits ein Rechtshilfeübereinkommen, vgl. Cohen, Gesichtspunkte (o. Fn. 29), S. 53 und Große, Eichmann-Prozess (o. Fn. 26), S. 118.

130 Sitzungsprotokoll, Sitzung 114, Teil 4.

131 Sitzungsprotokoll, Sitzung 114, Teil 4.

132 Vgl. die Vernehmungsprotokolle in Sitzungsprotokoll, Band V; für die Anklage war jeweils RA Shaul Shimron anwesend, ein ehemaliger israelischer Staatsanwalt, vgl. zum ganzen auch Cohen, Gesichtspunkte (o. Fn. 29), S. 45 ff.

133 Vgl. Cohen, Gesichtspunkte (o. Fn. 29), S. S. 51.

134 Vgl. Cohen, Gesichtspunkte (o. Fn. 29), S. 54.

135 Hausner, Gerechtigkeit (o Fn. 11), S. 573 f.

seine Befugnisse auch jederzeit überschritt, wenn er nur glaubte, im Sinne seiner Befehle zu handeln.[136] Hätte man nach einer Ausnahme für einen Juden oder etwas ähnlichem gesucht, so hätte man sich sicher nicht an ihn gewandt.[137]

Das wichtigste Beweismittel der Verteidigung war damit die Aussage des Angeklagten. Eichmann trat am 20.06.1961 in den Zeugenstand[138] und wurde von Servatius bis zum 07. Juli befragt. Das anschließende Kreuzverhör dauerte bis zum 20.07.1961, danach stellten die Richter ihre Fragen, bevor beide Parteien noch einmal kurz Gelegenheit zum Wiederverhör hatten.[139] In seinem Plädoyer führte der Verteidiger aus, diese Aussage sei absolut glaubwürdig. Der Angeklagte habe schwere Belastungen schon bei den Verhören durch die Polizei freiwillig eingeräumt und naheliegende Wege sich zu entlasten nicht beschritten. Auch seien seine Antworten im Kreuzverhör stets ruhig und sicher gewesen, was ausgeschlossen sei, wenn jemand ein Lügengebäude zu verteidigen suche.[140]

Der Case *der Verteidigung*

Dieses Vorbringen der Verteidigung erschöpfte sich im Wesentlichen in Argumenten, die mit Eichmanns Stellung in der Hierarchie der SS zu tun hatten.

Seine wichtigste Verteidigungslinie war der Höhere Befehl. Servatius meinte, dass Vorschriften wie Art. 8 NNG und Art. 8 des Londoner Statuts die Berufung auf Befehle ausschlössen, mache diese zu rechtswidrigen Ausnahmebestimmungen. Briten und Amerikaner hätten diese Berufung bis 1944 akzeptiert, Eichmann müsse sie als durch Eid gebundenem Angehörigen einer straffen Organisation ebenfalls offenstehen.[141] Die Judenverfolgungen seien politisch angeordnet gewesen und einen politischen Befehl könne man nicht als rechtswidrig erkennen. Blinder Gehorsam sei die grundlegende Funktionsweise aller Staaten, in Ausführung solcher politischer Befehle würden nach wie vor in aller Welt Unmenschlichkeiten begangen, zwischen Verbrechen und Tugend entscheide am Ende allein der Sieg. Diese Ausführungen gipfelten in seiner Behauptung, auch Israel habe „harte Maßnahmen" treffen müssen, als es um die Existenz des Staates ging.[142] So berief sich Eichmann, wann immer er einräumen musste, irgendetwas getan oder ge-

136 Sitzungsprotokoll, Aussage Winkelmann Teil 2. Die Aussagen der kommissarisch vernommenen Zeugen befinden sich im 5. Band des Sitzungsprotokolls.
137 Sitzungsprotokoll, Aussage Six Teil 2.
138 Was nicht räumlich zu verstehen ist, denn auf Antrag der Anklage beschloss das Gericht gemäß § 5 des Courts Law, dass der Angeklagte aus Sicherheitsgründen von seinem Platz im kugelsicheren Glaskasten aus seine Aussage zu machen habe, Sitzungsprotokoll, Sitzung 75, Teil 5 (Entscheidung Nr. 84).
139 Vgl. zu diesem Ablauf Cohen, Gesichtspunkte (o. Fn. 29), S. 27 ff.
140 Sitzungsprotokoll, Sitzung 114, Teil 4.
141 Sitzungsprotokoll, Sitzung 114, Teil 5.
142 Sitzungsprotokoll, Sitzung 114, Teil 6.

wusst zu haben, darauf, dass dies von oben befohlen worden sei. Sogar einzelne Deportationen seien ihm befohlen worden[143] und nach seiner Teilnahme an der Wannseekonferenz habe er sich gut, weil völlig unschuldig, gefühlt, denn nun hätten ja die führenden Personen ihre Befehle gegeben.[144] Überhaupt sei er durch seinen Eid ja nicht länger Herr seines Willens gewesen, die Verantwortung für seine Taten müsse die Staatsführung tragen.[145] Aufgrund des Eides der Untergebenen müsse das Gewissen der Staatschef haben.[146] Das Gericht konnte er so nicht überzeugen. Nach einem Hinweis auf Art. 8 NNG legte es unter Heranziehung u. a. des Londoner Statuts und von § 47 des deutschen Militärstrafgesetzbuches dar, dass die Befehle, auf die Eichmann sich berief, offensichtlich rechtswidrig waren und somit auch in dieser Hinsicht nicht zu seiner Entlastung taugten.[147]

Seine persönliche Stellung in diesem Staat schilderte Eichmann immer wieder als die eines kleinen Rädchens im großen Getriebe. Ohne jede eigene Entscheidungsbefugnis habe er stets nur für den Leiter seiner Dienststelle gehandelt, seine Machtlosigkeit sei hinlänglich bekannt gewesen, so dass er Hinweise hierauf nicht an jede Weisung anzuhängen brauchte.[148] In überaus komplizierten Ausführungen über die Geschäftsverteilung im Reichssicherheitshauptamt ließ er seine Funktion immer mehr verschwinden,[149] bis, wie Haim Gouri, ein Beobachter des Prozesses,[150] schreibt, er für die Zuhörer immer weiter untergegangen sei im endlosen und komplexen System von Verwaltungsstellen, Vorgesetzten und Untergebenen. Unter den Zuschauern sei man sich nicht einig gewesen, ob Servatius nun brillant oder unfähig sei.[151] Als er ausführte, nach der Wannseekonferenz habe er nur deshalb mit Heydrich und Müller Cognac trinkend am Kamin gesessen, weil Heydrich

143 Vgl. etwa Sitzungsprotokoll, Sitzung 98, Teil 5 oder Sitzung 93, Teil 4.

144 Sitzungsprotokoll, Sitzung 79, Teil 1.

145 Sitzungsprotokoll, Sitzung 105, Teil 4.

146 Sitzungsprotokoll, Sitzung 88, Teil 2.

147 Urteil Abs. Nr. 220. Für die Bestimmung dieser offensichtlichen Rechtswidrigkeit folgte das Gericht der Entscheidung in der Sache *Prosecutor v. Melinki et al.*, an der auch Benjamin Halevi beteiligt gewesen war. In dem Fall war israelischen Soldaten, die ein Massaker in einem arabischen Dorf angerichtet hatten, die Berufung auf höhere Befehle versagt worden, vgl. Urteil, Abs. Nr. 119 und Hauff, Richter (o. Fn. 34), S. 130 f.

148 Sitzungsprotokoll, Sitzung 114, Teil 5.

149 Sitzungsprotokoll, Sitzung 75, Teil 7 und Sitzung 76, Teil 1; vgl. hier auch die Ermahnung des Vorsitzenden, Eichmann müsse seine endlosen Schachtelsätze abkürzen, wenn er verstanden werden wolle.

150 Die Aufzeichnungen Gouris stellen, genau wie Hannah Arendts bekannter Bericht, frühe Formen moderner Prozessbeobachtung dar. Vgl. zu diesem gerade im Völkerstrafrecht aktuell bedeutenden Konzept Safferling/Graebke/Hansen/Hörmann, Das Monitoring-Projekt des Forschungs- und Dokumentationszentrums für Kriegsverbrecherprozesse (ICWC), Marburg, in: Zeitschrift für Internationale Strafrechtsdogmatik 2011, S. 564 ff. und Hansen, Zwischenbericht zur Verfahrensbeobachtung im Strafverfahren gegen Onesphore R. vor dem Oberlandesgericht Frankfurt, in: Safferling/Kirsch (Hrsg.), Völkerstrafrechtspolitik. Praxis des Völkerstrafrechts, S. 433 ff.

151 Gouri, Facing the Glass Booth. The Jerusalem Trial of Adolf Eichmann, Detroit 2004, S. 167.

das Protokoll sofort erledigt wissen wollte, brach unter den Zuschauern Gelächter aus.[152]

Über seine Befehle sei er niemals hinausgegangen,[153] von Natur aus habe er keinen Judenhass gekannt.[154] So hätten etwa die Vertreter der jüdischen Gemeinde in Wien „sehr gerne“ mit ihm „zusammengearbeitet“.[155]

Als er sich von hier aus dazu hinreißen ließ zu erläutern, wie er nach Möglichkeit auch noch Schlimmeres verhinderte, indem er etwa 20.000 Juden in ein Ghetto statt in ein Vernichtungslager schickte,[156] war der Widerspruch zu den soeben dargestellten Einlassungen perfekt. So musste er nicht nur eingestehen, nicht immer voll und ganz im Sinne seiner Befehle gehandelt zu haben, sondern auch seine Entscheidungsbefugnisse einräumen.[157] Es half auch nicht, dass ihm in Einzelfällen nachgewiesen wurde, dass er die Ausführung dieser Befehle sogar gegen Widerstände durchgesetzt hatte.[158]

Flankiert wurde seine Berufung auf Befehle von der Behauptung des Befehlsnotstandes. Im Unterschied zu höheren Rängen habe er sich dem Gehorsam nicht entziehen können und Desertion sei nicht zumutbar.[159] Tatsächlich habe er mehrfach darum ersucht, an die Front versetzt zu werden, dies sei jedoch stets abgelehnt worden.[160] Natürlich musste er zugeben, dass er millionenfachen Mord für ein schwereres Verbrechen als Eidbruch halte.[161]

Neben diesen immer wiederkehrenden Argumenten trug Servatius vor, die Handlungen des Angeklagten seien als Staatshandlungen zu werten, für die allein der Staat die Verantwortung trage.[162] Während gemäß Art. 7 des Londoner Statuts die Berufung hierauf noch ausgeschlossen gewesen sei, enthalte das NNG eine solche Vorschrift nicht.[163] Auch wenn Eichmann nicht zur politischen Führung gehört habe, müsse ihm das Handeln für den Staat zugutekommen.[164] Der Verteidiger berief sich dabei vor allem auf Hans Kelsen und dessen Doktrin, dass *par in parem non habet imperium*, dass also Staatsorgane nicht der Strafgewalt fremder Staaten unterworfen sein könn-

152 Sitzungsprotokoll, Sitzung 106, Teil 3; Schmorak, Der Prozess Eichmann. Dargestellt anhand der in Nürnberg und Jerusalem vorgelegten Dokumente sowie der Gerichtsprotokolle, Wien 1964, S. 26.

153 Etwa Sitzungsprotokoll, Sitzung 105, Teil 2.

154 Sitzungsprotokoll, Sitzung 106, Teil 6.

155 Sitzungsprotokoll, Sitzung 90, Teil 2.

156 Sitzungsprotokoll, Sitzung 78, Teil 3 und Sitzungsprotokoll, Sitzung 98, Teil 4.

157 Bspw. auch Sitzungsprotokoll, Sitzung 106, Teil 6.

158 Etwa Sitzungsprotokoll, Sitzung 106, Teil 6; auch das Gericht glaubte ihm seine behaupteten Rettungsabsichten nicht, vgl. etwa Urteil, Abs. Nr. 67.

159 Sitzungsprotokoll, Sitzung 114, Teil 6.

160 Z.B. Sitzungsprotokoll, Sitzung 106, Teil 7 und Sitzungsprotokoll, Sitzung 114, Teil 6; das Gericht hingegen stellte fest, er habe diese Absicht nie ernsthaft gehabt, Urteil Abs. Nr. 226.

161 Sitzungsprotokoll, Sitzung 95, Teil 5.

162 Sitzungsprotokoll, Sitzung 114, Teil 1.

163 Sitzungsprotokoll, Sitzung 114, Teil 1.

164 Sitzungsprotokoll, Sitzung 114, Teil 1.

ten.[165] Das Gericht allerdings schloss sich der Meinung des Anklägers an, dieses Vorbringen sei schon qua Völkergewohnheitsrecht ausgeschlossen,[166] überhaupt, führte es weiter aus, könne ein Staat, der eine „Endlösung“ plane, nicht wie ein *par in parem* (Gleicher unter Gleichen), sondern nur wie eine Verbrecherbande behandelt werden.[167]

Ein letztes verzweifeltes Argument konstruierte Dr. Servatius als er in seinem Plädoyer beantragte, die vorgeworfenen Taten als verjährt anzusehen. Das NNG schloss die Verjährung, außer bei der Mitgliedschaft in verbrecherischen Organisationen, aus,[168] der Anwalt berief sich aber auf eine 15-jährige Frist der Verfolgungsverjährung in Argentinien. Bei Festsetzung des 05.05.1945 als letztem Tattag sei die Verjährung also noch vor der Entführung Eichmanns eingetreten. Zur Wiederherstellung von dessen durch die Entführung verletzten Rechten fordert er nun eine Art Naturalrestitution. Eichmann solle so gestellt werden wie er im Falle einer ordnungsgemäßen Auslieferung stünde. Dann aber, so Servatius, wäre die Verjährung nach argentinischem Recht auch in Israel zu berücksichtigen.[169] Das Gericht erklärte nur, dass der Verjährungseinwand möglicherweise in einem Auslieferungsverfahren in Argentinien geholfen hätte, aber nach erfolgter Auslieferung in keinem Land der Welt mehr berücksichtigt würde.[170]

Das Ende des Verfahrens

Die Hauptverhandlung endete mit dem Plädoyer des Verteidigers am 14.08.1961. Sein Urteil verlas das Gericht über fünf Sitzungstage hinweg ab dem 11.12.1961. Es sprach Eichmann in allen Punkten schuldig, wenn es auch einige Teilfreisprüche enthielt.[171]

Aufgrund eines formellen Schuldinterlokuts kam es zu einer weiteren Verhandlung über das Strafmaß.[172] Dr. Servatius argumentierte, dass das NNG die Todesstrafe nicht absolut androhe wie sich aus den in Art. 11 ent-

165 Vgl. den Annex zu Band I in den Sitzungsprotokollen, ab S. 532 bzw. unter http://www.nizkor.org/hweb/people/e/eichmann-adolf/transcripts/Sessions/Defence-Submission-01-02.html (zuletzt abgerufen am 05.04.2015). Servatius beruft sich insbesondere auf Collective and Individual Responsibility in International Law with Particular Regard to War Criminals, in: California Law Review 1943, S. 530 ff.

166 Sitzungsprotokoll, Sitzung 112, Teil 6.

167 Urteil Abs. Nr. 28.

168 Art. 12 NNG.

169 Sitzungsprotokoll, Sitzung 114, Teil 6.

170 Urteil Abs. Nr. 53.

171 Etwa in Bezug auf die Eichmann vorgeworfene Verantwortlichkeit für die sog. Sonderaktion 1005, für Zwangssterilisationen oder für die Ermordung der Kinder von Lidice. Im letzten Fall freilich blieb die Verantwortung des Angeklagten für ihre Deportation bestehen. Vgl. Urteil, Abs. Nr. 148, 158, 213.

172 Unter einem Schuldinterlokut versteht man eine Aufteilung des Verfahrens in einen ersten Teil, in dem allein über die Schuld des Angeklagten verhandelt wird, und einen davon getrennten zweiten Teil, der die Festsetzung des Strafmaßes zum Gegenstand hat. Vgl. zum Verfahren insoweit Cohen, Gesichtspunkte (o. Fn. 29), S. 55 ff.

haltenen Milderungsgründen ergebe. Neben dem Handeln auf Befehl sollte für Eichmann vor allem sprechen, dass er, integriert durch Hierarchie und Gruppendynamik, Teil einer gewaltigen Maschinerie gewesen sei, die er unmöglich hätte aufhalten können.[173] Auch das Gericht hielt die Strafandrohung (Todesstrafe) nicht für absolut,[174] entschied aber dennoch auf ein Todesurteil, das es zwei Tage später, am 15 Dezember 1961, verkündete.

Gegen dieses Urteil legte die Verteidigung Rechtsmittel ein,[175] über das ab dem 22.03.1962 vor dem Obersten Gericht verhandelt wurde. Im Großen und Ganzen glich dieses Verfahren eher einer Revision,[176] auch wenn Servatius etwa die Möglichkeit erhielt, noch einmal die Ladung von Zeugen zu beantragen.[177] In der Sache trug der Verteidiger im Wesentlichen die selben Argumente wie im erstinstanzlichen Verfahren vor.[178] Nach Verwerfung dieses Rechtsmittels legte Servatius ein Gnadengesuch bei Staatspräsident Yitzhak Ben-Zvi ein,[179] welches dieser am 31.05.1962 zurückwies. Am ersten Juni 1962 – zwei Jahre und 21 Tage nach Eichmanns Ergreifung in Buenos Aires – wurde die Todesstrafe vollstreckt.

Zu diesem Zeitpunkt weilten Servatius und sein Assistent schon nicht mehr in Israel. Ob der Verteidiger es eilig hatte das Land zu verlassen, muss hier offenbleiben. Dass er in Israel mehrerer Leibwächter bedurfte,[180] könnte durchaus mit den teilweise sehr befremdlichen Formulierungen zu tun gehabt haben, die er von Zeit zu Zeit in den Verhandlungen gebrauchte. So trat nicht nur unter den Zuschauern eine erdrückende Stille ein[181] als er Gastötungen und die Beschaffung von Skeletten als medizinische Angelegenheiten bezeichnete. Benjamin Halevi unterbrach ihn mit der Bemerkung, es müsse ihm ein Fehler unterlaufen sein, doch Servatius bestand darauf, dass diese Tätigkeiten von Medizinern ausgeführt und das Töten überhaupt eine medizinische Angelegenheit sei.[182]

---

173 Sitzungsprotokoll, Sitzung 120, Teil 3.

174 Wobei es aber anders argumentierte, Sitzungsprotokoll, Sitzung 121, Teil 1.

175 Die Anklage verzichtete auf dieses auch ihr zustehende Recht.

176 Geprüft wird prinzipiell nur auf Rechtsfehler, Tatsachen können nur ausnahmsweise thematisiert werden, vgl. Cohen, Gesichtspunkte (o. Fn. 29), S. 71 f.

177 So beantragte er hier, Hans Globke als Zeugen zu hören und ließ damit eine Befürchtung wahr werden, die auf politischer Ebene schon lange bestanden hatte. Globke, Staatssekretär im Bundeskanzleramt und Adenauers wichtigster Mitarbeiter, hatte als Beamter im Reichsinnenministerium u.a. die sog. Nürnberger Rassegesetze kommentiert. Eine Ladung Globkes hätte die Beziehungen zwischen Tel Aviv und Bonn durchaus belasten können. Das Gericht lehnte den Antrag ab. Vgl. zum ganzen v.a. Winkler, Eichmann und seine Unterstützer (o. Fn. 12), S. 290 ff.

178 Daneben versuchte er, aus einigen internationalen Verträgen Rechte Eichmanns abzuleiten. Das Gericht ließ sich davon nicht überzeugen, hatte Israel diese doch zum Teil noch nicht einmal unterzeichnet.

179 Er war natürlich nicht der einzige. Neben Eichmann und seiner Familie kamen Zuschriften aus aller Welt beim Präsidenten an, vgl. Arendt, Eichmann (o. Fn. 23), S. 249.

180 Pendorf, Verteidiger (o. Fn. 17).

181 Gouri, Glass Booth (o. Fn. 151), S. 262.

182 Sitzungsprotokoll, Sitzung 114, Teil 2; vgl. für weitere Beispiele ähnlicher Art Gouri, Glass Booth (o. Fn. 151), S. 25 und Pendorf, Verteidiger (o. Fn. 17).

Solcher Art dürften die „überflüssigen“ Bemerkungen der Verteidigung gewesen sein, welche das Gericht „in den Ohren schmerzten“.[183] Gleichwohl brachte es ihr gegenüber seine große Anerkennung zum Ausdruck und dankte ihr für den sachlichen Umgang mit dem Prozessgegenstand.[184] Auch die Vertreter der Anklage und der polizeilichen Ermittlungseinheit 06 schüttelten Servatius höflich die Hand, nachdem er sein Plädoyer gehalten hatte.[185] In Israel und bei Gericht hinterließ die Verteidigung einen gemischten Eindruck.

Die Rolle der Verteidigung im Rückblick

Aus heutiger Sicht liegt ein wichtiger Teil der Bedeutung des Eichmannprozesses in der veränderten Wahrnehmung des Holocaust, die das Verfahren mit sich brachte. Während in Nürnberg noch der Angriffskrieg im Mittelpunkt des Verfahrens stand, rückte mit dem Prozess in Jerusalem nicht nur in Israel sondern weltweit die Shoah verstärkt ins Zentrum der Geschichte des Zweiten Weltkriegs.

Auch in modernen Völkerstrafprozessen streben Verfahrensbeteiligte Effekte solcher Art bisweilen als Ergebnis ihrer Arbeit an. Immer wieder lässt sich beobachten, wie das Spannungsfeld zwischen dem Kampf um Geschichtsbilder und der immensen Bedeutung, die unscheinbare Details für die juristische Bewertung individueller Schuld haben können, auch und gerade die Verteidigung vor Probleme stellt.

Tatsächlich wäre die Frage berechtigt, ob nicht ein Verteidiger, der am Geschichtsbild arbeitet, seinem Mandanten eher schadet als nutzt. Natürlich hat aber unter Umständen gerade der Angeklagte ein Interesse hieran. Wie geschildert schenkte Servatius etlichen Aussagen von Opferzeugen kaum Beachtung, fand er in ihnen doch schlicht keine unmittelbare Belastung seines Mandanten. Sehr viel Energie verwendete er hingegen auf prozessuale Einwände, Fragen der Gerichtsbarkeit und andere Vorbringen, die sich nicht unmittelbar mit dem Schuldvorwurf und dem Beweismaterial beschäftigten. Eichmann auf der anderen Seite war durchaus interessiert an dem Bild, das die Nachwelt von ihm haben würde, umso mehr als er sich keine allzu großen Illusionen über das zu erwartende Urteil machte. Seine unermüdliche Dokumentenarbeit freilich war nicht nur die wichtigste Informationsquelle seines Vertreters, sondern oftmals auch seine einzige.

Über den Umgang mit einer solchen Situation müssen auch heute jede Verteidigerin und jeder Verteidiger immer wieder neu entscheiden.

---

183 Urteil, Abs. Nr. 3.
184 Urteil, Abs. Nr. 3.
185 Gouri, Glass Booth (o. Fn. 151), S. 265.

Julia Gebhard[*]

Arguing Human Rights from the Bench? How Judges in International Criminal Courts Perceive International Human Rights Law

Introduction

In international criminal law, human rights are likely to become an issue for defence teams in mainly two areas. Procedural issues before the court, referring to the way in which pre-trial phase, trial and sentencing are conducted, can violate the human rights of the defendant and his or her right to a fair trial. Before the ICC, for example, proceedings have been stayed twice in the trial of Congolese rebel leader Thomas Lubanga Dyilo when the prosecutor refused to disclose information necessary for Lubanga's defence. Twice, the stay has been accompanied by the Trial Chamber's assessment that a fair trial of the accused was not possible before the ICC and twice, the quarrels evolved around the use of third parties in the investigative work. That this problem erupted repeatedly in the same case shows that the defence in international trials continues to be faced with unique problems, despite the fact that all modern international criminal courts and tribunals explicitly refer to the rights of the accused, albeit to a differing degree of sophistication. The ad hoc and hybrid tribunals, as well as the International Criminal Court (ICC), all dedicate an article to the rights of the accused during preparation and trial phase.[1] All these provisions are explicitly modelled after Art. 14 International Covenant on Civil and Political Rights (ICCPR) and only slightly adapted to fit the needs of an international criminal legal context.[2] Other 'procedural' human rights guarantees, taking the example of the Rome Statute of the ICC as the most detailed and elaborate of the Statute are Art. 20 (*ne bis in idem* –

---

* LL.M./Legal Officer, OSCE Office for Democratic Institutions and Human Rights (ODIHR); Member of the International Max Planck Research School on Retaliation, Mediation and Punishment (IMPRS-REMEP). The views expressed are those of the author and do not necessarily reflect the views of OSCE/ODIHR.

1 See Art. 21 ICTY Statute; Art. 20 ICTR Statute; Art. Art. 17 SCSL Statute; Art. 16 STL Statute; Art. 35 Law on the Establishment of Extraordinary Chambers in the Courts of Cambodia for the Prosecution of Crimes committed during the Period of Democratic Kampuchea; see also Art. 67 Rome Statute.

2 For the ICTY see Theodor Meron 'Human Rights Marches into New Territory: The Enforcement of International Human Rights in International Criminal Tribunals' Fourth Marek Nowicki Memorial Lecture (28 November 2008) <http://web.ceu.hu/legal/pdf%20documents/Nowicki/Meron_Enforcement%20of%20HRwarsawnowicki13nov08.pdf> (as last accessed on 10 June 2013; speech no longer accessible online); 'Report of the Secretary-General Pursuant to Paragraph 2 of Security Council Resolution 808 (1993)' UN Doc S/25704 para. 106.

the prohibition of double jeopardy, i.e. a defendant cannot be tried on the same or similar charges after a conviction or acquittal); Art. 22 (*nullum crimen sine lege* - no crime without a law, the prohibition of retroactive criminal prosecution, which is an intrinsic part of the principle of legality); Art. 23 (*nulla poena sine lege* – no punishment without the law, the prohibition of retroactive punishment, which is an intrinsic part of the principle of legality); Art. 24 (non-retroactivity); Art. 26 (exclusion of jurisdiction over persons under eighteen) Art. 64 (2) (Trial Chamber as the organ that must ensure fair and expeditious trial); Art. 66 (presumption of innocence); Arts 81-84 (right to appeal); Art. 85 (right to compensation in cases of unlawful arrest of detention). Human rights law has also been used by the ICC to outline the scope, rules and limitations of victim protection and has already been used to clarify the unique victim participation procedure before the ICC.[3]

In another, often overlooked way, human rights come into play also regarding substantive international criminal law, on which this paper concentrates. Substantive law refers to the provisions on the subject-matter of the Rome Statute of the ICC, i.e. the crimes over which the court has jurisdiction (genocide, crimes against humanity, war crimes and the crime of aggression). The way in which these crimes are defined by the court, for example, what requirements an act must fulfill in order to be categorized as an act of torture as a crime against humanity, can obviously have a severe impact on the defendant and the evaluations of his actions pursuant to international criminal law.

Human rights law and international criminal law are undeniably interconnected and yet the degree, the structure, the whole nature of this connection is debated. Yet, as the legal and dogmatic frameworks used to describe the relationship are unclear, it is understood that many of the crimes enlisted in modern-day statutes of international courts and tribunals are mass violations of human rights.[4] As the statutes are often conceptualized in a wide and

---

3 further William A Schabas *The International Criminal Court: A Commentary on the Rome Statute* (OUP Oxford 2010) 399-400; eg *Situation on the Democratic Republic of the Congo (Decision on the Applications for Participation in the Proceedings of VPRS 1, VPRS 2, VPRS 3, VPRS 4, VPRS 5 and VPRS 6)* ICC-01/04 UN (17 January 2006); *Prosecutor v Thomas Lubanga Dyilo (Decision on Victims' Participation)* ICC-01/04-01/06-1119 (18 January 2008) para. 35; *Prosecutor v Jean-Pierre Bemba (Fourth Decision on Victims' Participation)* ICC-01/05-01/08 6/39 (2 December 2008) para. 16; instruments referred to varied from the Convention on the Rights of the Child ([adopted 20 November 1989, entered into force 2 September 1990] 1577 UNTS 3) to soft law documents such as Commission on Human Rights 'Basic Principles and Guidelines on the Right to a Remedy and Reparation for Victims of Gross Violations of International Human Rights Law and Serious Violations of International Humanitarian Law' ([19 April 2005] ESCOR 61st Session Supp 3, 136); UNGA Res 40/34 'Declaration of Basic Principles of Justice for Victims of Crime and Abuse of Power' ([29 November 1985] GAOR 40th Session Supp 53, 213).

4 According to its Preamble and Art. 1 Rome Statute, the ICC is responsible for the prosecution of the most serious crimes of concern to the international community as a whole. This is an expression of a system of values and morals the international community as a

vague manner, courts are forced to look into extra-statutory sources in order to properly define and delineate the crimes under their jurisdiction, contributing to the decentralized production and diffusion of norms. Despite this necessity in decision-making and despite the vast crossovers in the areas of human rights law and international criminal law, there is scarce reference of human rights law in substantive international criminal law and from the existing references no clear system or dogmatic approach can be deduced.[5] From a defence perspective, this recourse to extra-statutory sources per se holds the risk of infringing upon the principle of legality particularly without a sound dogmatic approach. This principle is one of the cornerstones of criminal law and criminal justice as it protects persons from arbitrary punishment for actions they could not identify as sanctioned by way of criminal law when these actions were performed. In international criminal law as a relatively new field of law, this principle is both particularly important and at risk. Since the first establishment of international tribunals proper, after World War II, international criminal law had to constantly defend itself against accusation of arbitrarily assigning criminal sanctions to actions which had previously not been punishable out of political motivations. Indeed, in emerging fields of criminal law, the decision of what is a criminal act can be difficult, when this catalogue is continuously developed and expanded. For this reason, adherence to the principle is, in the international criminal law of the 21st century, both possible and crucial.

A Note on Methodology

Enormous freedoms and responsibilities are bestowed upon the judge in this field due its rudimentary nature. The variety of professional backgrounds and expertise of judges not only feeds into the fragmentation of norms but intensifies it. Because of the judges' preeminent role, interviews are crucial in order to understand what drives the actual practical application of human rights law or the lack thereof. Interviews also help to show how the precon-

---

whole seeks to protect. The codification of the values of the international community is, to a great extent, to be found in international human rights law. In the 1991 ILC Draft Code of Crimes against the Peace and Security of Mankind, the crimes now known as crimes against humanity were enlisted under the heading 'systematic or mass violations of human rights'.4 Furthermore, the human rights law movement and the focus of human rights institutions like the Inter-American Court of Human Rights and the Human Rights Committee on accountability of mass violations fertilized and spurred the development of legal concepts of international criminal law and are responsible for much of the political momentum that led to the ad hoc tribunals and later to the ICC; see also Carsten Stahn and Sven-R. Eiffler 'Über das Verhältnis von Internationalem Menschenrechtsschutz und Völkerstrafrecht anhand des Statuts von Rom' (1999) 82(1) Kritische Vierteljahresschrift für Gesetzgebung und Rechtswissenschaft 253-277, 267; William A Schabas *The International Criminal Court: A Commentary on the Rome Statute* (OUP Oxford 2010) 397.

5 See the author's PhD research project Julia Gebhard *Necessity or Nuisance? Recourse to Human Rights in Substantive International Criminal Law* (forthcoming).

ceived perception of the relationship of human rights law and international criminal law, which are themselves influenced by the background and experience of the judge, shaped said application, the understanding of when judges are mandated to apply human rights law and to what benefit.[6]

This paper is predominantly based on a qualitative study including 14 semi-structured expert interviews conducted with 12 judges at the International Criminal Tribunal for the Former Yugoslavia (ICTY) and the ICC between January 2010 and January 2012 (two judges agreed to be interviewed twice).[7] The selection of judges as interviewees was based on the following factors. The ICTY is the international criminal tribunal which assembled by far the largest body of case law (also exceeding the International Criminal Tribunal for Rwanda [ICTR]) and this case law fundamentally shaped international criminal law in the past and will continue to do so in the future. The ICC as the permanent forum of international criminal litigation will build up on this case law and further contribute to its development and sophistication. The research sought a balance between the two institutions, and includes judges with considerable experience acting as judges in international criminal courts and tribunals as well as those whose experience as judges in international criminal justice was fairly recent. In approaching the judges for an interview request, consideration was also paid to maximal possible diversity as to their professional background (academic, judge, prosecutor, diplomat etc.), field of expertise (public international law/criminal law), national background, legal system in the country of origin or education as well as diversity in gender and age. That being said, the number of interview partners is comparably low as there are in fact only a limited numbers of judges practising international criminal law.[8] To these judges, access is

6 Interviews with judges were chosen due to their distinguished role in the trial as envisaged by the Rome Statute and the ICTY Statute. In practice, judges also rely on the legwork done by their Legal Officers. The nature of the work and the degree to which Legal Officers shape the judges' decisions vary from judge to judge. It would be interesting to focus on Legal Officers, their background and if judges choose Legal Officers with similar expertise and background as their own (as far as they have the opportunity to choose in the recruitment process) or if they chose Legal Officers with different, but complementing backgrounds. As, in any case, judges have the overall authority over their decision and the last say in them, coupled with the authority bestowed upon them by the Rome Statute, judges were deemed to be the appropriate interview partners for the terms of this study.

7 All interviews with ICC judges were conducted during a four months stay of the author as a visiting professional at the International Criminal Court from January 2010 until April 2010. This programme is specifically designed for professionals to do their own research project on international criminal law. The author worked at the International Criminal Court as a staff member. During her time as an ICC staff member, no interviews with ICC staff were conducted. The interviews with ICTY judges were conducted between January 2010 and April 2010 and between May 2011 and January 2012. The interviews were used in the author's dissertation entitled "Necessity or Nuisance? Recourse to Human Rights in Substantive International Criminal Law", currently awaiting defence and publication.

8 The ICC, for example, has 18 serving judges and 14 former judges. Of the 18 serving judges, six judges have only been appointed to the bench after the last round of interviews was conducted in 2012.

restricted. There are a number of potential interview partners who generally declined to speak about the way their decision-making process is conducted.

Given these limitations, the present qualitative study does not claim to present a comprehensive picture of the perception of human rights law in international criminal law. However, the data can identify major tendencies in how the background and experience of judges can influence their understanding and interpretation of legal problems surrounding the role and application of human rights law in international criminal law. Data from the interviews was analyzed in light of and juxtaposed with other sources, applying the concept of triangulation. These sources included the documents such as judgments, official court documents and records and participations, conversations with legal practitioners and other experts of international criminal law on formal and informal levels and trial observation. Furthermore, judges volunteered their assessment of the various approaches of their colleagues in relation to their backgrounds, which again allows more general inferences and tendencies. While the interviews were not tape-recorded, notes were made during the interviews. The interviewees were assured of their anonymity.

Judicial Decision-Making in a Diverse Environment

A number of scholarly works, from legal, sociological and anthropological perspectives, have dealt with creation of prosecutorial and investigative strategies and judgments in courts and with the question what big a role a systematic exegesis really plays vs. the role attributed to external factors.[9] Mainly, these works have been dealing with the interpretation of national constitutions, thus with legal norms that are by definition rather broad in order to be

9 Eg Michael Bohlander and Christian Latour *The German Judiciary in the Nineties - A Study of the Recruitment, Promotion and Remuneration of German Judges* (Shaker Verlag 1998) Shaker Verlag; Christina Boyd, Lee Epstein and Andrew Martin 'Untangling the Causal Effects of Sex on Judging' (2010) 54 American Journal of Political Science 398-411; Nienke Grossmann 'Sex Representation on the Bench and the Legitimacy of the International Criminal Courts' (2011) 11 International Criminal Law Review 643-653; John Hagan, Ron Levi and Gebrielle Ferrales 'Swaying the Hands of Justice: The Internal and External Dynamics of Regime Change at the International Criminal Tribunal for the Former Yugoslavia' (2006) 31(3) Law and Social Inquiry 585-616; John Hagan and Ron Levi 'War Crimes and the Force of Law' (2005) 83(4) Social Forces 1499-1534; Kimi Lynn King and Megan Greeing ‚Gender Justice or Just Gender? The Role of Gender in the Sexual Assault Decisions at the International Criminal Tribunal of the Former Yugoslavia' (2007) 88 Social Science Quarterly 1049-1071; 'Uwe Kranenpohl ‚Die Bedeutung von Interpretationsmethoden und Dogmatik in der Entscheidungspraxis des Bundesverfassungsgerichts' 48 (2009) Der Staat 387–409; Rüdiger Lautmann *Freie Rechtsfindung und Methodik der Rechtsanwendung* (C Schon München 1967); Rüdiger Lautmann *Justiz—Die stille Gewalt: Teilnehmende Beobachtung und entscheidungssoziologische Analyse* (Athenäum Verlag Frankfurt am Main 1972); Ernst Gottfried Mahrenholz 'Probleme der Verfassungsauslegung, Verfassungsinterpretation aus praktischer Sicht' in Hans-Peter Schneider (ed) *Verfassungsrecht zwischen Wissenschaft und Richterkunst: Konrad Hesse zum 70. Geburtstag* (Heideberg Müller 1990) 53-65.

flexible enough to be applied to a variety of cases. Naturally, the nature of a national constitutional court differs from that of an international criminal court. To name the most obvious difference, a criminal court has, at all times, to ensure that it operates within the limits imposed on it through the principle of legality. Whereas constitutional courts can, to a large extent, be self-referential in the way that they refer to principles of a constitutional order which the courts constructed themselves out of the constitution.[10] Criminal courts, when concretising the given norms, need to refer to systems outside of their own legal discipline in a narrow sense. They consult, for instance, the answer found to similar questions posed to national legal systems or human rights law. Whereas constitutional courts can deliberately maintain a certain dogmatic vagueness in their decision so as to keep the body of case law flexible enough for their predecessors to apply it to new situations and future challenges the court is faced with. Criminal courts, to the contrary, are faced with the obligation to define a certain text in light of what a person, at the time he or she executed the act that lead to his/her indictment before the court, could have reasonably held to be legal or illegal. Criminal courts, therefore, have to interpret criminal law norms in a way so as they present them as a reliable and predictable body of law for a potential accused.

However, as international criminal law is a rather new legal discipline, the judges can often not resort to a lot of scholarly literature, commentaries or preceding cases, but have to define the limits and the scope of a specific crime themselves. In order to make the general terms of the Rome Statute or the ICTY/ICTR Statute sufficiently concrete to work with them in criminal proceedings, the judges are obliged to interpret the terms, keeping in mind the principle of legality. The leeway that the courts naturally have with this new body of law, when examining its limits and the terms of its application, will decrease on its own due to the growing number of case law in the area. Even though the courts are not bound by precedents within their own institution, let alone by case law decided at another international criminal court or tribunal, they tend to either adhere to previous decisions or, if the arguments used previously are dismissed, usually do so with an explicit explanation of why the court or tribunal decided not to follow what has previously been decided.

Furthermore, international criminal law derives from the most serious violations of human rights, and human rights law, like constitutional law, is generally formulated in a very broad manner, and, inter alia, indirectly, protects basic rights of a human person and therefore subject to extensive acts of interpretation by the judges who apply the law.

Additionally, both constitutional courts and international criminal courts and tribunals (or rather their appeals chambers) have to exercise an increased degree of self-control, as their judgments are not subject to the control of any

10 Uwe Kranenpohl ‚Die Bedeutung von Interpretationsmethoden und Dogmatik in der Entscheidungspraxis des Bundesverfassungsgerichts' 48 (2009) Der Staat 387-409, 398.

other court of higher instance. When it comes to the ICC, an aggravating factor, which called for a particularly high degree of interpretation by the practitioners, is that the Rome Statute is a compromise which has been drawn up by the States Parties under time pressure and therefore, at occasions, contains contradictory passages.

Hence, the tools available to the judges, in order to interpret the normative framework in which they operate, are similar, as is the inconsistency when it comes to working with those tools and methods. As has been observed in relation to the interpretation of national constitutions by national constitutional courts, 'the court, in truth, aims for the result which seems right to it. On the way to this [result], it adheres to basic exegetical rules or other principles of constitutional interpretation as pilot lights, but not as guarantees for the right result; they are buoys rather than pilots' (translation by the author).[11]

Therefore, the question, in the context of this work, is to what extent it can be expected that the way a judge evaluates the use of human rights law within substantive international criminal law is shaped by his or her professional and other background.

Traditionally, the events leading to a judicial decision-making process are categorized in accordance with seven different phases.[12] In the first phase, the problem is identified and the judge familiarizes himself or herself with the situation he or she is called upon to judge. In phase two, the judge explores the alternatives for a possible solution of the situation. In the third phase, the judge gathers the facts for the different alternatives, the judges explores the circumstances of the case out of the pleadings and hearings. In phase four, the judge looks at the normative framework applicable to the situation and explores whether the alternatives are legally correct. The judge chooses one of the alternatives in the fifth phase. In the sixth phase, the chosen alternative is explained, the judgment is reasoned and delivered. Finally, the post-decision process constitutes the seventh and last phase. The decision-maker receives criticism and learns for his or her decision in the future.[13] Even though this is simply a descriptive formula which does not apply to all cases, the phases cannot be clearly distinguished from each other and the decision-maker often does not consort to the different phases in a chronological order, the formula helps to categorize the different fundamental phases of judicial decision-making.[14]

11 Ernst Gottfried Mahrenholz 'Probleme der Verfassungsauslegung, Verfassungsinterpretation aus praktischer Sicht' in Hans-Peter Schneider (ed) *Verfassungsrecht zwischen Wissenschaft und Richterkunst: Konrad Hesse zum 70. Geburtstag* (Heideberg Müller 1990) 53-65, 60.

12 Ibid.

13 Rüdiger Lautmann *Justiz – Die stille Gewalt: Teilnehmende Beobachtung und entscheidungssoziologische Analyse* (Athenäum Verlag Frankfurt am Main 1972) 15.

14 Rüdiger Lautmann *Justiz—Die stille Gewalt: Teilnehmende Beobachtung und entscheidungssoziologische Analyse* (Athenäum Verlag Frankfurt am Main 1972) 15.

In the following, phases four and five are primarily scrutinized in order to inquire to what extent the professional and or personal background of the judges can play a role in the decision-making process in relation to the judges' perception of the importance of international human rights law in substantive international criminal law and the judges' general willingness to use human rights law in order to define crimes under international law. The most significant factors in relation to the background of the judges is highlighted and analysed based on the empirical data collected.

There are plenty of ways in which the composition of a bench can shape the outcome of the trial. This is not to assume that the individuals who serve as judges belong to different homogenous groups and can be defined or define themselves by belonging to this group first and foremost. This solitarist approach to groups of human beings inevitably shortens the view on the individuals belonging to that group who, in fact, belong to different groups and do not exclusively define themselves as a member of a single group.[15] Even less so, it would be possible for the individuals belonging to a certain group to define, in a fixed homogenous way, what the components are of which this group is made up.

Nevertheless, there are a number of dividing lines which could possibly be of relevance to the work of the ICC and the ad hoc tribunals and which could influence the decision-making of the judges. Apart from the professional or geographical background of the members of the bench, their understanding of the role of human rights law in their work of applying international criminal law could also be framed in terms of which basic legal system is used in their country of origin, whether it is Common Law or Civil Law and whether they have been working mostly as academics or practitioners.

Safeguarding Professional Diversity on the Bench at the ICC and the ICTY

Pursuant to Art. 36 (3) (b) Rome Statute, a judge at the International Criminal Court shall either

i. Have established competence in criminal law and procedure, and the necessary relevant experience, whether as judge, prosecutor, advocate or in other similar capacity, in criminal proceedings; or
ii. Have established competence in relevant areas of international law such as international humanitarian law and the law of human rights, and extensive experience in a professional legal capacity which is of relevance to the judicial work of the Court;

At the ICC, the focus is, pursuant to Art. 36 (5) Rome Statute, explicitly put on the judges with a criminal law background. They shall, in the first elec-

15 See Amartya Sen *Identity and Violence: The Illusion of Destiny* (WW Norton & Co New York 2006).

tion, make up the majority of at least nine judges whereas at least five of the judges shall have an international law background. In its first session between 3 and 7 February 2003, the Assembly of States Parties elected 18 judges for a term of office of three, six and nine years. On 26 and 27 January 2006, the Assembly elected six judges for a term of nine years. In 2009, 2011 and 2014 the Assembly of States Parties elected another six judges respectively in order to fill the vacancies that occurred when the term of office of their predecessors expired or they resigned prematurely. In its thirteenth session in June 2015, the Assembly of States Parties elected one more judge to fill a current vacancy.[16]. Currently, there are 12 judges from list A (criminal law) and six judges from list B (international law) serving at the ICC (one of the judges from List A is a judge still serving despite having finished her term to allow her to conclude proceedings).[17] However, some of the individuals listed as experts under list A do also have considerable experience under international law, so the lists do not make a clear cut between the experiences of the judges.

The assessment of whether a judge has the necessary qualification is to a large degree driven by the Coalition for the International Criminal Court (CICC), an association of civil society organizations which, since 2006, asks candidates to fill in questionnaires establishing their competence and motivation and organizes public seminars with and debates amongst the candidates.[18] These measures seek to contribute to the raising the respective candidates' expertise and assist the Assembly of State Parties in deciding about the competence of a candidate.[19] The questionnaire provided to the judges asks them, inter alia, about their different legal systems.[20] It also asks in detail about the experience in either criminal law (for List A candidates) or international law (for List B candidates) and invites the candidates to share their experience which would qualify them for running on the list they are not appointed on.[21] Additionally the nomination process is addressed and the candidate is requested to lay down what qualification a person needs to have

---

16 See http://www.icc-cpi.int/en_menus/asp/elections/Pages/election2015.aspx (28 October 2015).

17 See <http://www.icc-cpi.int/en_menus/icc/structure%20of%20the%20court/chambers/the%20judges/Pages/judges.aspx> (28 October 2015).

18 Coalition for the International Criminal Court 'Judges' <http://www.iccnow.org/?mod=electionjudges> (28 October 2015); Coalition for the International Criminal Court 'Coalition for the International Criminal Court Announces Global Campaign on ICC Elections: Global Coalition Committed to Ensuring Independent, Fair, Transparent, and Merit-based Elections' (27 January 2011) <http://www.iccnow.org/documents/ CICCElectionsCampaign_2011.pdf> (28 October 2015).

19 <http://www.iccnow.org/?mod=electionjudges> (28 October 2015).

20 Questions 7 a) and b) Coalition of the ICC 'Questionnaire for ICC Judicial Candidates: November 2013 Elections' <http://coalitionfortheicc.org/documents/CICC_Cathala_ Judicial_Questionnaire_2011_2.pdf> (28 October 2015).

21 Question 9 a) and b) Coalition of the ICC 'Questionnaire for ICC Judicial Candidates: November 2013 Elections' <http://coalitionfortheicc.org/documents/CICC_Cathala_ Judicial_Questionnaire_2011_2.pdf> (28 October 2015).

to be appointed to the highest judicial office in his or her respective country as stipulated in Art. 36 (3) (a) Rome Statute.[22] The CICC addresses the issue of further training and skill enhancement stating that at the ICC as a 'unique institution', 'even judges with significant prior experience …may not necessarily possess requisite skills and knowledge to manage these challenges'.[23] The questionnaire therefore explores the candidates' attitude towards the idea of 'ongoing workplace training aimed at promoting legal innovation and coordination amongst all judicial chambers in adjudicating complex questions relating to law and policy'.[24] Finally, the CICC questionnaire explicitly addresses advocating for, reference to and application of human rights law. Question 16 of the questionnaire asks 'Have you advocated for the adoption and/or implementation of human rights or international humanitarian law treaties or other instruments?'[25] Since 2011, Question 17 is included to specifically ask about the reference to human rights law: 'Have you ever referred to or applied any specific provision of international human rights or international humanitarian law treaties within any judicial decision you have issued within the context of your judicial activity or legal experience?'[26]

In addition, an independent high-expert panel was established by the CICC in 2011, which, for the first time, conducted assessments on whether each individual candidate matched the qualifications outlined in Art. 36 Rome Statute.[27] Before the 2011 elections of judges during the Tenth Session of the Assembly of States Parties, the Independent Panel, consisting of experts of international law and criminal law, most of them former international criminal judges or prosecutors, found that four of the nineteen candidates lacked sufficient qualification to be elected as judges of the ICC.[28] None of the candidates assessed as 'not qualified' by the Independent Panel were

---

22 Question 5 Coalition of the ICC 'Questionnaire for ICC Judicial Candidates: November 2013 Elections' <http://coalitionfortheicc.org/documents/CICC_Cathala_ Judicial_ Questionnaire_2011_2.pdf> (28 October 2015).

23 Question No. 12 Coalition of the ICC 'Questionnaire for ICC Judicial Candidates: November 2013 Elections' <http://coalitionfortheicc.org/documents/CICC_Cathala_ Judicial_Questionnaire_2011_2.pdf> (28 October 2015).

23 <http://www.iccnow.org/?mod=electionjudges> (28 October 2015).

24 Question 12 a) Coalition of the ICC 'Questionnaire for ICC Judicial Candidates: November 2013 Elections' <http://coalitionfortheicc.org/documents/CICC_Cathala_ Judicial_Questionnaire_2011_2.pdf> (28 October 2015).

24 <http://www.iccnow.org/?mod=electionjudges> (28 October 2015).

25 Question 16 Coalition of the ICC 'Questionnaire for ICC Judicial Candidates: November 2013 Elections' <http://coalitionfortheicc.org/documents/CICC_Cathala_ Judicial_ Questionnaire_2011_2.pdf> (28 October 2015).

26 Question 17 Coalition of the ICC 'Questionnaire for ICC Judicial Candidates: November 2013 Elections' <http://coalitionfortheicc.org/documents/CICC_Cathala_ Judicial_ Questionnaire_2011_2.pdf> (28 October 2015).

27 <http://www.iccnow.org/?mod=electionjudges> (28 October 2015).

28 Independent Panel on ICC Judicial Elections 'Report on International Criminal Court Judicial Nominations 2011' (26 October 2011) http://www.iccindependentpanel.org/sites/default/files/Independent%20Panel%20on%20ICC%20Judicial%20Elections%20-%20Report%2026%20October%202011.pdf (28 October 2015).

among the six judges elected to the bench by Assembly of States Parties between 12 and 21 December 2011. This goes to show the increasing influence and importance that NGOs have in the area of international criminal law, where civil society has continuously pushed for the improvement and enhanced implementation of international criminal law.[29] During the same session, the Assembly of States Parties also established an Advisory Committee on Nomination of Judges, which has a similar mandate as the Independent Panel on Judicial Elections. For the 2014 elections, the Advisory Committee evaluated all candidates.[30] None of the candidates whose minimum qualification was questioned by the Advisory Committee were elected as judges.

The majority of current judges under list A (experts of criminal law and procedure) does have no or only limited experience of the other category of relevant law. The same holds true for judges under list B (relevant areas of international law) regarding their expertise in criminal law. However, a minority of judges indicates extensive expertise in both categories and could therefore have appeared under a different list. The ICC states that 'the Trial and Pre-Trial Divisions are composed predominantly of judges with criminal trial experience'.[31] Indeed, four of the currently factually eight Trial Chambers consist exclusively of judges from list A, while in all the other chambers, judges from List A have a 2/3 majority.[32] Insofar the focus on criminal experience and expertise in the chambers is a deliberate move and mirrors the merit that the court attaches to criminal law as opposed to international law in its everyday work. One reason for this might be that that some of the interviewed judges saw the real challenges for the court in its procedural aspects, for which an expertise in criminal law and procedure and a mindset for the potential pitfalls of criminal trials in this respect is vital.[33] As one judge formulated: 'the devil is in the procedure'.[34] In this sense, it is regrettable that the majority of ICC trial chambers (at least nominally) do not include any international law expert at all. The group of international law experts is generally more heterogeneous than the criminal law group. Whereas some of the judges previously to serving at the bench, held high positions in international organizations pertaining to human rights or humanitarian law, others were

---

29 A good example of this was the recent attempt by the NGO Southern Africa Litigation Centre to prevent Sudanese President Omar al-Bashir, for who the ICC issued a standing arrest warrant, from leaving South Africa where he travelled for a meeting of the African Union.

30 Assembly of States Parties 'Report of the Advisory Committee on Nomination of Judges on the work of its third meeting' (29 November 2014) ICC-ASP/13/22 http://www.icc-cpi.int/iccdocs/asp_docs/ASP13/ICC-ASP-13-22-ENG.pdf (28 October 2015).

31 <http://icc-cpi.int/en_menus/icc/structure%20of%20the%20court/chambers/Pages/ chambers.aspx> (21 July 2015).

32 Nominally, the ICC currently has seven Trial Chambers. However, the Kenya Case is dealt with by two different benches, Trial Chamber V (a) and Trial Chamber V (b) composed of different judges.

33 Interview No 2.

34 Interview No 2.

scholars, diplomats or worked in fields related to international law which are, at first sight, more detached from international criminal law.

At the ICTY the situations is slightly different, as there is no explicit quota system dividing the bench into international law and criminal law experts in a provision which is otherwise very similar to the one in the Rome Statute. The respective provision in the ICTY Statute reads:

The permanent and *ad litem* judges shall be persons of high moral character, impartiality and integrity who possess the qualifications required in their respective countries for appointment to the highest judicial offices. In the overall composition of the Chambers and sections of the Trial Chambers, due account shall be taken of the experience of the judges in criminal law, international law, including international humanitarian law and human rights law.

The ICTY is currently composed of 20 permanent judges and 3 ad litem judges, who are appointed by the UN Secretary-General at the request of the President of the Tribunal to sit on one or more specific trials.[35] Compared to that of the ICC, the present composition of the ICTY is somewhat more homogenous. The majority of the present judges have served as judges in their respective national jurisdictions before being appointed as judges of the ICTY. Most of the judges additionally had experience with criminal trials and a certain expertise in criminal proceedings prior to coming to the ICTY.

General attitude of judges towards the importance of HRL in ICL

When asked about the general importance attributed to human rights law in international criminal law, most judges, at first sight, display a conviction that human rights law has a high degree of importance to their work. Many judges referred to the development of international criminal law and, the common roots of human rights, humanitarian law and international criminal law, as well as to crimes under international law as severe violations of human rights.[36] Some describe human rights as always present in the work of the court. Even if that might not always be visible in the decisions that are produced and might not be explicitly mentioned there, these judges claim human rights issues are always underlying and present in the internal discussions. [37]

However, even in this generally framed question on the importance of human rights law on international criminal law, one can already spot differences between judges whose expertise lays primarily in the area of international criminal law and those who are first and foremost international law-

35 At the ICTY, the numbers of judges are declining due to the imminent conclusion up of trials of first instance.

36 Interview No 6; Interview No 7; Interview No 12.

37 Interview No 13; Interview No 7.

yers. Whereas several judges, no matter which background, emphasized that their courts are criminal courts and not human rights courts and that therefore human rights play a somewhat ancillary role as compared to aspects of criminal law and procedure,[38] the criminal law experts often explicitly emphasized that their foremost task is to sit on a criminal court and some argue that the 'international element' is given too much weight, at least at the ICC.[39] It has also been stated that cases should be dealt with in a less academic manner, that the primary tasks of the ICC is to punish the perpetrators and help the victims, not 'to write beautiful decisions for academics'.[40] One judge describes human rights issues as 'not very urgent'.[41]

Interestingly, some of the judges pointed to the reciprocal effects of an increase in the use of human rights law in international criminal law for the field of human rights law. One judge used the example of the then UN Commissioner for Human Rights, Navanethem Pillay, who, as a former judge of the ICTY and the ICC, draws from her practical experience in international criminal law by stirring up discussions about the impunity of human rights violations in her work as UN High Commissioner for Human Rights.[42] However, the answer to questions regarding the mutual effect of an increased interlinkage between the areas of international criminal law and human rights law is not always positive. One judge, for example, wondered whether international criminal law could also have a negative influence on human rights law, as is attached to human rights an 'aura of punitivity' which could hamper practical human rights work and keep States from enter into human rights commitments in the first place.[43] This statement is particularly interesting in light of the fact that binding human rights law is often developed by political, legally not binding commitments that States enter into and that later evolve into a consensus within the international community. Attaching another level of criminal sanctions to human rights, does indeed bear the risk that States might shy away from any form of commitment to human rights issues. On the other hand, criminal sanctions are sometimes the only way to guarantee proper redress and justice to victims of human rights violations and to ensure that individuals who violate human rights, often at the highest levels of the executive power, do not act with impunity.

Specific relevance of the recourse to human rights law in substantive international criminal law

When asked about what areas of international criminal law could be most appropriate for the use of human rights law, most judges first pointed to pro-

38 Interview No 2; Interview No 5; Interview No 8; Interview No 10; Interview No 11.
39 Interview No 5; Interview No 10.
40 Interview No 5.
41 Interview No 2.
42 Interview No 3.
43 Interview No 4.

cedural points, mostly to the right to a fair and expeditious trial, including the right to defend oneself, questions regarding the disclosure of evidence or to procedural rules for the protection of victims.[44] Whereas the international law experts usually by themselves referred also to the relevance of human rights law in the substantial aspects of defining a crime and exploring the boundaries of customary international law on a certain crime, most of the criminal law experts agreed that human rights law could be used in such way after it had been suggested to them by the interviewer. Some, however, dismissed the importance of international human rights law in substantive international criminal law altogether and claimed that most of the problematic issues in these regard had already been solved.[45]

When asked about what parts of human rights law would be the most obvious to take recourse to in substantive matters, the prohibition of torture was one of the areas most often referred to.[46] Here, judges mentioned concrete and widely ratified conventions like the CAT[47] or the ICCPR.[48] Minority rights law was generally not mentioned by any of the judges initially. Some judges agreed, after the suggestion by the interviewer that international criminal law can draw from minority rights law.[49] Yet, a certain confusion regarding what the concept of minority rights entails could be observed: whereas one judge rightly pointed out that the recognition of genocide and apartheid were influenced by concerns about minority protection,[50] one judge incorrectly claimed that minority rights law also covers the protection of women and could therefore be of value to the Court.[51] One can easily see how such confusion about what the concept entails could prevent the court from seeking assistance in the case extra-statutory human rights law would have to be consulted.

Women's rights were the issue, which was most often mentioned by judges when asked areas of human rights of interest to substantive international criminal law.[52] However, the judges seemed to have only a vague idea where to find helpful instruments in this area. One judge mentioned Convention on the Elimination of All Forms of Discrimination against Women, in all other cases, the mention of women's rights seemed to have been guided merely by a vague idea of usefulness without any concrete provisions or concepts to draw from.[53]

---

44 Interview No 2; Interview No 3; Interview No 7; Interview No 8; Interview No 9; Interview No 11; Interview No 12.

45 Interview No 2; Interview No 6; Interview No 7.

46 Interview No 7; Interview No 10; Interview No 12.

47 Interview No 10; Interview No 12.

48 Interview No 10.

49 Interview No 7; Interview No 10; Interview No 12.

50 Interview No 12.

51 Interview No 7.

52 Interview No 2; Interview No 7; Interview No 10; Interview No 11; Interview No 13.

53 Interview No 7.

The question of how it can be used and what are the limits of a use of human rights law in light of the principle of legality is characterized by a certain dogmatic vagueness. Basically all judges mentioned Art. 21 (3) Rome Statute as the provision which allows them to use human rights even though, to a certain extent, the exact meaning of that provision and the possibilities it opens for judges to make reference to human rights seemed to be rather unclear. Art. 21(3) Rome Statute provides:

'The application and interpretation of law pursuant to this article must be consistent with internationally recognized human rights, and be without any adverse distinction founded on grounds such as gender as defined in article 7, para 3, age, race, colour, language, religion or belief, political or other opinion, national, ethnic or social origin, wealth, birth or other status'.

In particular, no judge mentioned that Article 21 (3) may not be the right provision for including human rights law into substantive international criminal law.[54] Many judges seemed to be satisfied with Art. 21 (3) Rome Statute as a sufficient legal basis for applying international human rights law. In particular, customary international law as a source seemed to not be of particular relevance to the judges and was rarely brought up. Asked about how human rights can be used in international criminal law, particularly with regard to Art. 21 (3) Rome Statute, the judges gave a variety of different answers many of which contradicted each other. Human rights were seen as 'underlying principles'[55], 'sources of inspiration'[56] 'almost binding principles'[57] 'persuasive, but non-binding inspiration'[58], 'sources of brainstorming on a legal issue'[59], 'guiding principles'[60] and 'underlying constitutional provision'[61].

Some judges saw it as 'two sides of the same coin'[62], others dismissed this rhetorical figure and instead insisted on a 'qualitative difference'[63] of the

54 See the authors PhD research project Julia Gebhard *Necessity or Nuisance? Recourse to Human Rights in Substantive International Criminal Law* (forthcoming); see also eg Margaret McAuliffe de Guzman 'Art. 21: Applicable law' in Otto Triffterer *Commentary on the Rome Statute of the International Criminal Court* (2nd edition Beck Munich 2008) 701-712, 711; William A Schabas *The International Criminal Court: A Commentary on the Rome Statute* (OUP Oxford 2010) 398; *Prosecutor v. Thomas Lubanga Dyilo (Judgment on the Appeal of Mr. Thomas Lubanga Dyilo against the Decision on the Defense Challenge to the Jurisdiction of the Court pursuant to Article 19(2)(a) of the Statute of 3 October 2006)* ICC-01/04-01/06-772 (14 December 2006) para. 36.

55 Interview No. 7; one judge additionally mentioned Art. 21 (2).

56 Interview No. 10.

57 Interview No. 7.

58 Interview No. 8; Interview No. 12.

59 Interview No. 9.

60 Interview No. 9.

61 Interviews No. 5, 7, 8 and 10; in Interviews No. 5 and 7, the term 'underlying constitutional provision' was brought up by the interviewer who asked the judges whether this is a term they could agree to in relation to human rights in international criminal law.

62 Interview No. 10.

63 Interview No. 11.

two regimes, which they saw as not being of equal value, but which 'complement and reinforce each other'[64] or 'complement and inform each other'.[65]

One judge openly admitted that reference to human rights law is made to support already existing convictions and views on a certain topic.[66] In the same vein, another judge said that what she was interested in is the impact of her decisions 'on the people' and not so much where they stem from.[67] This is congruent with the sociological findings regarding the decision-making process of judges in national legal systems[68] and also confirms an observation made by Antonio Cassese regarding the use of comparative law as an extra-statutory source of law at the ICTY.[69]

Professional and Personal Factors Contributing the Attitude towards International Human Rights Law

1. Public international law experts in human/(National) criminal law experts

As can be inferred from the analysis of the two previous sections, the dividing line between public international law experts and experts of criminal law was found to be one of the most decisive factors regarding the attitude towards human rights law. Experts of criminal law often seemed to be somewhat dismissive of the 'international element' of international criminal law and stated that this element is given too much weight in international criminal practice.[70] Human rights law in international criminal law was for most of the criminal law experts mostly a procedural issue, though most, but not all,[71] agreed that human rights law could also be used in the substantive definitions of crime when so suggested.

Generally, the criminal lawyers seemed to have less of a dogmatic problem with a recourse on international human rights law in order to define crimes, which, in general, they saw as not problematic.[72] In particular, they did often not see a dogmatic difference in the application of human rights law in substantive as opposed to procedural law. This might partly be due to the fact that the criminal lawyers interviewed also tended to have a purely practi-

---

64 Interview No. 11.

65 Interview No 12.

66 Interview No 1.

67 Interview No 9.

68 Rüdiger Lautmann Justiz – Die stille Gewalt: Teilnehmende Beobachtung und entscheidungssoziologische Analyse (Athenäum Verlag Frankfurt am Main 1972) 101.

69 'Mon experience est que souvent le droit comparé est utilisé pour confirmer une solution que l'on avait déjà trouvée' Antonio Cassese in Mireille Delmas-Marty and Antonio Cassese (eds) *Crimes Internationaux Et Jurisdictions Internationales* (Presses Unversitaires de France Paris 2002) 140.

70 Interview No 5 ; Interview No 10.

71 Interview No 2; Interview No 6; Interview No 7.

72 Interview No 5; Interview No 6; Interview No 7; Interview No 9.

cal background, whereas many of the international law experts have been working as academics prior to becoming judges at the ICTY or the ICC. One judge simply held that if the ECtHR came up with a decision which 'can equally work for the ICC' and can be used there, it becomes part of international criminal law.[73] One judge suggested narrowing down the quota in Art. 36 (3) (b) (i) to experts of international criminal law as opposed to general criminal law and procedure as a way to ensure quality throughout the bench.[74] In light of the limited number of established experts in the field on the one hand coupled with geographical quota requirements on the other hand, this suggestion does not seem viable at this point in time.

2. Common Law/Civil Law

The question whether they were educated in a common or in a civil law system was explicitly posed to the interviewees and some expressed opinions on whether and how this background influenced their work and the collaboration with their colleagues. Pursuant to Art. 36 (8) (a) (i) Rome Statute, the principle legal systems of the world shall be taken into account in the selection of the judges. Several of the judges emphasized that they see a dividing line between judges coming from civil law countries and judges with a common law background in their work.[75] This perception is backed by analyses of the deciding attitude of judges at the ICTY, which found clear differences between civil and common law judges in the way they refer to sources outside of international criminal law in order to back their arguments.[76]

One judge mentioned that there is more 'separation' by judges from common law countries: the judge was of the opinion that judges educated in common law systems were generally more willing than their colleagues from civil law countries to apply human rights regarding procedural, formalistic issues (rights of the accused regarding deadlines for submissions etc.) but that they strive for 'clean, clear criminal law' without referring to extra-statutory provisions.[77]

For another judge, the common law/civil law divide was interlinked with question of whether a judge came from a country which was a former British colony. This judge was of the opinion that judges coming from former British colonies applied Common law in a more dogmatically strict fashion than colleagues from the United Kingdom.[78] For most judges, List A and List B judges alike, this issue did, however, not pose a particular problem, even

73 Interview No 9.

74 Interview No 7.

75 Interview No 1; Interview No 6.

76 Michael Bohlander and Mark Findlay 'The Use of Domestic Sources as a Basis for International Criminal Law Principles' (2002) 2 Yearbook of International Law and Jurisprudence 3–26.

77 Interview No 1.

78 Interview No 6.

though one could suspect that judges with an expertise in international law might be more used to a flexible approach in this respect.

3. Academics/Practitioners

Closely related to whether judges are criminal law or international law experts is the question whether they have a theoretical, academic background or expert a purely practical one. This issue was brought up by several judges on their own account, as it was not part of a question put to the judges, and the ones who brought it up usually felt strongly about the subject.[79] All the judges who brought up this topic were appointed on List A as experts of criminal law and they were all practitioners who had served as judges or prosecutors in their respective countries. These judges emphasized that the courts and tribunals needed more practitioners and deemed work with practitioners easier than with 'professors'.[80] Two of these judges criticised the way of evaluation and decision-writing: judges were writing 'too much',[81] facts should be dealt with in a 'less academic manner'[82] but in a more practical way ('help victims, punish perpetrators'[83]) as it was not about 'writing beautiful decisions for academics'[84] or writing 'for the public'.[85] Additionally, a desire to 'write history' and 'lay down principles' at the expense of efficiency and goal-oriented action' was criticized.[86] Another List A judge, however, stressed the importance of keeping up with developments in academic scholarly literature in decision-making.[87] None of the judges appointed through List B did express any views on the distribution of practitioners and more theory-focused individuals on the bench.

4. Developing Country/Industrialized Country

Application of human rights law might also depend also on the geographical background of the judge. According to Art. 36 (8) (a) (iii) Rome Statute the Court shall take equitable geographical representation into account when selection the judges. One European judge argued that human rights did not play a major role in practical international criminal law, but since they, as he argued, gained importance in the European legal discourse they receive more attention.[88]

---

79 Interview No 5; Interview No 6; Interview No 13.
80 Interview No 13.
81 Interview No 6.
82 Interview No 5.
83 Interview No 5.
84 Interview No 5.
85 Interview No 6.
86 Interview No 5.
87 Interview No 9.
88 Interview No. 1.

However, the geographical background of the judge might not necessarily play a role in whether or not human rights law is referred to but rather which system of human rights protection is referenced. Several judges from the global south stated that international courts and tribunals frequently refer to case law of the European Court of Human Rights (ECtHR) and underused jurisprudence and provisions from other regional systems of human rights protection. One judge argued that in terms of usefulness to international criminal law, the American system of human rights protection was more advanced than the European one as the Inter-American Court of Human Rights (IACtHR) and the Inter-American Commission on Human Rights dealt with massive human rights violations on a regular basis and therefore, their case law had more to offer to international criminal law.[89] Another judge argued that due to the fact that all cases currently before the court deal with situations in African countries, more reference should be made to the African systems of human rights protection and the use of human rights jurisprudence and rules should generally be more diversified.[90]

5. Age

One judge saw age as another decisive matter in how open a judge was to extra-statutory sources or input from outside he or her initial area of expertise.[91] This judge saw a generational shift in international criminal law and argued that older judges from the same generation generally had a more conservative approach to applying human rights law. The same judge argued that judges, in their decision-making process, are influenced by their personal experiences. Examples of these factors which were mentioned by this judge to be of influence are gender, sexual orientation and disability.[92]

Concluding Remarks

The answers given by the judges in the interviews conducted were often characterized by a certain dogmatic vagueness. This vagueness is by no means surprising given the multitude of diverse education and professional experiences of the judges which lead to different priorities in their work and differing degrees of attention given to the issue of human rights in international criminal law. Furthermore, in an area as vast as international criminal law which combines a plurality of different fields, it is nearly impossible to possess the same degree of expertise on all up and coming issues in academia and practice. For this reason, a bench consisting of several individuals whose

---

89 Interview No 7.
90 Interview No 8.
91 Interview No 1.
92 Interview No 1.

expertise complements each other is of higher importance than in national criminal law where education is streamlined. On the other hand, due to the immense freedom that judges possess in the still emerging discipline of international criminal law, judges are under enormous pressure and their judgments regularly come under critical scrutiny. Therefore, it is even more important that the presence of international law experts on the bench is ensured. Currently, in the majority of Trial Chambers at the ICC only judges appointed from List A (experts in criminal law and procedure) are serving (even though one has to observe that most of these Trial Chambers have judges amongst them that do indeed also possess expertise in human rights law). It is also not evident why the ICC explicitly states that in its Trial Chambers, criminal law expertise is focused on, whereas in the Appeals Chamber, most judges are appointed from List B (experts in international law).

The judges with an expertise predominantly rooting in criminal law often pointed to the need for a more practical approach at ICC proceedings and to the fact that the court was not established to write 'beautiful decisions' which are well-reviewed in academic circles.[93] Whilst the truth within this perception is the fact that the ICC and the *ad hoc* and hybrid courts, like any other criminal courts, decide on the guilt of individuals for specific actions, the problem that these new sorts of courts face is that they, at the same time, have to constantly justify the existence of their area of law and need to bring their reasoning in line with the principle of legality. This requires an enormous effort of justification on behalf of the judges, which might be something that international lawyers, as opposed to criminal lawyers coming from national criminal justice systems, are used to.

Several times, the judges seemed to harbour skepticism towards the usefulness of human rights for their substantive work, in helping them to define crimes under international law. Several judges emphasized the importance of human rights law in international criminal procedure while, at the same time, downplaying its significance in terms of substantive law. Judges mentioned that according to them, the big problems regarding the definition of crimes are solved and the ICC will not have to deal with this issue majorly.[94] From a defence perspective, these statements should trigger a substantive amount of skepticism. On the one hand, it should be received positively by defence teams that the human rights of the accused in the pre-trial and trial period seems to have such a prominent role in the perception of the judges. This is particularly true for the ICC which has a chance to avoid some of the mistakes the ad hoc tribunals made in this respect, for example concerning the length of the trials. However, when one looks at the numerous innovations that the Rome Statute brings in comparison to previous statutes, stating that human rights law does not have any more to contribute to the substantive definition of crimes seems to be inaccurate. Particularly with regard to 'treaty

93 Interview No 5.
94 Interview No 2; Interview No 6; Interview No 7.

crimes' which have previously been enshrined in human rights treaties only (such as the crime of apartheid [crimes against humanity, Art. 7 (1) (j) Rome Statute] or intentional attacks on UN personnel or other personnel or material involved in an assistance or peacekeeping mission [war crimes, Art. 8 (2) (b) (iii) Rome Statute], and to a lesser degree, forced disappearance [crimes against humanity, Art. 7 (1) (i) Rome Statute]) or regarding gender-based persecution will the ICC have to consult sources outside the Rome Statute itself and will not be able to resort to case law issued by any other international criminal court or tribunal. This can lead to serious collisions with the principle of legality to the detriment of the accused. The very nature of the ICC as an international court, seen by some purely as a court functioning like any other criminal court and portrayed by others as an international court established to protect victims against mass violations seems to be disputed amongst judges. The vagueness and the conflicting ideas portray a spectrum of divergent opinions and dogmatic murkiness that should be worrisome to the attorneys representing accused persons.

As such, the approach of the CICC to assess candidates and work towards a comprehensive skill enhancement of judges seems to be the way forward. Incoherence in jurisprudence and legal norms in international law stems mostly from increasingly more separate legal regimes with a limited mandate.[95] International criminal courts and tribunals are few in numbers and with the establishment of a permanent International Criminal Court the numbers are likely to stagnate or, with the completion of the trials before the ICTR and the ICTY go down. As such, by ensuring that the question of how extra-statutory sources, in particular human rights law, can be used in international criminal law and what he limits of such an application are, international criminal law is confronted with the unique opportunity to counteract incoherent or conflicting jurisprudence at least to a certain degree and thereby avoid the level of fragmentation prevalent in more established fields like the law of the sea, human rights law or world trade law.[96] This is particularly crucial in international criminal law as enhanced fragmentation is likely to undermine the defendant's right to a fair trial.

95 Oliver Diggelmann and Tilman Altwicker 'Is There Something Like a Constitution of International Law? A Critical Analysis of the Debate on World Constitutionalism' (2008) 68 ZaöRV 623-650, 630.

96 Oliver Diggelmann and Tilman Altwicker 'Is There Something Like a Constitution of International Law? A Critical Analysis of the Debate on World Constitutionalism' (2008) 68 ZaöRV 623-650, 630; see also as referenced by Diggelmann and Altwicker Gerhard Hafner 'Pros and Cons Ensuing from Fragmentation of International Law' (2004) 25 Michigan Journal of International Law 849-863; George Abi-Saab 'Fragmentation or Unification: Some Concluding Remarks' (1999) 31 NYU Journal of International Law and Politics 919-932.

Marie O'Leary[*]

Compelling Fair Trials: The Necessity of Effective Court Powers to Ensure a Defendant's Right "to examine, or have examined, the witnesses against him or her"

1 Introduction

The principles of International Criminal Law dictate that witness testimony must be considered with full appreciation of the rights afforded to the suspect or accused person; namely, the right "[t]o have adequate time and facilities for the preparation of the defence" as preserved in Article 67(1)(b) of the Rome Statute and the right "[t]o examine, or have examined, the witnesses against him or her and to obtain the attendance and examination of witnesses on his or her behalf under the same conditions as witnesses against him or her" as enshrined in Article 67(1)(e). The very words of the latter require equality of the parties in the ability to compel testimony. As a treaty-based Court, the ICC relies on the cooperation of States to fully ensure these rights are upheld, not the least of which comes through assistance in securing witness testimony to hold effective proceedings aimed at seeking justice.

Until a recent decision by the Appeals Chamber of the *Ruto & Sang* case, it was not clear that the Rome Statute permitted a power of the ICC Chambers to compel witnesses to appear for testimony. The jurisprudence had previously declined to enunciate such a power, and academics equally had found the texts to be incongruent and, above all, lacking in an enforcement mechanism to ensure compliance. In short, the absence of any such express provision of 'subpoena'[1] in the Rome Statute created the potential for any case to be stalled, even paralyzed, by an unwilling witness. The issues on appeal in *Ruto & Sang*, then, were fodder for promoting effective proceedings, not only for the obvious reason of giving the Court a necessary tool to conduct proceedings effectively, but also in its ability to advance procedural equality of arms by providing a service to both parties equally in securing necessary witness evidence.

---

* B.A., J.D, Counsel/Legal Adviser in the Office of Public Counsel for the Defence of the International Criminal Court. The views expressed herein are those of the author alone and do not reflect the views of the International Criminal Court. The author would like to specially thank Ms. Aimel Yousfi-Roquencourt for her review and suggestions for this work.

1 Subpoena, typically a term held in common law to define "a writ commanding a person to appear before a court or other tribunal, subject to penalty for failing to comply", Black's Law Dictionary, 8th ed.

The Appeals Chamber, however, appears to have limited its interpretation of a 'subpoena' power, holding that witnesses can be compelled to attend only via videolink and/or *in situ*[2]. The lack of a clear recourse for non-compliance, even with such legally binding orders, leaves the situation in limbo, as the ICC remains beholden to a State's willingness and ability to execute and/or enforce punitive measures for non-compliance and places witnesses in a world of jurisdictional complexity. At the same time, it cannot go unnoticed that the cases of the ICC, to date, have demonstrated that the lure of relocation and/or recompense for testimony, as provided by the Court for witness safety and security, may have been equally, if not more, 'compelling' than any Court order. Without critical analysis of the impact of all factors which truly 'compel' a witness to testify before the Court, certain principles of fair proceedings may hang in the balance.

2 The Power to Compel Witnesses

2.1 Compelling Testimony

As a first point of these discussions, it is important to distinguish compelled testimony from compelled attendance; summoning an individual to a meeting or to the Court is not to be confused with the power of a Chamber to require testimony of an individual once he/she is at the seat of a court. The practice of the *ad hoc* Tribunals distinguishes the two situations: requiring attendance for testimony and compelling a present witness to testify to the questions or issues raised.[3] The latter, at the *ad hoc* Tribunals, is considered in the context of ICTY/R Rule 90, which provides for a witness objection to any statement of potential self-incrimination but states that a Chamber "may, however, *compel* the witness to answer the question".[4] It is within the discretion of the Chamber to compel testimony, even if it may incriminate a witness; however, a Chamber may choose to not exercise this discretionary power, for example, if a question has little relevance to the case and are only necessary to test a witness's credibility.[5]

For this type of 'compellability' where the witness is before the Court, the ICC texts are resoundingly clear. ICC Rule 65, entitled "*Compellability of witnesses*", specifically states that *"[a] witness who appears before the Court*

2 For definition and further discussion of "*in situ*", *see infra* § 2.3.

3 The Chambers have also distinguished between willingness to submit to an investigative interview and willingness to testify. *Prosecutor v Karadžić*, IT-95-5/18-T, Decision on Motion for Subpoena: Edin Garaplija, 26 November 2012, para. 13.

4 [Emphasis added.] ICTY Rule 90(E) contains a caveat that "*Testimony compelled in this way shall not be used as evidence in a subsequent prosecution against the witness for any offence other than false testimony.*"

5 *Ntagerura et al. v. Prosecutor,* ICTR-99-46-A, Appeals Judgement, 7 July 2006, paras 252-254.

is compellable by the Court to provide testimony" subject to privilege and self-incrimination provisions outlined in Rules 73-75.[6] The ICC Appeals Chamber has held that "once a witness is brought before the Court in accordance with the relevant provisions under domestic law, the Court would take over the exercise of jurisdiction and therefore rules 65 and 171" would apply.[7]

2.2 Compelled Attendance

2.2.1 The Subpoena Power of the ad hoc Tribunals

The first issuance of the Rules of Procedure and Evidence at the ICTY was silent on the term 'subpoena', but originally allowed for "*such orders, summonses and warrants as may be necessary for the purposes of an investigation or for the preparation or conduct of the trial*".[8] Just one year later, in early 1995, the same provision was revised to expressly include the term "subpoenas".[9] The parallel rule at the ICTR, adopted in June 1995, also employed the specific term of "subpoena".[10] Over the next 20 years, the ICTY/R Chambers have enjoyed wide discretion in the ability to issue, recall and enforce subpoenas to secure witnesses. The standard established is one for which applicant must demonstrate a legitimate forensic purpose demonstrated by a "reasonable basis for his belief that there is a good chance that the prospective witness will be able to give information which will materially assist him in his case, in relation to clearly identified issues relevant to the forthcoming trial"[11] and that the party "has made reasonable attempts to obtain the voluntary co-operation of the potential witness and has been unsuccessful".[12] Taking into account a number of considerations,[13] the *ad hoc* Chambers may choose to not issue a subpoena if the information may be obtainable by other

---

6 These provisions draw upon ICCPR, Article 14(3)(g) and other human rights instruments. *See Shabelnik v. Ukraine*, ECtHR App.16404/03, Judgment, 19 February 2009, para. 55 (privilege against self-incrimination is part of "*generally recognized international standards which lie at the heart of the notion of a fair trial under Article 6*" as such a right is "*in the protection of the accused against improper compulsion by the authorities, thereby contributing to the avoidance of miscarriages of justice [...]*").

7 *Prosecutor v. Ruto & Sang*, ICC-01/09-01/11-1598, Judgment on the appeals of William Samoei Ruto and Mr Joshua Arap Sang against the decision of Trial Chamber V (A) of 17 April 2014 entitled "Decision on Prosecutor's Application for Witness Summonses and resulting Request for State Party Cooperation, 9 October 2014, para. 111.

8 ICTY RPE (as adopted on 11 February 1994) IT/32, Rule 54.

9 ICTY RPE (as revised on 30 January 1995) IT/32/Rev.3, Rule 54.

10 ICTR RPE (as adopted on 29 June 1995), ITR/3/REV.1, Rule 54.

11 *Prosecutor v. Karadžić*, IT-95-5/18-T, Decision on Prosecution's Motion to Subpoena Milan Tupajić, 23 September 2011, para. 5 [internal citation omitted].

12 *Ibid.* at para. 7.

13 *Prosecutor v. Brđanin et al.*, IT-99-36-AR73.9, Decision on Interlocutory Appeal, 11 December 2002, paras 31-32.

means,[14] and have adopted a cautionary stance that "[s]ubpoenas should not be issued lightly, for they involve the use of coercive powers and may lead to the imposition of a criminal sanction".[15] However, the power to issue a subpoena has not been limited to calling a witness to testify at the seat of the Tribunals; ICTY Chambers have held that they may issue subpoenas for the purposes of investigative interviews[16] or even for the purposes of a meeting where the Judge can explain the importance of the testimony and the protections that may be afforded.[17] At the same time, certain categories of witnesses have been subject to specific, or excepting, standards – namely, interpreters (immune from subpoena),[18] International Committee of the Red Cross (ICRC) (immune from compelled testimony)[19] and war correspondents (where a balancing test is imposed).[20]

2.2.2 The Lack of 'Subpoena' Power at the ICC

In looking to the texts of the ICC, one will not find the term 'subpoena' as it has been used at the International *ad hoc* Tribunals. However, Article 64(6)(b) states:

> 6. In performing its functions prior to trial or during the course of a trial, the Trial Chamber may, as necessary:
> (b) Require the attendance and testimony of witnesses and production of documents and other evidence by obtaining, if necessary, the assistance of States as provided in this Statute;[21]

Despite direct language of "requiring attendance", the Court's jurisprudence relating to its ability to issue a 'subpoena' for testimony has been somewhat "ambiguous" in its first decade.[22] This is due largely to the reading of Article 64 in conjunction with other texts; notably, those texts which refer to 'volun-

---

14 *Prosecutor v. Halilović*, IT-01-48-AR73, Decision on the Issuance of Subpoenas, 21 June 2004, para. 5. *See also Prosecutor v. Karadžić*, IT-95-5/18-T, Decision on Prosecution's Motion to Subpoena Milan Tupajić, 23 September 2011, para. 7.

15 *Ibid.* at para. 6.

16 *Ibid.* at para. 5 *citing Prosecutor v. Krstić*, IT-98-33-A, Decision on Application for Subpoenas, 1 July 2003, para. 10.

17 *Prosecutor v. Krstić*, IT-98-33-A, Decision on Application for Subpoenas, 1 July 2003, para. 12.

18 *Prosecutor v. Delalić et al., IT-96-21, Decision on the Motion Ex Parte by the Defence of Zdravko Mucić Concerning the Issue of a Subpoena to an Interpreter,* 8 July 1997, para. 20.

19 *Prosecutor v. Simić et al.*, IT-95-9-PT, Decision on the Prosecution Motion Under Rule 73 for a Ruling Concerning the Testimony of a Witness, 27 July 1999.

20 *Prosecutor v. Brđanin et al.*, IT-99-36-AR73.9, Decision on Interlocutory Appeal, 11 December 2002, para. 50.

21 For further provisions on State Cooperation, *see, e.g.,* ICC Rome Statute, Part IX.

22 *Prosecutor v. Ruto & Sang*, ICC-01/09-01/11-1598, Judgement on the appeals of William Samoei Ruto and Mr Joshua Arap Sang against the decision of Trial Chamber V (A) of 17 April 2014 entitled "Decision on Prosecutor's Application for Witness Summonses and resulting Request for State Party Cooperation, 9 October 2014, para. 125.

tariness' of a witness in outlining State cooperation, especially Article 93(1)(e), Article 93(7)(a)(i) and Article 99(4).[23] The focus of the discussions also considered the *travaux préparatoires* with regard to 'voluntary appearance' and the State cooperation provision that is now Article 93(1)(e); a footnote of a foundational document of the Rome Statute instructs: "This includes the notion that witnesses or experts may not be compelled to travel to appear before the Court".[24] As observed by Gŏran Sluiter, "[t]he imposition of an obligation upon citizens to testify at the seat of the Court met with strong opposition" given the unsavoury result of forcing persons to travel across international borders.[25] In fact, the United Nations' *Report of the Ad Hoc Committee on the Establishment of an International Criminal Court* stressed that many States noted that, constitutionally, they could not force citizens to attend judicial proceedings in another country".[26] As a result of competing domestic legislation that would prevent full compliance in transferring witnesses to the seat of the Court against their will, such a provision was not accepted.[27]

In the Court's first trial, *Prosecutor v. Lubanga*, the bench dealt with a witness who was found to be unwilling to appear to testify and ultimately held that: "The Chamber has no power to compel the attendance of witnesses".[28] In the same discussions, even the Prosecution considered that the witness's unwillingness was "*the end of the road*".[29] Thereafter, in the Kenya

---

23 *See, e.g.*, Kreß, Claus, and Prost, Kimberly, "Article 93: Other forms of cooperation" in Triffterer, Otto (ed.), *Commentary on the Rome Statute of the International Criminal Court–Observers' Notes, Article by Article*, 2nd ed. (Beck/Hart 2008), p. 1576; Bitti, Gilbert, "Article 64: Functions and Powers of the Trial Chamber" in Triffterer, Otto (ed.), *Commentary on the Rome Statute of the International Criminal Court–Observers' Notes, Article by Article*, 2nd ed. (Beck/Hart 2008), page 1213; *Sluiter, Göran, "I beg you, please come testify" – The problematic absence of subpoena powers at the ICC, New Criminal Law Review, Vol. 12, Number 4 (2009), p. 600;* Schabas, William, *The International Criminal Court: A Commentary on the Rome Statute* (Oxford University Press 2010).

24 United Nations Diplomatic Conference of Plenipotentiaries on the Establishment of an International Criminal Court (1998), A/CONF.183/13 (Vol. III), p. 329, fn. 221, http://legal.un.org/diplomaticconferences/icc-1998/vol/english/vol_III_e.pdf (last accessed 28 September 2015), p. 329, fn. 221.

25 Sluiter, Göran, "I beg you, please come testify" – The problematic absence of subpoena powers at the ICC, New Criminal Law Review, Vol. 12, Number 4 (2009), pp. 597-598, 600.

26 U.N. Doc. A/50/22, 6 September 1995, http://www.legal-tools.org/uploads/tx_ltpdb/doc21168.pdf (last accessed: 28 September 2015), para. 233.

27 Sluiter, Göran, "I beg you, please come testify" – The problematic absence of subpoena powers at the ICC, New Criminal Law Review, Vol. 12, Number 4 (2009), pp. 597-598, 600.

28 *Prosecutor v. Lubanga*, ICC-01/04-01/06-T-355-ENG ET, Transcript, 20 May 2011, T.5:19. Previous to this, the same Chamber had held that the Chamber could require his attendance and testimony live before the Court (rather than via video link) given the witness's previous indication of willingness to travel to The Hague. *Prosecutor v. Lubanga,* ICC-01/04-01/06-2727-Red, para. 65.

29 *Ibid.* at T.2:5.

Situation, the Prosecutor again argued that "willingness" of the witness was a mandatory requirement with the Pre-Trial Chamber holding that "the Court may request a State Party to facilitate the *voluntary* appearance of a witness".[30] At the same time, however, that Pre-Trial Chamber reaffirmed that it possessed power to compel a witness if he/she "appears before it to provide testimony" within the meaning of Rule 65.[31] In academic circles, many have read the ICC texts in the same manner. William Schabas took the position that "[n]othing in the Statute provides for the compellability of witnesses, for example by issuance of subpoenae or similar orders to appear before the Court".[32] In 2010, Gӧran Sluiter contemplated this lack of a subpoena power noting that "[t]he absence of any subpoena power is so strikingly peculiar for the ICC, as I know of no system where criminal courts lack this power as a general rule".[33]

In the cases that followed arising out of the Kenya Situation, it seemed that certain 'inherent powers' of Article 64 were considered. Trial Chamber V(a) held that Article 64(2), when read with Article 64(6)(f), is to "be described as the general, residual power to do what is fair, reasonable and just in the particular circumstances confronting the Chamber".[34] Trial Chamber V(b) went on to determine that a certain flexibility must be permitted in procedural matters, in particular relating to Article 64, finding that "silence on a particular procedural issue does not necessarily imply that it is forbidden".[35]

2.3 The Ruto & Sang Decision

On 29 November 2013, the Prosecution filed a request, pursuant to Article 64(6)(b) and Article 93, asking the Trial Chamber for an order to "summon"

30 *Kenya Situation*, ICC-01/09, Second Decision on Application by Nine Persons to be Questioned by the Office of the Prosecutor, 31 January 2011, para. 20. [Emphasis added.]

31 *Ibid.*

32 Schabas, William, "Article 67: Rights of the Accused" in Triffterer, Otto (ed.), *Commentary on the Rome Statute of the International Criminal Court–Observers' Notes, Article by Article*, 2nd ed. (Beck/Hart 2008), p. 1265.

33 *Sluiter, Göran,* "Appearance of Witnesses and Unavailability of Subpoena Powers for the Court" in Bellelli, Roberto (ed.), *International Criminal Justice: Law and Practice from the Rome Statute to its Review* (Ashgate 2010), p. 469. *See also Sluiter, Göran, "I beg you, please come testify" – The problematic absence of subpoena powers at the ICC, New Criminal Law Review, Vol. 12, Number 4 (2009), pp. 590-591 (asking "how any criminal court could function with a permanent and structural absence of subpoena power"?).*

34 *Prosecutor v. Ruto & Sang*, ICC-01/09-01/11-777, Decision on Mr Ruto's Request for Excusal from Continuous Presence at Trial, 18 June 2013, para. 33.

35 *Prosecutor v. Kenyatta*, ICC-01/09-02/11-588, Decision on witness preparation, 2 January 2013, para. 31 *citing Prosecutor v. Bemba*, ICC-01/05-01/08-1039, Partly Dissenting Opinion of Judge Kuniko Ozaki on the Decision on the Unified Protocol on the practices used to prepare and familiarise witnesses for giving testimony at trial, 24 November 2010, para. 10.

seven witnesses to testify in the *Ruto & Sang* case.[36] In doing so, the Prosecutor advanced that it did not possess a "subpoena" power itself, but that the Chamber held the power to "require the attendance and testimony of witnesses" and held "an indisputable interest in hearing the witnesses' evidence to fulfil its mandate to discover the truth".[37]

From this filing, the Prosecution, the Defence teams, the Victims Representatives and the Government of Kenya embarked on what would become a year-long legal battle of well-considered arguments as to what the texts envisaged with regard to 'subpoena', compelled testimony, compelled attendance and the powers of the Chambers to enforce any such orders. The parties and participants dove deep into the issues of inherent powers of the Court and the intentions of the drafters in ensuring that the Rome Statute would not be created in such a way as to put States into a position that would violate their own laws. Aside from the factual specifics as relate to Kenya's own laws in allowing for such Court orders, several arguments were devoted to the textual trappings of the Rome Statute. The parties debated whether the word "voluntary", as contained in Article 93(1)(e), is such to require express consent of a witness to testify at all or if it merely precludes physical transfer of persons to the seat of the Court beyond his/her will.[38] Further, the Article 64(6)(b) provision that allows the Trial Chamber to "*[r]equire* the attendance and testimony of witnesses" was compared against the French version of the Rome Statute which translates more directly into English as to "*[o]rder* the attendance and testimony of witnesses" ("*[o]rdonner la comparution des témoins*").[39] [Emphasis added.]

The Trial Chamber, in its Decision of 17 April 2014, gave a deep analysis of the "object and purposes of the ICC", international law, customary international criminal procedural law, implied powers, the rule of good faith in interpretation of treaties, and the principle of complementarity.[40] In reaching a decision, the Majority held that the Chambers did have the power to compel witnesses "as a matter of obligation on them, to testify before this Trial Chamber by video-link or at a location in Kenya" and requested Kenya "to facilitate, by way of compulsory measure as necessary" their appearance in such manner.[41] The Trial Chamber held that "pursuant to article 93(1)(d) and (l) of the Statute, it can, by way of requests for cooperation, obligate

36 *Prosecutor v. Ruto & Sang*, ICC-01/09-01/11-1120-Red2-Corr, Corrected and amended version of "Prosecution's request under article 64(6)(b) and article 93 to summon witneses" (ICC-01/09-01/1-120-Conf-Exp), 5 December 2013.

37 *Ibid.* at para. 2.

38 *See, e.g., Prosecutor v. Ruto & Sang*, ICC-01/09-01/11-1274-Corr2, Decision on Prosecutor's Application for Witness Summons and resulting Request for State Party Cooperation, 17 April 2014, paras 116-119, 146-156.

39 *Ibid. at* paras 94-101.

40 *Prosecutor v. Ruto & Sang*, ICC-01/09-01/11-1274-Corr2, Decision on Prosecutor's Application for Witness Summons and resulting Request for State Party Cooperation, 17 April 2014.

41 *Ibid.* at p. 77.

Kenya both to serve summonses and assist in compelling the attendance (before the Chamber) of the witnesses summoned".[42]

Thereafter, the Appeals Chamber was called to review the Trial Chamber Decision on two issues 1) *"[w]hether a chamber has the power to compel the testimony of witnesses*" and 2) "*[w]hether [...] Kenya, a State party to the Rome Statute, is under an obligation to cooperate with the Court to serve summonses and assist in compelling the appearance of witnesses subject to a subpoena*".[43] In its decision on the two issues at hand, the Appeals Chamber held that examining principles of international criminal procedure or implied powers were incorrect as the Trial Chamber had rightly noted that Article 64(6)(b) provides for a conclusive legal basis;[44] in this respect, the Appeals Chamber agreed that "the plain wording of article 64 (6) (b) of the Statute indicates that the Trial Chambers have the power to compel the appearance of the witnesses before the Court, *in the sense of creating a legal obligation for the individual concerned*".[45] The Court supported this with the academic discussion that had taken place in the preceding years; as predicted by one commentator, the Court appears to have circumvented the core issue of an ICC 'subpoena' power by substituting a videolink option under its control.[46] What stands from the Appeals Chamber decision is that 1) Individuals can be legally bound to appear for testimony via videolink or *in situ*[47], and 2) States can be ordered to comply pursuant to the obligations to cooperate under to Article 93(1)(b). The Appeals Chamber's ruling, in sum total, was highly restricted and left burning the issue of whether the Court could compel a witness to testify at the seat of the Court; however, in doing so, the Appeals Chamber did take note of the more permissive nature of the Trial Chamber decision before them, stating:

> *[S]ome of the Trial Chamber's statements in the Impugned Decision could give rise to the understanding that such powers could also be used to oblige a State Party generally in respect of compelling witnesses to appear before the Court. The Appeals Chamber recalls that the issues on appeal are limited to the specific questions arising in the case at hand, namely witness appearance before*

---

42 *Ibid.* at para. 193.

43 *Prosecutor v. Ruto & Sang*, ICC-01/09-01/11-1598, Judgement on the appeals of William Samoei Ruto and Mr Joshua Arap Sang against the decision of Trial Chamber V (A) of 17 April 2014 entitled "Decision on Prosecutor's Application for Witness Summonses and resulting Request for State Party Cooperation, 9 October 2014, para. 11.

44 *Ibid.* at para. 105 *referring to Prosecutor v. Ruto & Sang*, ICC-01/09-01/11-1274-Corr2, Decision on Prosecutor's Application for Witness Summons and resulting Request for State Party Cooperation, 17 April 2014, para. 100.

45 *Ibid.* at para.107. *See also* para. 113.

46 Klamberg, Mark, *Evidence in International Criminal Trials: Confronting Legal Gaps and the Reconstruction of Disputed Events* (Martinus Nijhoff Publishers 2013), p. 246.

47 Article 3(3) of the Rome Statute provides: "The Court may sit elsewhere, whenever it considers it desirable, as provided in this Statute"; thus, the term '*in situ*' as discussed in these proceedings takes on the meaning of 'locally' in that the ICC proceedings themselves – in this case the taking of testimony – can be done in the domestic courts if ordered by an ICC Chamber.

the Trial Chamber sitting in situ *or by way of videolink. Accordingly, the Appeals Chamber's judgement is limited to those questions.*[48]

3 ICC Structure & Developments

3.1 The Continuing Lack of Subpoena and the Statutory Rights of the Defendant

As noted well-prior to the *Ruto & Sang* Appeals Chamber decision, an equality of arms issue may be seen in a lack of a true subpoena power.[49] In 2011, the IBA took note of this procedural vacancy on the fairness of proceedings calling to mind the incomplete picture that may be available to the judiciary for a determination of the truth should the Chamber lack authority to produce necessary witnesses; they further cautioned:

> *[...] even more troubling is the potential impact on the fairness of the proceedings – a clear example being circumstances where a witness who could give cogent potentially exculpatory evidence refuses to cooperate with the defence and to testify. Save for any efforts on the part of the relevant State, the ICC would be powerless to act.*[50]

Jurisprudentially, international criminal law has pronounced similarly. The *Tadić* Appeals Chamber Judgement at the ICTY discussed the importance of subpoena and summons powers, especially where there is non-compliance in cooperation, "to alleviate the difficulties faced by the parties so that each side may have equal access to witnesses".[51] That Appeals Chamber went so far as to say it could "conceive of situations where a fair trial is not possible because witnesses central to the defence case do not appear due to the obstructionist efforts of a State".[52] The ICTR Appeals Chamber, in particular, has found that the lack of effective subpoena power in a particular State factored into a referral decision as it could create hardship for a defendant in securing out-of-State witnesses "to the extent and in a manner which would jeopardize his right to a fair trial".[53] In the ICTR case of *Bagosora & Nsengiyumva*, the

---

48 *Prosecutor v. Ruto & Sang*, ICC-01/09-01/11-1598, Judgment on the appeals of William Samoei Ruto and Mr Joshua Arap Sang against the decision of Trial Chamber V (A) of 17 April 2014 entitled "Decision on Prosecutor's Application for Witness Summonses and resulting Request for State Party Cooperation, 9 October 2014, para. 31.

49 *Sluiter, Göran, "I beg you, please come testify" – The problematic absence of subpoena powers at the ICC, New Criminal Law Review, Vol. 12, Number 4 (2009)*, p. 602.

50 IBA/ICC Monitoring and Outreach Programme, *Enhancing efficiency and effectiveness of ICC proceedings: a work in progress*, January 2011, http://www.ibanet.org/Document/Default.aspx?DocumentUid=499255EC-D744-4847-A430-026BC22BFDEB (last accessed 28 September 2015), p. 24. *See also* pp. 11, 35.

51 *Prosecutor v. Tadić*, IT-94-1-A, Appeals Judgment, 15 July 1999, para. 52.

52 *Ibid.* at para. 55.

53 *Prosecutor v. Kanyarukiga*, ICTR-2002-78-R11bis, Decision on the Prosecution's Appeal Against Decision on Referral Under Rule 11bis, 30 October 2008, para. 30. The Trial

Appeals Chamber held that the Trial Chamber erred by failing to enforce a subpoena for which Mr. Bagosora "was thus deprived of the opportunity to present a potentially important witness".[54]

Pursuant to Article 64(2), an ICC Chamber has a duty to ensure fair proceedings that are conducted "with full respect for the rights of the accused and due regard for the protection of victims and witnesses". Even with a "legal obligation" placed upon a witness, without the ability of the Chamber to issue a correlating sanction for non-compliance of its summons, it remains incumbent on the resident State, or even the calling party,[55] to ensure the production of the witnesses necessary to its case. For this, the Defence are often at a disadvantage of resources as "external" (having limited access to directly participate in the framework agreements that define State cooperation to the Court, such as Memorandums of Understanding outlining the ability to conduct investigations in a specific territory) and lacking in sufficient staffing and/or resources to garner compliance (with no dedicated investigations team, it is difficult for the Defence team to maintain contacts with witnesses to build trust and establish relationship often necessary to ensuring a witness's willingness to testify). Furthermore, significant reliance on substitutive remedies of videolink or paper evidence in lieu of live testimony impacts several foundational rights of the Rome Statute.

3.1.1 Article 67(1)(e): "[...] to obtain the attendance and examination of witnesses on his or her behalf under the same conditions"

The disparity in its ability to investigate at all puts the Defence at a significant disadvantage in securing witnesses to testify. For 2015, the OTP Investigations Division alone had an approved €15,934,500 budget "ensuring quality in the administration of justice by supporting the OTP in carrying out impartial and expeditious investigations […]".[56] The investigations budget

---

Chamber in that case noted UNSC Resolution 1503 that called on States to cooperate with the *ad hoc* Tribunal, but concluded that it was not convinced that it would be in itself sufficient to ensure the availability of Defence witnesses. *Prosecutor v. Kanyarukiga*, ICTR-2002-78-R11bis, Decision on the Prosecution's Appeal Against Decision on Referral Under Rule 11*bis*, 30 October 2008, para. 32. This case was cited by the *Katanga* Defence in arguing that the ICC's inability to subpoena witnesses contributed to the inadmissibility of the case being held before the ICC at all. *Prosecutor v. Katanga & Ngudjolo*, ICC-01/04-01/07-949, Motion Challenging the Admissibility of the Case by the Defence of Germain Katanga, Pursuant to Article 19(2)(a) of the Statute, 11 March 2009, para. 24.

54 *Bagosora & Nsengiyumva v. Prosecutor*, ICTR-98-41-A, Appeals Judgement, 14 December 2011, para. 543.

55 *Sluiter, Göran, "I beg you, please come testify" – The problematic absence of subpoena powers at the ICC, New Criminal Law Review, Vol. 12, Number 4 (2009), p. 599. See also Fedorova, Masha, The Principle of Equality of Arms in International Criminal Proceedings, (Intersentia 2012), p. 218.*

56 ASP 13th Session, Approved Programmed Budget for 2015 of the International Criminal Court,- 24 March 2015, ICC-ASP/13/20, http://www.icc-cpi.int/iccdocs/ other/ICC_ Approved_Budget_2015.pdf (last accessed 28 September 2015), p. 48.

for each legal aid Defence team – for the life of the case – is presently budgeted at €73,006.[57] The staffing differences are mind-boggling when considering the Prosecution's staffing model applied for the 2014 and 2015 budget assumptions, namely:

> *an OTP investigation team involved in an active investigation (as opposed to a case in "hibernation") must have the equivalent of 26.5 staff members in order to operate effectively (17 staff members from the Investigations Division; 7.5 from the Prosecution Division; and one international cooperation adviser);*[58]

Compare this with the €73,006, which is meant to cover:

> *All costs associated with the investigation requirements of the defence team [...] [s]uch costs include the hourly fees of the professional investigator(s) or resource person(s) assigned to the team to conduct investigative work in the field; travel expenses, and the daily subsistence allowance of all team members in connection with* in situ *investigation work in the field.*[59]

While the Prosecution bears the burden of proof and must equally investigate exonerating evidence, there is still evident disparity in the number of full-time professional resources the Prosecution can allocate to a case to make contact with witnesses and engage them over a period of time, as opposed to a short-term contractor of the Defence who has less institutional backing. While monetary resources may not seem an open door to securing testimony (without violation of the law), it is the way that these funds are translated into human capital who establish relationships of trust with potential witnesses to ensure that they are at ease in the prospect of giving testimony. Defence

---

57 ASP 12th Session, Registry's single policy document on the Court's legal aid system, ICC-ASP/12/3, 4 June 2013 http://www.icc-cpi.int/iccdocs/asp_docs/ASP12/ICC-ASP-12-3-ENG.pdf (last accessed 28 September 2015), para. 46.

58 ASP 13th Session, Proposed Programme Budget for 2015 of the International Criminal Court Executive Summary - 17 July 2014, ICC-ASP/13/11, http://www.icc-cpi.int/iccdocs/asp_docs/ASP13/ICC-ASP-13-11-ENG.pdf (last accessed 28 September 2015), p. 7, para. 23. For Prosecution Teams, the model is "14 staff members (2 investigators per accused, which will increase the size of the team depending on the number of accused; 11 from the Prosecution Division; and one international cooperation adviser)." The Prosecution submits that "[c]ompared to team staffing levels at the UN international criminal tribunals and special courts, or to the investigation and prosecution of serious crime by domestic authorities, these staffing levels are extremely modest." *Ibid.*

59 ASP 12th Session, Registry's single policy document on the Court's legal aid system, ICC-ASP/12/3, 4 June 2013 http://www.icc-cpi.int/iccdocs/asp_docs/ASP12/ICC-ASP-12-3-ENG.pdf (last accessed 28 September 2015), para. 47. "The amount of €73,006 allocated to the defence for investigations is determined on the basis of the equivalent of 90 days' of fees for one professional investigator (corresponding to the remuneration of an investigator in the Office of the Prosecutor at the P-4 level), the remuneration of one resource person for the same period (corresponding to the remuneration of an assistant investigator in the Office of the Prosecutor at the G-5 level), the daily subsistence allowance for the same period (€20,970) and €13,000 for travel costs. This budget is considered to be a core budget covering the investigative needs of the defence, for example, for identifying potential witnesses and reaching a decision regarding their testimony, or acquiring relevant evidence for an average of 30 prosecution witnesses." *Ibid.*

teams simply do not have resources to approach witnesses in the same manner as the Prosecution, which can lead to greater inability to find and/or bring witnesses to the Court.

Aside from sheer ability to access witnesses, there are often hurdles the Defence encounters in finding witnesses who will testify 'for the Defence'. While there is no 'ownership' of a witness by a party,[60] it does not mean that witnesses don't sometimes feel to be seen as 'aligned' with one side if called by that party. There is, for one, the recognition that many witnesses would prefer being called to testify "for the Prosecution" rather than to testify "for someone accused of grave Article 5 crimes". Such impression is compounded not only by the visibility of these trials and the high-profile accused, but also in the highly political nature of many of the situations in which the Court is engaged. In some cases at the ICTY, witnesses had to be subpoenaed on this basis alone.[61]

Finally, the organisational structure of the Court places the Office of the Prosecutor, as an organ, closer to the States themselves which affords the Prosecutor greater ability to access the witnesses themselves through established relationships and to secure measures that may be tied to a witness's willingness to testify, such as relocation discussions. The Defence, as not in a position to negotiate with States directly, must rely on the Registry or the Chambers as its interlocutor.

3.1.2 Article 67(1)(e): "To examine, or have examined, the witnesses against him or her [...]"

Unfortunately, the true subpoena power to compel witnesses to provide testimony in person is not equivalent to summoning them for videolink testimony. The *ad hoc* Tribunals, in particular, have noted that videolink should be the exception to the rule, stressing its impact on the right of confrontation; one early ICTY Trial Chamber decision noted:

> *It is important to re-emphasise the general rule requiring the physical presence of the witness. This is intended to ensure confrontation between the witness and the accused and to enable the Judges to observe the demeanour of the witness when giving evidence.*[62]

In fact, the *ad hoc* Tribunals have held that there is lesser weight to be vested in testimony taken via videolink, considering "[t]he distance of the witness from the solemnity of the courtroom proceedings and the fact that the witness is not able to see all those present in the courtroom at the same time, but only those on whom the video camera is focused, may detract from the reliance

---

60 *Prosecutor v. Mrkšić et al.*, IT-95-13/1-AR73, Decision on Defence Interlocutory Appeal on Communication with Potential Witnesses of the Other Party, 30 July 2003, para. 15.

61 When subpoenaed, the witness could sometimes be referred to as a 'Chambers' witness.

62 *Prosecutor v. Delalić et al.*, Decision on the Motion to Allow Witnesses K, L and M to Give their testimony by Means of Video-Link Conference, 28 May 1997, para. 17.

placed upon his or her evidence".[63] The Appeals Chamber in the ICTR *Kanyarukiga* case noted that while Rwanda had videolink facilities for out-of-State witnesses, the Trial Chamber was not in error to find that this solution was not fully satisfactory "given that it is preferable to hear direct witness testimony, and that it would be a violation of the principle of equality of arms if the majority of Defence witnesses would testify by video-link while the majority of Prosecution witnesses would testify in person".[64]

An even more concerning development is the proliferation of paper testimony at the ICC. With the 2013 amendment of ICC Rule 68 – allowing written testimony to enter into the record without the possibility of cross-examination in certain circumstances – inability to secure a witness's live testimony may give way to a request for their statement to substitute. In fact, an Assembly of States Parties Report at the 12th Session (in which the newly formulated Rule 68 was adopted) specifically called for Rule 68 to be "more flexible and efficient" especially noting "[t]he difficulties inherent in introducing prior recorded testimony under the current rule 68 are exacerbated by the fact that the Chamber has no power to compel a witness to appear before the Court".[65] It went on to state:

> *Rule 65 provides that once a witness appears before the Court, that witness may be compelled to provide testimony, however no general subpoena power exists in the Rules. In contrast, the ICTY Rules do allow the Chamber to issue subpoenas. The difficulty in compelling a witness to appear before the Court increases the need to develop more flexible and efficient processes for the introduction of prior recorded testimony, while also having due regard to the principles of fairness and the rights of the accused.*[66]

Further, the Prosecutor directly referenced the use of Rule 68 as an alternative in the ongoing *Ruto & Sang* discussions of a power to compel testimony. In one written submission, the Prosecutor specifically raised the potential use of the newly amended Rule 68(2)(d), arguing:

> *Moreover, the Prosecution has informed the Court and the Defence in advance of the probability that some of the witnesses are likely to testify to the contrary of a prior statement, therefore enabling the Court to satisfy itself of the absence of any improper motive and to intervene if necessary. Moreover, rule 68(2) of the ICC Rules, as with ICTY rule 92*quinquies *adopted after the Popovic Ap-*

---

63 *Ibid.*

64 *Prosecutor v. Kanyarukiga*, ICTR-2002-78-R11bis, Decision on the Prosecution's Appeal Against Decision on Referral Under Rule 11bis, 30 October 2008, para. 33.

65 ASP 12th Session, Study Group on Governance: Working Group on Lessons Learnt: Second report of the Court to the Assembly of States Parties, ICC-ASP/12/37/Add.1, 31 October 2013, http://www.icc-cpi.int/iccdocs/asp_docs/ASP12/ICC-ASP-12-37-Add1-ENG.pdf (last accessed 28 September 2015), p. 21.

66 *Ibid.*

peals Decision, specifically permits the admission of the prior recorded testimony of a witness who has been subjected to interference.[67]

Drafted in the absence of any developed public case law of Rule 92*quinquies* at the ICTY, Rule 68(2)(d) was presented with a dangerously low threshold in relation to witnesses who refuse to testify in that a mere citation of interference could, *prima facie*, pave the way for the witness's non-attendance. In fact, substantiated threats are not required to justify the issuance of a subpoena at the *ad hoc* Tribunals.[68] In fact, in what is seemingly the first public pronouncement pursuant to Rule 68(2)(d), the *Ruto & Sang* Trial Chamber held that a higher standard of proof, such as beyond reasonable doubt, was not necessary to evaluate assertions of interference; rather, it held "to establish the factual thresholds required for introducing prior recorded testimony, evidence of sufficient specificity and probative value must be provided to satisfy the Chamber that the requirements under Rule 68 of the Rules are met".[69]

Thus, if inability to secure the physical presence of witnesses gives rise to an increase in 'paper' testimony, it could violate not only the Accused's rights of confrontation, but the Rome Statute's original principle of orality that "testimony of a witness at trial shall be given in person" with only Rule 68 as an 'exception'.[70]

3.2 Enforcement

Leaving aside the lesser-quality of videolink evidence, the question remains as to what measures can be taken against an individual or State in non-compliance of a summons to appear in that manner. The powers as found by the Appeals Chamber, while significant to clarifying the responsibilities of individuals and States, are not immediately synonymous with the ability to effectively implement such orders. In consideration of complementarity and absent its own police force, the Court relies on the cooperation of the States – both members and non-members – to effectuate the orders of the Bench.

---

67 *Prosecutor v. Ruto & Sang*, ICC-01/09-01/11-1202, Prosecution's further submissions pursuant to the Prosecution's request under article 64(6)(b) and article 93 to summon witnesses, 14 March 2014, para 34.

68 *Prosecutor v. Simba*, ICTR-01-76, Decision on the Defence Request for Subpoenas, 4 May 2005, para 2.

69 *Prosecutor v. Ruto & Sang*, ICC-01/09-01/11-1938-Corr-Red2, Decision on Prosecution Request for Admission of Prior Recorded Testimony, 19 August 2015, para 37. At the time of drafting, this Decision is on appeal on 11 issues, including, *inter alia*, "Whether the correct standard of proof for determining interference was 'evidence of sufficient specificity and probative value". *Prosecutor v. Ruto & Sang*, ICC-01/09-01/11-1953-Red, Decision on the Defence's Applications for Leave to Appeal the 'Decision on Prosecution Request for Admission of Prior Recorded Testimony', 10 September 2015, para 4(h).

70 ICC Rome Statute, Article 69(2). *See also* Kreß, Claus, and Prost, Kimberly, "Article 93: Other forms of cooperation" in Triffterer, Otto (ed.), *Commentary on the Rome Statute of the International Criminal Court–Observers' Notes, Article by Article*, 2nd ed. (Beck/Hart 2008), p. 1576.

3.2.1 Individual non-compliance

Notably, the ICC does not possess the same remedies for non-compliance as enjoyed by the Chambers of the *ad hoc* Tribunals. At the ICTY/R, non-compliance with a 'subpoena', which equally created a 'legal obligation for the individual concerned' could result in arrest and transfer to the seat of the Court for contempt proceedings. For example, a Majority Bench in the case of *Prosecutor v. Tolimir* issued an *Order in Lieu of Indictment* initiating contempt proceedings against Mr. Dragomir Pećanac, pursuant to ICTY Rule 77, for his failure to comply with a subpoena to appear for testimony.[71] Mr. Pećanac was arrested by the Republic of Serbia, brought before the Tribunal and ultimately convicted, by Majority, for his non-compliance; he was sentenced to three months of imprisonment.[72]

While ICTY/R Rule 77 grants specific contempt power to the sitting bench, in addition to its inherent powers,[73] the ICC Chambers have repeatedly held that Article 70 investigations into *Offences Against the Administration of Justice* must be brought by the Prosecution. In *Lubanga*, for example, the Defence recently requested the Appeals Chamber for an *amicus* to investigate an intermediary's actions resulting in the false testimony presented at trial; the *Lubanga* Appeals Chamber reaffirmed that it had no such power, holding "that the decision whether to initiate or conduct investigations on alleged offenses as provided by article 70 of the Statute lies within the purview of the Prosecutor".[74] Naturally, as noted by commentators, *"[i]t is far from ideal that the prosecution of offences against the administration of justice should lie exclusively in the hands of the OTP [...]"*.[75] Of primary concern, this prevents the Chambers from taking any direct action when it appears that offences against the administration of justice may have occurred, in this case, any inference of "obstructing or interfering with the attendance or testimony of a witness".[76]

---

71 *Prosecutor v. Dragomir Pećanac*, IT-05-88/2-R77.2, Order Issuing a Public Redacted Version of the "Order in Lieu of Indictment", 19 October 2011 (Judge Nyambe dissenting).

72 *Prosecutor v. Dragomir Pećanac*, IT-05-88/2-R77.2, Judgement on Allegations of Contempt, 9 December 2011 (Judge Nyambe dissenting). Thereafter, Mr. Pećanac testified before the Tribunal in the *Tolimir* case in January 2012.

73 *See Prosecutor v. Blaškić,* IT-95-14, Judgement on the Request of the Republic of Croatia for Review of the Decision of Trial Chamber II of 18 July 1997, 29 October 1997, para. 59.

74 *Prosecutor v. Lubanga*, ICC-01/04-01/06-3114, Decision on the request of the Defence in relation to investigations conducted pursuant to article 70 of the Statute, 17 June 2014, para. 19.

75 Hiéramente, Mayeul, Müller, Philipp & Ferguson, Emma, *Barasa, Bribery and Beyond: Offences against the Administration of Justice at the International Criminal Court*, International Criminal Law Review 14 (2014), p. 1136 *citing* Defence for Lubanga, *Prosecutor v. Lubanga*, ICC-01/04-01/06-2715, 1 April 2011.

76 ICC Rome Statute, Article 70(1)(c).

However, the Appeals Chamber did not enumerate Article 70 in the ramifications that could flow from non-compliance with a legally-binding order for an individual to provide testimony, but rather, held that refusal to appear "would constitute, at most, misconduct within the meaning of article 71 of the Statute".[77] Dismissing arguments of Article 22 *nullum crimen sine lege*, the Appeals Chamber held that "it would be for the State enforcing a request to stipulate such sanctions in the domestic law" and, as dictated by domestic law, an individual would benefit from sufficient notice of the consequences.[78]

With regard to Article 71, which delineates "Sanctions for misconduct before the court" including "disruption of its proceedings or deliberate refusal to comply with its directions", two points may negate its use for the purposes of compelling attendance. First, Article 71 refers only to "persons present before it", seemingly referring only to someone who is already present before the Chamber and, therefore, similar to the Rules applicable to 'compelling testimony'.[79] While this phrase could be extended to those appearing via videolink, or potentially in a domestic deposition, it is not likely that such phrase could be extended to include those subject to a summons.[80] Second, the provision – which appears to apply more to disturbing the actual courtroom proceedings – allows only for a fine or administrative sanction to disruption only within the courtroom setting; pursuant to Rule 171(4), the maximum fine permissible is €2.000 per day, and may be cumulative "on each day that the misconduct continues". Aside from the fact that the remedy of excluding a non-compliant person from the Courtroom is precisely the opposite of attempting to get someone before the Chamber for testimony, monetary sanctions may not be as 'compelling' as potential incarceration especially considering the potential for the average witness to be completely unable to ever pay such fines.

Considering the Appeals Chamber's direction of domestic sanctions to suffice for recourse, it is unclear if a potential witness would receive sufficient notice with regard to non-compliance. Certainly, it would be wise to clearly spell out actions that the national jurisdiction can take if the witness

---

77 *Prosecutor v. Ruto & Sang*, ICC-01/09-01/11-1598, Judgement on the appeals of William Samoei Ruto and Mr Joshua Arap Sang against the decision of Trial Chamber V (A) of 17 April 2014 entitled "Decision on Prosecutor's Application for Witness Summonses and resulting Request for State Party Cooperation, 9 October 2014, para. 109.

78 *Ibid.* at para. 110.

79 *See Prosecutor v. Ruto & Sang*, ICC-01/09-01/11-1344-Corr, Corrigendum to Sang Defence appeal against the Decision on Prosecutor's Application for Witness Summonses and resulting Request for State Party Cooperation, 26 June 2014, para. 10.

80 *See* Schabas, William, *The International Criminal Court: A Commentary on the Rome Statute* (Oxford University Press 2010), pp. 859- 860; Triffterer, Otto, "Article 71: Sanctions for misconduct before the Court" in Triffterer, Otto (ed.), *Commentary on the Rome Statute of the International Criminal Court–Observers' Notes, Article by Article*, 2nd ed., (Beck/Hart 2008), para. 19.

does not comply; if directed from the Court itself directly to the individual,[81] it would be reasonable to expect that the individual may not understand that domestic consequences may flow from non-compliance.[82] Furthermore, such domestic sanction for inaction by the witness could lead to disparate treatment among witnesses based on residence; for example, what punishment for non-compliance could flow from a State that does not have a penalty for refusing to testify?

3.2.2 State non-compliance

Even less evident in the *Ruto & Sang* ruling is what power the Court has to enforce compliance of a State in executing its order. The Appeals Chamber has taken the position that even if the States Parties are not obliged to execute the order, it does not prevent the Court from rendering the edict to member States "*to provide assistance in compelling witnesses to appear before the Court*".[83] The Appeals Chamber specifically turned to the cooperation provision of Article 93(1)(b), which requires States Parties to assist in "[t]he taking of evidence, including testimony under oath, and the production of evidence [...]".[84]

In the specific case of the witnesses summoned in *Ruto & Sang*, non-compliance of the Government of Kenya does not appear to have been a subsequent issue; however, were that not the case, what would be the Chamber's recourse? This question of ensuring compliance was raised in the filings before the Appeals Chamber; citing to the commentary of the Rome Statute, the *Ruto* Defence submitted that "[t]he better view…is that the Trial Chamber may well, pursuant to article 64 para. 6(b) create an international obligation of persons to appear before the Court, but that States are under no duty to

---

81 *See Prosecutor v. Ruto & Sang*, ICC-01/09-01/11-1274-Corr2, Decision on Prosecutor's Application for Witness Summonses and resulting Request for State Party Cooperation, 17 April 2014, Disposition, p. 78: "*DIRECTS the Registry to prepare and transmit, in consultation with the Prosecutor, the necessary subpoenas to the concerned witnesses (with or without the assistance of the Government of Kenya)*".

82 This is especially true as an average citizen of any country may neither know that he/she is bound to the ICC nor automatically understand the local consequence (assuming a federal standard would be applied by the State) of refusing to testify before a court of law. *See Prosecutor v. Haradinaj et al.*, IT-04-84, Transcript, 20 November 2007, T.10958-10959 (as example that even a licensed practicing domestic attorney may not have an immediate full appreciation of the jurisdictional interplay between international criminal law and domestic provisions for a refusal to testify in an International Tribunal).

83 *Prosecutor v. Ruto & Sang*, ICC-01/09-01/11-1598, Judgement on the appeals of William Samoei Ruto and Mr Joshua Arap Sang against the decision of Trial Chamber V (A) of 17 April 2014 entitled "Decision on Prosecutor's Application for Witness Summonses and resulting Request for State Party Cooperation, 9 October 2014, para. 112.

84 *Ibid.* at paras 129-132. The Appeals Chamber found it did not need to consider the Government of Kenya's arguments regarding impossibility of implementation given its governing domestic laws. *Ibid.* at para. 133.

enforce that obligation".[85] This is supported by the plain language of the relevant language of Article 64(6)(b) of the Rome Statute, which refers only to the limited power of the Court "obtaining, if necessary, the assistance of States as provided in this Statute". However, the language of Article 93(1)(b) perhaps provides a stronger requirement in that "States Parties *shall*, in accordance with the provisions of this Part and under procedures of national law, *comply* with requests by the Court to provide the following assistance in relation to investigations or prosecutions". [Emphasis added.]

What has remained constant over time is that the Court is not willing to dictate to the national authorities how to execute any such cooperation with the Court.[86] This is supported by customary international law which would prevent a State or international organisation from placing an order upon another State.[87] As shown in the cases against *Omar Al Bashir* and *Saif Gaddafi*, when faced with non-compliance of a State relating to a U.N.-referred case, the Court has relied on referral of that State to the U.N. Security Council.[88] Beyond availability of that measure, it is unclear how the Court could take further action to secure compliance save notice to the Assembly of States Parties of a non-cooperating State.

---

85 *Prosecutor v. Ruto & Sang*, ICC-01/09-01/11-1345, Defence appeal against the "Decision on Prosecutor's Application for Witness Summonses and resulting Request for State Party Cooperation", 5 June 2014, para.16 *citing* Kreß, Claus, and Prost, Kimberly, "Article 93: Other forms of cooperation" in Triffterer, Otto (ed.), *Commentary on the Rome Statute of the International Criminal Court–Observers' Notes, Article by Article*, 2nd ed. (Beck/Hart 2008), pp. 1576-1577; *referencing* Bitti, Gilbert, "Article 64: Functions and Powers of the Trial Chamber" in Triffterer, Otto (ed.), *Commentary on the Rome Statute of the International Criminal Court–Observers' Notes, Article by Article*, 2nd ed. (Beck/Hart 2008), p. 1213; Schabas, William, *The International Criminal Court: A Commentary on the Rome Statute* (Oxford University Press 2010), p. 768.

86 Kenya Situation, Second Decision on Application by Nine Persons to be Questioned by the Office of the Prosecutor, ICC-01/09, 31 January 2011, para. 21.

87 Rastan, Rod, *Testing Co-operation: The International Criminal Court and National Authorities*, Leiden Journal of International Law, Vol. 21, Issue 2 (2008), pp. 431, 436.

88 *Prosecutor v. Al Bashir*, ICC-02/05-01/09-195, Decision on the Cooperation of the Democratic Republic of the Congo Regarding Omar Al Bashir's Arrest and Surrender to the Court, 9 April 2014 (referral of a State Party to the Rome Statute, DRC, to the UNSC for failure to arrest and surrender Al Bashir to the ICC); *Prosecutor v. Saif Gaddafi*, ICC-01/11-01/11-577, Decision on the non-compliance by Libya with requests for cooperation by the Court and referring the matter to the United Nations Security Council, 10 December 2014 (referral of a non-State Party to the Rome Statute, Libya, to the UNSC for failure to surrender Saif Gaddafi to the ICC and to return original privileged documents to the Defence). As U.N.-created, the *ad hoc* Tribunals similarly utilised the U.N. Security Council as a last measure of ensuring cooperation. *See Prosecutor v. Semanza*, ICTR-97-20-1, Decision on Semanza's Motion for Subpoenas, Depositions, and Disclosure, 20 October 2000, para. 23: "*Thus, a Trial Chamber, under Article 28 of the Statute and Rule 54, has the authority to issue subpoenas of witnesses, but must rely primarily on state cooperation and state judicial mechanisms to execute and enforce subpoenas, short of referring a matter to the Security Council under Rule 7bis(A).*".

However, it is 'compelling' circumstances that may have prevented these sought-after witnesses in *Ruto & Sang* from live testimony in the first place. Notably, in the Majority Decision on Subpoena, the Chamber determined that the Defence request for an "order to the Prosecution to disclose the evidence in its possession which shows that intimidation, bribery or other improper influence has been the proximate cause of witness non-cooperation" was not necessary as the reason for the summons is simply "the search for the truth".[89] However, as shown in what followed from the witnesses being summoned to testify via videolink was that some recanted their previous testimony citing inducement. The Defence specifically noted that it did not hold the belief that this was any improper action of the Prosecution; however, the circumstances do raise significant questions of what 'compels' testimony – is it the carrot or the stick?

Consider, for example, when Witness 5 refused to testify in the *Lubanga* case without being paid a certain sum of money; the argument ended there.[90] Therefore, without that 'carrot', his testimony was not received and there was no 'stick'.[91] Contrast this with the ICTR case of *Karemera et al.* where the Trial Chamber held that financial demands equated 'unwillingness' and a subpoena was the proper recourse.[92]

For this topic, it should be noted that the *Ruto & Sang* Trial Chamber has held that information of support may be relevant to credibility and must be disclosed by the Prosecution;[93] however, the same has not held true for support provided by the Victims and Witnesses Unit. On 9 September 2014, the Trial Chamber made an oral ruling denying the Defence information it requested regarding the assistance and benefits provided by the Victims and Witnesses Unit (VWU) to certain witnesses (namely Witnesses 604, 495, 516, and 524 – all who were subject to summons) holding: "Whether or not any witness is impressed by the assistance, or the prospect of it, in that way

---

89 *Prosecutor v. Ruto & Sang*, ICC-01/09-01/11-1274-Corr2, Decision on Prosecutor's Application for Witness Summons and resulting Request for State Party Cooperation, 17 April 2014, para. 194.

90 *Prosecutor v. Lubanga*, ICC-01/04-01/06-T-355-ENG ET, Transcript, 20 May 2011, T.5-6.

91 It is not without noting that the testimony of persons who will do so only while engaged in 'bargaining' or contingent on sums paid may not be seen as the most altruistic testimony, and, ergo, perhaps may even raise questions of reliability.

92 *Prosecutor v. Karemera et al.*, ICTR-98-44-T, Decision on Joseph Nzirorera's Motion for Reconsideration of Oral Decision on Motion to Compel Full Disclosure of ICTR Payments for the Benefit of Witnesses G and T, 29 May 2008, para. 8.

93 *Prosecutor v. Ruto & Sang*, ICC-01/09-01/11-1514, Joint Defence Request for Leave to Appeal the Oral Decision of 9 September 2014 on Disclosure of Assistance and Benefits provided by the Victims and Witnesses Unit to Prosecution witnesses 604, 495, 516 and 524, 15 September 2014, para. 15.

remains a matter for legitimate questions by counsel without prejudice to the VWU's assessment as to the reasonableness of the assistance."[94]

Days later, Witness 604, subject to a summons, appeared via videolink and, on cross-examination, the following exchange occurred:

> *Defence Counsel:* "Mr. Witness, were you surprised at the amounts of money that you were being paid?"
> *Witness 604:* "Yes."
> *Defence Counsel:* "And it is this kind of money, sir, that you described in your testimony as fantastic and wonderful, monies which led you to tell lies against Honourable William Ruto?"
> *Witness 604:* "Yes."[95]

Thereafter, the Defence requested to appeal the oral decision regarding VWU support as "the witnesses often do not know the difference between funds coming from the Prosecution and funds provided by the VWU", including Witness 604.[96] They have submitted that "[m]any of the witnesses who are testifying now or in the upcoming sessions have recanted and claim they initially gave false testimony and then changed their minds, often as a result of a dispute over money with the Prosecution and/or VWU".[97]

While it is inevitable that certain witnesses may be compelled for the wrong reason – benefit or punishment – the real problem may be in the existing structures, that the parties hold all of the carrots in securing testimony and the Chamber holds no sticks. In a perfect world, neither would be necessary; but given reality, better defined positive and negative 'incentives' must be discussed in relation to the Court's endeavours of seeking the truth and holding fair and expeditious criminal trials. This is especially true with a backdrop of Article 70 contempt proceedings ongoing against five persons, including Defence team members, from the *Bemba* case;[98] as commentators have rightly suggested:

94 *Ibid.* at para. 1.

95 *Prosecutor v. Ruto & Sang*, ICC-01/09-01/11-T-136-Red-ENG WT, Transcript, 15 September 2014, T.27.

96 *Prosecutor v. Ruto & Sang*, ICC-01/09-01/11-1514, Joint Defence Request for Leave to Appeal the Oral Decision of 9 September 2014 on Disclosure of Assistance and Benefits provided by the Victims and Witnesses Unit to Prosecution witnesses 604, 495, 516 and 524, 15 September 2014, para. 17.

97 *Ibid.* at para. 19.

98 In the *Bemba et al.* Article 70 case, one of the men, is allegedly culpable of: "recruiting [...], instructing, persuading or otherwise influencing [certain witnesses], including *by way of transfers of money and the possibility of a relocation in Europe*, to state false information or withhold true information before TCIII". *Prosecutor v. Bemba et al.*, ICC-01/05-01/13-749, Decision pursuant to Article 61(7)(a) and (b) of the Rome Statute, 11 November 2014, Disposition (a)(v), p. 53. [Emphasis added.] One Defence team in that case has requested information about assistance provided by the Prosecution to the witnesses in the main case ostensibly seeking a gauge of 'improper influence' or 'positive compulsion'. *Prosecutor v. Bemba et al.*, ICC-01/05-01/13-520, Request Seeking the Prosecution to Provide to the Kilolo Defence Specific Information Relating to Its Reimbursement of Prosecution Witnesses, 27 June 2014. Per the subsequent order of the Single Judge, the

As a matter of legal certainty, it would be helpful to identify what can be considered a legally acceptable incentive and what is deemed an offence under Article 70. Is it merely the fact that 'money corrupts' or is the offence rather constituted by the conduct that is sought for on the part of the witness?[99]

5 Conclusion

It is obvious that, for an effective power of the Court to both 'establish the truth' and ensure 'equality of arms' among the parties, it is imperative that the States implement the orders as to the service of documents as a part of their Article 93 obligations identified by the Appeals Chamber. For this, the *Ruto & Sang* Trial Chamber has since specifically encouraged States "to update their national laws in accordance with the Summons Judgment".[100] However, it may be incumbent upon the Court to revise its texts and/or practices to ensure consistency and equality in the event of non-compliance. In doing so, they may choose to modify the Rome Statute to grant power to the Chamber to issue charges, *sua sponte*, for any non-execution of a Court's order by an individual; this power would be welcomed not only for the matter of the enforcement of summons, but also would grant the Court a direct power to investigate other contemptuous actions before it relating to the evidence. By taking this power out of the hands of the Prosecutor alone, it permits the Defence a small modicum of equality of arms in challenging those who may be perverting the course of justice. Additionally, it may be worthwhile for the Court to develop the definition and practice of *in situ* hearings for reluctant witnesses (pursuant to Article 3(3) and Article 62) to avoid both the inherent problems of videolink testimony and the firm preclusion of summoning persons across international borders. Finally, the Court could seek ways to ensure better equality of resources among the Prosecution and Defence with regard to the investigative duties of the parties.

Regardless of the ultimate measures, the matter of what is actually influencing a witness's choice to testify, or otherwise reluctance, should be monitored and discussed. As the first trials of the Court have shown issues of improper 'compulsion', certainly, it is in the Court's interest to ensure that it

---

Prosecution disclosed to the Chamber and Registry, *confidentially and ex parte*, the records sought which contained 669 documents with a chart detailing "the source identity, the witness to which it relates, the date, the title, the amount of expenses incurred by the Prosecution, the expense category, and the currency of the transaction that detailed", *Prosecutor v. Bemba et al.*, ICC-01/05-01/13-609, Prosecution's Submission of Information relating to the Reimbursement of the Prosecution Witnesses in the case of The Prosecutor v. Jean-Pierre Bemba Gombo, 4 August 2014.

99 Hiéramente, Mayeul, Müller, Philipp & Ferguson, Emma, *Barasa, Bribery and Beyond: Offences against the Administration of Justice at the International Criminal Court*, International Criminal Law Review 14 (2014), p. 1126.

100 *Prosecutor v. Ruto & Sang*, ICC-01/09-01/11-1817-Red, Decision on Prosecution Request for Issuance of a Summons for Witness 727 of 17 February 2015, 17 February 2015, para. 29.

has its own, proper, form of influence to counteract or control the proceedings to guarantee optimal results in fair and expeditious trials.

Masha Fedorova[*]

Disclosure of Information as an Instrument Ensuring Equality of Arms in International Criminal Proceedings

1. Introduction

In criminal cases in order for a defendant to answer the public accusation he must not only have knowledge of the specific charges against him but also be aware of the grounds of this accusation. Without access to this information the accused is denied an adequate opportunity to defend himself and fairness as a fundamental tenet of any modern criminal justice system cannot be sustained. Different systems adopt different means in facilitating defence access to relevant information and to ensure adequate facilities for defence to prepare for trial. Criminal justice systems based on the civil law tradition usually adopt a dossier (case-file) approach, while systems based on the common law tradition rather incorporate a 'disclosure' regime to facilitate exchange of information between procedural parties. The rationale of ensuring fair and effective conduct of administration of justice underlies, however, all of the systems.

Almost all international criminal courts, particularly the International Criminal Tribunals for the former Yugoslavia (ICTY) and Rwanda (ICTR) and the International Criminal Court (ICC) implement a disclosure regime. The practice of disclosure in international criminal proceedings has been one of the most controversial and extensively debated legal issues to date. In fact, it has been observed that "[f]rom the perspective of the defence, resolving disclosure-related issues at the ICC may often be the most pressing task confronting counsel in the process of defending his or her client".[1] It is not an overstatement to notice that the disclosure (mal)practice continues to be one great sources of frustration for the parties involved and the institutional stability seen from the perspective of equality of arms.[2] To defence, 'disclosure'

---

* LLM (2004), PhD (2012), assistant professor criminal law and criminal procedure at Radboud University, Nijmegen, The Netherlands. This paper draws on my PhD research, which was funded by the Netherlands Organisation for Scientific Research (see M. Fedorova, *'The Principle of Equality of Arms in International Criminal Proceedings'*, Antwerp: Intersentia, 2012).

1 K.A.A. Khan and A.A. Shah, Defensive Practices: Representing Clients before the International Criminal Court, *Law and Contemporary Problems* 76, 191, 2013, p. 218.

2 E.g. M.A. Newton, Evolving Equality: The Development of the International Criminal Bar, *Stanford Journal of International Law* 47, 2011, p. 416. C.C. Jalloh and A. DiBella, Equality of Arms in International Criminal Law: Continuing Challenges, in: *The Ashgate Research Companion to International Criminal Law – Critical Perspectives*, 2013, pp. 251-287. K.A.A. Khan and A.A. Shah, Defensive Practices: Representing Clients before the International Criminal Court, *Law and Contemporary Problems* 76, 191, 2013, pp. 191-233; K. Gibson & C. Lussiaa-Berdou, 'Disclosure of Evidence', in: K. Khan, C. Bu-

is an essential fair trial guarantee[3] as a properly functioning disclosure practice ensures the realisation of defence rights, particularly the rights to have knowledge of the charges against one and to have adequate facilities to prepare a defence. Realisation of these rights constitutes a necessary step towards fulfilment of the principle of equality of arms.[4] Moreover, in more practical terms, it is a means of accessing the needed information from the prosecution and constitutes a driving force for defence investigations and strategies.[5] To understand 'disclosure' one cannot merely have regard to the legal framework in place, as it is the application of the disclosure regime by procedural participants that shapes it in practical terms. This chapter focuses on the disclosure regimes of the three international criminal courts, the two ad hoc tribunals and the ICC, from a defence perspective. The main objective is to delineate how the disclosure regime has affected a meaningful application of the principle of equality of arms. Therefore, particular attention will be paid to disclosure practice and more specifically, the way the international criminal courts have dealt with disclosure violations.

The chapter is structured as follows. Before examining the disclosure regime at the international criminal courts, its rationales and interpretation is considered from a human rights perspective (section 2). Then in section 3, the prosecutorial disclosure obligations and the exceptions to them, are analysed on the basis of the courts' legal frameworks and jurisprudence. Of particular importance is the scope of the prosecutorial obligation to disclose potentially favourable evidence to the defence and the development of this practice, as this goes to the heart of prosecution's role as a 'Minister of Justice'. Before drawing some general conclusions in section 5, section 4 will elaborate on the remedies or sanctions that are attached to disclosure violations.

2. 'Disclosure' from a human rights perspective

The prosecutorial advantage of being able to initiate an investigation, the principally greater resources and the powers belonging to the state that are associated with a public prosecutor's office necessitate some 'equalizing' of

---

isman & C. Gosnell (eds.), *Principles of Evidence in International Criminal* Justice (2010), pp. 306-374. D. Schaffer, A Review of Experiences of the Pre-Trial and Appeals Chambers of the International Criminal Court Regarding the Disclosure of Evidence, *Leiden Journal of International Law* 21 (2008), pp. 151-163.

3 E.g. ICTY, *Prosecutor* v. *Lukic et al.,* Case No. I-98-32/1-T, Decision on Milan Lukié's Motion to Suppress Testimony for Failure of Timely Disclosure with Confidential Annexes A and B, 3 November 2008, par. 15.

4 ICTY, Krajisnik and Plavsic, Decision on Prosecution Motion for Clarification in Respect of Application of Rule 65*ter*, 66 (B) and 67 (C), IT-00-39&40 PT, 1 August 2001, par. 7.

5 ICTY, *Prosecutor v. Kordic and Cerkez*, Decision on Appellant's Notice and Supplemental Notice of Prosecution's Non-Compliance with its Disclosure Obligation under Rule 68 of the Rules, IT-65-14/2-A, 11 February 2004, par. 17 (mentioning the prosecutor's "superior, and sometimes even sole access to this material").

arms between the prosecutor and the defence to provide a fair opportunity for the latter to put forward a meaningful defence.[6] The right to have adequate time and facilities for the preparation of one's defence is one of the corollaries of the principle of equality of arms and the right to a fair trial.[7] Equality of arms is underlined by the equality of access to information: both parties must have equal access to materials, which are relevant to the case.[8] Consequently, the accused has the right to adequate time and facilities to prepare his defence and "to have at his disposal, for the purposes of exonerating himself or of obtaining a reduction of his sentence, all relevant elements that have been or could be collected by the competent authorities."[9] This means that the defendant has the right to have knowledge of all the material that is relevant to the determination of the charges, both inculpating and exculpatory.[10]

What constitutes 'adequate time and facilities' is a case-specific determination and the scope of the term 'facilities' is potentially very far-reaching: there is no clear delineation of what falls specifically under this right and what is covered by other minimum rights.[11] The temporal scope of application of the right to the full disclosure of prosecutorial evidence runs from the early stages of the criminal process, when the accused is to have adequate access to the investigation file so as to be able to challenge provisional detention.[12] The 'facilities' need to be adequate and are, thus, "restricted to those

---

6 E.g. ECtHR, *Jespers v. Belgium*, App. No. 8403/78, Commission's report of 14 December 1981, D&R 27, par. 55, referring to *Ofner and Hopfinger v. Austria,* App. No. 524/59 and 617/59, Report of 23 November 1962, Yearbook 6 (1963), p. 680, *Pataki and Dunshirn v. Austria*, App. Nos. 596/59 and 789/60, Report of 28 March 1963, Yearbook 6(1963), pp. 730-732. See also Human Rights Committee, *Paul Perterer v. Austria*, Comm. No. 1015/2001, Views of 20 July 2004, par. 10.6.

7 This right is laid down in virtually identical texts in Articles 14(3)(b) ICCPR, 6(3)(b) ECHR, and 8(2)(b) ACHR. ECtHR, *Edwards v. The United Kingdom,* App.No. 13071/87, 16 December 1992, par. 36; Human Rights Committee, *Little v. Jamaica*, Communication No. 283/1988, Views of 19 November 1991, par. 8.3. HRC, *Sawyers and McLean v. Jamaica,* Communications Nos. 226/1907 and 256/1981, Views of 11 April 1991, par. 13.6.

8 Cf. J. D. Jackson, The Effect of Human Rights on Criminal Evidentiary Processes: Towards Convergence, Divergence or Realignment?, *Modern Law Review*, Vol. 68,nr. 5, 2005, pp. 751-752 [footnote reference to *Jespers v. Belgium*]. Human Rights Committee, *Perterer v. Austria,* Communication No. 1015/2001, Views of 20 July 2004, par.10.6; ECtHR, *Mattoccia v. Italy*, App. No. 23969/94, Judgment of 25 July 2000, par. 60. See also S. Trechsel, *Human Rights in Criminal Proceedings*, (Oxford: Oxford University Press), 2005, p. 217-218; Van Dijk et al., (eds.), *Theory and Practice of the European Convention on Human* Rights, 4th ed. (Antwerp: Intersentia, 2006), pp. 632-633.

9 ECtHR, *Jespers v. Belgium,* App. No. 8403/78, Commission's report of 14 December 1981, D&R 27, par. 56.

10 ECtHR, *Edwards v. The United Kingdom,* App.No. 13071/87, 16 December 1992.

11 For example, the right to freely access and communicate with counsel is sometimes dealt with as constituting a 'facility', see S. Trechsel, *Human Rights in Criminal Proceedings*, (Oxford: Oxford University Press), 2005, p. 210.

12 E.g. ECtHR, *Mooren v. Germany*, App. No. 11364/03, Judgment of the Grand Chamber, 9 July 2009, par. 124-125; ECtHR, *Garcia Alva v. Germany*, App. No. 23541/94, Judgment of 13 February 2001, par. 39; *Niedbala v. Poland*, App. No. 27915/95, Judgment of 4 July 2000; ECtHR, *Imbrioscia v. Switzerland*, App. No. 13972/88, Judgment of 24 November

which assist or may assist [the accused] in the preparation of his defence."[13] While the case law of the human rights bodies offers only limited guidance for the evaluation of the adequacy of the facilities provided to the defence, the procedural context becomes even more important for a proper evaluation of the element of 'adequacy'.

The basic rule on the disclosure of evidence, that "in principle …the prosecution authorities should disclose to the defence all material evidence in their possession for or against the accused"[14] is, however, not absolute. Other interests may be involved, which necessitate the weighing of the defence's right to have access to information against those other interests. National security considerations and protection of victims and witnesses have been accepted as legitimate grounds for restriction of defence rights.[15] However, measures restricting the rights of the accused must be strictly necessary and any difficulties caused by the limitation of defence rights must be sufficiently counterbalanced in order to ensure a fair trial for the accused.[16] A procedure in which it is only the prosecutor who determines whether certain evidence should be withheld from the accused on public interest grounds has been found to violate the right to a fair trial.[17] When the trial judge assesses the appropriateness of the non-disclosure of certain materials to the defence, the ECtHR has stressed the importance of (1) weighing the public interest against the interest of the accused; and (2) affording the defence an opportunity to participate in the decision-making process to the maximum extent possible.[18] Relevant factors to be investigated include "whether those materials would have been of any assistance for the defence, and whether their disclosure would, at least arguably, have harmed any identifiable public interest."[19] Central for the proper decision-making is whether the non-disclosure was counterbalanced by adequate procedural guarantees and whether it was sufficiently justified.[20]

1993, par. 39; ECtHR, *Lamy v. Belgium*, App. No. 10444/83, Judgment of 30 March 1989.

13 ECtHR, *Jespers v. Belgium,* App. No. 8403/78, Commission's report of 14 December 1981, D&R 27, par. 57: "Despite the slight difference in meaning between the adjective in the French text ["*nécessaire*"] and the one in the English text ['adequate']."

14 ECtHR, *Rowe and Davis v. United Kingdom*, App. No. 28901/95, 16 February 2000, par. 60.

15 E.g. ECtHR, *Moiseyev v. Russia*, App. No.62936/00, Judgment of 9 October 2008, par. 216.

16 ECtHR, *Rowe and Davis v. United Kingdom*, App. No. 28901/95, 16 February 2000, paras. 60-61; ECtHR, *Moiseyev v. Russia*, App. No.62936/00, Judgment of 9 October 2008, par. 216.

17 ECtHR, *Rowe and Davis v. The United Kingdom*, App. No. 28901/95, Judgment of 16 February 2000, par. 66.

18 E.g. ECtHR, *Mirilashvili v. Russia*, App. No. 6293/04, Judgment of 11 December 2008, par. 205.

19 Ibid., par. 206.

20 E.g. Ibid., paras. 203, 209; ECtHR, *Edwards and Lewis v. United Kingdom,* App. Nos. 39647/98 and 40461/98, Judgment of 27 October 2004.

3. *Prosecutorial disclosure in international criminal law*

3.1 ICTY and ICTR

a. General obligations

In the framework of the ad hoc tribunals, the prosecution must hand over to the defence during the pre-trial stage all materials supporting the indictment, copies of witness statements it intends to rely on, and exculpatory evidence.[21] The legal framework presents two types of disclosure obligations: (1) a positive obligation to disclose certain materials; and (2) an obligation to facilitate the inspection of certain materials by the other party. Defence access to prosecutorial disclosure is generally effectuated through the Electronic Disclosure System' (EDS),[22] which, has not been unproblematic for defence to access and to use in terms of being able to conduct effective searches for relevant materials through the considerable amount of information placed in EDS.[23]

With regard to the positive disclosure obligation, within 30 days of the initial appearance, the prosecutor shall disclose all the supporting material accompanying the indictment, as well as all prior statements obtained by the prosecutor from the accused (Rule 66 (A)(i)).[24] Within a time limit set by the Pre-Trial Judge or Trial Chamber, copies of the statements of witnesses who the prosecution intends to call at trial must also be disclosed (Rule 66(A)(ii) ICTY and ICTR RPE).[25] Due to its positive nature, this obligation imposes the duty to explicitly draw defence's attention to this materials, it does not

---

21 ICTY, *Prosecutor v. Krstić*, Appeals Chamber, Decision on Prosecution's Motion to Be Relieved of Obligation to Disclose Sensitive Information Pursuant to Rule 66 (C), IT-98-33-A, 27 March 2003, par. 4.

22 ICTY Practice Direction on 'Establishing Restrictions on Dissemination of Material Disclosure to the Defence by the Prosecutor on the 'Electronic Disclosure System', IC/219/Rev/1, 6 November 2003.

23 See e.g. ICTY, *Prosecutor v. Limaj et al.*, Decision on Joint Defence Motion on Prosecution's Late and Incomplete Disclosure, IT-03-66-T, 7 June 2005; ICTY, *Prosecutor v. Mladic*, Decision on Submissions relative to the proposed "EDS" Method of Disclosure, IT-09-92-T, 26 June 2012.

24 Rule 66 (A) (i) ICTY and ICTR RPE. ICTY, *Prosecutor v. Blaškić*, Decision on the Defence Motion for Sanctions for the Prosecutor's Failure to Comply with Sub-Rule 66(A) of the Rules and the Decision of 27 January 1997 Compelling the Production of all Statements of the Accused, IT-95-14, 15 July 1998.

25 As well as copies of all transcripts and written statements taken in accordance with Rule 92*bis*, Rule 92*ter*, and Rule 92*quater*. Witness statements under Rule 66(A)(ii) refer to "all previous statements of all Prosecution witnesses, in whatever form." ICTR, *Prosecutor v. Bizimungu et al.*, Decision on Prosper Mugiraneza's Motion to Require Strict Compliance with Rule 66(A)(ii), ICTR-99-50-I, 5 May 2004, par. 7; ICTY, *Prosecutor v. Milutinović et al.*, Decision on Ojdanić Motion for Disclosure of Witness Statements and for Finding of Violation of Rule 66(A)(ii), IT-05-87, 29 September 2006, par. 14. In addition, at the ICTY, no less than six weeks before the Pre-Trial Conference, the Prosecution must file, *inter alia*, the list of exhibits (Rule 65*ter*(E)(iii)). See ICTY, *Prosecutor v. Krajišnik and Plavšić*, Decision on Prosecution Motion for Clarification in Respect of Application of Rules 65, 66(B) and 67(C), T. Ch., IT-00-39 & IT-00-40/1, 1 August 2001.

suffice for the prosecutor to place the materials on the EDS for the defence to search for them.[26] Moreover, the prosecution must disclose to the defence, "as soon as practicable", all exculpatory material, i.e. "material known to the Prosecutor which in any way tends to suggest the innocence or mitigate the guilt of the accused or may affect the credibility of prosecution evidence".[27]

With regard to the obligation to facilitate inspection, the prosecution, on request, must permit the defence to inspect the documents in its possession or under its control that (1) "are material to the preparation of the defence," and those that (2) "are intended for use by the Prosecutor as evidence at trial"[28] or (3) "were obtained from or belonged to the accused" (Rule 66(B)). With regard to Rule 66(B) the Appeals Chamber considered that "purely inculpatory material is not necessarily immaterial for the preparation of the Defence"; the prosecution has to consider: "(a) whether the issues to which the material related are subject to a ground of appeal", or "(b) whether the material could reasonably lead to further investigation by the Defence and the discovery of additional evidence admissible under Rule 115 of the Rules."[29] The defence needs to establish a legitimate forensic purpose for seeking additional material and that material needs to be in the possession of the prosecutor.[30]

b. Limitations on disclosure: protection of other interests

The right to have access to information relevant to the case is not absolute. Disclosure of information might, for example, have negative consequences for the security of witnesses or jeopardise state security interests. In such cases, right of the accused to have access to information can be limited.

The *ad hoc* tribunals' framework, under Rule 66(C) RPE, allows the prosecution to apply to the Trial Chamber *in camera* to be relieved from the disclosure obligations in respect of information "the disclosure of which may prejudice further or ongoing investigations, or for any other reasons may be

---

26 A 'courtesy copy' does not mitigate the Prosecutor's failure to comply with the disclosure obligations. ICTY, *Prosecutor v. Lukić and Lukić*, Decision on Milan Lukić's Motion to Suppress Testimony for Failure of Timely Disclosure with Confidential Annexes A and B, IT-98-32/1-T, T. Ch. III, 3 November 2008, par. 17.

27 Rule 68 ICTY and ICTR RPE. This duty is further elaborated in section 3.1.c.

28 E.g. ICTR, *Prosecutor v. Bagasora*, Decision on Interlocutory Appeal Relating to Disclosure Under Rule 66(B) of the Tribunal's Rules of Procedure and Evidence, IT-98-41-AR73, 25 September 2006, par.12.

29 ICTR, *Prosecutor v. Bizimungu et al.*, Decision on Prosper Mugiraneza's Motion to Require Strict Compliance with Rule 66(A)(ii), ICTR-99-50-I, T. Ch., 5 May 2004, par. 16, referring to ICTY, *Prosecutor v. Krstić*, Confidential Decision on the Prosecution's Motion to be Relieved of Obligation to Disclose Sensitive Information Pursuant to Rule 66(C), IT-98-33-A, A. Ch., 27 March 2003, p. 4.

30 E.g. ICTY, *Prosecutor v. Delalić et al.*, Decision on the Motion of the Accused Zejnil Delalić for the Disclosure of Evidence, IT-96-21-T, T. Ch. II, 26 September 1996, paras. 8-9; ICTR, *Prosecutor v. Karemera,* Decision on the Prosecution's Interlocutory Appeal Concerning Disclosure Obligations, ICTR-98-44-AR73.11, 23 January 2008.

contrary to the public interest or affect the security interests of any State."[31] Moreover, exempted from disclosure is the internal work prepared by a party in connection with the investigation or preparation of the case (Rule 70(A) RPE).[32] Written notes made by an investigator, although falling under Rule 70(A) RPE, are disclosable in as far as they refer to witness statements. [33] To the extent that questions were put directly to a witness and notes were made thereof, they fall outside the ambit of Rule 70(A) RPE.[34] According to the Appeals Chamber in *Niyitegeka*, questionnaires put to the prosecution's witnesses were disclosable as witness statements.[35]

In light of the sheer size of the crimes charged before international criminal tribunals and the fact that witness evidence is one of essential sources of evidence before these courts, protection of witnesses has been of major concern for these tribunals. The disclosure requirement is expressly subjected to Rule 53 (public non-disclosure) and Rule 69 (the protection of victims and witnesses – including *inter partes* non-disclosure or delayed disclosure).[36] The most common protective measure applied in the *ad hoc* tribunals' practice, in relation to disclosure, is the late or redacted disclosure of witness-identifying information. In fact, the "system of redacted disclosure is accepted as a virtually unavoidable consequence of the Tribunal's criminal proceedings."[37] According to Rule 69 ICTY RPE, the prosecutor can request protective measures, such as the non-disclosure or late disclosure of the identity of a witness in the pre-trial phase.[38] The disclosure of unredacted witness statements in order to provide the accused with adequate means to prepare for trial, proceeds either shortly before the commencement of the trial (approxi-

---

31 See also Rule 66(C) ICTR.

32 E.g. ICTR, *Prosecutor v. Nahimana et al.*, Public Redacted Version of the Decision on Motions Relating to the Appellant Hassan Ngeze's and the Prosecution's Request for Leave to Present Additional Evidence of Witnesses ABC1 and EB, ICTR-99-52, 27 November 2006, par. 12.

33 ICTY, *Prosecutor v. Blaškić*, IT-95-14-PT, Decision on the Production of Discovery Materials, 27 January 1997, par. 40; Also in ICTR, *Prosecutor v. Ndayambaje*, Decision on Defence Motion for Disclosure, Rules 66, 70(A), and 73 of the Rules, Case No. ICTR-96-8-T, 25 September 2001.

34 ICTR, *Prosecutor v. Niyitegeka*, Appeals Judgement, ICTR-96-14-A, 9 July 2004, paras. 30-36.

35 ICTR, *Prosecutor v. Niyitegeka*, Appeals Judgement, ICTR-96-14-A, 9 July 2004, paras. 33-34. In contrast see the Trial Chamber in Ndayambaye which considered the Prosecutor's witness questionnaires to be covered by the Rule 70(A) exception. See ICTR, *Prosecutor v. Ndayambaje*, Decision on Defence Motion for Disclosure, Rules 66, 70(A), and 73 of the Rules, ICTR-96-8-T, 25 September 2001, paras. 13-16.

36 See e.g. ICTY, *Prosecutor v. Tadic*, Decision on Prosecutor's Motion requesting Protective Measures for Witness "R", IT-94-1-T, 31 July 1996; ICTY, *Prosecutor v Brdjanin and Talic,* Decision on Motion by Prosecution for Protective Measures, IT-99-36-PT, 3 July 2000.

37 G. McIntyre, 'Equality of Arms – Defining Human Rights in the Jurisprudence of the International Criminal Tribunal for the Former Yugoslavia' (2003) 16 *Leiden Journal of International Law* 269, p. 287.

38 Rule 69(C) ICTY& ICTR RPE. Rule 75 deals with protective measures at trial.

mately 30 days)[39] or on a 'rolling basis' prior to testimony of individual witnesses.[40] Although it is undisputed that the interests involved deserve full attention from the organs of the tribunals, the practice of redactions has put a severe strain on tribunals' resources and more specifically has presented various practical challenges to defence in terms of time and resources necessary to evaluate disclosure on its relevance and usefulness as well as time spend on litigating disclosure issues.[41]

Protection of state security interests constitutes another, in terms of defendants' disclosure rights, reductive element that has shaped tribunals' disclosure regimes..[42] Rule 70(B) ICTY RPE was created to encourage state cooperation[43] by excluding from disclosure obligations material that has been obtained confidentially and "solely for the purpose of generating new evidence". The idea is that without such protection, crucial information could be withheld from the Tribunal and, as such, the Tribunal's ability to fulfil its function would be in jeopardy.[44] Thus, without the consent of the information provider, the prosecutor cannot disclose this evidence to the defence and cannot tender it in evidence without prior disclosure to the defence.[45] The protection of Rule 70 extends to an informant's identity, the general subject of his knowledge and also the substance of the shared knowledge, as presented for example in a witness statement.[46] The Trial Chamber possesses only limited discretion to "police the application of Rule 70 in order to pre-

39 E.g. ICTY, *Prosecutor v. Milutinovic et al*, Decision on Prosecution's Motion for Protective Measures, IT-99-37-PT, 17 July 2003.

40 See also ICTR, *Prosecutor v. Bogasora*, Decision and Scheduling Order on the Prosecution Motion for Harmonization and Modification of Protective Measures for Witnesses, ICTR-98-41-T, 5 December 2001 (imposing a 35-day deadline for disclosure of unredacted witness statements before the testimony of the relevant witnesses).

41 E.g. ICTY, *Prosecutor v. Haradinaj*, Decision on Motions on Behalf of Idriz Balaj and Lahi Brahimaj to Recieve Ten Unredacted Witness Statements, IT-04-84-PT, 3 May 2006. Also K. Gibson & C. Lussiaa-Berdou, 'Disclosure of Evidence', in: K. Khan, C. Buisman & C. Gosnell (eds.), *Principles of Evidence in International Criminal* Justice (2010), pp. 306-374.

42 For an historic overview L. Moranchek, Protecting National Security Evidence while Prosecuting War Crimes: Problems and Lessons for International Justice from the ICTY, 31 *The Yale Journal of International Law* 477, (2006), pp. 477-501.

43 ICTY, *Prosecutor v. Milošević*, Public Version of Confidential Decision on the Interpretation and Application of Rule 70, IT-02-54-AR108bis & AR73.3, A. Ch., 23 October 2002, par. 18ii, 19. R. Goldstone, A View from the Prosecution, 2 *Journal of International Criminal Justice* 380 (2004), p. 381.

44 ICTY, *Prosecutor v. Brđjanin and Talić*, Public Version of the Confidential Decision on the Alleged Illegality of Rule 70, IT-99-36-T, 6 May 2002, par. 18.

45 E.g. ICTR, *Prosecutor v. Nahimana et al.*, Public Redacted Version of the Decision on Motions Relating to the Appellant Hassan Ngeze's and the Prosecution's Request for Leave to Present Additional Evidence of Witnesses ABC1 and EB, ICTR-99-52, 27 November 2006, par. 12.

46 ICTY, *Prosecutor v. Milošević*, Public Version of Confidential Decision on the Interpretation and Application of Rule 70, IT-02-54-AR108bis & AR73.3, A. Ch., 23 October 2002, par. 22-23.

vent its misapplication."[47] Applying an objective test, the Trial Chamber may ascertain the confidential basis of information by considering (1) the information itself, (2) accepting the prosecution's assertion; (3) the information provider's confirmation; and (4) any indication from the face of the document itself.[48] In practice, the tribunals have struggled with adjusting both legal framework as well as judicial interpretation of it to the realities of international criminal prosecutions. The tribunals' dependence on state cooperation in providing valuable intelligence information has subjected them to political pressure from states. According to Goldstone, the tribunals' first prosecutor, "[a]rrangements to receive police information, and, even more so, intelligence information, required lengthy, complex and detailed negotiations."[49] Notably, the United States 'stance in this has provided "the most dramatic example of state hesitation to provide secret evidence to international tribunals without protections", but other states have been hesitant too.[50] Gradually, the rules have been changed, while the rights of the defence have been more restricted for the sake of ensuring state cooperation. The "creeping erosion of defendants' rights to discovery"[51], at ICTY, has cumulated in a rule changes in 2003 and 2004, whereby even the disclosure of exculpatory evidence was subjected to the Rule 70 restrictions allowing the prosecutor to apply in camera for relief from disclosure obligations for protection of ongoing investigations, public interests and state security interests (Rule 68(iv)).

c. Disclosure of exculpatory evidence

The prosecutor's duty to disclose exculpatory evidence to the defence is of universal application.[52] Fundamental to a fair trial and central to the prosecution's duty as "ministers of justice assisting in the administration of justice"[53]', the duty to disclose exculpatory evidence is an essential requirement to preserve equality of arms between the parties.[54] Perhaps unsurprisingly,

47 Ibid., par. 26.

48 Ibid., par. 29.

49 R. Goldstone, A View from the Prosecution, 2 *Journal of International Criminal Justice* 380 (2004), p. 381.

50 L. Moranchek, Protecting National Security Evidence while Prosecuting War Crimes: Problems and Lessons for International Justice from the ICTY, 31 *The Yale Journal of International Law* 477, (2006), pp. 485.

51 Ibid., pp. 489.

52 A. Orie, Accusatorial v. Inquisitorial Approaches in International Criminal Proceedings Prior to Establishment of the ICC and the Proceedings before the ICC, in: A. Cassese, P. Gaeta and J.RW.D. Jones (eds.), *The Rome Statute of the International Criminal Court: A Commentary*, Oxford University Press, Vol. II, 2002, pp. 1439-1495, p. 1483; G. Sluiter, H. Friman, S. Linton, S. Zappala and S. Vasiliev, *International Criminal Procedure*, 2013, p. 54; See also J. Jones, 'Disclosure in A. Cassese (ed.), *Oxford Companion to international Criminal Justice,* 2009.

53 ICTY, *Prosecutor v. Kordić and Ćerkez*, Decision on Motions to Extend Time for Filing Appellant's Briefs, IT-95-14/2-A. A. Ch., 11 May 2001, par. 14.

54 S. Zappala, The Prosecutor's Duty to Disclose Exculpatory Materials and the Recent Amendement of Rule 68 ICTY RPE, 2 *Journal of International Criminal Justice*, 2004, pp. 620-630, pp. 622-623.

the disclosure of exculpatory material is one of the most litigated areas in international criminal practice. In their case law, the ad hoc tribunals have constantly underlined that the Prosecution's obligation to disclose exculpatory material "is not a secondary one, to be complied with after everything else is done; is it as important as the obligation to prosecute."[55]

The duty to hand over exculpatory evidence is positive and continuous obligation, which applies even in the case of an appeal or after the termination of the trial.[56] Prosecution must disclose to the defence any material which (1) may suggest the innocence or (2) mitigate the guilt of the accused; or (3) may affect the credibility of the prosecution evidence.[57] He has a discretionary power to determine which materials fall within the Rule 68 obligations and there is a rebuttable presumption that the Prosecution is operating in good faith.[58] The reference to the 'actual knowledge' in Rule 68 narrows the disclosure obligation to material that is in 'possession or control' of the prosecution.[59] Rule 68 certainly does not impose an obligation on the prosecution to search for material of which it has no knowledge and to replace defence investigations,[60] nor does it entitle the defence to embark on a "fishing expedition".[61]

---

55 ICTY, *Prosecutor v. Kordić and Ćerkez*, Decision on Motions to Extend Time for Filing Appellant's Briefs, IT-95-14/2-A. A. Ch., 11 May 2001, par. 14. See also ICTR, *Prosecutor v. Bizimungu et al.*, Judgment and Sentence, ICTR-99-50-T, T. Ch., 30 September 2011, par. 134, references in footnote 205.

56 ICTY, *Prosecutor v. Blaškić*, Decision on the Appellant's Motions for the Production of Material, Suspension or Extension of the Briefing Schedule, and Additional Filings, IT-95-14-A, 26 September 2000, par. 32.

57 E.g. ICTR, *Prosecutor v. Karemera et al.*, Decision on Interlocutory Appeal Regarding the Role of the Prosecutor's Electronic Disclosure Suite in Discharging Disclosure Obligations, ICTR-98-44-AR73.7, 30 June 2006, par. 9; ICTY, *Prosecutor v. Blaškić*, Confidential Decision on Prosecution's Application to Seek Guidance from the Appeals Chamber regarding Redaction of the Statement of "Witness Two" for the Purposes of Disclosure to Paško Ljubičić under Rule 68, IT-95-14-A, 30 March 2004, par. 32.

58 E.g. ICTY, *Prosecutor v. Kordic and Cerkez,* Case No. IT-95-14/2-A, Judgement, 17 December 2004, par. 183; ICTR, *Nahimana et al. v. Prosecutor*, Decision on Appellant Jean-Bosco Barayagwiza's Motions for Leave to Present Additional Evidence pursuant to Rule 115 of the Rules of Procedure and Evidence, ICTR-99-52-A, 8 December 2006, par. 34; ICTY, *Prosecutor v. Kordić and Čerkez*, Appeal Judgment, IT-95-14/2-A, 17 December 2004, par. 183; ICTY, *Prosecutor v. Blaškić*, Appeal Judgment, IT- 95-14-A, 29 July 2004, par. 264; ICTY, *Prosecutor v. Krstić*, Appeal Judgment, IT-98-33-A, 19 April 2004, par. 190.

59 ICTY, *Prosecutor v. Blaškić*, IT-95-14-PT, Decision on the Production of Discovery Materials, 27 January 1997, paras. 47, 50. S. Zappala, The Prosecutor's Duty to Disclose Exculpatory Materials and the Recent Amendement of Rule 68 ICTY RPE, 2 *Journal of International Criminal Justice*, 2004, pp. 620-630, p. 624.

60 ICTY, *Prosecutor v. Blagojević et al.*, Joint Decision on Motions Related to Production of Evidence, IT-02-60-PT, 12 December 2002, par. 26. The defence, according to the Trial Chamber, is not bound by the prosecutor's characterisation of material as exculpatory, and in fact, it is defence counsel who bears the "primary responsibility for investigating the charges against an accused, including seeking and gathering information related to those charges." Moreover, the Trial Chamber emphasized that "Rule 68 also does not translate into a right for the defence to "receive all of the Prosecution's evidence that could be *use-*

Initially, the ICTY judges prioritized disclosure obligations over protection of confidentiality.[62] In 2004 a second amendment to Rule 68 was effected at ICTY, which subjected the application of Rule 68 to Rule 70.[63] This was judges' solution in relation to the conflicts between the prosecutor's respect for the confidentiality of sources and information and his disclosure obligations. Subjecting the Rule 68 disclosure to confidentiality agreements under Rule 70(B) ICTY seems to reverse the initial priority and gives the prosecutor some leeway to withhold potentially exculpatory materials that have been provided to him on a confidential basis with the purpose of generating new evidence. Although the amendment was "intended to further the interests of justice, providing safeguards for on-going or future investigations, increasing the expediency of proceedings, and protecting the confidentiality interests of states or other sensitive sources," it was questioned "whether the new Rule 68 is consistent with the right of the accused to a fair trial, with the role of the Prosecutor in international criminal law, and, ultimately, with the proper administration of justice."[64] Without an obligation to investigate both incriminating and exculpatory information, it remains unclear what the ICTY prosecutor's obligations are with regard to exculpatory elements that were obtained under the cloak of confidentiality, and are unsupported by additional evidence (for whatever reason). Ideally, the prosecutor should investigate the potentially exculpatory leads in order to disclose the evidence to defence; or apply to the Trial Chamber to be relieved of his disclosure obligations in that regard. The prosecutor's ethical standards, objective as well as subjective, may play the most crucial role in the resolution of this issue.

The prosecutor must make Rule 68-disclosure determination on the basis of fairness considerations;[65] however, only when the defence can show the wrongfulness of this decision will the Chamber interfere.[66] Of course, the

---

ful in the defence against charges in the Amended Indictments" (*Id.*, footnote reference omitted).

61 ICTR, *Nahimana et al. v. Prosecutor*, Decision on Motions Relating to the Appellants Hassan Ngeze's and the Prosecution's Requests for Leave to Present Additional Evidence of Witness ABC1 and EB, ICTR-99-52-A, 27 November 2006, par. 11, and footnote 38 references. ICTY, *Prosecutor v. Hadžihasanović et al,* Decision on Appeal from Refusal to Grant Access to Confidential Material in Another Case, ., IT-01-47-AR73, 23 April 2002, p. 3. See also ICTR, *Prosecutor v. Bizimungu et al.*, ICTR-99-50-T, Decision on Bicamumpaka's Motion for Disclosure of Exculpatory Evidence (MDR Files), 17 November 2004, paras. 11-14.

62 ICTY, *Prosecutor v. Brđjanin and Talić*, Public Version of the Confidential Decision on the Alleged Illegality of Rule 70, IT-99-36-T, 6 May 2002, paras. 19-21.

63 Effected in July 2004. No such amendment has been made at the ICTR.

64 S. Zappala, The Prosecutor's Duty to Disclose Exculpatory Materials and the Recent Amendement of Rule 68 ICTY RPE, 2 *Journal of International Criminal Justice*, 2004, pp. 620-630, p. 624.

65 ICTY, *Prosecutor v. Oric*, Decision on Ongoing Complaints About Prosecutorial Non-Compliance with Rule 68 of the Rules, IT-03-68-T, 13 December 2005.

66 ICTR, *Prosecutor v Bagilishema*, Decision on the Motion for a Review of the Decision by the President of the Appeals Chamber; on the Motion pursuant to Article 73 of the Rules

opportunities for defence to check whether the prosecution complies with its disclosure obligations are limited. For example, in *Blaškić*, the Trial Chamber ordered the prosecutor to respond to defence questions about the possession and nature of certain materials.[67] According to the Trial Chamber, it was not sufficient for the prosecutor to declare that she "recognizes her obligations under the Rules and has complied with them."[68]

When applying to the Trial Chamber to evaluate prosecution's disclosure practice the defence needs to meet a certain threshold: of (1) defining or identifying with reasonable specificity the material sought; (2) if disputed, showing *prima facie,* that the material is in the possession or control of the prosecutor; and (3) if disputed, showing *prima facie* that the material is of potentially exculpatory nature.[69] Each of the steps presents the defence with difficulties, because the defence is particularly unapt to monitor prosecutorial disclosure practice in light of its tight time and resources.[70] Although the Chambers have emphasized the fundamental nature of the prosecutorial disclosure of exculpatory evidence,[71] and have interpreted the relevant material broadly, encompassing any information that could be relevant to defence of the accused,[72] they too were mindful of the strain that broad disclosure obligations place upon the prosecutor. With this in mind the Appeals Chamber considered that "that Rule 68 does not require the Prosecution to identify the material being disclosed to the Defence as exculpatory."[73] The downside for

of Procedure and Evidence Praying to Chamber to Order the Prosecutor to Disclose to the Defence the Tapes Containing the Recordings of Radio Muhabura; On the Motion for Review of the Decision by the President of the Appeals Chamber, ICTR-95-1A-A, 6 February 2002.

67 ICTY, *Prosecutor v. Blaškić*, IT-95-14-PT, Decision on the Production of Discovery Materials, 27 January 1997, par. 47.

68 Ibid.

69 ICTR, *Prosecutor v. Juvénal Kajelijeli*, Case No. ICTR-98-44A-A, Judgement (AC), 23 May 2005, par. 262; *Prosecutor v. Radoslav Brdjanin*, Case No. IT-99-36A, Decision on Appellant's Motion for Disclosure Pursuant to Rule 68 and Motion for an Order to the Registrar to Disclose Certain Materials (AC), 7 December 2004.

70 K. Gibson & C. Lussiaa-Berdou, 'Disclosure of Evidence', in: K. Khan, C. Buisman & C. Gosnell (eds.), *Principles of Evidence in International Criminal* Justice (2010), pp. 326-335.

71 In later case law, the importance of disclosure obligations to a fair trial has been underscored, see e.g. ICTY, *Prosecutor v. Krstić*, Appeal Judgment, IT-98-33-A, 19 April 2004, par. 180; ICTY, *Prosecutor v. Orić*, Decision on Ongoing Complaints About Prosecutorial Non-Compliance With Rule 68 of the Rules, IT-03-68-T, T. Ch., 13 December 2005, par. 20; ICTY, *Prosecutor v. Stakić*, Appeals Chamber Judgment, IT-97-24-A, 22 March 2006, par. 188; ICTY, *Prosecutor v. Karadzić*, Decision on Accused's Motion for Additional Time to Prepare Cross examination of Momčilo Mandić, IT-95-5/18-T, 2 July 2010, par. 4.

72 ICTR, *Prosecutor v. Kalimanzira,* Appeals Chamber Judgment, ICTR-05-88-A, A.Ch., 20 October 2010, par. 18, 20; ICTR, *Karemera et al*, Decision on 'Joseph Nzirorera's Appeal from Decision on Tenth Rule 68 Motion, 14 May 2008, para 12, citing with approval *Prosecutor v. Bagosora et al*, Case No. ICTR-98-41-T, Decision on Disclosure of Defence Witness Statements in the Possession of the Prosecution Pursuant to Rule 68 (A), 8 March 2006, par. 5.

73 ICTY, *Prosecutor v. Krstić*, Appeal Judgment, IT-98-33-A, 19 April 2004, par. 190.

defence is that it has to work through a magnitude of materials that the Prosecution has placed on EDS.[74] In *Karemera et al.,* the Appeals Chamber considered that "the Prosecution has for all intents and purposes buried the exculpatory materials."[75] According to the Appeals Chamber, an electronic search machine could not replace the prosecutor's individualized assessment of the material. While the Appeals Chamber did not provide clear guidance on the extent of the prosecution's identification obligation, it did suggest making a separate file with exculpatory material.

Where the defence manages to satisfy all three conditions mentioned above, and the Chamber determines that the prosecutor failed to disclose these materials 'as soon as practicable', a violation of disclosure obligations is established. In practice, there are ample examples of prosecutorial disclosure violations and particularly the practice of disclosure of exculpatory evidence has proved receptive to violations.[76] Such a violation, however, does not automatically lead to imposition of a remedy for the defence, an issue that will be considered in section 4.

3.2 ICC

a. General obligations

At the ICC, the disclosure regime takes its predecessors practice into account but makes several important adjustments to accommodate the realities of prosecutions before the ICC.[77] Pre-trial disclosure consists of the pre-confirmation hearing disclosure and pre-trial disclosure.[78] Before the confirmation of charges hearing the prosecutor needs to provide the defence with a document detailing the charges (DCC) and the list of supporting evidence which the prosecution intends to rely upon at the hearing should be disclosed

---

74 E.g. ICTR, *Prosecutor v. Karemera et al.*, Decision on Interlocutory Appeal Regarding the Role of the Prosecutor's Electronic Disclosure Suite in Discharging Disclosure Obligations, ICTR-98-44-AR73.7, 30 June 2006, par. 13 (defence challenge to the EDS).

75 Ibid., par. 15.

76 See among many authorities ICTY, *Prosecutor v. Karadzic,* Public redacted Version of "Decision on Accused's Ninety-Third Disclosure Violation Motion" issues on 13 October 2014, IT-95-5/18-T, T.Ch., 20 March 2015; ICTR, *Prosecutor v Bizimungu et al.,* Judgment and Sentence, ICTR-99-50-T, T.Ch., 30 September 2011, paras. 175, 177.

77 Article 67(1)(a) and (b) ICC Statute specifies the right of the accused to be informed promptly and in detail of the charges and to have adequate time and facilities to prepare a defence.

78 The ICC's legal framework does not contain express rules on disclosure in relation to the issuance of an arrest warrant and in relation to applications for interim release. However, the judges have affirmed the defence right to have access to documents which are essential for the purposes of applying for interim release and challenging the validity of the arrest warrant, but having regard to the sensitive nature of such disclosure its scope might be limited. ICC, *Prosecutor v. Mbarushimana*, Prosecution Response to the 'Defence Request for Disclosure', ICC-01/04-01/10-31, 5 January 2011, PTC I, p. 17; ICC, *Prosecutor v. Bemba*, ICC-01/05-01/08, Judgment on the Appeal of Mr Jean-Pierre Bemba Gombo against the decision of the Pre-Trial Chamber III entitled 'Decision on application for interim release', 16 December 2008, A.Ch., par. 26.

no later than 30 days before the confirmation hearing (art. 61(3) ICC Statute, Rule 121(2)(3) ICC RPE).[79] This 30 days deadline has been approached by the prosecution as the final deadline for disclosure, which has become prosecutions "standard operating procedure".[80] Considering the requirement for defence to file its list of evidence fifteen days before that confirmation of charges hearing (Rule 121(6) RPE), this prosecution's practice of late disclosure has had a significant negative effect on defences time and resources for preparation for the confirmation of charges hearing. Notably, in *Kenyatta* the Prosecution disclosed its DCC 30 days prior to the confirmation hearing, an 'in-depth analysis chart' of 6,600 pages length to assist the defence and judges in understanding the prosecution's case, 1,300 pages incriminatory disclosure and 1,200 pages of witness statements' transcripts.[81]

The Pre-Trial Chamber monitors the disclosure practice (121(2) ICC RPE) and may issue additional orders on the disclosure of information for the hearing.[82] The *inter partes* disclosure process is complemented by the obligation to communicate evidence to the Chamber.[83] In protecting the defence from being overburdened with massive disclosure, the Pre Trial Chamber considered that

> "the most important factor in both safeguarding the rights of the defence and enabling the Chamber to exercise its function is not for Prosecutor to disclose the greatest volume of evidence, but to disclose the evidence which is of true relevance to the case, whether that evidence be incriminating or exculpatory. In fact, disclosure of a considerable volume of evidence for which it is difficult or impossible to comprehend the usefulness for the case merely puts the defence in a position where it cannot genuinely exercise its rights, and serves to hold back the proceedings." [84]

Thus, the prosecutor must subject the disclosure material to "a sufficiently detailed legal analysis," which should be presented as a summary table showing the "relevance of evidence presented in relation to the constituent elements of the crimes with which the person is charged."[85]

---

79 The standard the prosecution has to meet is "substantial grounds to believe that the defendant committed the crimes charged", Art. 61(5) ICC Statute.

80 K.A.A. Khan and A.A. Shah, Defensive Practices: Representing Clients before the International Criminal Court, *Law and Contemporary Problems* 76, 191, 2013, p. 202.

81 Ibid., p.191, footnote 46 and accompanying text.

82 ICC, *Prosecutor v. Bemba*, Decision on the Evidence Disclosure System and Setting a Timetable for Disclosure between the Parties, ICC-01/05-01/08-55, 31 July 2008, p. 22.

83 Rule 121(2)(c) ICC RPE. ICC, *Prosecutor v. Lubanga Dyilo*, Decision on the Final System of Disclosure and the Establishment of a Timetable, ICC-01/04-01/06-102, 15 May 2006, par. 65-66. ICC, *Prosecutor v. Bemba*, Decision on the Evidence Disclosure System and Setting a Timetable for Disclosure between the Parties, ICC-01/05-01/08-55, 31 July 2008, paras. 43, 47. In *Lubanga* the Single Judge rejected the defence's request for full access to the entire investigation file of the prosecutor in that case. (Idem, Annex par. 15).

84 ICC, *Prosecutor v. Bemba*, Decision on the Evidence Disclosure System and Setting a Timetable for Disclosure between the Parties, ICC-01/05-01/08-55, 31 July 2008, par. 67.

85 Ibid., paras. 66, 70.

After the confirmation of charges, the pre-trial disclosure is governed by Article 67(2) (disclosure of exculpatory evidence); Rule 76-77 (the Prosecutor's disclosure obligations) and Rules 78-80 (defence disclosure) and inspection (Rules 77-78), which imposes on the relevant party the obligation (i) to allow the other party to inspect the relevant books, photographs, maps, and tangible objects, and (ii) to provide those copies requested during inspection.[86] Similar to Rule 66(B), Rule 77 ICC RPE requires the prosecutor to permit the defence to inspect any books, documents, photographs and other tangible objects in the prosecutor's possession or control which (1) are material to the preparation of the defence, (2) are intended for use at the confirmation hearing or at trial, or (3) were obtained from or belonged to the suspect/accused.[87] The prosecutor is required to provide copies or photographs of the pieces of evidence requested during the inspection.[88] Furthermore, the record of the proceedings of the Pre-Trial Chamber is transmitted to the Trial Chamber (Rule 130 RPE) and the Trial Chamber can order the disclosure of information not previously disclosed (Art. 64(3)(c)) or the production of additional evidence (Art. 64(6)(d) ICC Statute).

b. Limitations on disclosure: protection of other interests

Rule 81 ICC RPE details the general restrictions on disclosure obligations:[89] (1) not subjected to disclosure are the internal documents; (2) disclosure may be limited where it would prejudice ongoing investigations, in which case the prosecutor shall apply to the Chamber *ex parte* for a ruling on the matter; (3) the disclosure of materials subject to confidentiality agreements may be limited as well as (4) disclosure of material that might endanger victims or witnesses.[90] Importantly, the Rule 81 emphasizes that the undisclosed material

86 ICC, *Prosecutor v. Lubanga Dyilo*, Decision on the Final System of Disclosure and the Establishment of a Timetable, ICC-01/04-01/06-102, 15 May 2006, p. 4.

87 See also ICC, *Prosecutor v. Lubanga Dyilo,* Decision on the scope of the prosecution's disclosure obligations as regards defence witnesses, ICC-01/04-01/06-2624, 12 November 2010, par. 13.

88 See e.g. ICC, *Prosecutor v. Abu Garda*, Decision Scheduling a Hearing on Issues relating to Disclosure between the Parties, ICC-02/05-02/09-18, 30 May 2009, PTC I, par. 5. ICC, *Prosecutor v. Lubanga Dyilo,* Decision on the scope of the prosecution's disclosure obligations as regards defence witnesses, ICC-01/04-01/06-2624, 12 November 2010, par. 16.

89 In *Lubanga* the Single Judge issued a decision laying out the principles of application of Rule 81 (2) and (4) ICC RPE. See ICC, *Prosecutor v. Lubanga Dyilo,* Decision Establishing General Principles Governing Applications to Restrict Disclosure pursuant to Rule 81 (2) and (4) of the Rules of Procedure and Evidence, ICC-01/04-01/06-108-Corr, 30 May 2006, par. 13.

90 When making an assessment of whether to authorize non-disclosure of witness identities to the defence, the Chamber has to take into account the following three most important considerations: (1) the endangerment of the witness or of members of his or her family that the disclosure of the identity of the witness may cause; (2) the necessity of the protective measure; and (3) why the Pre-Trial Chamber considered that the measure would not be prejudicial to or inconsistent with the rights of the accused and a fair and impartial trial. Moreover, an assessment of subsidiarity must be made; if "less restrictive protective measures are sufficient and feasible, a Chamber must choose those measures over more

may not be introduced into evidence without adequate prior disclosure to the accused. The operation of any protective measures is subject to ultimate control by the Chambers.[91] To ensure the safety, well-being, dignity and privacy of victims and witnesses (Art. 68(1), Rule 81, 87), the Court can take protective measures such as conduct *in camera* proceedings, grant anonymity, allow summary of evidence or information instead of disclosing them (Art. 61(5)), and other appropriate protective measures.[92]

One of the common protective measures, just as at the *ad hoc* tribunals, is the practice of redacting any identifying information from the evidence, which practice has certainly been "sweeping and resource-intensive".[93] In *Katanga & Ngudjolo* the Appeals Chamber rejected the Pre-Trial Chamber's ruling that Rule 81(4), in its literal interpretation, does not include third individuals (called by the prosecution as 'innocent third parties' who are named in the statements of prosecution witnesses) other than prosecution witnesses, victims and members of their family.[94] The Appeals Chamber extended Rule 81(4) protections "to persons who may be placed at risk as a result of the activities of the Court, but 'who are not victims, current or prospective prosecution witnesses or sources, or members of their families'."[95] Appeals Cham-

---

restrictive measures." The analysis should be conducted on a case-by-case basis. And the Chambers have an obligation to periodically review the decision authorizing the redactions in case of changing circumstances. ICC, *Prosecutor v. Lubanga Dyilo*, Judgment on the appeal of Mr. Thomas Lubanga Dyilo against the decision of Pre-Trial Chamber I entitled "First Decision on the Prosecution Requests and Amended Requests for Redactions under Rule 81", ICC-01/04-01/06-773, A. CH., 14 December 2006, par. 21, 33. ICC, *Prosecutor v. Katanga and Ngudjolo Chui*, Judgment on the appeal of the Prosecutor against the decision of Pre-Trial Chamber I entitled "First Decision on the Prosecution Request for Authorisation to Redact Witness Statements", ICC-01/04-01/07-475, 13 May 2008 paras. 67, 71, 73.

91 ICC, *Prosecutor v. Katanga and Ngudjolo*, Judgement on the Appeals of the Prosecutor against the "Decision on Evidentiary Scope of the Confirmation Hearing, Preventive Relocation and Disclosure under Article 67(2) of the Statute and Rule 77 of the Rules" of Pre-Trial Chamber I, 26 November 2008, ICC-01/04-01/07-776, par. 93.

92 In *Lubanga* case the Single Judge considered the prosecutor's practice of providing the defence with redacted documents, without the authorization of the Pre-Trial Chamber, as inappropriate. ICC, *Prosecutor v. Lubanga Dyilo*, Decision on the Prosecution Practice to Provide to the Defence Redacted Versions of Evidence and Materials without Authorization by the Chamber, PTC I. (Judge Steiner), ICC-01/04-01-06-355, 25 August 2006 [*Lubanga* Decision on the Practice of Redactions].

93 K.A.A. Khan and A.A. Shah, Defensive Practices: Representing Clients before the International Criminal Court, *Law and Contemporary Problems* 76, 191, 2013, p. 206.

94 ICC, *Prosecutor v. Katanga and Ngudjolo Chui*, Judgment on the appeal of the Prosecutor against the decision of Pre-Trial Chamber I entitled "First Decision on the Prosecution Request for Authorisation to Redact Witness Statements", ICC-01/04-01/07-475, 13 May 2008 [*Katanga and Ngudjolo Chui* Appeal Decision on Redactions].

95 ICC, *Prosecutor v. Katanga and Ngudjolo Chui*, Judgment on the appeal of the Prosecutor against the decision of Pre-Trial Chamber I entitled "First Decision on the Prosecution Request for Authorisation to Redact Witness Statements", ICC-01/04-01/07-475, 13 May 2008 paras. 40, 55. Referring to the jurisprudence of the ECtHR, the ICC Appeals Chamber reasoned that whether or not a redaction would be appropriate has to be determined on a case-by-case basis, while making a careful assessment so as "to ensure that any measures restricting the rights of the Defence that are taken to protect individuals at risk are

ber elaborated the appropriate factors for the Pre-Trial Chamber to consider when faced with such requests for a redaction, so as to provide clear guidance.[96] One of the additional factors is the following: "in balancing the various interests at stake, the Pre-Trial Chamber must make sure that adequate safeguards are in place to protect the interests of the suspect so as to comply, as far as possible, with the requirements of adversarial proceedings and equality of arms.[97]" The addition of 'as far as possible' seems to refer to the particular stage of the proceedings, namely the pre-confirmation of charges phase, where the rights accorded to an accused have a more limited application as compared to the trial proceedings.

From the perspective of defence, the extended application of far-reaching redactions, the "almost reflexive imposition" of these redactions, and the cumbersome process of imposition and the piecemeal approach to lifting of redactions has been a particularly worrying aspect of defence practice before the ICC.[98] In an attempt to minimize the burden upon the Court created by the case-by-case approval of every redaction applied for by the prosecution, Trial Chamber in the *Kenya* cases has authorized categorical redaction of information to be imposed *inter partes*.[99] Defence counsel have indicated that the intended speedier disclosure came "with a significant new burden in the defence having to review the *proprio motu* redactions imposed by the prosecution, with little information as to the specific underlying justification for the redactions".[100]

c. Disclosure of exculpatory evidence

Where at the ad hoc tribunals the duty of the prosecutor to act as a Minister of Justice only extends towards the disclosure of exculpatory evidence, the ICC has taken a step forward in that regard by obliging the prosecutor to search explicitly for both incriminatory and exculpatory evidence (Article 54(1) ICC Statute). In addition, Article 67(2) imposes an ongoing duty upon

---

strictly necessary and sufficiently counterbalanced by the procedures taken by the Pre-Trial Chamber." (Idem, par. 59).

96 ICC, *Prosecutor v. Katanga and Ngudjolo Chui*, Judgment on the appeal of the Prosecutor against the decision of Pre-Trial Chamber I entitled "First Decision on the Prosecution Request for Authorisation to Redact Witness Statements", ICC-01/04-01/07-475, 13 May 2008 paras. 70-73.

97 *Katanga and Ngudjolo Chui* Appeal Decision on Redactions, par. 73.

98 See for an elaborate discussion K.A.A. Khan and A.A. Shah, Defensive Practices: Representing Clients before the International Criminal Court, *Law and Contemporary Problems* 76, 191, 2013, pp. 205-218.

99 ICC, *Prosecutor v Samoei Ruto and Arap Sang*, Decision on the Protocol Establishing a Redaction Regime, Case No. ICC-01/09-01/11-458, 27 September 2012. See also ICC, *Prosecutor v. Gbagbo*, Decision on the Protocol Establishing a Redaction Regime, ICC-02/11-01/11-737, 15 December 2014; ICC, *Prosecutor v. Bemba Gombo, Kilolo Musamba, Mangenda Kobongo, Babala Wandu and Arido,* Protocol Establishing a Redaction Regime, ICC-01/05-01/13-959-Anx, 22 May 2015.

100 K.A.A. Khan and A.A. Shah, Defensive Practices: Representing Clients before the International Criminal Court, *Law and Contemporary Problems* 76, 191, 2013, p. 214.

the prosecutor to disclose, as soon as practicable, evidence in the prosecutor's possession or control which he or she believes shows or tends to show (1) the innocence of the accused, (2) or mitigate the guilt of the accused, or (3) which may affect the credibility of prosecution evidence.[101] Compared to Rule 68, Article 67(2) is more explicitly presented in the framework of the accused's rights; it explicitly refers to material that must be in the prosecutor's possession or control[102] and instead of 'actual knowledge' the prosecutor's 'belief' about the exculpatory nature of the material triggers the disclosure obligation. Although the general rule is for the prosecutor to assess the value of the evidence and to decide upon its relevance to the defence,[103] the judges are the final arbiters in case of doubt.[104]

In *Lubanga* the Trial Chamber considered that an accused has "an absolute entitlement" to the disclosure of exculpatory materials, which encompass all the materials that "may contribute to a resolution of material issues in the case in favour of the accused".[105] The disclosure must take place as soon as the prosecutor identifies the material[106] and is of an ongoing nature. [107] Although ideally, the investigation should be completed by the time of the confirmation of charges,[108] this is neither required by the legal provisions nor corresponds to the realities of investigations.[109] According to the Appeals

---

101 This has been considered as a clear definition of 'exculpatory' evidence, see ICC, *Prosecutor v. Lubanga Dyilo*, Decision on the Consequences of non-disclosure of Exculpatory Materials covered by Article 54(3)(e) agreements and the application to stay the prosecution of the accused, together with certain other issues raised at the Status Conference on 10 June 2008, 13 June 2008, par. 88-89.

102 Ad hoc tribunals' case law has adopted this same requirement.

103 ICC, *Prosecutor v. Lubanga Dyilo*, Decision on the Consequences of Non-disclosure of Exculpatory Materials Covered by Article 54(3)(e) Agreements and the Application to Stay the Prosecution of the Accused, together with Certain Other Issues Raised at the Status Conference on 10 June 2008, ICC-01/04-01/06-1401, T. Ch., 13 June 2008, par. 87.

104 ICC, *Prosecutor v. Lubanga Dyilo*, Redacted version of "Decision on the prosecution's filing entitled "Prosecution's provision of information to the Trial Chamber" filed on 3 September 2007", Annex 1, ICC-01/04-01/06, T. Ch. I, 26 September 2007, par. 12. Rule 83 ICC RPE adds that "[t]he Prosecutor may request as soon as practicable a hearing on an *ex parte* basis before the Chamber dealing with the matter for the purpose of obtaining a ruling under Article 67, paragraph 2."

105 ICC, *Prosecutor v. Lubanga Dyilo*, Decision Issuing a Confidential and a Public Redacted Version of Decision on Disclosure issues, responsibilities for protective measures and other procedural matters, ICC-01/04-01/06, 8 May 2008, par. 94.

106 ICC, *Prosecutor v. Lubanga Dyilo*, Decision on the Final System of Disclosure and the Establishment of a Timetable, ICC-01/04-01/06-102, 15 May 2006, p. 5, Annex paras. 119, 124 -131.

107 ICC, *Prosecutor v. Lubanga Dyilo*, Decision Regarding the Timing and Manner of Disclosure and the Date of Trial, ICC-01/04-01/06, 9 November 2007.

108 ICC, *Prosecutor v. Callixte Mbarushimana*, Case No. ICC-01/04-01/10, Judgment In The Appeal of the Prosecutor against the Decision of Pre-Trial Chamber I of 16 December 2011, entitled "Decision on the Confirmation of Charges", 30 May 2012, par. 44.

109 ICC, *Prosecutor v. Lubanga Dyilo*, Judgment on the Prosecutor's appeal against the decision of Pre-Trial Chamber I entitled "Decision Establishing General Principles Governing Applications to Restrict Disclosure pursuant to Rule 81 (2) and (4) of the Rules of Procedure and Evidence", ICC-01/04-01/06, 13 October 2006, paras. 54, 55.

Chamber, such a restriction upon prosecution's investigations could deprive the Court of crucial evidence, both inculpatory and exculpatory.[110] Thus, the prosecutor can continue his investigations after the confirmation of charges and remains under the obligation to disclose any inculpatory evidence he intends to use at trial or which is exculpatory, sufficiently in advance of the trial so as to give adequate preparation time to the accused.[111] However, before the confirmation of charges hearing, the prosecutor is expected to disclose all the evidence that is potentially exonerating or material to the preparation of the defence.[112] In the *Mbarushimana* and the *Kenya* cases the Pre-Trial Chamber considered it fair to oblige the prosecution to organise his office to effect total disclosure at the pre-confirmation stage in a timely fashion.[113] In addition, the Chamber ordered the prosecution to provide the defence with summaries explaining the relevance of all disclosed potentially exculpatory material.[114] The prosecutor disagreed arguing that it is "manifestly unequal to require the prosecution to bear its own burden to establish substantial evidence to hold the person for trial and also to bear the burden to affirmatively guide the defence to understand and fashion a responsive case".[115] The defence argued that the prosecution's summaries helped to

110 ICC, *Prosecutor v. Lubanga Dyilo*, Judgment on the Prosecutor's appeal against the decision of Pre-Trial Chamber I entitled "Decision Establishing General Principles Governing Applications to Restrict Disclosure pursuant to Rule 81 (2) and (4) of the Rules of Procedure and Evidence", ICC-01/04-01/06, 13 October 2006, paras. 53-54.

111 Article 64(3) (c) ICC Statute.

112 ICC, *Prosecutor v. Samoei Ruto, Kiprono Kosgey and Arap Sang*, Decision Setting the Regime for Evidence Disclosure and Other Related Matters, ICC-01/09-01/11-44, PTC II, 6 April 2011; ICC, *Prosecutor v. Callixte Mbarushimana*, Decision on issues relating to disclosure, ICC-01/04-01/10-87, PTC I, 30 March 2011. In *Lubanga*, the Chamber took a more restricted explaining that, before the confirmation of charges hearing, the prosecutor is expected to disclose at least the 'bulk' of the exculpatory evidence defence. ICC, *Prosecutor v. Lubanga Dyilo*, Decision on the Confirmation of Charges, ICC-01/04-01/06-803-EN, 29 January 2007, par. 154.

113 ICC, *Prosecutor v. Samoei Ruto, Kiprono Kosgey and Arap Sang*, ICC-01/09-01/11-74, Decision on the Prosecution's Application for Leave to Appeal the "Decision Setting the Regime for Evidence Disclosure and Other Related Matters", PTC II, 2 May 2011, par. 27.

114 ICC, *Prosecution v. Callixte Mbarushimana*, ICC-01/04-01/10-93, Prosecution's Application for leave to Appeal the 'Decision on issues relating to disclosure, ICC-01/04-01/10-87, PTC I, 5 April 2011, par. 17; ICC, *Prosecutor v. Samoei Ruto, Kiprono Kosgey and Arap Sang*, ICC-01/09-01/11-44, Prosecution's Application for Leave to Appeal the "Decision Setting the Regime for Evidence Disclosure and Other Related Matters", PTC II , 13 April 2011, par. 27.

115 ICC, *Prosecution v. Callixte Mbarushimana*, ICC-01/04-01/10-93, Prosecution's Application for leave to Appeal the 'Decision on issues relating to disclosure, ICC-01/04-01/10-87, PTC I, 5 April 2011, par. 17. The prosecutor's applications for leave to appeal have been denied, arguing that the disclosure orders were not so burdensome as to affect the fairness of the proceedings. See also ICC, *Prosecutor v. Samoei Ruto, Kiprono Kosgey and Arap Sang*, ICC-01/09-01/11-50, Prosecution's Application for leave to appeal the 'Decision Setting the Regime for Evidence Disclosure and Other Related Matters', ICC-01/09-01/11-44, PTC I, 13 April 2011, par. 5; ICC, *Prosecutor v. Callixte Mbarushimana*, ICC-01/04-01/10-116, Decision on the Prosecution's application for leave to Appeal the 'Decision on issues relating to disclosure', ICC-01/04-01/10- 87, PTC I, 21 April 2011,

mitigate the inequality of resources between the parties[116] and were protecting the defence from being "overwhelmed by the disclosure of potentially irrelevant material."[117] The Chambers' approach to such explanatory summaries has however been rather inconsistent [118]. Although these explanatory summaries undeniably pose an additional burden on the prosecution, this 'burden' could rightly be considered as a mere consequence of the role of the ICC prosecutor in light of Article 54(1)(a) and the principle of equality of arms. As a Minister of Justice the prosecutor must assist the court in its truth-finding mission, whereas the inherently weaker position of the accused necessitates 'equalising' of arms so as to be able to adequately prepare the case. It is indeed the defendant who must be able to "understand and fashion a responsive case" and should be placed in a position to do so by having *adequate* facilities to prepare.[119].
As already extensively documented, the practice of disclosure of exculpatory evidence has presented challenges in the context of the ICC from the start.[120]

---

par. 29; ICC, *Prosecutor v. Samoei Ruto, Kiprono Kosgey and Arap Sang*, ICC-01/09-01/11-74, Decision on the 'Prosecution's Application for leave to Appeal the "Decision Setting the Regime for Evidence Disclosure and Other Related Matters"', ICC-01/09-01/11-44, PTC I, 2 May 2011. ICC, *Prosecutor v. Bahr Idriss Abu Garda*, ICC-02/05-02/09-35, Second Decision on issues relating to Disclosure, PTC I ,15 July 2009, paras.15 and 16; ICC, *Prosecutor v. Callixte Mbarushimana*, ICC- 01/04-01/10-87, Decision on issues relating to disclosure, PTC I, 30 March 2011, par. 11 and p. 15.

116 ICC, *Prosecution v. Callixte Mbarushimana*, ICC-01/04-01/10-94, Defence Response to the Prosecution's Request for Leave to Appeal Decision ICC-01/04-01/10-87, PTC I, 10 Aprill 2011, par. 9.

117 ICC, *Prosecutor v. Samoei Ruto, Kiprono Kosgey and Arap Sang*, ICC-01/09-01/11-74, Decision on the Prosecution's Application for Leave to Appeal the "Decision Setting the Regime for Evidence Disclosure and Other Related Matters", PTC II, 2 May 2011, par. 14.

118 ICC, *Prosecutor v. Bahr Idriss Abu Garda*, ICC-02/05-02/09-35, Second Decision on issues relating to Disclosure, PTC I ,15 July 2009, paras.15 and 16; ICC, *Prosecutor v. Callixte Mbarushimana*, ICC- 01/04-01/10-87, Decision on issues relating to disclosure, PTC I, 30 March 2011, par. 11 and p. 15. In addition, some Pre-Trial Chambers have required that all disclosed exculpatory material be communicated to the Chamber, irrespective of whether the prosecution intended to rely on that material at the confirmation hearing; others have not done so. See ICC, *Prosecutor v. Samoei Ruto, Kiprono Kosgey and Arap Sang*, ICC-01/09-01/11-44, Decision Setting the Regime for Evidence Disclosure and Other Related Matters, PTC III, 6 April 2011, par. 6; ICC, *Prosecutor v. Bahr Idriss Abu Garda*, ICC-02/05-02/09-35, Second Decision on issues relating to Disclosure, PTC I, 15 July 2009, at par. 9; ICC, *Prosecutor v. Callixte Mbarushimana*, ICC-01/04-01/10-87, Decision on issues relating to disclosure, PTC I, 30 March 2011, par. 9 subparagraph (c).

119 ICC, *Prosecution v. Callixte Mbarushimana*, ICC-01/04-01/10-93, Prosecution's Application for leave to Appeal the 'Decision on issues relating to disclosure, ICC-01/04-01/20-87, PTC I, 5 April 2011, par. 17.

120 E.g. A. Heinze, *International Criminal Procedure and Disclosure*, Duncker & Humblot, 2014, pp. 452-476; K. Ambos, The First Judgment of the International Criminal Court (*Prosecutor v.* Lubanga): A Comprehensive Analysis of the Legal Issues, 12 *International Criminal Law* Review (2012), pp. 115-153; M. Fedorova, 'Reconciling the Prosecutor's Duty to Search for Truth with the Principle of Equality of Arms at the ICC', in: Coster van Voorhout, J., Grijsen, C., Hirsch Ballin, M., Van Noorloos, M., Pijnen, R. and Ver-

The first *Lubanga* case generated two stays of proceedings by the Trial Chamber (which were however reversed on appeal). The first stay was imposed as a consequence of prosecutorial misuse of Article 54(3)(e) ICC Statute, which provides for an opportunity not to disclose information that has been obtained confidentially and only for the purpose of generating new evidence.[121] The argument centred on the tension between the possibility to limit disclosure of materials that been obtained under the cloak of confidentiality (Article 54(3)(e)) and prosecution's disclosure obligations (Art. 67(2)), as well as on the role of Chamber in resolving this tension. The prosecutor had collected documents from the UN, under the promise of confidentiality, and ended up in the situation of not being able to disclose potentially exculpatory evidence to the defence or the Chamber due to lack of consent from the information provider. These documents were essential for the initiation of the investigations in the DRC.[122] The Trial Chamber was not amused that the prosecutor has accepted the condition of confidentiality even towards the judges; and after repeated disclosure orders, it found that it could no longer secure the fairness of proceedings.[123] The Chamber considered that prosecution's use of Article 54(3)(3) power was too broad and ultimately incorrect.[124] The Chamber was clearly optimistic about the possibilities of disclosure of potentially exculpatory evidence in a situation of only limited use of the confidentiality agreements. Although the tension between confidentiality and disclosure cannot be excluded completely, if Article 54(3)(e) is used properly, the tension would be minimal, according to the Chamber, and "[i]n any event, if the prosecution is unable to disclose evidence of this kind which is covered by these agreements, the issue should always be raised with the Chamber in accordance with Rule 83."[125] It must be noted that this is what

vaele, J. (eds.), *Shifting Responsibilities in Criminal Justice: Critical Portrayals of the Changing Role and Content of a Fragmented Globalizing Law Domain*, The Hague: Eleven International Publishing, 2012; A. Whiting, Lead Evidence and Discovery before the International Criminal Court: The Lubanga Case, UCLA Journal of International Law and Foreign Affairs 14, (2009) pp. 207-233; K. Ambos, Confidential Investigations v. Disclosure obligations: The Lubanga Case and National Law, 4 *New Criminal Law* Review (2009), pp. 543-568; D. Schaffer, A Review of Experiences of the Pre-Trial and Appeals Chambers of the International Criminal Court Regarding the Disclosure of Evidence, *Leiden Journal of International Law* 21 (2008), pp. 151-163.

121 For an overview of the framework of the ICTY in relation to confidential agreements and the disclosure of exculpatory evidence (Rule 70 and 68), see Whiting, 2009, pp. 211-215.

122 ICC, *Prosecutor v. Lubanga Dyilo,* Transcript, ICC-01/04-01/06-102, 2 October 2007, p. 7.

123 ICC, *Prosecutor v. Lubanga Dyilo*, Decision on the Consequences of Non-disclosure of Exculpatory Materials Covered by Article 54(3)(e) Agreements and the Application to Stay the Prosecution of the Accused, together with Certain Other Issues Raised at the Status Conference on 10 June 2008, ICC-01/04-01/06-1401, T. Ch., 13 June 2008.

124 *Lubanga* First Stay of Proceedings Trial Decision, par. 76.

125 *Lubanga* First Stay of Proceedings Trial Decision, par. 76.

the prosecutor actually did when he presented his conundrum to the Chamber.[126]

The Appeals Chamber confirmed the Trial Chamber's interpretation of Article 54(3)(e) ICC Statute, and emphasized that "the investigatory activities of the Prosecutor must be directed towards the identification of evidence that can eventually be presented in open court, in order to establish the truth and to assess whether there is criminal responsibility under the Statute."[127] Notwithstanding the importance of the confidentiality agreements to conducting investigations into conflict areas, the Chambers must, in any case, be able to resolve the possible tension between confidentiality and disclosure.[128] The Appeals Chamber expressed particular concern regarding the fact that the prosecutor had agreed to 'exclude' the judges by not disclosing confidential materials even to the Chamber.[129] It is the Chamber that bears the final say with regard to "whether the material would have to be disclosed, had it not been obtained under Article 54(3)(e) of the Statute."[130] If the Chamber decides in favour of disclosure but the information providers refuse to lift confidentiality, the judges will then have to decide on potential counter-balancing measures to protect the rights of the accused, including evaluating potential alternative evidence.[131] The Appeals Chamber, although confirming

---

126 ICC, Separate Opinion of Judge Pikis, Judgment on the Appeals of the Prosecutor against the decision of Trial Chamber I entitled "Decision on the Consequences of Non-disclosure of Exculpatory Materials Covered by Article 54(3)(e) Agreements and the Application to Stay the Prosecution of the Accused, together with Certain Other Issues Raised at the Status Conference on 10 June 2008, *Prosecutor v. Thomas Lubanga Dyilo*, Case No. ICC-01/04-01/06-OA 13, 21 October 2008, par. 11.

127 ICC, *Prosecutor v. Lubanga Dyilo*, Judgment on the Appeals of the Prosecutor against the decision of Trial Chamber I entitled "Decision on the Consequences of Non-disclosure of Exculpatory Materials Covered by Article 54(3)(e) Agreements and the Application to Stay the Prosecution of the Accused, together with Certain Other Issues Raised at the Status Conference on 10 June 2008, ICC-01/04-01/06-OA 13, 21 October 2008, par. 41. In his separate opinion Judge Pikis contended that the prosecution has done "little, if anything" to conduct any further investigations on the potentially exculpatory information so as to be able to discharge the disclosure obligations towards the accused. ICC, Separate Opinion of Judge Pikis, Judgment on the Appeals of the Prosecutor against the decision of Trial Chamber I entitled "Decision on the Consequences of Non-disclosure of Exculpatory Materials Covered by Article 54(3)(e) Agreements and the Application to Stay the Prosecution of the Accused, together with Certain Other Issues Raised at the Status Conference on 10 June 2008, *Prosecutor v. Thomas Lubanga Dyilo*, Case No. ICC-01/04-01/06-OA 13, 21 October 2008, par. 42.

128 See *Lubanga* First Stay of Proceedings Appeals Decision, par. 43.

129 ICC, *Prosecutor v. Lubanga Dyilo*, Judgment on the Appeals of the Prosecutor against the decision of Trial Chamber I entitled "Decision on the Consequences of Non-disclosure of Exculpatory Materials Covered by Article 54(3)(e) Agreements and the Application to Stay the Prosecution of the Accused, together with Certain Other Issues Raised at the Status Conference on 10 June 2008, ICC-01/04-01/06-OA 13, 21 October 2008, par. 45.

130 Ibid., par. 48.

131 Ibid., paras. 48, 95.

the Trial Chambers approach, classified the stay of proceedings as conditional, and reversed the decision on release of the accused.[132]

In sum, whenever the prosecutor is confronted with material offered to him on the basis of confidentiality, taking into account specific circumstances such as the expected content and nature of the documents, he will have to decide on the specific conditions under which he can accept these materials considering his other obligations.[133] It follows that to some extent these decisions subject Article 54(3)(e) to Article 67(2) ICC Statute. From the perspective of the defence, the judge's approach to the relationship between Articles 54(3)(e) and 67(2) is encouraging. However, one is to hope that both the prosecutor and the information providers would not shy away from respectively collecting and disclosing potentially exculpatory evidence which could only be obtained under the cloak of confidentiality.[134] Otherwise, this will have a devastating effect on both the truth-finding in and the fairness of the process.

Some one and a half years later, the *Lubanga* Trial Chamber imposed a second stay of proceedings because the prosecutor had repeatedly not complied with the Chamber's order to disclose the identity of an intermediary that the defence wished to call to the stand.[135] The prosecutor referred to his autonomous duty of protection of that individual and therewith challenged the Chambers' function as the final arbiter of fairness.[136] It was the defence who challenged the propriety of the conduct of the intermediaries used by the prosecution to "facilitate contact between the Prosecution and a witness or

---

132 Ibid. The prosecution was able to obtain disclosure consent to the Trial Chamber from the information providers in the end. The Trial Chamber ordered several measures for disclosure of that material to defence, such as redaction of documents, summaries, and disclosure of analogous documents, and lifted the stay of proceedings one the prosecutor complied with these measures. ICC, *Prosecutor v. Lubanga*, Reasons for Oral Decision Lifting the Stay of Proceedings, Case No. ICC-01/04-01/06, 23 January 2009, pp.25, 33-35, 59.

133 ICC, *Prosecutor v. Lubanga Dyilo*, Judgment on the Appeals of the Prosecutor against the decision of Trial Chamber I entitled "Decision on the Consequences of Non-disclosure of Exculpatory Materials Covered by Article 54(3)(e) Agreements and the Application to Stay the Prosecution of the Accused, together with Certain Other Issues Raised at the Status Conference on 10 June 2008, ICC-01/04-01/06-OA 13, 21 October 2008, par. 51.

134 A reason for the ICTY judges to eventually subject the disclosure obligations under Rule 68 to confidentiality agreements possible under Rule 70(B) ICTY RPE.

135 ICC, *Prosecutor v. Lubanga Dyilo*, Redacted Decision on the Prosecution's Urgent Request for Variation of the Time-Limit to Disclose the Identity of Intermediary 143 or Alternatively to Stay Proceedings Pending Further Consultations with the VWU, ICC-01/04-01/06-2517-Red, T. Ch. I, 8 July 2010 [*Lubanga* Second Stay of Proceedings Trial Decision].

136 ICC, *Prosecutor v. Lubanga Dyilo*, Prosecution's Urgent Request for Variation of the Time-Limit to Disclose the Identity of Intermediary 143 or Alternatively to Stay Proceedings Pending Further Consultations with VWU, , ICC-01/04-01/06-2512, T. Ch. I, 8 July 2010, p. 3. ICC, *Prosecutor v. Lubanga Dyilo*, Redacted Decision on the Prosecution's Urgent Request for Variation of the Time-Limit to Disclose the Identity of Intermediary 143 or Alternatively to Stay Proceedings Pending Further Consultations with the VWU, ICC-01/04-01/06-2517-Red, T. Ch. I, 8 July 2010, par. 31.

any other source of information".[137] Consequently, the Chamber ordered the prosecution to (1) disclose the identity of one intermediary "to enable the defence to conduct necessary and meaningful investigations and to secure a fair trial for the accused,"[138] once the necessary protective measures had been implemented, (2) call two intermediaries to the stand to testify, and (3) call an OTP representative to testify generally on the use of intermediaries.[139] The Chamber reiterated that once seized of a case, the Trial Chamber alone has the power to order and vary protective measures as it has the overarching responsibility to ensure a fair trial.[140] The prosecutor's claim of a separate authority in that regard is obviously misconceived and "involves a profound, unacceptable and unjustified intrusion into the role of the judiciary."[141]

In this instance again, the Appeals Chamber agreed with the Trial Chamber on the merits, but saw the imposition of a stay of proceedings as premature.[142] According to the Appeals Chamber, the prosecutor obviously and deliberately disobeyed, and any argument to the contrary "is, at best, disingenuous [and] at worst, [...] an expression of [...] a more profound and enduring concern [...]."[143] The Appeals Chamber reiterated that it is the Trial Chamber who is "the ultimate guardian of a fair and expeditious trial" and that, notwithstanding the prosecutor's statutory duties, in any perceived conflict between those duties and the Trial Chamber's orders, the latter must prevail.[144] On an optimistic note, the prosecutor's explicit recognition that he would rather face adverse consequences as a party to proceedings than fall short of ensuring the protection of broader public interests can be seen as an expression of his role as a "Minister of Justice" rather than a partisan advocate. Whether the prosecutor was prepared to allow the trial to be halted permanently, rather than obeying the Chamber's orders, is another question which is somewhat too speculative.[145] However, the prosecutor clearly took the wrong path regarding his assessment of the primacy of the Trial Chamber's evaluation of protective measures.

---

137 ICC, *Prosecutor v. Lubanga Dyilo*, Prosecution Proposed Procedure for Dealing with Intermediaries, ICC-01/04-01/06-2362, 19 March 2010, introduction. ICC, *Prosecutor v. Lubanga Dyilo*, Redacted Decision on Intermediaries, ICC-01/04-01/06-2434-Red2, 31 May 2010, par. 135.

138 *Lubanga* Decision on Intermediaries, par. 143.

139 *Lubanga* Decision on Intermediaries, par. 150.

140 *Lubanga* Second Stay of Proceedings Trial Decision, par. 24.

141 *Lubanga Dyilo* Second Stay of Proceedings Trial Decision, par. 27.

142 *Lubanga* Second Stay of Proceedings Appeals Decision, par. 59.

143 ICC, *Prosecutor v. Lubanga Dyilo*, Judgment on the Appeal of the Prosecutor against the Decision of Trial Chamber I of 8 July 2010 entitled "Decision on the Prosecution's Urgent Request for Variation of the Time-Limit to Disclose the Identity of Intermediary 143 or Alternatively to Stay Proceedings Pending Further Consultations with the VWU, ICC-01/04-01/06 OA 18, A. Ch., 8 October 2010, par. 46 [*Lubanga* Second Stay of Proceedings Appeals Decision].

144 *Lubanga* Second Stay of Proceedings Appeals Decision, paras. 47-48.

145 Considering the Prosecutor's contention that the stay had been imposed on a conditional basis, see Trial Transcript of 15 July 2010, ICC-01/04-01/06-T-314-ENG.

In several cases the defence has expressed substantiated concerns about prosecution's "reckless investigative techniques,"[146] his failure to investigate incriminating and exonerating evidence equally[147] and to investigate the truthfulness of his own witnesses and intermediaries.[148] The judges were "highly disturbed" by some prosecutorial disclosure incidents[149] and have acknowledged the 'negligence' on the part of prosecution.[150] In *Muthaura* case, important disclosure oversight led to withdrawal of charges against the accused.[151] In *Bemba* case, the judges expressed their 'astonishment' about the disclosure irregularities, which led to postponement of the confirmation of charges hearing.[152] Deep concerns about prosecutorial disclosure were also expressed in *Samoei Ruto and Joshua Arap Sang* case.[153] Whether or not the prosecutor has been acting *bona fide,* the prosecutorial investigation and disclosure practice today is fit for drastic changes. It is at least questionable whether the prosecutor lives up to his role as a "Minister of Justice" assisting

146 ICC, Decision on Article 54(3)(e) Documents Identified as Potentially Exculpatory or Otherwise Material to the Defence's Preparation for the Confirmation Hearing, *Prosecutor v. Germain Katanga and Mathieu Ngudjolo Chui*, Case No. ICC-01/04-01/07, 20 June 2008, par. 123.

147 Cf. C. Buisman, The Prosecutor's Obligation to Investigate Incriminating and Exonerating Circumstances Equally: Illusion or Reality?, 27 *Leiden Journal of International Law* , 2014, pp. 205-226.

148 ICC, Decision on defence application for a permanent stay of the proceedings due to abuse of process, *Prosecutor v. Uhuru Muigai Kenyatta*, Case No. ICC-01/09-02/11-868-Red, T.Ch. V(B), 5 December 2013, par. 44 including footnote reference. The charges against *Kenyatta* case have been withdrawn on 5 December 2014 due to lack of inculpating evidence.

149 See e.g. ICC, *Prosecutor v. Germain Katanga and Mathieu Ngudjolo Chui*, Decision on the 19 June 2008 Prosecution Information and other Matters concerning Article 54(3)(e) and 67(2) of the Statute and rule 77 of the Rules, Case No. ICC-01/04-01/07, 25 June 2008, par. 21.

150 E.g. ICC, *Prosecutor v. Lubanga Dyilo*, Judgment pursuant to Article 74 of the Statute, ICC-01/04-01/06-2842, 14 March 2012, par. 482; ICC, *Prosecutor v. Lubanga Dyilo*, Redacted Decision on the "Defence Application Seeking a Permanent Stay of the Proceedings, ICC-01/04-01/06-2690-Red, 2 March 2011. See also Minority Opinion of Judge Christine Van den Wyngaert, Prosecutor v Katanga, Jugement rendu en application de l'article 74 du Statut, ICC-01/04-01/07-3436-AnxI, 7 March 2014.

151 In the *Muthaura* case, an 'disclosure error' of material that casted substantial doubts on the statement of one of prosecution's key witnesses, was disclosed to the defence a year past the confirmation of charges hearing and eventually lead to the withdrawal of charges against the accused. *The Prosecutor v. Uhuru Muigai Kenyatta and Francis Kirimi Muthaura,* Case No. ICC-01/09- 02/11, Prosecution notification of withdrawal of the charges against Francis Kirimi Muthaura, 11March 2013. See for an elaborate discussion of the course of these proceedings: K.A.A. Khan and A.A. Shah, Defensive Practices: Representing Clients before the International Criminal Court, *Law and Contemporary Problems* 76, 191, 2013, pp. 208-213.

152 ICC, *Prosecutor v. Jean-Pierre Bemba Gombo*, Case No. ICC-01/05-01/08, Decision on Postponement of the Confirmation Hearing, 17 October 2008, paras. 22-23.

153 ICC, *Prosecutor v. William Samoei Ruto and Joshua Arap Sang*, Case No. ICC-01/09-01/11, Decision concerning the start date of trial, 8 March 2013, par. 13; ICC, *Prosecutor v. William Samoei Ruto and Joshua Arap Sang*, Case No. ICC-01/09-01/11, Decision on prosecution requests to add witnesses and evidence and defence requests to reschedule the trial start date, 3 June 2013, paras. 90, 94.

the Court to arrive at the truth.[154] Notwithstanding, defence's role as a 'watchdog' of fair proceedings clearly cannot be underestimated.

4. Remedying and sanctioning disclosure violations

In light of the importance of strict adherence to the disclosure obligations for the fairness of proceedings, an important question concerns how to remedy disclosure violations. Moreover, sanctioning these violations could be considered an appropriate method to prevent any reoccurrence of the damaging behaviour. Whereas the measures taken to remedy or to sanction will often overlap in the area of disclosure violations, they are not necessarily interchangeable, as the first has a reparatory nature and the latter a punitive and preventive one. This section will consider the legal framework to remedy and sanction disclosure violations and take a closer look at how international criminal courts have approached this issue.

a. ICTY & ICTR

Mindful of the complex nature of the disclosure regime, the ICTY judges have introduced Rule 68*bis* ICTY RPE: "The pre-trial Judge or the Trial Chamber may decide *proprio motu*, or at the request of either party, on sanctions to be imposed on a party which fails to perform its disclosure obligations pursuant to the Rules."[155] In the case law, the Chambers have considered the application of this rule possible in cases of persistent disregard or lack of diligence on the part of the prosecution of its Rule 68 obligations that obstruct the proceedings or the interests of justice.[156] Notably, the rule talks about the imposition of sanctions rather than remedies, which directs the attention to the more punitive, deterrent effect of the measures taken rather than their reparatory nature.[157]

When challenging the prosecutor's compliance with his disclosure obligations the defence bears the burden of substantiating a disclosure violation as well as establishing that the violation had caused material prejudice to the defence amounting to an infringement of the right to a fair trial, which is a prerequisite for imposition of any remedies of sanctions.[158] Particularly the

---

154 Cf. C. Buisman, The Prosecutor's Obligation to Investigate Incriminating and Exonerating Circumstances Equally: Illusion or Reality?, 27 *Leiden Journal of International Law* , 2014, pp. 205-226.

155 Adopted on 13 December 2001. This rule was not introduced at ICTR.

156 ICTR, *Prosecutor v. Ndindiliyimana et al.,* Decision on Defence Motions Alleging Violation of the Prosecutor's Disclosure Obligations pursuant to Rule 68, ICTR-00-56-T, T.Ch.II, 22 September 2008, par. 14.

157 Rule 46 with possible measures to be taken in case of misconduct of a counsel.

158 E.g. ICTR, *Prosecutor v. Ndindiliyimana et al.,* Decision on Defence Motions Alleging Violation of the Prosecutor's Discloasure Obligations pursuant to Rule 68, ICTR-00-56-T, 22 September 2008, par. 14; ICTY, *Prosecutor v. Radoslav Brdjanin*, Case No. IT-99-36A, Decision on Appellant's Motion for Disclosure Pursuant to Rule 68 and Motion for

practice of disclosure of exculpatory evidence has been receptive to violations. To establish a violation of Rule 68 obligations, the defence must (1) identify specifically the material sought; (2) present a *prima facie* showing of its probable exculpatory nature; and (3) prove that the material requested is in the custody or under the control of the prosecution.[159] Whenever these requirements are fulfilled and the Chamber is satisfied that the material has not been disclosed "as soon as practicable", it finds a violation of the disclosure obligations under Rule 68.[160] For the purpose of establishing the exculpatory nature of the material, the Appeals Chamber has considered that the defence need only to show that the material is *prima facie* or "potentially" exculpatory"[161] and not whether the material was 'on its face'[162] or 'in fact' exculpatory.[163] The appropriate standard is "whether there is any possibility, in light of the submissions of the parties, that the information could be relevant to the defence of the accused."[164] As such, Rule 68, "as a rule of disclosure rather than admissibility of evidence, imposes a categorical obligation to disclose any document or witness statement that contains exculpatory material."[165] Low probative value of material does not stand in the way of classifying it as potentially exculpatory for the purpose of establishing a Rule 68 violation.[166]

---

an Order to the Registrar to Disclose Certain Materials, 7 December 2004; ICTY, *Prosecutor v. Blaškić*, Decision on the Production of Discovery Materials, IT-95-14-PT, 27 January 1997, par. 49.

159 E.g. ICTR, *Prosecutor v. Nshogoza*, Decision on Defence Motion for Order to Prosecutor to Comply with his Disclosure Obligations and Motion for Stay of Proceedings Due to the on-going Violation of the Prosecutor's disclosure obligations, ICTR-07-91-T, T. Ch., 10 February 2009, par. 16; ICTR, *Prosecutor v. Augustin Ndindiliyimana et al,* Decision on Defence Motions Alleging Violation of the Prosecutor's Disclosure Obligations Pursuant to Rule 68, ICTR-00-56-T, T. Ch., 22 September 2008, par. 13 [references omitted]; ICTR, *Prosecutor v. Karemera et al.*, Decision on Joseph Nzirorera's Appeals from Decision on Tenth Rule 68 Motion, ICTR-98-44-AR73.13, A. Ch., 14 May 2008, par. 9; ICTY, *Prosecutor v. Brđjanin*, Decision on Appellant's Motion for Disclosure pursuant to Rule 68 and Motion for an Order to the Registrar to Disclose Certain Materials, 7 December 2004, p. 3.

160 See e.g. ICTY, *Prosecutor v. Karadžić,* Decision on Accused's Thirty-Seventh to Forty-Second Disclosure Violation Motions With Partially Dissenting Opinion of Judge Kwon, IT-95-5/18-T, T. Ch., 29 March 2011, paras. 25, 38.

161 ICTR, *Prosecutor v. Kalimanzira*, Appeals Chamber Judgement, ICTR-05-88-A, A. Ch., 20 October 2010, par. 20.

162 ICTY, *Prosecutor v. Krstić*, Appeal Judgment, IT-98-33-A, 19 April 2004, par. 179.

163 ICTR, *Prosecutor v. Kalimanzira*, Appeals Chamber Judgement, ICTR-05-88-A, A. Ch., 20 October 2010, paras. 19-20.

164 ICTR, *Prosecutor v. Karemera et al.*, Decision on Joseph Nzirorera's Appeals from Decision on Tenth Rule 68 Motion, ICTR-98-44-AR73.13, A. Ch., 14 May 2008, par. 12, citing ICTR, *Prosecutor v. Bagosora et al.*, Decision on Disclosure of Defence Witness Statements in the Possession of the Prosecution Pursuant to Rule 68(A), ICTR- 98-41-T, 8 March 2006, par. 5.

165 ICTR, *Prosecutor v. Karemera et al.*, Decision on Joseph Nzirorera's Appeals from Decision on Tenth Rule 68 Motion, ICTR-98-44-AR73.13, A. Ch., 14 May 2008, par. 12.

166 Low probative value is, however, taken into account when establishing, or rather not establishing, any material prejudice. ICTR, *Prosecutor v. Kalimanzira*, Appeals Chamber Judgement, ICTR-05-88-A, A. Ch., 20 October 2010, paras. 20-22.

As mentioned, as soon as the exculpatory nature of the materials is established, for the purpose of finding a violation, the judges have to make an assessment of whether this material has been disclosed as soon as practicable. A substantive examination takes place only when the prosecutor indicates when he received this material and makes a submission on the reasons of late disclosure. The judges have recognized that delay may occur due to the enormous amount of documents in prosecution's possession. The assessment has focused on the reasons provided by the prosecutor for his inability to quickly identify and/or access the exculpatory materials, and any indication of a *mala fide* practice.[167] The threshold is high for the prosecution to successfully argue that he has disclosed the material as soon as practicable. A delay of approximately three month has been found to violate the 'as soon as practicable' requirement.[168] Even in cases where the prosecutor has received the materials under the cloak of confidentiality (Rule 70) and only recently was given consent to disclose them to the defence, the Chambers were tough considering that "this does not excuse the original failure by the Prosecution to identify this document and seek the required clearance earlier."[169]

Notwithstanding the rather unproblematic establishment of the violation of the "as soon as practicable"-requirement, clearly the rather difficult criterion to satisfy in order to effectuate a remedy for the established Rule 68 disclosure violation has been the requirement of 'prejudice' suffered from that violation.[170] It concerns a very case-specific assessment; thus only several elements relevant for that assessment will be mentioned. First, for the purposes of assessing whether the defence has suffered any material prejudice, the Appeals Chamber has drawn a distinction between material "of a public character in the public domain" and materials "reasonably accessible to the Defence."[171] Only this second category falls within the scope of Rule 68, with regard to which the Chamber emphasized that "unless exculpatory material is reasonably accessible to the accused, namely, available to the Defence with the exercise of due diligence, the Prosecution has a duty to disclose the material itself."[172] From this reasoning it follows, on the one hand, that where the defence would be able to gain access to materials that are not of a public character, but can easily be accessed, no material prejudice

167 E.g. ICTY, *Prosecutor v. Krstić*, Appeal Judgment, IT-98-33-A, 19 April 2004, par. 197.

168 ICTY, *Prosecutor v. Krstić*, Appeal Judgment, IT-98-33-A, 19 April 2004, paras. 196, 198. However, in ICTY, *Prosecutor v. Blaškić,* Appeal Chamber Judgment, IT-95-14-A, 29 July 2004, paras. 270, 273-275, a delay of almost eight month after Trial Chamber's judgment was not "inordinate amount of time.".

169 ICTY, *Prosecutor v. Karadžić,* Decision on Accused's Forty-Ninth and Fiftieth Disclosure Violation Motions, IT-95-5/18-T, T. Ch., 30 June 2011, paras. 42, 44.

170 For example, see the many defence motions in the Karadzic case alleging a disclosure violation. Also, ICTR, *Prosecutor v. Renzaho,* Judgment and Sentence, ICTR-97-31-T, T.Ch., 14 July 2009, paras. 36-51.

171 ICTY, *Prosecutor v. Blaškić,* Appeal Chamber Judgment, IT-95-14-A, 29 July 2004, par. 296.

172 Ibid.

could arise. On the contrary, in light of the case law on the subject matter, where the material was not reasonably accessible to the defence and gave rise to a Rule 68 violation, the prejudice suffered by the defence is subject to evaluation and does not automatically follow from the fact that the defence could not access the materials. Second, the specific nature of the materials has been taken into account to the extent that when "their content is not of such significance that their late disclosure has had a detrimental impact on the Accused's overall preparation for trial or the approach to his defence," no prejudice will be established.[173] Third, the judges have paid attention to whether the defence has enough time to analyse the materials and whether it has an opportunity to challenge it on cross-examination;[174] and whether the defence could call to testify.[175] Fourth, on appeal, no prejudice from a violation of a disclosure obligation would arise when the defence was able to seek the admission of additional evidence, even if that evidence was not admitted.[176]

In case prejudice is established, the determination of a suitable remedy is also a highly case-specific matter falling within Trial Chamber's discretion and is appraised taking into account (1) the scope and significance of the violation with regard to the charges, (2) the persistence of the violations, and (3) the timing of the disclosure in light of the stage of the proceedings.[177] Examples of possible remedy for disclosure violations include recalling relevant witnesses for further cross-examination, calling additional witnesses, drawing reasonable inferences in favour of the accused from the belatedly disclosed exculpatory evidence, excluding relevant part of the prosecution' evidence, and as a last resort, ordering a stay of proceedings and dismissing the charges against the accused.[178]

In practice, in several cases disclosure violations have led to remedial actions.[179] In *Bizimungu et al.* the Trial Chamber concluded that the defence

---

173 ICTY, *Prosecutor v. Karadžić,* Decision on Accused's Forty-Ninth and Fiftieth Disclosure Violation Motions, IT-95-5/18-T, T. Ch., 30 June 2011, par. 47. *Cf.* ICTR, *Niyitegeka v. The Prosecutor*, Decision on Third Request for Review, ICTR-96-14-R, A. Ch., 23 January 2008, par. 28, no material prejudice was established because the exculpatory evidence did not warrant review.

174 ICTY, *Prosecutor v. Krstić*, Appeal Judgment, IT-98-33-A, 19 April 2004, paras. 192, 197.

175 ICTY, *Prosecutor v. Blaškić,* Appeal Chamber Judgment, IT-95-14-A, 29 July 2004, par. 282.

176 ICTY, *Prosecutor v. Krstić*, Appeal Judgment, IT-98-33-A, 19 April 2004, par. 187.

177 *Karemera et al.*, Decision on Joseph Nzirorera's Interlocutory Appeal (AC), 28 April 2006 (*Karemera* Decision of 28 April 2006), paras. 8-9.

178 ICTR, *Prosecutor v Bizimungu et al.,* Judgment and Sentence, ICTR-99-50-T, T.Ch., 30 September 2011, par. 143; ICTR, *Prosecutor v. Ndindiliyimana*, Decision on Defence Motions Alleging Violation of the Prosecutor's Disclosure Obligations Pursuant to Rule 68, ICTR-00-56-T, 22 September 2008, par. 61. See also e.g. ICTY, *Prosecutor v. Orić*, Decision on Ongoing Complaints About Prosecutorial Non-Compliance with Rule 68 of the Rules Case No. IT-03-68-T, 13 December 2005.

179 For an overview, see ICTR, *Prosecutor v. Bizimungu et al.,* Judgment and Sentence, ICTR-99-50-T, T. Ch., 30 September 2011, paras. 170-174.

suffered material prejudice because prosecutor's late disclosure of exculpatory material prevented the defence from exercising its right to call and examine witnesses.[180] This prejudice was further enhanced because of the clearly exculpatory nature of the evidence with regard to the charges, and because the delay in disclosure occurred during the drafting of the judgment.[181] As a remedial action, the Chamber considered it appropriate to draw a reasonable inference in favour of the Accused from the exculpatory material, as this would "strike an appropriate balance between remedying the material prejudice caused to the Accused by the Prosecution's late disclosure of exculpatory material, and respecting the quality of the evidence adduced by all parties as it relates to the affected allegations."[182] These inferences were not based on a positive evaluation of the evidence, but the Chamber did not enter findings on incriminating evidence that was affected by the exculpatory evidence because of the prosecutorial disclosure violations. "On a final note" the Chamber reprimanded the Office of the Prosecution for this "inexcusable" conduct and his failure to design adequate procedures for the reexamination in light of Rule 68 of evidence from different cases.[183] Such reprimands have been issued in other cases too: in *Haradinaj et al.* for example, the Trial Chamber reprimanded a senior prosecution Trial Attorney personally.[184]

Moreover, the *Karadzic* case presents a notable example, where the defence has filed, at least, 96 disclosure violation motions, many of which have resulted in the finding of disclosure violations.[185] The Chamber oftentimes reprimanded the prosecutor for these violations by stating that "[t]he reasons proffered by the Prosecution for the failure to identify and disclosure the Rule 68 documents have often been completely inadequate"[186] and that the delay in disclosure "is clearly unacceptable, and [...] reflects badly on its [Prosecution's] disclosure practices".[187] When considering adequate remedy the

180 Ibid., par. 166.

181 Ibid., par. 167.

182 Ibid., par. 174.

183 Ibid., paras. 175, 177.

184 ICTY, *Prosecutor v. Haradinaj et al.,* Decision on Joint Defence Motion for Relief from Rule 68 Violations by the Prosecution and for Sanctions to be Imposed Pursuant to Rule *68bis,* IT-04-84his-T, 12 October 2011. However, after the prosecution's request for reconsideration, the Chamber vacated this reprimand as a "clear error of reasoning" arguing that it missed the power to issue a personal reprimand under Rule 68*bis*, as opposed to Rule 46 that allows for "a disciplinary measure in cases of serious disclosure violations." ICTY, *Prosecutor v. Haradinaj et al.,* Decision on Prosecutor's Motion for Reconsideration of Relief ordered pursuant to Rule 68*bis* with Partially Dissenting Opinion of Judge Hall, IT-04-84bis-T, 27 March 2012, paras. 40-42.

185 ICTY, *Prosecutor v. Karadzic*, Decision on Accused's Ninety-Sixth Disclosure Violation Motion 96, IT-95-5/18-T, 21 January 2015.

186 ICTY, *Prosecutor v. Karadzic*, Decision on Accused's Fourty-Ninth and Fiftieth Disclosure Violation Motions, IT-95-5/18-T, T.Ch., 30 June 2011, par. 53.

187 ICTY, *Prosecutor v. Karadzic,* Public redacted Version of "Decision on Accused's Ninety-Third Disclosure Violation Motion" issues on 13 October 2014, IT-95-5/18-T, T.Ch., 20 March 2015, par. 16. See also e.g. ICTR, *Prosecutor v. Karemera et al.,* Deci-

Chambers took into account that the cumulative effect of the disclosure violations was "likely to have placed a strain on the resources of the Accused in the preparation of his defence".[188] To remedy the prejudice against the accused arising out of disclosure violations, the Chambers have sometimes postponed witness testimony and suspended the proceedings to provide the defence with an opportunity to deal with the new (voluminous) disclosure.[189]

Interestingly, the presiding judge has issued a partially dissenting opinion to all the decisions in *Karadzic* where the majority declared a violation without finding any prejudice suffered by the accused, on the grounds that such majority's declaratory finding "is unnecessary, moot or even frivolous" and as such "serves no purpose".[190] Judge Kwon argued that a finding of a violation in itself constitutes a remedy which is unwarranted in cases where no prejudicial effect is established. [191] Moreover, such a finding could only have an adverse effect on the accused's behaviour and "would only encourage the Accused to continue filing unnecessary motions" while "[i]n a trial of this size and scope, where hundreds of witnesses are being called and tens of thousands of pages of documents are being tendered, it is unwarranted to seek a declaratory finding of disclosure violation every time that a potentially exculpatory document is belatedly disclosed in violation of Rule 68 without demonstrating any prejudice on the part of the Accused".[192] Although the judge makes a valid point that a declaratory finding of a violation can be conceived of as a remedy in itself, and his approach could facilitate trial efficiency, considering the fundamental importance of disclosure of (exculpatory) evidence for the preservation of equality of arms, his proposal must be rejected.

First of all, the judges should pay attention to the cumulative effect of individualized disclosure violations, arguably more so than done to date.[193] Additionally, the defence should not feel discouraged to bring the disclosure violations to the attention of the judges as that could result in any (systemic) disclosure regime flaws being concealed and therefore neglected. On the contrary, only through exposing these flaws can a way be found to properly address those and hopefully to implement long term changes. Although, un-

---

sion on Joseph Nzirorera's Interlocutory Appeal, ICTR-98-44-AR73.6, 28 April 2006, par. 63.

188 ICTY, *Prosecutor v. Karadzic,* Decision on Accused's Eighteenth to Twenty-First Disclosure Violation Motions, IT-95-5/18-T, T.Ch., 2 November 2010, par. 43.

189 ICTY, *Prosecutor v. Karadzic,* Decision on Accused's Eighteenth to Twenty-First Disclosure Violation Motions, IT-95-5/18-T, T.Ch., 2 November 2010, par. 43; ICTY, *Prosecutor v Karadzic*, Oral Decision, IT-95-5/18-T, T.Ch.,3 November 2010, T.8907-8908.

190 Partially Dissenting Opinion of Judge Kwon to ICTY, *Prosecutor v Karadzic*, Decision on Accused's Thirty-Seventh to Fourty-Second Disclosure Violation Motions with partially Dissenting Opinion of Judge Kwon, 29 March 2011.

191 Ibid., par. 5.

192 Ibid., par. 7.

193 See e.g. ICTR, *Prosecutor v. Bizimungu et al.,* Judgment and Sentence, ICTR-99-50-T, T.Ch., 30 September 2011.

derstandably, in international criminal trials the massive amount of documents that might be subject to disclosure can interfere and offset even the most *bona fide* intentions of the parties in relation to disclosure, in order to avoid a perception of implied tolerance and "a climate of impunity" the judges should pay more attention to their power to *sanction* disclosure violations, rather than only provide for a remedy in a particular case.[194] On a practical note, a more elaborate sanctioning regime, designed according to the seriousness of disclosure violation and that is more rigorously implemented could prove beneficial to provide for ensuring compliance with the disclosure obligations. To that a more 'personal' approach might be inevitable: Prosecution counsel should be held personally accountable for disclosure misconduct, which approach is more often implemented with regard to the defence counsel.[195]

b. ICC

The ICC Statute does not contain a provision explicating the possible remedies or sanctions to be provided in case of disclosure violations; this decision belongs to the implicit discretionary power of the judges.[196] As to the consequences of the non-disclosure of exculpatory evidence, the Trial Chamber indicated that when non-disclosed exculpatory evidence materially impacts the Chamber's determinations as to the guilt or innocence of the accused, the prosecutor will have to withdraw any charges.[197] In fact, the prosecutor relied on this suggestion of 'adverse consequences' when he was not able to disclose potentially exculpatory material to the defence and the Trial Chamber in the *Lubanga* case. The *Lubanga* 'disclosure crises' discussed above have clearly shown that the Trial Chambers did not shy away from taking most exceptional measure of staying the proceedings in order to ensure the fairness of the trial process. This far-reaching power has been based on internationally recognised human rights norms and the abuse of process doctrine.[198] The test

---

194 Partially dissenting opinion of Judge Hall, ICTY, *Prosecutor v. Haradinaj et al.,* Decision on Prosecutor's Motion for Reconsideration of Relief ordered pursuant to Rule 68*bis* with Partially dissenting Opinion of Judge Hall, IT-04-84bis-T, 27 March 2012, par. 4.

195 See also e.g. K. Gibson & C. Lussiaa-Berdou, 'Disclosure of Evidence', in: K. Khan, C. Buisman & C. Gosnell (eds.), *Principles of Evidence in International Criminal* Justice (2010), pp. 338.

196 A. Heinze, *International Criminal Procedure and Disclosure*, Duncker&Humblot, 2014, p. 452 (arguing that the inherent power can be derived from a combined reading of Rule 121(8) ICC RPE and Article 64(8)(b) ICC Statute). Moreover, just as at the *ad hoc* tribunals, the ICC has the power to take disciplinary measures (Art. 47 ICC Statute, Rule 24, 25 ICC RPE) or sanctions for misconduct before the Court (Art. 71 ICC Statute).

197 ICC, *Prosecutor v. Lubanga Dyilo*, Decision Regarding the Timing and Manner of Disclosure and the Date of Trial, ICC-01/04-01/06, 9 November 2007, par. 19.

198 See also ICC, *Prosecutor v. Banda and Jerbo*, decision on the Defence Request for a temporary stay of proceedings, ICC-02/05-03/09-409, 26 October 2012; ICC, *Prosecutor v. Callixte Mbarushimana*, Decision on the "Defence request for a permanent stay of proceedings", ICC-01/04-01/10-264, 1 July 2011; ICC, Prosecutor v. Lubanga Dyilo, Re-

established for the imposition of s stay of proceedings is whether (1) it would be 'odious' or 'repugnant' to the administration of justice to allow the proceedings to continue, or (2) the rights of the accused have been breached to the extent that a fair trial has been rendered impossible.[199]

No other instances of recognised 'mistakes' on behalf of the prosecution with regard to its disclosure obligation have risen to the level of severity so as to justify a stay of proceedings.[200] However, the Chambers have taken other measures to address disclosure malpractice, such as the re-calling of witnesses, postponing the proceedings and ordering the prosecution to review its files again in order to certify that no disclosable material is left undisclosed.[201] Just as at the ad hoc tribunals, the ICC Chambers have oftentimes cautioned, warned or reprimanded the Prosecution office for disclosure malpractice, rather than particular prosecutions attorneys.[202]As argued above, a more developed and stringently applied sanctioning regime could benefit disclosure practice at the ICC too.[203] Consistency in the application of such a regime could provide a better incentive to implement structural changes to the prosecutorial disclosure practice, than the *ad hoc* case-by-case reprimands practiced to date.

5. Concluding remarks

This chapter focused on the disclosure regimes of three international criminal courts: International Criminal Tribunals for the former Yugoslavia and Rwanda (ICTY and ICTR) and International Criminal Court (ICC), from a defence perspective. The main objective was delineating how the disclosure

---

dacted Decision on the "Defence Application Seeking a Permanent Stay of the Proceedings, ICC-01/04-01/06-2690-Red, 2 March 2011.

199 ICC, *Prosecutor v. Lubanga Dyilo*, Judgment on the Appeal of Mr. Thomas Lubanga Dyilo against the Decision on the Denfece Challenge to the Jurisdiction of the Court pursuant to Article 19(2)(a) of the Statute of 3 October 2006, ICC-01/04-01/06-772, 14 December 2006, paras. 27, 30, 37.

200 ICC, *Prosecutor v. Lubanga Dyilo*, Redacted Decision on the "Defence Application Seeking a Permanent Stay of the Proceedings, ICC-01/04-01/06-2690-Red, 2 March 2011, par. 212.

201 ICC, *Prosecutor v. Lubanga Dyilo*, Decision on the prosecution's disclosure obligations arising out of an issue concerning witness DRC-OTP-WWWW-0031, 7 December 2010, ICC-01/04-01/06-2656-Conf. A public redacted version was issued on 20 January 2011, ICC-01/04-01/06-2656-Red. ICC, *Prosecutor v. Uhuru Muigai Kenyatta*, Decision on defence application pursuant to Article 64(4) and related requests, Case No. ICC-01/09-02/11, 26 April 2013, par. 97. See also references in paragraph 3.2.c above.

202 ICC, *Prosecutor v. Uhuru Muigai Kenyatta*, Decision on defence application pursuant to Article 64(4) and related requests, Case No.ICC-01/09-02/11, 26 April 2013, par. 89-90; ICC, *Prosecutor v. Uhuru Muigai Kenyatta*, Decision on Prosecution's application for a finding of noncompliance pursuant to Article 87(7) and for an adjournment of the provisional trial date, Case No. ICC-01/09-02/11,31 March 2014, par. 88.

203 This regime could form *lex specialis* of the sanctioning framework provided for in Article 71 ICC Statute.

regime has affected a meaningful application of the principle of equality of arms. Particular, although highly selective, attention is paid to disclosure practice and more specifically, the way the international criminal courts have dealt with disclosure violations. Due to unequal positioning of both parties, structurally as well as procedurally, any violation on the part of prosecution of its disclosure obligations potentially undermines meaningful achievement of equality of arms and endangers the fairness of proceedings. Moreover, inefficient disclosure practice has had a detrimental effect on the expeditiousness of the proceedings.[204]

What transpires from the above overview of disclosure practice is that the obligations of the prosecution are broadly set up within the legal framework and have even been extended in the case law of the courts. Although applauded from the perspective of the right to have access to the materials underlying an accusation, the broadly set up disclosure obligations in combination with the digital modus of disclosing, has presented various practical challenges to defence which go to the ability of defence teams to adequately prepare for trial. Enormous amounts of documents disclosed close to or even past the disclosure deadlines, the regime of redactions and the practice of confidential documents have presented particular challenges to defence preparations. Moreover, the disclosure violations sanctions regime has not reached its full potential yet, to say the least, which seems mostly attributable to the fundamental importance of international crimc prosecution.[205] Notwithstanding ICC prosecutor's duty to investigate incriminating and exonerating evidence equally, it transpires from the practice that the prosecutor's approach to disclosure has been primarily driven by an adversarial attitude. In the strive towards a more effective application of 'disclosure' of information in order to better ensure equality of arms, a leap towards a common *dossier* (case file) system might prove unavoidable.[206]

204 Letter dated 29 May 2006 from the President of the International Tribunal for the Prosecution of Persons Responsible for Serious Violations of International Humanitarian Law Committed in the Territory of the Former Yugoslavia since 1991, addressed to the President of the Security Council, ANNEX I Assessment and Report of Judge Fausto Pocar, President of the International Criminal Tribunal for the Former Yugoslavia, Provided to the Security Council Pursuant to Paragraph 6 of Council Resolution 1534 (2004), S/2006/353, 31 May 2006, par. 25.

205 *Cf.* B.L. Gershman, The New Prosecutors, *53 University of Pittsburgh Law Review*, 1992, p. 439.

206 See also A. Heinze, *International Criminal Procedure and Disclosure*, Duncker & Humblot, 2014.

Eleni Chaitidou and Elisa Hoven[*]

The Person's Liberty at Stake – A Tour d'Horizon on the Rights of the Arrested Person under the Rome Statute

I. Introduction

The issuance of a warrant of arrest may occur unnoticed from the public's attention, but any arrest and surrender of a suspect to the International Criminal Court (ICC), or the first appearance of a suspect following a summons to appear, are special events in the Court's calendar. Indeed, the success of the Court is often assessed on the basis of the arrests effectuated (or the appearance of a suspect) as they trigger visibly the commencement of judicial proceedings before the Court. The legal questions and practical efforts behind a successful arrest and surrender are not always the focus of public interest. This article endeavors to present a selection of issues related to the person's liberty as they would typically unfold in proceedings before the ICC. It begins with the Prosecutor's application for a warrant of arrest or a summons to appear. Even though the latter is not a coercive measure depriving the person of his or her liberty, it is worthwhile to enquire how Pre-Trial Chambers have understood the preconditions of and interplay between the two options available under the Rome Statute. Once the person is arrested, arrest proceedings in the custodial State take place, and, upon their completion, the person is transferred to the Court's detention centre in The Hague. Soon thereafter, the person makes his or her initial appearance before the Pre-Trial Chamber. During that first hearing, he or she is informed of the minimum rights guaranteed under the Rome Statute, including the right to request interim release pending the commencement of trial. Should the detainee submit a request to this effect, he or she triggers a periodic judicial review exercise during which the competent chamber examines whether the preconditions for detention are still met. Finally, one aspect of the Rome Statute is discussed which has received only little attention in the Court's case law to date, namely the right to compensation to an arrested person.

---

* Eleni Chaitidou is Legal Officer in Chambers of the International Criminal Court (Pre-Trial and Trial Division). Dr. Elisa Hoven is an assistant professor (Juniorprofessor) at the Institute for Criminal Law and Criminal Procedure, University of Cologne and worked as a Visiting Professional at the International Criminal Court. The views expressed herein are those of the authors alone and do not reflect the views of the International Criminal Court.

II. Prologue: The Differentiation between a "Situation" and a "Case"

Unlike other international(ized) tribunals, the Court is not assigned with one situation. Rather, the ICC has been designed to be a permanent court with universal vocation, empowered to select the situations in which it intervenes. A corollary of this unique conception is the distinction between the 'situation' and one or more 'cases' emanating therefrom. A 'situation' denotes a conflict scenario, defined by territorial, temporal, and, as the case may be, personal parameters,[1] in which one or more crimes subject to the jurisdiction of the Court appear to have been committed. A 'situation' (and not a 'case') is referred to the Court by way of a State Party or Security Council referral;[2] in the following, the Prosecutor conducts a preliminary examination pursuant to article 53(1) of the Rome Statute[3] with a view to ascertaining whether there is a reasonable basis to proceed. If so, the Prosecutor shall commence the investigation. A third possibility to trigger the exercise of jurisdiction of the Court is that the Prosecutor, having concluded the article 53(1) preliminary examination in the affirmative, has been given authorization by the Pre-Trial Chamber to initiate an investigation *proprio motu* (on his or her own initiative) in accordance with article 15.[4] The investigation is the exclusive province of the Prosecutor[5] during which he or she enquires into the commission of crimes and the individual criminal responsibility of potential perpetrators. Judicial proceedings at the situation level only take place in relation to specific issues, such as the preservation of evidence in the context of a unique investigative opportunity (article 56(1) or (3)) or the protection and privacy of victims and witnesses (article 57(3)).[6] Proceedings at the situation level

1 Pre-Trial Chamber I, Decision on the Applications for Participation in the Proceedings of VPRS 1, VPRS 2, VPRS 3, VPRS 4, VPRS 5 and VPRS 6, 17 January 2006, ICC-01/04-101-tENG-Corr, para. 65; Pre-Trial Chamber II, Decision on victims' applications for participation a/0010/06, a/0064/06 to a/0070/06, a/0081/06 to a/0104/06, and a/0111/06 to a/0127/06, 10 August 2006, ICC-02/05-101, paras 88-103; A Marchesi/E Chaitidou, Article 14 MN 25, in O Triffterer/K Ambos (eds), The Rome Statute of the International Criminal Court – A Commentary (3rd ed, 2015).

2 Articles 13(a) and (b) of the Rome Statute.

3 Rome Statute of the International Criminal Court = UNTS vol. 2187, p. 3. All articles mentioned in this article without reference to the legal instrument are those of the Rome Statute. Article 53(1) establishes three criteria which the Prosecutor must adhere to when conducting the preliminary examination. The Prosecutor must assess whether (i) the crime(s), as alleged, fall(s) within the jurisdiction of the Court; (ii) the potential cases emanating from this situation would be admissible before the Court; and (iii) whether "taking into account the gravity of the crime and the interests of victims, there are nonetheless substantial reasons to believe that an investigation would not serve the interests of justice".

4 Article 13(c).

5 Appeals Chamber, Judgment on victim participation in the investigation stage of the proceedings in the appeal of the OPCD against the decision of Pre-Trial Chamber I of 7 December 2007 and in the appeals of the OPCD and the Prosecutor against the decision of Pre-Trial Chamber I of 24 December 2007, 19 December 2008, ICC-01/04-556, para. 51.

6 Pre-Trial Chamber II, Victims Decision on Victims' Participation in Proceedings Related to the Situation in the Republic of Kenya, 3 November 2010, ICC-01/09-24, para. 12.

remain separate from those relating to a particular 'case'. All relevant documents and decisions are registered in the 'situation record'.[7]

A concrete 'case' emerges if the Prosecutor has identified a particular individual and the alleged conduct for which he or she is held responsible.[8] 'Case' proceedings start with the Prosecutor's request seeking the issuance of a warrant of arrest or a summons to appear pursuant to article 58. Accordingly, with the article 58 application a 'case record' is opened.[9] However, in the Court's practice, the article 58 application still forms part of the pertinent 'situation record'. The justification for this approach is twofold: (i) if the Pre-Trial Chamber declines to issue the requested warrant of arrest or summons to appear, a case record must not be opened; (ii) if in one and the same year an article 58 request is submitted 'under seal' or 'confidential' in relation to one suspect, and another article 58 request is subsequently submitted publicly in relation to another suspect, the Registry's assignment of case numbers could reveal to the public that a case record was opened in one and the same year against one or more individuals in that situation without notice to the public. This would jeopardize the confidentiality of the 'under seal'/'confidential' proceedings[10] and would invite speculation as to who might be targeted by an 'under seal'/'confidential' warrant of arrest. These considerations have led to the practice to open a 'case record' and to assign a case number only when the Chamber issues the warrant of arrest or summons to appear. Thus, the warrant of arrest or summons to appear is often the first document contained in the case record.[11] With a view to keeping the article 58 application together with the actual warrant of arrest or summons to appear, the Chamber subsequently orders the transfer of the article 58 application and related other documents into the 'case record'.

---

7 See regulation 20(1) of the Regulations of the Registry. Pursuant to regulation 27(1) of the Regulations of the Registry, the acronym "ICC" is followed by the serial numbers of the situation in a given year (e.g., 01/04 = first situation in the year 2004).

8 See, for example, Pre-Trial Chamber II, Decision on the admissibility of the case against Abdullah Al-Senussi, 11 October 2013, ICC-01/11-01/11-466-Red, para. 66(i); Appeals Chamber, Judgment on the appeal of the Republic of Kenya against the decision of Pre-Trial Chamber II of 30 May 2011 entitled "Decision on the Application by the Government of Kenya Challenging the Admissibility of the Case Pursuant to Article 19(2)(b) of the Statute", ICC-01/09-02/11-274 (OA), para. 39.

9 See regulation 20(2) of the Regulations of the Registry. Pursuant to regulation 27(1) of the Regulations of the Registry, the serial number of the situation (e.g., ICC-01/04) is followed by the serial number of the case in a given year (e.g. 01/15 = first case in the year 2015).

10 Regulation 14(c) of the Regulations of the Registry.

11 The only exception to date is the *Ongwen* case record to which all filings relevant to *Ongwen* were transferred from the *Kony et al.* case (a case in which *Ongwen* was originally prosecuted together with others) in chronological order, starting with the Prosecutor's application, as foreseen in regulation 20(2) of the Regulations of the Registry.

III. The Issuance of a Warrant of Arrest or Summons to Appear

1. The Impetus: The Prosecutor's Application

Under the statutory framework, there is no possibility to hold trials *in absentia.*[12] Only the confirmation of charges hearing can be held without the presence of the suspect, according to article 61(2). To ensure a person's presence before the ICC, the Prosecutor may request the Pre-Trial Chamber to issue a warrant of arrest or a summons to appear. Article 58(2) sets out in great detail the requirements for the application seeking the issuance of a warrant of arrest. There is no equivalent provision in the Statute in respect of the Prosecutor's application for a summons to appear. However, considering that the summons to appear is an alternative to the warrant of arrest, appropriate guidance may still be drawn from article 58(2), with the exception of setting out the reasons on the necessity of arrest pursuant to article 58(2)(e).[13] The application is therefore discussed in relation to both avenues under article 58(1) and (7).

The process leading to the issuance of a warrant of arrest or summons can only be triggered by the Prosecutor. The Pre-Trial Chamber cannot issue a warrant of arrest or summons *proprio motu.*[14] The Statute does not establish any time limit within which the Prosecutor must submit an application. Indeed, as the wording of article 58(1) suggests, the Prosecutor may approach the Chamber "[a]t any time after the initiation of the investigation".[15] When this is the case depends to a great extent on the conduct and progress of the

12 Article 63. However, the Court has accepted the absence of the accused at trial under limited circumstances, see Appeals Chamber, Judgment on the appeal of the Prosecutor against the decision of Trial Chamber V(a) of 18 June 2013 entitled "Decision on Mr Ruto's Request for Excusal from Continuous Presence at Trial", 25 October 2013, ICC-01/09-01/11-1066 (OA5) (with two Judges dissenting); the Court's ruling was later translated into new provisions, see rules 134*bis* to 134*quater* of the Rules of Procedure and Evidence. The Rules of Procedure and Evidence = ICC-ASP/1/3 and Corr.1, as amended by resolutions ICC-ASP/11/Res.2 and ICC-ASP/12/Res.7. All rules mentioned in this article without reference to the legal instrument are those of the ICC's Rules of Procedure and Evidence.

13 See also W Schabas, Article 58, in W Schabas (ed), The International Criminal Court – A Commentary on the Rome Statute (OUP, 2010), p. 712.

14 See also Ch Hall/C Ryngaert, Article 58 MN 5, in O Triffterer/K Ambos (eds), The Rome Statute of the International Criminal Court – A Commentary (3rd ed, 2015). However, see below for the discussion whether the Chamber, once seized of a request, can decide to resort to either article 58(1) or (7) on its own motion. Equally, a different matter is the Chamber's authority to replace a summons to appear with a warrant of arrest in case the person does not comply with the conditions imposed, as is discussed below.

15 See also Ch Hall/C Ryngaert, Article 58 MN 6, in O Triffterer/K Ambos (eds), The Rome Statute of the International Criminal Court – A Commentary (3rd ed, 2015); Ch Safferling, International Criminal Procedure, (OUP, 2012), p. 291.

investigation in relation to the person against whom a warrant of arrest or summons to appear is considered.[16]

The Statute also remains silent as to the classification of the application as either 'public',[17] 'confidential' or 'under seal'.[18] Under the statutory regime, all of these options are possible. Factors such as the prospective chances of success for apprehending the suspect, or the possible impact on victims and witnesses, or security concerns for the suspect, if the application were to be known, may militate in favor of lodging and treating the application 'under seal' or 'confidential' for a certain time. The chosen course of action is regularly explained to the competent Chamber.[19] Where the basis for keeping the application 'under seal' or 'confidential' no longer exists, the application is reclassified as 'public', if need be with redactions to protect sensitive information.

According to article 58(2) the application must contain (i) the name of the person sought and other relevant identifying information; (ii) a specific reference to the crimes which the person is alleged to have committed; (iii) a concise statement of the facts which are alleged to constitute those crimes; (iv) a summary of the evidence and other information which establish reasonable grounds to believe that the person committed the crimes as purported by the Prosecutor; and, finally, (v) an explanation of the Prosecutor as to why the arrest of the person is necessary. In case of a summons, the latter requirement must be read to encompass the reasons why the summons is deemed sufficient to ensure the person's appearance (article 58(7), second sentence). These substantive prerequisites are the minimum content of the Prosecutor's application.[20] The Appeals Chamber clarified that information and evidence in relation to the admissibility of the case does not need to be

---

16 The investigation in a situation is the umbrella undertaking which comprises one or more derivative investigations against potential suspects. Unlike the *ad hoc* tribunals, the situations at the ICC do not have an end-date but remain ongoing for as long as the Prosecutor investigates against persons suspected to bear responsibility for crimes under the jurisdiction of the Court. As a corollary, investigations into a situation may last for several decades.

17 For example, on 14 July 2008, the Prosecutor filed a public summary of the first application against Omar Hassan Ahmad Al Bashir, President of Sudan, and gave a press statement, see "ICC Prosecutor presents case against Sudanese President, Hassan Ahmad AL BASHIR, for genocide, crimes against humanity and war crimes in Darfur", ICC-OTP-20080714-PR341 (available on the website of the Court).

18 See regulation 14 of the Regulations of the Registry. Documents 'under seal' and 'confidential' have in common that they are confidential and are not to be disclosed to the public. The difference between the two classifications pertains to the circle of persons who know of the existence (and content) of the documents; in relation to 'under seal' only a limited number of persons will be aware of it.

19 Regulation 23*bis* (1) of the Regulations of the Court.

20 Appeals Chamber, Judgment on the Prosecutor's appeal against the decision of Pre-Trial Chamber I entitled "Decision on the Prosecutor's Application for Warrant of Arrests, Article 58", 13 July 2006, ICC-01/04-169 (OA), para. 45.

included in the application, since such considerations are not part of the article 58 proceedings.[21]

Pre-Trial Chamber II in the *Mudacumura* case highlighted that the application must comply with the legal requirement of specificity.[22] This concerns in particular the pleading of specific crimes and the description, as precise as possible, of the conduct underlying the crimes, including their spatial parameters. This would mean, for example, that in the request the Prosecutor must set out in sufficient detail the conduct of the suspect which is alleged to fulfil the definition of the crimes (what did he or she do or omit, and in relation to which crime?). Also, the description of the crime(s) must be sufficiently clear, informing the Chamber about the temporal and spatial scope of the crime(s) that are mentioned in the article 58 request (what happened when and where?). The Chamber stated that it would not use its authority to deprive a person of his or her liberty if the requirement of specificity was not met.[23] The imprecise pleading of the facts was the reason for the Chamber to dismiss *in limine* (from the outset) the Prosecutor's first application in the *Mudacumura* case. Upon submission of a new revised application, the warrant of arrest against *Mudacumura* was issued. The specificity of pleading the factual course of conduct for which the arrest of a suspect is sought is a point which at times surfaces later again in the context of the confirmation of charges or trial. It is indeed imperative that the Prosecutor define the contours of the case, as required by the Statute, at any given stage of the proceedings.

The application must be accompanied by evidence and information which will, in the view of the Prosecutor, convince the Judges to issue the warrant of arrest or summons to appear.[24] It is incumbent upon the Prosecutor to select those pieces of evidence which in his or her opinion will meet the requisite 'threshold of suspicion' applicable at this stage. The relatively low threshold for issuing a warrant of arrest or summons to appear under article 58(1)[25] and the fact that the investigation at the article 58 stage is still ongo-

---

21 *Ibid.*

22 Pre-Trial Chamber II, Decision on the Prosecutor's Application under Article 58, 31 May 2012, ICC-01/04-613, para. 5. The same requirement was reiterated later in the *Bemba et al.* case, see Pre-Trial Chamber II, Warrant of arrest for Jean-Pierre BEMBA GOMBO, Aimé KILOLO MUSAMBA, Jean-Jacques MANGENDA KABONGO, Fidèle BABALA WANDU, and Narcisse ARIDO, 20 November 2013, ICC-01/05-01/13-1-Red2-tENG, para. 11.

23 Pre-Trial Chamber II, Decision on the Prosecutor's Application under Article 58, 31 May 2012, ICC-01/04-613, para. 8.

24 "*The availability of evidential material establishing grounds leading to a reasonable belief that the arrestee committed a crime or crimes in accordance of article 58(1) of the Statute is a* sine qua non *for the issuance of a warrant of arrest*", Separate Opinion of Judge Georghios M Pikis, para. 4, annexed to Appeals Chamber, Judgment on the appeal of Mr. Thomas Lubanga Dyilo against the decision of Pre-Trial Chamber I entitled "Décision sur la demande de mise en liberté provisoire de Thomas Lubanga Dyilo", 13 February 2007, ICC-01/04-01/06-824 (OA7).

25 See below "The Chamber's Response: The Warrant of Arrest".

ing have a bearing on the nature of the material submitted. Material that has been submitted at this stage of the proceedings consisted mostly of press articles, reports of non-governmental or international organizations, such as the United Nations, and, to a lesser degree, witness statements. In case the Chamber is not fully satisfied, it may request the submission of further material[26] or simply reject the application[27]. In the latter case, the Prosecutor may resubmit the application on the basis of additional evidence.

At this stage of the proceedings, the application and supporting material is filed *ex parte*, without notification to the person concerned. The Chamber regularly ensures that all this material is made available to the suspect soon after the surrender or voluntary appearance before the Court.[28] For protection reasons, the application and supporting material may require the redaction of certain information. However, the *ex parte* nature has the downside that it prevents from the outset any possible intervention of the suspect prior to the issuance of the warrant of arrest or summons to appear. Indeed, in the Kenya cases, where the Prosecutor chose not to interview the suspects under article 55(2), the persons were also not permitted to make any submissions before Pre-Trial Chamber II at the time it entertained the article 58(7) applications.[29] It remarked that "*under the statutory framework of the Court, there is no legal basis for a person under the Prosecutor's investigation to submit observations at the current stage of proceedings. (...) The only communication envisaged at the article 58 stage is conducted between the Pre-Trial Cham-*

26 Pre-Trial Chamber I, Redacted Version of the Decision concerning Supporting Materials in Connection with the Prosecution's Application REDACTED pursuant to article 58, 9 March 2006, ICC-01/04-01/06-27, p. 3; Pre-Trial Chamber I, Decision concerning Supporting Materials in Connection with the Prosecution's Application for Warrants of Arrest pursuant to article 58, 20 January 2006, ICC-01/04-02/06-323-Red; Pre-Trial Chamber I, Decision Requesting Additional Supporting Materials in relation to the Prosecution's Request for a Warrant of Arrest against Omar Hassan Al Bashir, 15 October 2008, ICC-02/05-160. In the *Hussein* case, Pre-Trial Chamber I requested that material referred to but not annexed to the Prosecutor's article 58 application should be submitted to the Chamber, see Pre-Trial Chamber I, Decision requesting supporting materials for the "Prosecutor's Application under Article 58", 27 January 2012, ICC-02/05-239.

27 Pre-Trial Chamber I, Decision on the Prosecutor's Application for a warrant of arrest, Article 58, 10 February 2006, para. 9, as annexed to *id.*, Decision concerning Pre-Trial Chamber I's Decision of 10 February 2006 and the Incorporation of Documents into the Record of the Case against Mr Thomas Lubanga Dyilo, 24 February 2006, ICC-01/04-01/06-8-Corr.

28 See for example, Pre-Trial Chamber II, Decision Requesting the Prosecutor to Submit Observations on the Possible Reclassification of Certain Documents, 21 March 2011, ICC-01/09-01/11-7; Pre-Trial Chamber II, Transcript of Hearing, 15 April 2013, ICC-01/04-02/06-T-3, p. 13, lines 15-22.

29 Pre-Trial Chamber II, Decision on Application for Leave to Submit Amicus Curiae Observations, 18 January 2011, ICC-01/09-35 (leave to appeal this decision was denied by the Chamber, see Decision on a Request for Leave to Appeal, 11 February 2011, ICC-01/09-43); see also *ibid.*, Decision on the "Application for Leave to Participate in the Proceedings before the Pre-Trial Chamber relating to the Prosecutor's Application under Article 58(7)", 11 February 2011, ICC-01/09-42; Decision on Application for Leave to Participate under Articles 58,42(5), (7)-(8)(a) of the Rome Statute and Rule 34(l)(d) and (2) of the Rules of Procedure and Evidence, 18 February 2011, ICC-01/09-47.

ber and the Prosecutor".[30] It is debatable whether such a strict approach is compatible with the right to be heard under internationally recognized human rights (article 21(3)).

2. *The Chamber's Response: The Warrant of Arrest*

Upon examination of the application and the evidence or information submitted, the Chamber issues a warrant of arrest. There is no time limit within which the warrant must be issued.[31] Much will depend on the workload of the Chamber, the scope of the case and the time needed to review the evidentiary material submitted. This may explain the time consumed between the lodging of the Prosecutor's application and the actual issuance of the warrant of arrest. *Schabas* has argued that "extraordinary delays" in responding to the Prosecutor's application may be incompatible with the rights of the suspect to be tried without undue delay.[32] However, this conclusion is quite far-reaching. As explained above, there is no case before the actual issuance of the warrant of arrest, and the individual, who most of the time is not aware of the existence of an application, is not negatively affected in his or her rights prior to the issuance of such warrant.[33] All the more so since, as shown in the *Mudacumura* case, the Prosecutor's application may be rejected.

The Pre-Trial Chamber will issue a warrant if it is satisfied of the existence of two cumulative conditions: (i) "there are reasonable grounds to believe that the person has committed a crime within the jurisdiction of the Court"; and (ii) "the arrest of the person appears necessary". In case the two conditions of article 58(1) are fulfilled, the Pre-Trial Chamber is under an obligation to issue the warrant of arrest. This is underlined by the use of the word "shall" in the introductory sentence of article 58(1).[34] Accordingly, the

---

30 Pre-Trial Chamber II, Decision on Application for Leave to Submit Amicus Curiae Observations, 18 January 2011, ICC-01/09-35, para. 10.

31 Pre-Trial Chamber I announced the date on which it would issue and publicize its first decision on the Prosecutor's article 58 application in relation to *Bashir*. It felt compelled to take this unusual steps in the face of a growing number of rumours surrounding the Court's response to the Prosecutor's application regarding a sitting head of State, see Pre-Trial Chamber I, Public notice of the Decision on the Prosecution's Application under article 58 of the Statute, 23 February 2009, ICC-02/05-193.

32 W Schabas, Article 58, in W Schabas (ed), The International Criminal Court – A Commentary on the Rome Statute (OUP, 2010), p. 711.

33 Should the person be interviewed during the course of investigation, article 55 ensures that the rights of the person are respected. "*The issue of a warrant of arrest or a summons to appear paves the way for the commencement of judicial proceedings respecting the crimes the person is believed to have committed*", Separate Opinion of Judge Georghios M. Pikis, para. 7, annexed to Appeals Chamber, Judgment on the appeal of Mr. Thomas Lubanga Dyilo against the decision of Pre-Trial Chamber I entitled "Décision sur la demande de mise en liberté provisoire de Thomas Lubanga Dyilo", 13 February 2007, ICC-01/04-01/06-824 (OA7).

34 Appeals Chamber, Judgment on the Prosecutor's appeal against the decision of Pre-Trial Chamber I entitled "Decision on the Prosecutor's Application for Warrants of Arrest, Article 58", 13 July 2006, ICC-01/04-169 (OA), para. 44.

Chamber has no discretion to decline the request for reasons other than evidentiary or legal.[35]

a) The first condition: reasonable grounds that suspect committed a crime

As regards the first condition in article 58(1)(a), the Pre-Trial Chamber must be satisfied, based on the material provided, that there are reasonable grounds to believe that the person committed one or more crimes, as alleged by the Prosecutor. The interpretation of the statutory evidentiary threshold of "reasonable grounds" is the lowest applicable in case proceedings[36] and, as it is not otherwise defined in the statutory documents, has been construed by resorting to internationally recognized human rights (article 21(3)). As a result, the notion is informed mainly by the jurisprudence of the European Court of Human Rights and that of the Inter-American Court of Human Rights concerning the right to liberty.[37] Most frequently, it is equated with the "reasonable suspicion" standard as stipulated in article 5(1)(c) of the (European) Convention for the Protection of Human Rights and Fundamental Freedoms ("ECHR") which is understood to require "the existence of some facts or information which would satisfy an objective observer that the person concerned may have committed the offence".[38] In the Court's language this has been translated to mean that "[t]he facts placed before the Chamber must be cogent to the extent of creating a reasonable belief that the person committed the crimes".[39] Mere suspicion is not enough. In the *Bashir* case, the Appeals Chamber stressed that the ruling Chamber does not have to be

---

35 Ch Hall/C Ryngaert, Article 58 MN 10, in O Triffterer/ K Ambos (eds), The Rome Statute of the International Criminal Court – A Commentary (3rd ed, 2015); W Schabas, Article 58, in W Schabas (ed), The International Criminal Court – A Commentary on the Rome Statute (OUP, 2010), p. 705.

36 Appeals Chamber, Judgment on the appeal of the Prosecutor against the "Decision on the Prosecution's Application for a Warrant of Arrest against Omar Hassan Ahmad Al Bashir", 3 February 2010, ICC-02/05-01/09-73 (OA), para. 30. The standard "reasonable basis to proceed" within the meaning of articles 53(1) and 15(4) is considered to be even lower, but it concerns proceedings taking place at the situation level, see, for example, Pre-Trial Chamber II, Decision Pursuant to Article 15 of the Rome Statute on the Authorization of an Investigation into the Situation in the Republic of Kenya, 31 March 2010, ICC-01/09-19-Corr, paras 27-35.

37 See, for example, Pre-Trial Chamber III, Decision on the Prosecutor's Application for a Warrant of Arrest against Jean-Pierre Bemba Gombo, 10 June 2008, ICC-01/05-01/08-14-tENG, para. 24; Pre-Trial Chamber III, Decision on the Prosecutor's Application Pursuant to Article 58 for a warrant of arrest against Laurent Koudou Gbagbo, 30 November 2011, ICC-02/11-01/11-9-Red, para. 27; Pre-Trial Chamber II, Decision on the Prosecutor's Application under Article 58, 13 July 2012, ICC-01/04-02/06-36-Red, para. 16. Viewed critically by *Schabas*, W Schabas, Article 58, in W Schabas (ed), The International Criminal Court – A Commentary on the Rome Statute (OUP, 2010), pp. 706-707.

38 For example, European Court of Human Rights (ECtHR), *Fox, Campbell and Hartley v United Kingdom*, Judgment of 30 August 1990, vol. 182, Series A, p. 16, para. 32; *K.-F. v. Germany*, Judgment of 27 November 1997, Reports 1997-VII, para. 57.

39 Appeals Chamber, Judgment in the Appeal of Mathieu Ngudjolo Chui of 27 March 2008 against the Decision of Pre-Trial Chamber I on the Application of the Appellant for Interim Release, 9 June 2008, ICC-01/04-01/07-572 (OA4), para. 18.

certain that the person concerned committed the crimes. Rather, the evidence must only establish *a* reasonable conclusion, possibly amongst several other reasonable conclusions available, and not the *only* reasonable conclusion.[40]

The Pre-Trial Chamber reviews the Prosecutor's allegations comprehensively and in light of the supporting material as regards the crimes and criminal responsibility of the suspect[41] set forth in the application.[42] However, it may not add new facts that it discovers when reviewing the material submitted as it is not vested with investigative powers. On the other hand, the Chamber is not bound by the Prosecutor's *legal* characterization of the facts and may advance its own reading of the facts in the warrant of arrest.[43] But even if the Chamber would accept the Prosecutor's legal characterization at the warrant of arrest stage, this does not mean that this characterization may not change at a later stage.[44] Indeed, new evidence collected during the investigation may warrant such reconsideration. The following example may illustrate the changing nature of the legal characterization of facts while the investigation is ongoing. In the decision authorizing the commencement of an investigation (article 15) in the situation in the Republic of Côte d'Ivoire, the Chamber had accepted the Prosecutor's assessment that crimes against humanity had been committed according to a 'State policy'. At the warrant of arrest stage in the *Laurent Gbagbo* case, however, the Chamber accepted the

40 Appeals Chamber, Judgment on the appeal of the Prosecutor against the "Decision on the Prosecution's Application for a Warrant of Arrest against Omar Hassan Ahmad Al Bashir", 3 February 2010, ICC-02/05-01/09-73 (OA), para. 33. For a discussion, see W Schabas (ed), The International Criminal Court – A Commentary on the Rome Statute (OUP, 2010), p. 707-708.

41 See also W Schabas, Article 58, in W Schabas (ed), The International Criminal Court – A Commentary on the Rome Statute (OUP, 2010), p. 706; Ch Safferling, International Criminal Procedure, (2012), p. 292.

42 See, for example, Pre-Trial Chamber I, Decision on the Prosecutor's Application for a warrant of arrest, Article 58, 10 February 2006, paras 10-11, as annexed to *id.*, Decision concerning Pre-Trial Chamber I's Decision of 10 February 2006 and the Incorporation of Documents into the Record of the Case against Mr Thomas Lubanga Dyilo, 24 February 2006, ICC-01/04-01/06-8-Corr; Pre-Trial Chamber III, Decision on the Prosecutor's Application Pursuant to Article 58 for a warrant of arrest against Charles Blé Goudé, 6 January 2012, ICC-02/11-02/11-3, para. 14; Pre-Trial Chamber III, Decision on the Prosecutor's Application Pursuant to Article 58 for a warrant of arrest against Simone Gbagbo, 2 March 2012, ICC-02/11-01/12-2-Red, para. 14.

43 For example, Pre-Trial Chamber III, Decision on the Prosecutor's Application for a Warrant of Arrest against Jean-Pierre Bemba Gombo, 10 June 2008, ICC-01/05-01/08-14-tENG, para. 25; Pre-Trial Chamber II, Decision on the Prosecutor's Application for Summons to Appear for William Samoei Ruto, Henry Kiprono Kosgey and Joshua Arap Sang, 8 March 2011, ICC-01/09-01/11-1, paras 37 and 44. In the latter case, the Chamber declined to follow the Prosecutor's assessment that Sang was to be held accountable as a principal and accessorial perpetrator but determined that there were reasonable grounds to believe that he was (only) an accessory to the crimes alleged.

44 Similarly, W Schabas, Article 58, in W Schabas (ed), The International Criminal Court – A Commentary on the Rome Statute (OUP, 2010), p. 706.

Prosecutor's proposition that the crimes had been committed pursuant to an 'organizational policy'.[45]

The Chamber's comprehensive review of the Prosecutor's allegations allows the Judges to accept or reject all or some of the allegations made. In the Court's jurisprudence, it has occurred with some frequency that Pre-Trial Chambers rejected certain allegations already at this early stage. In the *Mudacumura* case, for example, Pre-Trial Chamber II included in the warrant of arrest the counts of war crimes but declined to include crimes against humanity as it denied the existence of an 'organizational policy' within the meaning of article 7.[46] Equally, in the *Bemba* case, the competent Chamber rejected the Prosecutor's assessment that the evidence supported the existence of 'other forms of sexual violence' as crime against humanity and war crime and did not include those counts in the warrant of arrest.[47] Finally, it may happen that a Pre-Trial Chamber accepts certain factual allegations but rejects others in relation to one and the same crime(s) or mode(s) of liability, thus limiting the course of conduct described in the warrant of arrest.[48] However, the fact that the Chamber does not include a particular crime or form of participation in the warrant of arrest does not preclude the Prosecutor, subject to the requirements of the rule of speciality (article 101), from later presenting those factual allegations on the basis of new evidence in the confirmation proceedings, in the document containing the charges (article 61(3)(a)) or by

45 Pre-Trial Chamber III, Decision on the Prosecutor's Application Pursuant to Article 58 for a warrant of arrest against Laurent Koudou Gbagbo, 30 November 2011, ICC-02/11-01/11-9-Red, para. 48. Notwithstanding this determination, the Chamber pointed to its authority to revisit the issue of State or organizational policy at a later stage.

46 Pre-Trial Chamber II, Decision on the Prosecutor's Application under Article 58, 13 July 2012, ICC-01/04-01/12-1-Red, paras 23-29.

47 Pre-Trial Chamber III, Decision on the Prosecutor's Application for a Warrant of Arrest against Jean-Pierre Bemba Gombo, 10 June 2008, ICC-01/05-01/08-10-tENG, paras 40 and 63.

48 The following example is borrowed from the *Kenyatta* case where the competent Pre-Trial Chamber issued summonses to appear against then three suspects *Muthaura*, *Kenyatta* and *Ali*. In the accompanying decision, the crime of rape in the location of Naivasha was not included in the summary of facts as "the Prosecutor failed to provide evidence substantiating his allegation that rape was committed as part of the attack in Naivasha", see Pre-Trial Chamber II, Decision on the Prosecutor's Application for Summonses to Appeal for Francis Kirimi Muthaura, Uhuru Muigai Kenyatta and Mohammed Hussein Ali, 8 March 2011, ICC-01/09-02/11-1, para. 26. Moreover, the Chamber rejected to include the events which allegedly had taken place in the locations "Kisumu" and "Kibera". The Chamber held: "[T]he Prosecutor (…) failed to provide an accurate factual and legal submission which would require the Chamber to examine whether the acts of violence were part of an attack pursuant to or in furtherance of a State policy. Apart from the foregoing, it is even more compelling that the material presented by the Prosecutor does not provide reasonable grounds to believe that the events which took place in Kisumu and/or Kibera can be attributed to Muthaura, Kenyatta and/or Ali under any mode of liability embodied in article 25(3) of the Statute", see Pre-Trial Chamber II, Decision on the Prosecutor's Application for Summonses to Appeal for Francis Kirimi Muthaura, Uhuru Muigai Kenyata and Mohammed Hussein Ali, 8 March 2011, ICC-01/09-02/11-1, paras 31-32.

way of an amendment of the charges (article 61((4)).[49] This means that the factual scope of the case may be enlarged at a later procedural stage.

Two more points warrant brief mention in the context of article 58(1)(a). First, before delving into the requirements of article 58(1)(a), the Chamber typically satisfies itself that it has jurisdiction to issue a warrant of arrest in the case. This requirement stems from article 19(1); but it is also embedded in the wording of article 58(1)(a) making reference to 'a crime within the jurisdiction of the Court'. Therefore, before embarking on its article 58 assessment, the Chamber will regularly determine whether the statutory parameters of jurisdiction have been met. To this end, the four facets of jurisdiction are examined, namely jurisdiction *ratione materiae* (article 5), *ratione temporis* (article 11), *ratione personae* or *ratione loci* (article 12(2)), the last two of which are in the alternative.[50]

Second, the Chamber may not enquire whether the case is admissible as a precondition of issuing the warrant of arrest. This question arose in one of the first cases before the Court. The Prosecutor submitted a request to issue a warrant of arrest against both *Lubanga* and *Ntaganda* for having had recruited and used child soldiers in armed hostilities. While the Chamber was responsive in relation to *Lubanga*, it refused to issue a warrant of arrest against *Ntaganda* on the grounds that the case against him did not reach the 'gravity' threshold of the Statute (article 17(1)(d)). More specifically, the Chamber reasoned that the case against *Ntaganda* lacked gravity because he was not one of the highest-ranking perpetrators.[51] At the appellate stage, the Pre-Trial Chamber's decision was reversed. Of relevance to our discussion is the Appeals Chamber's holding not to introduce the admissibility criteria in article 58 as a substantive prerequisite for issuing a warrant of arrest. It clarified that the substantive requirements in article 58 are exhaustively listed, and that

49 Pre-Trial Chamber II, Decision on the Prosecutor's Application for Summons to Appear for William Samoei Ruto, Henry Kiprono Kosgey and Joshua Arap Sang, 8 March 2011, ICC-01/09-01/11-1, para. 33.

50 In its judgment of 14 December 2006, the Appeals Chamber held: *"[t]he notion of jurisdiction has four different facets: subject-matter jurisdiction also identified by the Latin maxim jurisdiction* ratione materiae, *jurisdiction over persons, symbolized by the Latin maxim jurisdiction* ratione personae, *territorial jurisdiction – jurisdiction* ratione loci *– and lastly jurisdiction* ratione temporis. *These facets find expression in the Statute. The jurisdiction of the Court is laid down in the Statute: Article 5 specifies the subject-matter of the jurisdiction of the Court, namely the crimes over which the Court has jurisdiction, sequentially defined in articles 6, 7, and 8. Jurisdiction over persons is dealt with in articles 12 and 26, while territorial jurisdiction is specified by articles 12 and 13(b), depending on the origin of the proceedings. Lastly, jurisdiction ratione temporis is defined by article 11*"; see Appeals Chamber, Judgment on the Appeal of Mr. Thomas Lubanga Dyilo against the Decision on the Defence Challenge to the Jurisdiction of the Court pursuant to Article 19(2)(a) of the Statute of 3 October 2006, Appeals Chamber, 14 December 2006, ICC-01/04-01/06-772 (OA4), paras 21-22.

51 Pre-Trial Chamber I, Decision on the Prosecutor's Application for Warrants of Arrest, Article 58, 10 February 2006, ICC-01/04-02/06-20.

admissibility is not one of them.[52] The Appeals Chamber however accepted that the Pre-Trial Chamber had discretionary powers to rule on admissibility under article 19(1), second sentence. That said, the Appeals Chamber cautioned to assess admissibility under this provision as a separate procedural step, in particular when the article 58 proceedings are conducted *ex parte* without the involvement of the suspect. In this scenario, the Appeals Chamber emphasized, sufficient weight must be given to the interests of the suspect who has not been heard and may not even know of the existence of admissibility proceedings before the Court. According to the Appeals Chamber, whatever the decision of the Pre-Trial Chamber on admissibility, the interests of the suspect would be curtailed.[53] The Appeals Chamber acknowledged the advantage for the suspect not to be subjected to a warrant of arrest due to the inadmissibility of the case; however it opined that the Pre-Trial Chamber may not "come to the aid" of the suspect as there are other procedural avenues available through which his or her interests can be maintained, namely a challenge of admissibility by the suspect under article 19(2)(a).[54] With a view to reconciling the need for restraint and the discretionary powers under article 19(1), second sentence, the Appeals Chamber coined the formulation that admissibility be considered in instances "*where a case is based on the established jurisprudence of the Court, uncontested facts that render a case clearly inadmissible or an ostensible cause impelling the exercise of proprio motu review*".[55] Following this judgment, the Pre-Trial Chamber issued a warrant of arrest against *Ntaganda*.[56] Admissibility concerns were never again raised

---

52 Appeals Chamber, Judgment on the Prosecutor's appeal against the decision of Pre-Trial Chamber I entitled "Decision on the Prosecutor's Application for Warrants of Arrest, Article 58", 13 July 2006, ICC-01/04-169 (OA), paras 44-45.

53 *"[I]f the Pre-Trial Chamber makes a determination that the case against a suspect is admissible without the suspect participating in the proceedings, and the suspect at a later stage seeks to challenge the admissibility of a case pursuant to article 19(2)(a) of the Statute, he or she comes before a Pre-Trial Chamber that has already decided the very same issue to his or her detriment. A degree of predetermination is inevitable. If, on the other hand, the Pre-Trial Chamber decides that the case against the suspect is inadmissible, the situation for the suspect could be even worse: pursuant to article 82(1)(a) of the Statute, decisions with respect to admissibility can be appealed by the Prosecutor as matter of right; the present appeal is an appeal of this kind. If the Appeals Chamber overturns the Pre-Trial Chamber's decision and determines that the case is admissible, the suspect would be faced with a decision by the Appeals Chamber that the case is admissible. The right of the suspect to challenge the admissibility of the case before the Pre-Trial Chamber ad – potentially – the Appeals Chamber thus would be seriously impaired*"; Appeals Chamber, Judgment on the Prosecutor's appeal against the decision of Pre-Trial Chamber I entitled "Decision on the Prosecutor's Application for Warrants of Arrest, Article 58", 13 July 2006, ICC-01/04-169 (OA), para. 50.

54 *Ibid.*, para. 51.

55 *Ibid.*, para. 52.

56 Pre-Trial Chamber I, Warrant of arrest, 22 August 2006, ICC-01/04-02/06-2-Anx-tENG. A second warrant of arrest was issued against Ntaganda by Pre-Trial Chamber II, Decision on the Prosecutor's Application under Article 58, 13 July 2012, ICC-01/04-02/06-36-Red.

in other warrant of arrest proceedings.[57] While it is true that admissibility criteria are not explicitly mentioned in article 58, it is of importance to recall that article 19(1), second sentence, remains applicable nevertheless. The criteria set up by the Appeals Chamber under which conditions the Pre-Trial Chamber may exercise its discretion regarding admissibility are nowhere to be found in the statutory texts and have the potential to curtail the Chamber's powers to reject a case on the grounds that it is not admissible.

b) The second condition: grounds to arrest and detain the suspect

We now turn our focus to the second condition stipulated in article 58(1), namely whether the Pre-Trial Chamber is satisfied, based on the information provided by the Prosecutor, that "the arrest of the person appears necessary". The grounds for which arrest may be necessary are specified exhaustively in three sub-paragraphs of article 58(1)(b). Accordingly, arrest appears necessary

> *(i) To ensure the person's appearance at trial;*
> *(ii) To ensure that the person does not obstruct or endanger the investigation or the court proceedings; or*
> *(iii) Where applicable, to prevent the person from continuing with the commission of that crime or a related crime which is within the jurisdiction of the Court and which arises out of the same circumstances.*

Appearance in this context "revolves around the possibility, not the inevitability of a future occurrence".[58] It requires "an element of prediction",[59] a prognosis on the part of the Chamber that any of the scenarios envisaged under article 58(1)(b) may occur. The grounds set out above are in the alternative;[60] it suffices if only one of them is fulfilled. Most of the time, however, Chambers do not discuss the grounds separately, explicating on which factual allegations exactly they base their decision for either ground. Rather, they

57 See recently, Pre-Trial Chamber I, Mandat d'arrêt à l'encontre d'Ahmad AL FAQI AL MAHDI, 18 September 2015, ICC-01/12-01/15, para. 12; A detailed analysis of the question of admissibility in the context of the issuance of a warrant of arrest can be found in M. M. El Zeidy, Some Remarks on the Question of Admissibility of a Case during Arrest Warrant Proceedings before the International Criminal Court, LJIL 19 (2006), pp. 741-751.

58 Appeals Chamber, Judgment in the Appeal of Mathieu Ngudjolo Chui of 27 March 2008 against the Decision of Pre-Trial Chamber I on the Application of the Appellant for Interim Release, 9 June 2008, ICC-01/04-01/07-572 (OA4), para. 21.

59 Appeals Chamber, Judgment on the appeal of Mr. Thomas Lubanga Dyilo against the decision of Pre-Trial Chamber I entitled "Décision sur la demande de mise en liberté provisoire de Thomas Lubanga Dyilo", 13 February 2007, ICC-01/04-01/06-824 (OA7), para. 137.

60 Appeals Chamber, Judgment on the appeal of Mr. Thomas Lubanga Dyilo against the decision of Pre-Trial Chamber I entitled "Décision sur la demande de mise en liberté provisoire de Thomas Lubanga Dyilo", 13 February 2007, ICC-01/04-01/06-824 (OA7), para. 139.

refer often collectively to a series of factual allegations and conclude that the arrest is necessary on two or all three grounds set out in article 58(1)(b), thus making it overly burdensome for the suspect to effectively challenge the decision to arrest at a later stage.[61] For example, in the *Bemba* case, Pre-Trial Chamber III referred collectively to a series of factors, such as *Bemba's* past and present political position, his financial resources, the possibility to rely on his movement's network as well as the financial destitution of victims, and concluded summarily that detention was necessary to ensure *Bemba's* appearance at trial and to prevent him from obstructing or endangering the investigation or court proceedings.[62] In this regard, it would be more helpful for the suspect if the Chambers specified with greater clarity their findings in relation to each of the grounds.[63]

The first ground under article 58(1)(b), namely to ensure the person's appearance at trial, is found most frequently in the Court's case law and is typically assessed by undertaking a prognosis whether the suspect will abscond or avoid arrest. Factors such as the suspect's financial resources, professional background, past and present political position, and international contacts are taken into account in making such a determination.[64] The seriousness or gravity of the allegations and possible sentence, if the person is found guilty, have also been accepted as relevant factors, as they are likely to provide an incentive for the suspect to abscond.[65] In addition, the fact that a

61 *Safferling* opines that "[o]n the whole, the ICC's evaluation of the grounds for detention in the decisions to issue a warrant of arrest is rather vague", Ch Safferling, International Criminal Procedure, (OUP, 2012), p. 295.

62 Pre-Trial Chamber III, Decision on the Prosecutor's Application for a Warrant of Arrest against Jean-Pierre Bemba Gombo, 10 June 2008, ICC-01/05-01/08-14-tENG, paras 87-90; Pre-Trial Chamber III equally assessed summarily the grounds under article 58(1)(b) in the *Blé Goudé* case and the *Simone Gbagbo* case, see Pre-Trial Chamber III, Decision on the Prosecutor's Application Pursuant to Article 58 for a warrant of arrest against Charles Blé Goudé, 6 January 2012, ICC-02/11-02/11-3, paras 40-43; Pre-Trial Chamber III, Decision on the Prosecutor's Application Pursuant to Article 58 for a warrant of arrest against Simone Gbagbo, 2 March 2012, ICC-02/11-01/12-2-Red, paras 42-45.

63 See also the example of Pre-Trial Chamber II in the *Kony et al.* case where the Chamber laconically referred to the existence of the Lord's Resistance Army for 18 years and the inclination of commanders to launch retaliatory strikes in order to conclude that all grounds under article 58(1)(b) were met, Pre-Trial Chamber II, Warrant of arrest for Joseph Kony issued on 8 July 2005 as amended on 27 September 2005, 27 September 2005, ICC-02/04-01/05-53, paras 43-44.

64 For example, Pre-Trial Chamber III, Decision on the Prosecutor's Application for a Warrant of Arrest against Jean-Pierre Bemba Gombo, 10 June 2008, ICC-01/05-01/08-14-tENG, para. 87; Pre-Trial Chamber III, Decision on the Prosecutor's Application Pursuant to Article 58 for a warrant of arrest against Laurent Koudou Gbagbo, 30 November 2011, ICC-02/11-01/11-9-Red, paras 85-86.

65 Appeals Chamber, Judgment in the Appeal of Mathieu Ngudjolo Chui of 27 March 2008 against the Decision of Pre-Trial Chamber I on the Application of the Appellant for Interim Release, 9 June 2008, ICC-01/04-01/07-572 (OA4), para. 21; *id.*, Judgment on the appeal of Mr. Thomas Lubanga Dyilo against the decision of Pre-Trial Chamber I entitled "Décision sur la demande de mise en liberté provisoire de Thomas Lubanga Dyilo", 13 February 2007, ICC-01/04-01/06-824 (OA7), para. 136; In the *Bemba* case, the Appeals Chamber drew upon the confirmation of charges decision (article 61(7)(a)) to con-

suspect remains at large despite the existence of a previous ICC warrant of arrest also weighs in when seeking to ensure the person's appearance at trial.[66] A further strong indication for affirming article 58(1)(b)(i) is the fact that the suspect absconded after domestic authorities had issued a warrant of arrest (for other crimes), as was the case in the *Blé Goudé* case. Here, *Blé Goudé's* flight was taken as a strong indicator that the suspect would also evade proceedings before the ICC.[67] By contrast, *Lubanga* was in detention in the Democratic Republic of the Congo ("DRC") and could not flee, but his publicly voiced concern about the prospect of being prosecuted by the ICC was taken as an indication that he would abscond.[68] By the same token, *Muammar Gaddafi's* and *Saif Al-Islam Gaddafi's* public pronouncements were taken into account for confirming that unless arrested, they would not willingly appear before the Court.[69] On the other hand, in case the Chamber was informed of the suspect's assurance to cooperate with the Court, such assurance has been treated with caution and weighed against other relevant factors. In the *Mbarushimana* case, for example, such assurance was not successful; *Mbarushimana's* assurance was outweighed by the fact that he was holding a French residency permit which allowed him to travel freely in the Schengen area of the European Union, and the fact that there existed a network of supporters who had the means to assist him in absconding.[70] A (purported) network of supporters is an important consideration in the Chamber's assessment of article 58(1)(b)(i). Supporters are seen to potentially provide the suspect with the necessary means, either practical or financial, to flee and evade justice.[71] Further, Pre-Trial Chamber I in the *Harun/Kushayb*

firm the risk of absconding, *id.*, Judgment on the appeal of the Prosecutor against Pre-Trial Chamber II's "Decision on the Interim Release of Jean-Pierre Bemba Gombo and Convening Hearings with the Kingdom of Belgium, the Republic of Portugal, the Republic of France, the Federal Republic of Germany, the Italian Republic, and the Republic of South Africa", 2 December 2009, ICC-01/05-01/08-631-Red (OA2), para. 70.

66 Pre-Trial Chamber II, Decision on the Prosecutor's Application under Article 58, 13 July 2012, ICC-01/04-02/06-36-Red, para. 80.

67 Pre-Trial Chamber I, Decision on the Prosecutor's Application Pursuant to Article 58 for a warrant of arrest against Charles Blé Goudé, 6 January 2012, ICC-02/11-02/11-3, para. 41.

68 Pre-Trial Chamber I, Decision on the Prosecutor's Application for a warrant of arrest, Article 58, 10 February 2006, ICC-01/04-01/06-8-Corr, para. 100.

69 Pre-Trial Chamber I, Decision on the "Prosecutor's Application Pursuant to Article 58 as to Muammar Mohammed Abu Minyar GADDAFI, Saif Al-Islam GADDAFI and Abdullah AL-SENUSSI", 27 June 2011, ICC-01/11-01/11-1, paras 93 and 97.

70 Pre-Trial Chamber I, Decision on the Prosecutor's Application for a Warrant of Arrest against Callixte Mbarushimana, 28 September 2010, ICC-01/04-01/10-1, para. 47.

71 For example, Pre-Trial Chamber III, Decision on the Prosecutor's Application for a Warrant of Arrest against Jean-Pierre Bemba Gombo, 10 June 2008, ICC-01/05-01/08-14-tENG, para. 87; Pre-Trial Chamber I, Decision on the Prosecutor's Application for a Warrant of Arrest against Callixte Mbarushimana, 28 September 2010, ICC-01/04-01/10-1, para. 47; Pre-Trial Chamber III, Decision on the Prosecutor's Application Pursuant to Article 58 for a warrant of arrest against Laurent Koudou Gbagbo, 30 November 2011, ICC-02/11-01/11-9-Red, para. 85; Pre-Trial Chamber I, Mandat d'arrêt à l'encontre d'Ahmad AL FAQI AL MAHDI, 28 September 2015, ICC-01/12-01/15-1-Red, para. 14.

case also considered *Kushayb's* ongoing detention at the national level to be an obstacle to the person's appearance at trial before the ICC and therefore considered it necessary to issue a warrant of arrest.[72] Also the State's cooperation history with the ICC has been drawn upon, most prominently in the *Darfur/Sudan* cases, when discussing article 58(1)(b)(i).[73] In the *Bashir* case, the fact that the government of Sudan, over which *Bashir* presides, was refusing to cooperate with the Court and the suspect's defiance of the Court sufficed to determine that the suspect's appearance at trial needed to be ensured by means of arrest.[74]

The second ground listed in article 58(1)(b)(ii) concerns the possibility that the suspect obstruct or endanger the investigation or the court proceedings by, for example, interfering with witnesses either personally or through others over whom the suspect has authority.[75] The possibility to act through others is not diminished if the suspect is held in detention as his or her capacity to communicate with others is not precluded.[76] It is also not necessary to demonstrate that an actual attempt to this effect has taken place. The Statute requires only that arrest "appears necessary" in order to ensure the absence of obstruction; therefore, the *possible* occurrence of such obstruction is sufficient.[77] As the Appeals Chamber highlighted, article 58(1)(b)(ii) indicates that there must be a link between the detained person and the risk of witness interference.[78] Hence, in the *Bemba* case, Pre-Trial Chamber III made (also) reference to the existence of a (purported) network of supporters and concluded that *Bemba* may be able to influence witnesses through his supporters; in this context the Chamber found it important to point to the suspect's past behavior without, however, further explaining in what this past behavior

72 Pre-Trial Chamber I, Decision on the Prosecution Application under Article 58(7) of the Statute, 27 April 2007, ICC-02/05-01/07-1-Corr, para. 133.

73 Pre-Trial Chamber I, Decision on the Prosecutor's application under article 58 relating to Abdel Raheem Muhammad Hussein, 1 March 2012, ICC-02/05-01/12-1-Red, para. 44.

74 Pre-Trial Chamber I, Decision on the Prosecution's Application for a Warrant of Arrest against Omar Hassan Ahmad Al Bashir, 4 March 2009, ICC-02/05-01/09-3, paras 228-232.

75 *Safferling* describes the purpose of article 58(1)(b)(ii) as "*preventing the destruction of evidence, the intimidation of victims and witnesses as well as collusion with accomplices. Its scope includes all kinds of behavior capable of jeopardizing the conduct of the investigation and with that the proceedings as a whole*", see Ch Safferling, International Criminal Procedure, (OUP, 2012), p. 296.

76 Pre-Trial Chamber I, Decision on the Prosecutor's Application for a warrant of arrest, Article 58, 10 February 2006, ICC-01/04-01/06-8-Corr, para. 101.

77 Ch Hall/C Ryngaert, Article 58 MN 17, in O Triffterer/K Ambos (eds), The Rome Statute of the International Criminal Court – A Commentary (3rd ed, 2015).

78 Appeals Chamber, Judgment on the appeal of Mr Jean-Pierre Bemba Gombo against the decision of Trial Chamber III of 26 September 2011 entitled "Decision on the accused's application for provisional release in light of the Appeals Chamber's judgment of 19 August 2011", 23 November 2011, ICC-01/05-01/08-1937-Red2 (OA9), para. 67 (the public redacted version of the judgment was released on 15 December 2011).

consisted.[79] It also took into account the fact that many victims and witnesses are destitute and that it would be easy for *Bemba* to locate them.[80] In the *Harun/Kushayb* case, the alleged concealing of evidence to protect the government's policy was considered to be indicative of *Harun's* intention to obstruct court proceedings.[81] In the *Bashir* case, the suspect's control of the State apparatus was enough to assume that "he is in a position to attempt to obstruct proceedings and to possibly threaten witnesses".[82] In the *Laurent Gbagbo* case, Pre-Trial Chamber III went further and relied upon the fact that investigations by the United Nations and media, in relation to alleged crimes similar to those for which the ICC warrant of arrest was sought, were obstructed by the suspect's supporters, without however substantiating that this was attributable to the suspect himself.[83] This raises the question as to what extent a chamber may draw upon facts which do not reveal any link with the suspect him- or herself and assume, without further evidence, a past or future involvement of the suspect in order to confirm the fulfilment of article 58(1)(b)(ii).

Finally, the third ground contained in article 58(1)(b)(iii) involves the assessment whether arrest is necessary so as to prevent the suspect from continuing with the commission of crimes within the jurisdiction of the Court. In the Court's jurisprudence, this ground has been invoked the least. The Statute requires that the crimes committed must be either the same crimes for which a warrant of arrest is sought, or related crimes arising out of the same circumstances. Frequently, the suspect's official position, activities and continued influence over others will be determinative in finding whether there is a risk that the suspect may continue with the commission of the crime(s) unless

79 Pre-Trial Chamber III, Decision on the Prosecutor's Application for a Warrant of Arrest against Jean-Pierre Bemba Gombo, 10 June 2008, ICC-01/05-01/08-14-tENG, para. 89. In the *Mbarushimana* case, the Chamber paid heed to the position of the suspect and his contacts with members of the armed group in the field who had access to witnesses, see Pre-Trial Chamber I, Decision on the Prosecutor's Application for a Warrant of Arrest against Callixte Mbarushimana, 28 September 2010, ICC-01/04-01/10-1, para. 48. The same approach was taken in the *Blé Goudé* case, Pre-Trial Chamber I, Decision on the Prosecutor's Application Pursuant to Article 58 for a warrant of arrest against Charles Blé Goudé, 6 January 2012, ICC-02/11-02/11-3, para. 42.

80 Pre-Trial Chamber III, Decision on the Prosecutor's Application for a Warrant of Arrest against Jean-Pierre Bemba Gombo, 10 June 2008, ICC-01/05-01/08-14-tENG, para. 88.

81 Pre-Trial Chamber I, Decision on the Prosecution Application under Article 58(7) of the Statute, 27 April 2007, ICC-02/05-01/07-1-Corr, para. 131.

82 Pre-Trial Chamber I, Decision on the Prosecution's Application for a Warrant of Arrest against Omar Hassan Ahmad Al Bashir, 4 March 2009, ICC-02/05-01/09-3, para. 233. The same position was taken in the *Hussein* case, Pre-Trial Chamber I, Decision on the Prosecutor's application under article 58 relating to Abdel Raheem Muhammad Hussein, 1 March 2012, ICC-02/05-01/12-1-Red, para. 47.

83 Pre-Trial Chamber III, Decision on the Prosecutor's Application Pursuant to Article 58 for a warrant of arrest against Laurent Koudou Gbagbo, 30 November 2011, ICC-02/11-01/11-9-Red, paras 85-86.

arrested.[84] *Bashir's* position as commander-in-chief of the Sudanese armed forces, in light of reports that crimes were still being committed in Darfur at the time, in the view of Pre-Trial Chamber I justified the conclusion that the issuance of the warrant of arrest was necessary to prevent *Bashir* from continuing to commit further crimes.[85] Interestingly, the same Chamber declined to find that Sudan's minister of defence, *Hussein*, would continue with the commission of the crimes, arguing that the Prosecutor had not presented any evidence to this effect.[86] In the *Blé Goudé* case, it was the suspect's alleged control over about "20,000 pro-Gbagbo combatants" who fled to Ghana, in light of his critical statements about the Court's proceedings against *Laurent Gbagbo* and reported acts of violence committed by pro-Gbagbo youth, that led Pre-Trial Chamber I to conclude that there was a "real possibility" that *Blé Goudé* would use the resources to commit further crimes within the jurisdiction of the Court.[87] Previous public statements also played a role in the *Simone Gbagbo* case where the suspect's alleged statement "to fight until the end" during the post-election period coupled with her political connections was seen to lend support to the "real possibility" that she would continue to commit crimes if released from detention at the national level.[88] Likewise, in the *Laurent Gbagbo* case, Pre-Trial Chamber III argued that the suspect, even though in detention at the time of the Prosecutor's application, would continue to commit crimes, basing its conclusion on the fact that many of his supporters had access to weapons and that he continued at the time to consider himself to be the president of the Côte d'Ivoire.[89]

The type of material providing the necessary information supporting any of the grounds for arrest is worth a closer look. It is not unusual that relevant information stems from press articles, reports of non-governmental or international organizations and other open-source material.[90] In the *Lau-*

---

84 For example, Pre-Trial Chamber I, Decision on the Prosecutor's Application for a Warrant of Arrest against Callixte Mbarushimana, 28 September 2010, ICC-01/04-01/10-1, para. 49.

85 Pre-Trial Chamber I, Decision on the Prosecution's Application for a Warrant of Arrest against Omar Hassan Ahmad Al Bashir, 4 March 2009, ICC-02/05-01/09-3, paras 235-236.

86 Pre-Trial Chamber I, Decision on the Prosecutor's application under article 58 relating to Abdel Raheem Muhammad Hussein, 1 March 2012, ICC-02/05-01/12-1-Red, para. 50.

87 Pre-Trial Chamber I, Decision on the Prosecutor's Application Pursuant to Article 58 for a warrant of arrest against Charles Blé Goudé, 6 January 2012, ICC-02/11-02/11-3, para. 42.

88 Pre-Trial Chamber III, Decision on the Prosecutor's Application Pursuant to Article 58 for a warrant of arrest against Simone Gbagbo, 2 March 2012, ICC-02/11-01/12-2-Red, para. 44.

89 Pre-Trial Chamber III, Decision on the Prosecutor's Application Pursuant to Article 58 for a warrant of arrest against Laurent Koudou Gbagbo, 30 November 2011, ICC-02/11-01/11-9-Red, para. 86.

90 Instructive on this point is the reference to the evidential material supporting the Chamber's decision accompanying the summons to appear against *Abu Garda*, Pre-Trial Chamber I, Decision on the Prosecutor's Application under Article 58, 7 May 2009, ICC-02/05-02/09-15-AnxA, for example, pages 8, 10 and 12.

rent Gbagbo case, for example, the Chamber, when discussing the possibility for the suspect to abscond, relied solely on press articles reporting on his alleged political contacts and financial resources. Whether those reports are credible and can be relied upon is usually not discussed further or in detail. As article 58 proceedings are conducted *ex parte* without the participation of the defence, the suspect is not able at this stage to contest the material on the basis of which the arrest is issued. Rather, the suspect will have the first opportunity to challenge the allegations supporting the suspect's detention only when he or she requests the review of detention under article 60(2).

c) Some further remarks on warrants of arrest

The Statute foresees that only one document, the warrant of arrest, be issued according to article 58. In practice, however, the warrant is regularly accompanied by a decision which offers in more detail the Chamber's motivation as regards points of facts and law, including the Chamber's reasoning for not including a particular crime or form of participation in the warrant of arrest. This was considered a practical approach as only the warrant of arrest would need to be transmitted to the executing national authorities and, therefore, translated into the official language of the cooperating State, thus expediting the process and reducing costs.[91] Pre-Trial Chamber II, however, in the cases of *Ntaganda*[92] and *Mudacumura*[93] recently opted to issue the decision together with the warrant of arrest in one document. Going a step further, in the *Barasa, Bemba et al.* and *Al Mahdi* cases, only a warrant of arrest was issued without any decision.[94] This recent change in approach may signify a development towards a more practical and routine functioning approach of the ICC.

The warrant of arrest is regularly issued with the same classification as the Prosecutor's application, if the Chamber is convinced about the reasons

---

91 This practice was introduced as early as the *Lubanga* case, see Pre-Trial Chamber I, Decision concerning Pre-Trial Chamber I's Decision of 10 February 2006 and the Incorporation of Documents into the Record of the Case against Thomas Lubanga Dyilo, 24 February 2006, ICC-01/04-10/06-8-Corr. Other early examples can be found in: Pre-Trial Chamber I, Decision on the evidence and information provided by the Prosecution for the issuance of a warrant of arrest for Germain Katanga, 5 November 2007, ICC-01/04-01/07-55; Pre-Trial Chamber III, Decision on the Prosecutor's Application for a Warrant of Arrest against Jean-Pierre Bemba Gombo, 10 June 2008, ICC-01/05-01/08-14-tENG.

92 Pre-Trial Chamber II, Decision on the Prosecutor's Application under Article 58, 13 July 2012, ICC-01/04-02/06-36-Red.

93 Pre-Trial Chamber II, Decision on the Prosecutor's Application under Article 58, 13 July 2012, ICC-01/04-01/12-1-Red.

94 Pre-Trial Chamber II, Warrant of arrest for Walter Osapiri Barasa, 2 August 2013, ICC-01/09-01/13-1-US-Exp (the warrant was made public in redacted form on 2 October 2013, ICC-01/09-01/13-1-Red2); Pre-Trial Chamber II, Warrant of arrest for Jean-Pierre Bemba Gombo, Aimé Kilolo Musamba, Jean-Jacques Mangenda Kabongo, Fidèle Babala Wandu and Narcisse Arido, 20 November 2013, ICC-01/05-01/13-1-Red2-tENG; Pre-Trial Chamber I, Mandat d'arrêt à l'encontre d'Ahmad AL FAQI AL MAHDI, 28 September 2015, ICC-01/12-01/15-1-Red (the unredacted version of the warrant of arrest was issued on 18 September 2015).

justifying such classification. This means that warrants of arrest may also be issued and remain 'under seal'/'confidential' for as long as this classification is maintained by the Chamber.[95] As discussed in the context of the Prosecutor's application, this is done in particular to increase the chances of apprehending the suspect[96] or for protecting victims and witnesses[97] or the Prosecutor's ongoing investigation[98]. The issuance of 'under seal'/'confidential' warrants of arrest, however, is an effective measure only as long as States provide timely cooperation in the execution of those warrants. If there is no arrest by national authorities, the 'under seal'/'confidential' warrant of arrest will remain a dead letter, unnoticed by the public. The reasons for choosing the classification of 'under seal'/'confidential' or 'public' will depend on the specificities of each case. A public warrant of arrest, or its re-classification to 'public' at a given moment, may be considered suitable to direct public awareness and increase pressure on national authorities to execute the ICC warrant of arrest as soon as possible.[99] Also, the making 'public' of the warrant of arrest will take place after the suspect has been arrested by national authorities or protective measures have been implemented which mitigate the risk to witnesses and victims.[100]

Finally, some words are devoted to the legal force and vacating of warrants of arrest. A warrant of arrest remains in effect unless ordered otherwise (article 58(4)). The necessity to pronounce on the validity of a warrant arose for the first time in the event a suspect died. In this case, the Pre-Trial Chambers declared the warrant of arrest to have no legal effect as the Court has only jurisdiction over natural persons (article 25(1)) who are alive. The suspects *Lukwiya*, *Muammar Gaddafi* and *Odhiambo* died before they could be arrested and surrendered to the Court.[101] In those instances, the proceedings

95 For a critical view on the practice of under seal warrants of arrest, see O Fourmy, 'Powers of the Pre-Trial Chamber', in: Cassese/Gaeta/Jones, The Rome Statute of the International Criminal Court: A Commentary, vol. II, (OUP, 2002), 1207 at 1223.

96 Pre-Trial Chamber II, Warrant of arrest for Walter Osapiri Barasa, 2 August 2013, ICC-01/09-01/13-1-Red2, para. 26; Pre-Trial Chamber II, Warrant of Arrest for Jean-Pierre BEMBA GOMBO, Aimé KILOLO MUSAMBA, Jean-Jacques MANGENDA KABONGO, Fidèle BABALA WANDU and Narcisse ARIDO, 20 November 2013, ICC-01/05-01/13-1-Red2-tENG, para. 24.

97 Pre-Trial Chamber II, Request for Arrest and Surrender of Joseph Kony issued on 8 July 2005 as amended on 27 September 2005, 27 September 2005, ICC-02/04-01/05-29, p. 3.

98 Pre-Trial Chamber II, Warrant of arrest for Walter Osapiri Barasa, 2 August 2013, ICC-01/09-01/13-1-Red2, para. 26.

99 Pre-Trial Chamber II, Decision on the Prosecutor's Application for Unsealing of the Warrants of Arrest, 13 October 2005, ICC-02/04-01/05-52, para. 14.

100 For example, Pre-Trial Chamber III, Decision to Unseal the Warrant of Arrest for Mr Jean-Pierre Bemba Gombo, 24 May 2008, ICC-01/05-01/08-5; Pre-Trial Chamber I, Decision to Unseal the Warrant of Arrest Against Germain Katanga, 18 October 2007, ICC-01/04-01/07-24; Pre-Trial Chamber I, Decision to unseal the warrant of arrest against Bosco Ntaganda, 28 April 2008, ICC-01/04-02/06-18.

101 Pre-Trial Chamber II, Decision to terminate the proceedings against Raska Lukwiya, 11 July 2007, ICC-02/04-01/05-248; Pre-Trial Chamber I, Decision to Terminate the Case Against Muammar Mohammed Abu Minyar Gaddafi, 22 November 2011, ICC-01/11-

against these suspects were terminated and all relevant documents rendered without effect.[102]

The legal situation is less clear as to the validity of the warrant of arrest when a case has been declared inadmissible before the ICC. In the *Al-Senussi* case, in which Libya had successfully challenged the admissibility of the case before the ICC, the Court declared that the warrant of arrest ceased to have any effect henceforth.[103] However, in contrast to the case where the suspect died, proceedings following a decision of inadmissibility may be revived at the ICC following the Prosecutor's submission of "a request for a review of the decision [on admissibility] when he or she is fully satisfied that new facts have arisen which negate the basis on which the case had previously been found inadmissible under article 17" (article 19(10)). In other words, should the Prosecutor successfully demonstrate to the relevant Chamber, for example, that domestic proceedings have not been conducted genuinely with the aim to bring the person to justice, the Prosecutor could be entitled to seize the Court again. If that happens, and if a previous warrant of arrest was declared ineffective, the Prosecutor must request the issuance of a new warrant of arrest. Since the Pre-Trial Chamber cannot issue a warrant of arrest on its own, it is incumbent upon the Prosecutor to re-submit an application under article 58.

A third possibility to vacate the warrant of arrest is expressly foreseen in article 61(10). This provision applies in case one or more charges have been declined to be confirmed by the Pre-Trial Chamber against the suspect (article 61(7)(b)) or in case the Prosecutor has withdrawn any of the charges (articles 61(4) and 61(9)). In the *Mbarushimana* case, Pre-Trial Chamber I declined to confirm the charges against the suspect, and consequently, declared that the warrant of arrest against him "cease[d] to have effect in its entirety".[104] As a corollary, any cooperation request is equally without effect and is to be withdrawn.

d) State cooperation

The warrant of arrest is further accompanied by a cooperation request for arrest and surrender which is transmitted to those States which could effectuate the arrest and surrender of the suspect to the Court.[105] This request for

---

01/11-28; Pre-Trial Chamber II, Decision terminating proceedings against Okot Odhiambo, 10 September 2015, ICC-02/04-01/05-431.

102 In case of multi-suspect cases, the Registrar is also ordered to strike out the name of the deceased suspect from the case name for all subsequent filings and decisions.

103 Pre-Trial Chamber I, Decision following the declaration of inadmissibility of the case against Abdullah Al-Senussi before the Court, 7 August 2014, ICC-01/11-01/11-567, para. 6. Regretfully, the Chamber omitted to premise its vacation of the warrant of arrest on a legal basis. It could have done so by referring to article 58(4).

104 Pre-Trial Chamber I, Decision on the confirmation of charges, 16 December 2011, ICC-01/04-01/10-465-Red, p. 149.

105 See also regulations 76 and 77 of the Regulations of the Registry. Attention must be paid to the fact that in the event a warrant of arrest is issued for offences against the admin-

cooperation in the arrest and surrender of the suspect must contain a copy of the warrant of arrest, information describing the person sought and documents necessary for meeting the requirements for the surrender process in the requested State (article 91(2)). While in the early operation of the Court this cooperation request was prepared by the Pre-Trial Chamber,[106] later practice developed to instruct the Registrar to prepare and transmit such requests to States.[107] Clearly, under the Statute, only States Parties are duty-bound to comply with such cooperation request (articles 86 and 89). Non-States Parties may, on a voluntary basis, agree to cooperate with the Court in a given instance (article 87(5)). In case the Security Council determined that a non-State Party shall cooperate with the Court, such obligation stems from a combined reading of the Security Council resolution, the Charter of the United Nations and the relevant articles under part IX of the Statute.[108] In case a State Party faces difficulties in the execution of a request for arrest and surrender, it may consult with the Court, as provided for in article 97.

A State which has jurisdiction over the case may (even prior to the surrender of the suspect to the Court) lodge a challenge to the admissibility of the case and inform the Court that it intends not to execute the request for surrender of the suspect. While an admissibility ruling is pending, the State requested to cooperate with the Court may postpone the execution of the request for surrender of the person, as foreseen in article 95, provided an admissibility challenge has been properly made.[109] This suspension does not in any other way impact on the validity of the warrant of arrest. In case the

---

istration of justice, article 70(2), second sentence, prescribes that the "conditions for providing international cooperation to the Court with respect to its proceedings under [article 70] shall be governed by the domestic laws of the requested State". Rule 167(1) stipulates that the Court "may" request a State to provide any form of international cooperation or judicial assistance in those forms of set forth in part IX of the Statute. Hence, the following remarks refer primarily to the issuance of warrants of arrest for article 5 crimes.

106 See for example, Pre-Trial Chamber III, Demande d'arrestation provisoire de M. Jean-Pierre Bemba Gombo adressée au Royaume de Belgique, 23 May 2008, ICC-01/05-01/08-3; *id.*, DEMANDE D'ARRESTATION ET DE REMISE DE JEAN-PIERRE BEMBA GOMBO ADRESSÉE AU ROYAUME DE BELGIQUE, 10 June 2008, ICC-01/05-01/08-16.

107 The content of a request for arrest and surrender is set out in article 91. Article 92 allows that in urgent cases, pending the presentation of the request for surrender and the documents supporting the request, the Court may request provisional arrest. Ch Safferling, International Criminal Procedure, (OUP, 2012), p. 297.

108 See e.g., Pre-Trial Chamber I, Decision on the non-compliance by Libya with requests for cooperation by the Court and referring the matter to the United Nations Security Council, 10 December 2014, ICC-01/11-01/11-577, para. 21; Pre-Trial Chamber II, Decision on the Prosecutor's Request for a Finding of Non-Compliance Against the Republic of the Sudan, 9 March 2015, ICC-02/05-01/09-227, paras 13-15.

109 Pre-Trial Chamber I, Decision on the postponement of the execution of the request for surrender of Saif Al-Islam Gaddafi pursuant to article 95 of the Rome Statute, 1 June 2012, ICC-01/11-01/11-163, para. 37; *id.*, Decision on Libya's postponement of the execution of the request for arrest and surrender of Abdullah Al-Senussi pursuant to article 95 of the Rome Statute and related Defence request to refer Libya to the UN Security Council, 14 June 2013, ICC-01/11-01/11-354, paras 26-27.

Court finds the case to be admissible before the ICC, the requested State is duty-bound to cooperate with the Court.

3. *The Chamber's Alternative: The Summons to Appear*

A summons to appear, pursuant to article 58(7), is an alternative to seeking a warrant of arrest if the Pre-Trial Chamber is satisfied that there are reasonable grounds to believe that a summons is sufficient to ensure the person's presence.[110] For many practical reasons, this alternative is a procedural option worth exploring. Apart from the advantages for the suspect him- or herself (see below), the Court is not further concerned with aspects of detention, review of detention and other related matters. Nevertheless, the issuance of a summons depends on whether the legal prerequisites are met. They are briefly explained in the following.

Similar to what was discussed in the context of a warrant of arrest, the Chamber must examine two conditions: (i) that there are reasonable grounds to believe that the suspect committed the crimes in question; and (ii) that the summons is sufficient to ensure that the person will appear. In case the two conditions of article 58(7) are fulfilled, the Pre-Trial Chamber is under an obligation to issue the summons to appear. As we discussed the first condition and other ancillary matters already in the context of the warrant of arrest, we shall direct our attention to the second condition.

A summons is not an invitation which the suspect may consider but a judicial order compelling the suspect to appear before the Court at a specific date. For the suspect, the summons has the advantage that he or she remains in liberty; the suspect can stay with his or her family and continue to engage in his or her professional activities. By contrast, an arrest entails a significant constraint on the suspect's personal liberties. In that case, the suspect is transferred to the custody of the Court and held in the Court's detention centre in The Hague until he or she is released or transferred to a prison of another State after conviction.[111] Considering the drastic effects on the person's liberty, it has been argued that the summons is the rule, while arrest must be the exception.[112] However, as *Schabas* has observed, the issuance of a warrant of arrest is the norm in ICC practice: at the time of writing, the Court issued 31 warrants of arrest against 28 individuals[113] and only 9 summonses to appear.

---

110 Pre-Trial Chamber I, Decision on the Prosecution Application under Article 58(7) of the Statute, 27 April 2007, ICC-02/05-01/07-1-Corr, para. 116.

111 Articles 103 *et seq.*

112 W Schabas, Article 58, in W Schabas (ed), The International Criminal Court – A Commentary on the Rome Statute (OUP, 2010), p. 712.

113 This number includes the two warrants of arrest issued against *Ntaganda* and *Bashir* respectively and considers also those warrants against *Lukwiya* and *Odhiambo* (Uganda situation) and *Muammar Gaddafi* (Libya situation) which later seized to have an effect, as the suspects had died. It does not consider the warrant of arrest against *Banda* which will be discussed below.

The reason for this development is perhaps to be found in the requirement that the Prosecutor provide sufficient and convincing information that the suspect can and will voluntarily appear before the Court. As Pre-Trial Chamber I summarized in the *Harun/Kushayb* case, the "*application of article 58(7) of the Statute is restricted to cases in which the person can and will appear voluntarily before the Court without the necessity of presenting a request for arrest and surrender as provided for in articles 89 and 91 of the Statute. (...) The Chamber can only issue a summons to appear if the [Prosecutor's] Application and its supporting material provide sufficient guarantees that the person will appear before the Court*".[114] In other words, the Chamber must satisfy itself that the summons "*would be equally effective as a warrant of arrest to ensure the person's appearance before the Court*".[115] The Chamber must give sufficient reasoning when accepting the effectiveness of a summons to appear. In the *Ruto/Kosgey/Sang* case[116] and *Muthaura/Kenyatta/Ali* case,[117] Pre-Trial Chamber II approved the Prosecutor's request to issue a summons to appear against all six suspects, arguing that it saw no indication that the persons "*are either perceived as flight risks or likely to evade personal service of the summonses or refrain from cooperating if summoned to appear*".[118] Likewise, Pre-Trial Chamber I in the *Abu Garda* case stated that it was satisfied that there were reasonable grounds to believe that a summons to appear was sufficient to ensure *Abu Garda's* appearance before the Court.[119] The brevity of the Chambers' findings is worth noting. It seems that the Chambers simply *decided* to agree with the Prosecutor's proposition that a summons would be sufficient.[120] More can perhaps be inferred from the decision on the Prosecutor's application under article 58 in the *Harun/Kushayb* case, where the Prosecutor had requested a summons to appear against the two suspects (without however ruling out the possibility to

---

114 Pre-Trial Chamber I, Decision on the Prosecution Application under Article 58(7) of the Statute, 27 April 2007, ICC-02/05-01/07-1-Corr, paras 117-118.

115 Pre-Trial Chamber I, Decision on the Prosecution Application under Article 58(7) of the Statute, 27 April 2007, ICC-02/05-01/07-1-Corr, para. 116.

116 The charges were not confirmed against *Kosgey* and the case is continued against *Ruto* and *Sang* before Trial Chamber V(a).

117 The charges were not confirmed against *Ali* by Pre-Trial Chamber II and the Prosecutor withdrew the charges against *Muthaura* shortly after he was committed to trial. Subsequently, the charges were also withdrawn against *Kenyatta* and the case proceedings terminated by Trial Chamber V(b).

118 Pre-Trial Chamber II, Decision on the Prosecutor's Application for Summons to Appear for William Samoei Ruto, Henry Kiprono Kosgey and Joshua Arap Sang, 8 March 2011, ICC-01/09-01/11-1, para. 56; *id.*, Decision on the Prosecutor's Application for Summonses to Appear for Francis Kirimi Muthaura, Uhuru Muigai Kenyatta and Mohammed Hussein Ali, 8 March 2011, ICC-01/09-02/11-1, para. 55.

119 Pre-Trial Chamber I, Decision on the Prosecutor's Application under Article 58, 7 May 2009, ICC-02/05-02/09-15-AnxA, para. 31.

120 The same approach was followed in the *Banda/Jerbo* case where Pre-Trial Chamber I issued a summons to appear against then two suspects, Pre-Trial Chamber I, Second Decision on the Prosecutor's Application under Article 58, 27 August 2009, ICC-02/05-03/09-1, para. 34.

resort to a warrant of arrest). At the time, *Harun* was minister of State for humanitarian affairs, while *Kushayb* was held in detention pursuant to a warrant of arrest issued by the Sudanese authorities. In relation to *Kushayb*, the Chamber held that if a suspect is already detained by national authorities prior to the Prosecutor's application, the Pre-Trial Chamber may only issue a warrant of arrest; issuing a summons to appear would be contrary to the objective of article 58(7) since the conditions restricting liberty do not apply to persons already detained.[121] Moreover, a person already detained cannot appear voluntarily before the ICC, nor can surrender be effectuated in this situation under the statutory regime, including temporary surrender under rule 183.[122] This approach was also followed by Pre-Trial Chamber III in the *Simone Gbagbo* case.[123] Similar concerns were raised in the *Banda* case, where Trial Chamber IV replaced the summons with a warrant of arrest (see below) although the accused had expressed his willingness to attend trial. The Chamber found that "*an individual can be obstructed in his willingness or freedom to appear at trial by means other than detention. If these obstacles are such that there are no longer guarantees that he will appear, the Chamber may issue a warrant of arrest*".[124]

A further interesting point is whether the competent Chamber can select freely between the routes available under article 58(1) and (7). If the Prosecutor proposes arguments for both routes, the Chamber is free to assess the facts independently and choose the avenue it deems justified by the facts at hand. But how is the Chamber to react if the Prosecutor submits an application for only one of the article 58 routes and the Chamber disagrees with this suggestion? It has been suggested that the Chamber may not issue a summons to appear unless explicitly requested by the Prosecutor. "*A summons to appear is not at issue in proceedings for the arrest of a person. Nor is a summons to appear an alternative open to the Chamber, upon application of the Prosecutor, for the issuance of a warrant of arrest.*"[125] However, the Statute does not assert such prohibition (or self-restraint) *expressis verbis*. Moreover, a restrictive approach may conflict with article 21(3), which dictates that the Statute, including article 58, be interpreted and applied in conformity with interna-

---

121 Pre-Trial Chamber I, Decision on the Prosecution Application under Article 58(7) of the Statute, 27 April 2007, ICC-02/05-01/07-1-Corr, para 120.

122 *Ibid.*, para. 121. In the view of the Chamber, (temporary) surrender presupposes the issuance of a warrant of arrest.

123 Pre-Trial Chamber III, Decision on the Prosecutor's Application Pursuant to Article 58 for a warrant of arrest against Simone Gbagbo, 2 March 2012, ICC-02/11-01/12-2-Red, para. 40.

124 Trial Chamber IV, Warrant of arrest for Abdallah Banda Abakaer Nourain, 11 September 2014, ICC-02/05-03/09-606, para. 23.

125 Appeals Chamber, Judgment in the Appeal of Mathieu Ngudjolo Chui of 27 March 2008 against the Decision of Pre-Trial Chamber I on the Application of the Appellant for Interim Release, 9 June 2008, ICC-01/04-01/07-572 (OA4), para. 13. See also W Schabas, Article 58, in W Schabas (ed), The International Criminal Court – A Commentary on the Rome Statute (OUP, 2010), p. 712.

tionally recognized human rights.[126] The question is therefore why should the Chamber be prevented from issuing a summons to appear when the Prosecutor has requested a warrant of arrest but the Chamber finds that arrest, based on the facts available, is not necessary. Does it not appear odd to compel the Chamber to order the arrest of a person whose appearance at trial can be ensured by way of a summons? It is suggested here that the Chamber should be at liberty to decide independently. As this question touches upon the deprivation of liberty, the Judges must have the final word and cannot be restricted by the Prosecutor's motivation. This question has not come up in the Court's jurisprudence, since the Prosecutor typically proposes to enquire into both routes under article 58(1) and (7), for example, in the *Abu Garda* and *Banda/Jerbo* cases. The same argumentation may hold true in case the Prosecutor requests a summons to appear only, but the Chamber opines that the prerequisites of article 58(7) are not met. Here too, the Chamber should have authority to issue a warrant of arrest, provided that facts that justify detention have been presented. It makes no sense in this situation for the Chamber to reject the Prosecutor's request for a summons and to await a new application for a warrant of arrest. Precious time may be lost during which the suspect could have been apprehended. This scenario appeared in the *Harun/Kushayb* case, where the Prosecutor requested the issuance of a summons for both suspects. Pre-Trial Chamber I disagreed with the Prosecutor's proposition as it was not satisfied that a summons is equally effective, and issued a warrant of arrest.[127]

The summons to appear may be issued "with or without conditions restricting liberty (other than detention) if provided for by national law". Some of these conditions are listed in rule 119(1). Conditions may range from travel and contact restrictions to posting a bond in the amount determined by the Chamber. The implementation and supervision of those conditions remains with the national authorities on whose territory the suspect is located.[128] In the *Abu Garda* case and *Banda/Jerbo* case, Pre-Trial Chamber I established as conditions that the suspects (i) refrain from discussing any issue related to the counts contained in the summons to appear; (ii) refrain from making political statements while within the premises of the Court or any other location assigned to them;[129] (iii) may not leave without permission the Court's

126 One may also argue *a majore ad minus* that the summons is included implicitly as the less intrusive measure in the application for a warrant of arrest.

127 Pre-Trial Chamber I, Decision on the Prosecution Application under Article 58(7) of the Statute, 27 April 2007, ICC-02/05-01/07-1-Corr, paras. 116-125.

128 Ch Hall/C Ryngaert, Article 58 MN 44, in O Triffterer/K Ambos (eds), The Rome Statute of the International Criminal Court – A Commentary (3rd ed, 2015).

129 The prohibition of making political statements may seem peculiar at first sight as it is not clear why the suspects' freedom of expression would generally be limited by criminal proceedings pending before the ICC. However, the reference to "the premises of the Court or any other location assigned to them" could imply that Pre-Trial Chamber I intended to prohibit any political statements of the suspects in relation to and for the duration of the pending proceedings. Indeed, their position as 'suspects' in ongoing criminal proceedings

premises or any other location assigned to them for the whole period of their stay in The Netherlands; and (iv) to comply with all instructions of the Registrar.[130] Those conditions seem to address the suspects' first appearance before the Court but did not subject the suspects under any other condition for the future. In contrast, Pre-Trial Chamber II in the *Ruto/Kosgey/Sang* case and the *Muthaura/Kenyatta/Ali* case established conditions which affected the suspects' conduct beyond their first appearance. It imposed as conditions that the suspects (i) have no contact directly or indirectly with any victim or witness of the crimes for which they have been summoned; (ii) refrain from, *inter alia*, corruptly influencing witnesses or tampering with evidence; (iii) refrain from committing further crimes; and (iv) attend all hearings as required. The first two conditions soon provoked the adoption of special measures, when the suspects, not knowing the identity of victims and witnesses, wished to undertake investigative activities during which it was possible that they would unintentionally contact those individuals. Hence, before approaching a person, the defence teams were required to submit a request to the Victims and Witnesses Unit with a view to receiving clearance that they may proceed with contacting that person.

In all cases mentioned above, the Pre-Trial Chambers reserved their right to replace the summons to appear with a warrant of arrest in case of non-compliance, either upon request or *proprio motu*.[131] Indeed, the circumstances under which a summons was originally issued may change over time and the Judges may need to react with a view to ensuring that the person appears before the Court. This may happen not only at the pre-trial phase but also at trial. A recent example is the *Banda* case where, due to the lack of cooperation of Sudan, *Banda*, albeit willing, was prevented from appearing before the ICC. In the face of this scenario, Trial Chamber IV explained: "*The sufficiency of the summons is subject to ongoing review by the Chamber, not least in light of its overarching duty to ensure that the course of justice [is] not disrupted and brought to a halt. Where the circumstances so require, the Chamber may issue a warrant of arrest at any point in time prior*

---

implies a degree of self-restraint when commenting publicly on matters which are under judicial inquiry. That said, any restriction beyond that measure could be deemed irreconcilable with the suspects' internationally recognized human rights (article 21(3)).

130 Pre-Trial Chamber I, Decision on the Prosecutor's Application under Article 58, 7 May 2009, ICC-02/05-02/09-15-AnxA, p. 18; Pre-Trial Chamber I, Second Decision on the Prosecutor's Application under Article 58, 27 August 2009, ICC-02/05-03/09-1, pp. 19-20.

131 Pre-Trial Chamber I, Decision on the Prosecutor's Application under Article 58, 7 May 2009, ICC-02/05-02/09-15-AnxA, para. 32; *id.*, Second Decision on the Prosecutor's Application under Article 58, 27 August 2009, ICC-02/05-03/09-1, para. 35; Pre-Trial Chamber II, Decision on the Prosecutor's Application for Summons to Appear for William Samoei Ruto, Henry Kiprono Kosgey and Joshua Arap Sang, 8 March 2011, ICC-01/09-01/11-1, para. 56; *id.*, Decision on the Prosecutor's Application for Summonses to Appear for Francis Kirimi Muthaura, Uhuru Muigai Kenyatta and Mohammed Hussein Ali, 8 March 2011, ICC-01/09-02/11-1, para. 55.

to or even after the commencement of trial".[132] Accordingly, Trial Chamber IV[133] reviewed the sufficiency of the existing summons to appear, as pronounced by Pre-Trial Chamber I, and replaced it with a warrant of arrest in conformity with rules 119(5), third sentence, in conjunction with rule 119(4).

A summons is served on the person according to article 58(7), fourth sentence. For this to happen, the summons is to be transmitted to the requested State, as the Court cannot perform an official act on the territory of a State without such notification. The State, in turn, is obliged to serve this judicial document to the person concerned, pursuant to article 93(1)(d). That said, a State of its own volition may agree to allow Court officials to serve the summons directly. Due to the nature of a summons to appear, it is issued publicly.

In the event of a summons, the suspect must appear for his or her initial appearance (article 60(1)) and any other hearing, either at the pre-trial or trial phase, as ordered. The person concerned is, however, free to leave the Court when the hearing is over and remains otherwise subject to the conditions imposed by the Court. The host State must facilitate the presence of the suspect on its territory and the Court makes the necessary arrangements. The following observations in this article do not concern the scenario where a summons to appear has been issued but relate only to the existence of a warrant of arrest.

IV. Arrest Proceedings in the Custodial State

Once the ICC issued a warrant of arrest and the cooperation request(s) have been notified to States, matters lie henceforth in the hands of States. As noted above, a State having received a request for arrest (or for provisional arrest, pending documentation) must immediately take steps to arrest the suspect in accordance with its laws and the provisions of Part IX of the Statute (article 59(1)).[134] Articles 59(1) and 99(1) make clear that the arrest, despite having been executed on the basis of an ICC warrant of arrest, remains a sovereign act of the custodial State following national laws.[135] In principle, any wrongdoing in this process is attributable to the State.

---

132 Trial Chamber IV, Warrant of arrest for Abdallah Banda Abakaer Nourain, 11 September 2014, ICC-02/05-03/09-606, para. 16(v).

133 The warrant of arrest or summons to appear is issued by the Pre-Trial Chamber, in accordance with article 58. However, by virtue of articles 61(11) and 64(6)(a), such powers may be exercised also by the Trial Chamber.

134 The arrest may be executed on the basis of the ICC warrant of arrest itself or, as national legislation may prescribe, on the basis of a national warrant of arrest into which the ICC warrant of arrest was transformed.

135 Indeed, States Parties are obliged under articles 86 and 88 to amend their procedural laws to accommodate the ICC's requests; see also M. El Zeidy, Critical Thoughts on Article 59(2) of the ICC Statute, JICJ 4 (2006), p. 453.

Once arrested, the suspect is not transferred immediately to the Court in a cloak-and-dagger operation. It may, in fact, take several months or years until the suspect is surrendered to the Court. The reason for this delay lies in the surrender proceedings in the custodial State. Pursuant to article 59(2), the person arrested must be brought promptly before a competent judicial authority in the custodial State.[136] The competent national authorities shall determine, in accordance with national laws, whether (i) the warrant applies to the person arrested; (ii) whether the person has been arrested in accordance with the proper process; and (iii) whether the person's rights have been respected. Article 59 remains silent as to how national judicial authorities may react if they identify a violation of the proper process or the rights of the suspect, as referred to in article 59(2).[137] It has been argued that a breach of law cannot prevent surrender to the Court but that the State might award compensation to the arrested person.[138] As set out in article 59(7), the person shall be delivered to the Court as soon as possible. The ICC Appeals Chamber clarified in the *Lubanga* case that the "*Court does not sit in the process (...) on judgment as a court of appeal on the identificatory decision of the [national] judicial authority. Its task is to see that the process envisaged by [national] law was duly followed and that the rights of the arrestee were properly respected. Article 99(1) of the Statute lays down that the enforcement of the warrant must follow the process laid down by the law of the requested State*".[139]

When brought before the competent national authority in the custodial State, the person arrested has the right to apply for interim release before national courts pending surrender as clarified in article 59(3).[140] In reaching a decision on such application, article 59(4), first sentence, instructs the national authorities of the custodial State to consider whether, despite the gravity of the alleged crimes, there are any "urgent and exceptional circumstances" that may justify interim release (such as the medical condition of the suspect or a family emergency), provided there exist necessary safeguards which ensure that the custodial State can fulfill its duty to surrender the person to the Court. The Pre-Trial Chamber must be notified of any such request for interim release and shall make recommendations to the competent authority in the

---

136 Article 59(2) is inspired by article 9(3) International Covenant on Civil and Political Rights and article 5(3) of the ECHR.

137 M. El Zeidy, Critical Thoughts on Article 59(2) of the ICC Statute, JICJ 4 (2006), p. 455.

138 Ch Hall/C Ryngaert, Article 59 MN 14, in O Triffterer/K Ambos (eds), The Rome Statute of the International Criminal Court – A Commentary (3rd ed, 2015). See also on this matter: M. El Zeidy, Critical Thoughts on Article 59(2) of the ICC Statute, JICJ 4 (2006), pp. 455-457.

139 Appeals Chamber, Judgment on the Appeal of Mr. Thomas Lubanga Dyilo against the Decision on the Defence Challenge to the Jurisdiction of the Court pursuant to article 19(2) (a) of the Statute of 3 October 2006, 14 December 2006, ICC-01/04-01/06-772 (OA4), para. 41.

140 The person may also renounce on this right.

custodial State, in accordance with article 59(5).[141] The competent authority in the custodial State shall give full consideration to such recommendations, including any recommendations on measures to prevent the escape of the person, before rendering its decision.[142]

When considering an application for interim release, however, the national authority may not consider whether the warrant of arrest was properly issued in accordance with article 58(1)(a) and (b), as clarified by article 59(4), second sentence. This means that the national court may not examine whether there are "reasonable grounds to believe" that the person committed the crimes which form part of the warrant of arrest or whether arrest was indeed necessary. These points can only be ascertained by the ICC Chamber which has issued the warrant and which, accordingly, should be in a position to review and lift it.[143] Another important consideration for preventing national authorities from examining the conditions set out in article 58(1) is to avoid undermining the competence of the ICC by domestic political influence. On the other hand, this restriction at the national level is counterbalanced by allowing the person, pending surrender, to challenge the legality of the warrant of arrest before the Pre-Trial Chamber which issued the warrant of arrest, pursuant to rule 117(3).[144] After having obtained the views of the Prosecutor, the Pre-Trial Chamber decides on the application without delay. Interestingly, suspects detained by national authorities have, until today, not availed themselves of this procedural remedy. Perhaps this is owed to the fact that surrender took place relatively quickly, leaving no time to file a challenge under rule 117(3) before the ICC.

One aspect in relation to article 59 is easily overlooked, and deserves to be emphasised here, namely the provision's non-applicability in the context of article 70 offences. Rule 165(2) explicitly rules out the applicability of article 59 (and any rules hereunder) with the consequence that suspects of offences against the administration of justice do not enjoy any *statutory* rights under article 59 during arrest proceedings in the custodial State, pending their transferral to the Court. Rather, during this time, their rights can only derive from national laws.

141 See, for example, Pre-Trial Chamber III, Recommendations adressées à la Chambre des mises en accusation de la Cour d'Appel de Bruxelles en vertu de l'article 59 du Statut de Rome, 3 June 2008, ICC-01/05-01/08-13; Pre-Trial Chamber I, Recommendations adressées à la Chambre d'instruction de la Cour d'Appel de Paris en vertu de l'article 59 du Statut de Rome, 18 October 2010, ICC-01/04-01/10-15.

142 "Although these recommendations are not strictly binding, the wording of [article 59(5)] illustrates their importance and the duty to take full account of them", Ch Safferling, International Criminal Procedure, (OUP, 2012), p. 298.

143 Ch Hall/C Ryngaert, Article 59 MN 17 and 22, in O Triffterer/K Ambos (eds), The Rome Statute of the International Criminal Court – A Commentary (3rd ed, 2015).

144 Pre-Trial Chamber II, Decision on the "Defence challenge to the warrant for the arrest of Walter Osapiri Barasa", 10 September 2015, ICC-01/09-01/13-35, para. 2.

V. Interim Release of the Person Subject to a Warrant of Arrest

Before transferring the suspect to the custody of the Court, various arrangements with the custodial State must be made by the ICC Registry. Often, while still being on the territory of the custodial State awaiting transfer, the suspect is served with a copy of the warrant of arrest as well as a copy of the Statute (rule 117(1)) in a language which he or she fully understands and speaks, if necessary. Upon arrival at the Court's detention centre, the person is medically examined and informed of his or her rights, including the free choosing of counsel and the right to request legal aid from the Court, if he or she cannot afford to pay counsel. During this process, the Registry's Counsel Support Section plays a crucial role in providing all the necessary support, if need be, with the assistance of an interpreter. It is established practice at the ICC that the Pre-Trial Chamber is comprehensively informed by way of a Registry report of all aspects of the suspect's transfer to the Court, including his or her arrival at the detention centre. The report is usually submitted prior to or immediately after the suspect's initial appearance. Thus, the Chamber stays informed of this aspect of the proceedings and may be apprised of any irregularities, as the case may be.

The first thing an arrested person seeks to regain is his or her liberty, one of the most precious of the fundamental rights to which any human being is entitled. It is therefore only natural that the question of detention and release is soon raised by the arrestee upon arrival in the Netherlands. To this end, the order of provisions in article 60 is instructive insofar as it indicates the sequence in which the arrested person must address the issue of detention.

1. The Application for Interim Release under Article 60(2)

The first occasion at which the arrestee can raise the issue is during the initial appearance of the suspect (article 60(1)), where he or she is informed, amongst other, of the right to request interim release under article 60(2). That provision reads:

> *A person subject to a warrant of arrest may apply for interim release pending trial. If the Pre-Trial Chamber is satisfied that the conditions set forth in article 58, paragraph 1, are met, the person shall continue to be detained. If it is not satisfied, the Pre-Trial Chamber shall release the person, with or without conditions.*

The Chamber shall decide upon such application without delay, after having obtained the observations of the Prosecutor.[145] If victims are participating in the case, they too may provide their views on the matter.[146] If the arrestee, however, does not apply for interim release, the Chamber is, in principle, not

145 Rule 118(1).
146 Article 68(3).

obliged to – and will not – decide *proprio motu* on the person's continued detention.[147] In practice, almost all arrested persons requested soon after their arrival at the Court to be released, with or without conditions. So far, only *Blé Goudé* did not request to be released during the entire pre-trial phase and, hence, the Pre-Trial Chamber did not pronounce on his continued detention until he was committed to a Trial Chamber.

With an application under article 60(2), the arrested person has the opportunity to challenge the Chamber's determinations under article 58(1) in its entirety, *i.e.* whether the person has committed the crimes (article 58(1)(a)) and whether detention is necessary (article 58(1)(b)).[148] The Chamber, in turn, must enquire *anew* into the existence of the facts justifying detention, based on the material placed before it.[149] Decisions on continued detention or release pursuant to article 60(2) are not of discretionary nature.[150] If the Chamber is satisfied that the conditions for detention are met, it shall keep the arrestee in detention (article 60(2), second sentence). If the Chamber considers the matter otherwise, it shall release him or her, with or without conditions (article 60(2), third sentence). We discussed earlier the importance to set out in the decision on the warrant of arrest (or the warrant of arrest itself, if no accompanying decision is issued) with sufficient detail the reasons in support of article 58(1). The clearer the Chamber reasoned, the easier it is for the arrested person to challenge effectively his or her arrest (and the appellate body to review the decision). A further related consideration, as briefly discussed already in the context of the warrant of arrest, is the type and probative value of evidence used. Reliance on hearsay evidence stemming from open-source material without any further details as to, for exam-

---

147 For a different (but to date singular) view, see Pre-Trial Chamber I, Decision on the powers of the Pre-Trial Chamber to review *proprio motu* the pre-trial detention of Germain Katanga, 18 March 2008, ICC-01/04-01/07-330, pp. 8-9. In order to avoid, however, that – absent an application for interim release – the person is detained for an unreasonably long time, the relevant Chamber may address the matter in reference to other provisions, such as articles 60(4) or 21(3) and 67(1)(c). This seems to be accepted by the Appeals Chamber, Judgment on the appeal of Mr. Thomas Lubanga Dyilo against the decision of Pre-Trial Chamber I entitled "Décision sur la demande de mise en liberté provisoire de Thomas Lubanga Dyilo", 13 February 2007, ICC-01/04-01/06-824 (OA7), para. 98.

148 Appeals Chamber, Judgment on the appeal of Mr. Thomas Lubanga Dyilo against the decision of Pre-Trial Chamber I entitled "Décision sur la demande de mise en liberté provisoire de Thomas Lubanga Dyilo", 13 February 2007, ICC-01/04-01/06-824 (OA7), para. 97. For a different view see W Schabas, Article 58, in W Schabas (ed), The International Criminal Court – A Commentary on the Rome Statute (OUP, 2010), p. 725.

149 Appeals Chamber, Judgment on the appeal of Mr Laurent Koudou Gbagbo against the decision of Pre-Trial Chamber I of 13 July 2012 entitled "Decision on the 'Requête de la Défense demandant la mise en liberté provisoire du président Gbagbo'", 26 October 2012, ICC-02/11-02/11-278-Red (OA), para. 23.

150 Appeals Chamber, Judgment on the appeal of Mr. Thomas Lubanga Dyilo against the decision of Pre-Trial Chamber I entitled "Décision sur la demande de mise en liberté provisoire de Thomas Lubanga Dyilo", 13 February 2007, ICC-01/04-01/06-824 (OA7), para. 134.

ple, the source of the information or the methodology applied when gathering the information, is not unusual and has been controversially discussed in the Court's jurisprudence. While Pre-Trial Chamber II, for example, takes a flexible approach arguing that the evidence "*in relation to the necessity of continued detention for the purpose of article 58(1)(b) of the Statute does not have to be of the same nature and strength as the evidence required to establish reasonable grounds to believe that the person has committed one or more crimes*",[151] there are other voices cautioning to use such type of evidence without paying attention to the Statute's evidentiary rules.[152]

2. *The Periodic Review of the Chamber's Ruling on Detention under Article 60(3)*

In case the Chamber denied the article 60(2) request for interim release, a periodic review process begins which obliges the Chamber to re-evaluate the conditions for detention either upon request of the suspect or the Prosecutor, or on its own motion. This is foreseen in article 60(3) which stipulates:

> *The Pre-Trial Chamber shall periodically review its ruling on the release or detention of the person, and may do so at any time on the request of the Prosecutor or the person. Upon such review, it may modify its ruling as to detention, release or conditions of release, if it is satisfied that changed circumstances so require.*

The purpose of the periodic review mechanism is explained by the Appeals Chamber in the following:

> "*[J]ustified detention for the ruling under article 60(2) of the Statute may change over time. It is the purpose of the periodic review under article 60(3) of the Statute to ensure that detention that was ordered in accordance with the Statute does not become unwarranted because of a change of circumstances. Hence, it is an essential procedural safeguard against detention that is not in accord with the Statute and internationally recognised human rights. This procedural safeguard must also be seen in the context of the detained person's right to be presumed innocent*".[153]

---

151 Pre-Trial Chamber II, Decision on the Defence's Application for Interim Release, 18 November 2013, ICC-01/04-02/06-147, para. 47.

152 See the two dissenting opinions of Judges Anita Ušacka and Christine van den Wyngaert, annexed to Appeals Chamber, Judgment on the appeal of Mr Bosco Ntaganda against the decision of Pre-Trial Chamber II of 18 November 2013 entitled "Decision on the Defence's Application for Interim Release", 5 March 2014, ICC-01/04-02/06-271-Red (OA).

153 Appeals Chamber, Judgment on the appeal of Mr Jean-Pierre Bemba Gombo against the decision of Trial Chamber III of 28 July 2010 entitled "Decision on the review of the detention of Mr Jean-Pierre Bemba Gombo pursuant to Rule 118(2) of the Rules of Procedure and Evidence", 19 November 2010, ICC-01/05-01/08-1019 (OA4), para. 49.

Article 60(3) is complemented by rule 118(2) which dictates that such periodic review must take place at least every 120 days.[154] But the review can also take place at an earlier point in time. A hearing on this matter may be held at the request of the Prosecutor, the detained person or at the Chamber's own initiative, as provided in rule 118(3), third sentence. A hearing *must* be held, however, at least once a year, pursuant to rule 118(3), fourth sentence. Following the plain wording of the Court's instruments, the review of detention shall be conducted by the Pre-Trial Chamber. In the Court's practice, however, such review is also exercised by Trial Chambers,[155] at least until the trial hearings commence.[156] Trial Chamber III accepted to review the detention of *Bemba* while the trial was underway arguing that such review may be conducted "at any time" upon request of the detained person pursuant to article 60(3) together with article 61(11).[157] Interestingly, Trial Chamber III added that the commencement of trial hearings "extinguishes the automatic review that is required at least every 120 days" at the pre-trial stage pursuant to rule 118(2).[158]

It is clear from the order of the provisions in article 60, that the ruling under article 60(3) "*follow[s] from, and [is] dependent upon, a ruling on a previous application by the detained person for interim release*".[159] Hence, the point of departure is the Chamber's ruling under article 60(2), as subsequently modified.[160] Yet, the scope of the review under article 60(3) is narrower than that to be carried out in reaching a decision pursuant to article 60(2): the object of review in the context of article 60(3) focuses on whether 'changed circumstances' warrant a modification of the previous ruling under article 58(1), and if so, whether they warrant the termination of detention.[161]

---

154 Rule 118(2) reads: "*The Pre-Trial Chamber shall review its ruling on the release or detention of a person in accordance with article 60, paragraph 3, at least every 120 days and may do so at any time on the request of the person or the Prosecutor.*"

155 See articles 61(11) and 64(6)(a).

156 See recently, Trial Chamber I, Decision on the "Requête urgente aux fins de fixation d'une nouvelle date d'audience portant sur le réexamen des conditions de maintien en detention", 8 October 2014, ICC-02/11-01/11-693.

157 Trial Chamber III, Public Redacted Version of the "Decision on Applications for Provisional Release" of 27 June 2011, 16 August 2011, ICC-01/05-01/08-1565-Red, para. 45.

158 *Ibid.*, para. 46.

159 Appeals Chamber, Judgment on the appeal of Mr. Thomas Lubanga Dyilo against the decision of Pre-Trial Chamber I entitled "Décision sur la demande de mise en liberté provisoire de Thomas Lubanga Dyilo", 13 February 2007, ICC-01/04-01/06-824 (OA7), para. 94.

160 Article 60(2) decisions may be modified in the course of the proceedings. Hence, the notion 'ruling on detention' within the meaning of article 60(3) must be interpreted as the initial decision under article 60(2) as well as any other subsequent modifications made to that decision under article 60(3); K Khan, Article 60 MN 15 and 16, in O Triffterer/K Ambos (eds), The Rome Statute of the International Criminal Court – A Commentary (3rd ed, 2015).

161 Appeals Chamber, Judgment on the appeal of Mr Jean-Pierre Bemba Gombo against the decision of Trial Chamber III of 28 July 2010 entitled "Decision on the review of the detention of Mr Jean-Pierre Bemba Gombo pursuant to Rule 118(2) of the Rules of Procedure and Evidence", 19 November 2010, ICC-01/05-01/08-1019 (OA4), para. 1: "*A*

'Change of circumstances' entails a "*change in some or all of the facts underlying a previous decision on detention, or a new fact satisfying a Chamber that a modification of its prior ruling is necessary*".[162] In ruling on this matter, the Chamber must weigh the arguments raised by the arrested person against those of the Prosecutor "*who must bring to the attention of the Chamber any other relevant information of which he [or she] is aware and which relates to the question of detention or release*".[163] The periodic review does not require the Chamber to make findings on the circumstances already decided upon in its previous ruling. Rather, it must review whether those circumstances have changed. Upon review, the Chamber is vested with discretionary powers to modify its ruling as to detention, release or conditions of release, as indicated in the use of the word "may" in article 60(3), second sentence.[164]

Where the person has remained in custody for an unreasonably long time (and this delay is not attributable to the Prosecutor within the meaning of article 60(4), see below), it is possible for the relevant Chamber to consider the suspect's release, with or without conditions, under article 60(3). This interpretation is possible – indeed imperative – following the dictates of article 21(3) to interpret and apply the Statute consistent with internationally recognized human rights.[165] This exegesis of the law finds its origin in the *Bemba et al.* case where four suspects, charged with offences against the administration of justice under article 70, were released from detention on 21 October 2014 by the Single Judge, acting on behalf of Pre-Trial Chamber II.[166] Prior to this decision, he had denied the suspects' requests for release, and had affirmed that the conditions of article 58(1)(b) were continuously met. By the time the decision to release was taken, the suspects had spent

---

Chamber carrying out a periodic review of a ruling on detention under article 60(3) (...) must revert to that ruling and determine whether there has been any changes in the circumstances underpinning the ruling and whether there are any new circumstances that have a bearing on the conditions under article 58(1) of the Statute".

162 Appeals Chamber, Judgment on the appeal of the Prosecutor against Pre-Trial Chamber II's "Decision on the Interim Release of Jean-Pierre Bemba Gombo and Convening Hearings with the Kingdom of Belgium, the Republic of Portugal, the Republic of France, the Federal Republic of Germany, the Italian Republic and the Republic of South Africa", 2 December 2009, ICC-01/05-01/08-631-Red (OA2), para. 60.

163 Appeals Chamber, Judgment on the appeal of Mr Jean-Pierre Bemba Gombo against the decision of Trial Chamber III of 28 July 2010 entitled "Decision on the review of the detention of Mr Jean-Pierre Bemba Gombo pursuant to Rule 118(2) of the Rules of Procedure and Evidence", 19 November 2010, ICC-01/05-01/08-1019 (OA4), para. 51.

164 For a restrictive interpretation, see Ch Safferling, International Criminal Procedure, (OUP, 2012), p. 306.

165 Appeals Chamber, Judgment on the appeals against Pre-Trial Chamber II's decisions regarding interim release in relation to Aimé Kilolo Musamba, Jean-Jacques Mangenda, Fidèle Babala Wandu, and Narcisse Arido and order for reclassification, 29 May 2015, ICC-01/05-01/13-969 (OA5, OA6, OA7, OA8, and OA9), para. 43.

166 Pre-Trial Chamber II, Decision ordering the release of Aimé Kilolo Musamba, Jean-Jacques Mangenda Kabongo, Fidèle Babala Wandu and Narcisse Arido, 21 October 2014, ICC-01/05-01/13-703.

several months to almost one year in detention.[167] The Single Judge acted *proprio motu*. He based his argumentation, *inter alia*, on article 60(4) and the consideration that the "*duration of the detention has to be balanced* inter alia *against the statutory penalties applicable to the offences at stake in these proceedings and that, accordingly, the further extension of the period of the pre-trial detention would result in making its duration disproportionate*".[168]

Upon appeal of the Prosecutor, the Appeals Chamber clarified that in the absence of an inexcusable delay on the part of the Prosecutor, reference to article 60(4) was misplaced; rather, article 60(3), in conjunction with article 21(3), provides the correct legal framework within which this issue must be entertained. The Appeals Chamber also added that in the context of the review exercise pursuant to article 60(3), the relevant Chamber may not consider the lapse of time, on its own, as a "changed circumstance" which overrides any other factor. Instead, as described above, the Chamber must review "*whether the conditions of article 58(1)(a) and (b) of the Statute, which were found to be met in the initial article 60(2) assessment, have changed such that detention is no longer justified*".[169] Hence, the time already spent in detention must be considered

> "*along with the risks that are being reviewed under article 60(3) of the Statute, in order to determine whether, all factors being considered, the continued detention 'stops being reasonable' and the individual accordingly needs to be released. In the context of the legal framework of the Court, such a determination requires balancing the risks under article 58(1)(b) of the Statute that were found to still exist against the duration of detention, taking into account relevant factors that may have delayed the proceedings and the circumstances of the case as a whole. The potential penalty for the offences charged may be a factor to take into account in assessing whether the time in detention is reasonable. Nevertheless, this factor cannot be assessed in isolation, but would need to be considered in light of all of the circumstances of the case*".[170]

As a result, the Appeals Chamber reversed the decision of the Single Judge and remanded the matter to the Trial Chamber to which the four suspects had been committed in the meantime. As the suspects had been at liberty since the decision of the Single Judge in October 2014, the Appeals Chamber was of the view that "*it would not be in the interests of justice for the suspects to be re-arrested because of the reversal of the [Single Judge's decision]*".[171]

167 Article 70(3) establishes that for offences of the administration of justice, the potential penalty is, *inter alia*, imprisonment "not exceeding five years".

168 Pre-Trial Chamber II, Decision ordering the release of Aimé Kilolo Musamba, Jean-Jacques Mangenda Kabongo, Fidèle Babala Wandu and Narcisse Arido, 21 October 2014, ICC-01/05-01/13-703, p. 4.

169 Appeals Chamber, Judgment on the appeals against Pre-Trial Chamber II's decisions regarding interim release in relation to Aimé Kilolo Musamba, Jean-Jacques Mangenda, Fidèle Babala Wandu, and Narcisse Arido and order for reclassification, 29 May 2015, ICC-01/05-01/13-969 (OA5, OA6, OA7, OA8, and OA9), para. 44.

170 *Ibid.*, para. 45 (footnote omitted).

171 *Ibid.*, para. 57.

As expected, the Trial Chamber upheld the release of the accused concerned, subject to conditions, but based its decision on the proper legal bases.[172] .

3. Conditional Release

Releasing a detained person, with or without conditions, is an avenue that Chambers have not explored too often. A reasonable explanation is to be found in the recurring findings that the risk to abscond or potential interference with witnesses is assessed to be high and cannot be otherwise mitigated. Moreover, the State, where the suspect would be released, would need to accept the person on its territory and enforce the conditions imposed by the Court. The Appeals Chamber therefore underlined that the competent Chamber has discretion to consider conditional release which it must "*exercise judiciously and with full cognizance of the fact that a person's liberty is at stake*".[173] Conditional release is possible in two situations: *"(1) where a Chamber, although satisfied that the conditions under article 58(1)(b) are not met, nevertheless considers it appropriate to release the person subject to conditions; and (2) where risks enumerated in article 58(1)(b) exist, but the Chamber considers that these can be mitigated by the imposition of certain conditions of release*".[174] It follows that conditions are not punitive in nature but are meant to mitigate the risks under article 58(1)(b). Conditions to be considered are enumerated in rule 119(1), albeit in a non-exhaustive way, and must be specified and imposed by the Chamber.[175] Where a State has indicated its general willingness and ability to accept the detained person on its territory and enforce conditions, the Chamber must seek observations from that State as to its ability to enforce specific conditions identified by the Chamber.[176] On the other hand, where a State has offered to accept a detained

172 Trial Chamber VII, Decision Regarding Interim Release, 17 August 2015, ICC-01/05-01/13-1151.

173 Appeals Chamber, Judgment on the appeal of Mr Laurent Koudou Gbagbo against the decision of Pre-Trial Chamber I of 13 July 2012 entitled "Decision on the 'Requête de la Défense demandant la mise en liberté provisoire du président Gbagbo'", 26 October 2012, ICC-02/11-01/11-278-Red (OA), para. 79. The ill health of the detained person can also be a factor in the exercise of the Chamber's discretion, see *ibid.*, para. 87.

174 Appeals Chamber, Judgment on the appeal of Mr Jean-Pierre Bemba Gombo against the decision of Trial Chamber III of 27 June 2011 entitled "Decision on Applications for Provisional Release", 19 August 2011, ICC-01/05-01/08-1626-Red (OA7), para. 55.

175 The conditions cannot be identified by the receiving State which is willing to accept the detained person on its territory, see Appeals Chamber, Judgment on the appeal of Mr Jean-Pierre Bemba Gombo against the decision of Trial Chamber III of 27 June 2011 entitled "Decision on Applications for Provisional Release", 19 August 2011, ICC-01/05-01/08-1626-Red (OA7), paras. 53-54.

176 *Ibid.*, para. 1; Appeals Chamber, Judgment on the appeal of Mr Jean-Pierre Bemba Gombo against the decision of Trial Chamber III of 26 September 2011 entitled "Decision on the accused's application for provisional release in light of the Appeals Chamber's judgment of 19 August 2011", 23 November 2011, ICC-01/05-01/08-1937-Red2 (OA9), para. 35 (the public redacted version of the judgment was released on 15 December 2011).

person and to enforce conditions, it is incumbent upon the competent Chamber to consider conditional release.[177]

Conditional release was tested at the Court for the first time in 2009 in the *Bemba* case. Before issuing the decision concerned within the 120-day period, the Single Judge, acting on behalf of Pre-Trial Chamber II, solicited the observations of six States to which *Bemba* sought to be released as well as the host State (rule 119(3), regulation 51 of the Regulations of the Court) as to whether they were willing to accept the detainee on their territory; the Court received negative answers. When issuing the decision, the Single Judge, having assessed the facts at stake, accepted 'changed circumstances' and ordered *Bemba's* conditional release. As no State had been forthcoming to accept *Bemba* on its territory, the implementation of the ruling on conditional release was deferred "pending a decision in which State [*Bemba*] will be released and which set of conditions shall be imposed on him".[178] The matter was to be discussed further in a hearing with the States concerned. In the meantime, the Prosecutor lodged an appeal (article 82(1)(b)), the Appeals Chamber suspended the implementation of the Single Judge decision (article 82(3)) and, after deliberation, reversed it. What is of interest here are the interpretative findings of the Appeals Chamber as regards the procedure in ordering conditional release. Should the Chamber grant conditional release, the Chamber must, at the same time, identify the State to which the person will be released together with the appropriate conditions which make conditional release feasible. The Appeals Chamber followed the Single Judge in acknowledging that the assessment of release and condition-setting is a two-tiered process, but considered that the result of such assessment can only be "*a single unseverable decision that grants conditional release on the basis of specific and enforceable conditions. Put differently, (...) release is only possible if specific conditions are imposed*".[179] Indeed, such conditions had not been imposed by the Single Judge who had intended to discuss this matter with the States concerned in the hearing. The approach established by the Appeals Chamber implies that in order to grant conditional release, it is required to have identified *previously* a State willing to accept the person con-

177 Appeals Chamber, Judgment on the appeal of Mr Laurent Koudou Gbagbo against the decision of Pre-Trial Chamber I of 13 July 2012 entitled "Decision on the 'Requête de la Défense demandant la mise en liberté provisoire du président Gbagbo'", 26 October 2012, ICC-02/11-01/11-278-Red (OA), para. 79.

178 Pre-Trial Chamber II, Decision on the Interim Release of Jean-Pierre Bemba Gombo and Convening Hearings with the Kingdom of Belgium, the Republic of Portugal, the Republic of France, the Federal Republic of Germany, the Italian Republic and the Republic of South Africa, 14 August 2009, ICC-01/05-01/08-475.

179 Appeals Chamber, Judgment on the appeal of the Prosecutor against Pre-Trail Chamber II's "Decision on the Interim Release of Jean-Pierre Bemba Gombo and Convening Hearings with the Kingdom of Belgium, the Republic of Portugal, the Republic of France, the Federal Republic of Germany, the Italian Republic and the Republic of South Africa", 2 December 2009, ICC-01/05-01/08-631-Red (OA2), para. 105.

cerned as well as enforce specific conditions identified by the Chamber.[180] There is some merit in taking this approach, considering that the Court is fully dependent on State cooperation without which the decision on conditional release cannot be implemented. The downside of this approach is, however, that the relevant Chamber, in the course of the 120-day interval as from the previous decision remanding the person, will have to enter into a dialogue with States on conditional release *prior* to actually deciding whether or not to release the person detained. It also has effectively put the right to interim release "into the hands" of States which are at liberty to decline to accept a detained person on their territory without justifying their position further. The human right of the individual is thus ultimately subjected to the interests of the State.

4. *Conditional Release for Humanitarian Reasons*

The Court has exceptionally granted short-term release due to humanitarian reasons. *Bemba* was released from detention for 24 hours to attend his father's funeral in Belgium in 2009,[181] and again for 24 hours in 2011 to attend his stepmother's funeral in Belgium[182]. In both instances, the relevant chambers relied on their inherent powers outside article 60(3). On the other hand, *Bemba* was denied twice a 24-hour release from detention to travel in June and September 2011 to the Democratic Republic of the Congo to obtain a voting card and register as a candidate for upcoming elections.[183] The first time, Trial Chamber III assessed whether this request could be granted exceptionally on the basis of humanitarian reasons and denied it. That decision was upheld on appeal but the Appeals Chamber, for reasons not explained, reviewed the Trial Chamber's decision under article 60(3).[184] Following the Appeals Chamber ruling, Trial Chamber III assessed a similar request the second time under the angle of article 60(3). The approach taken in the latter instance is not entirely convincing. A 24-hour conditional release for a specific, limited purpose is difficult to reconcile with the purpose of article 60(3) as the detainee returns to the Court's detention centre as soon as the purpose

180 *Ibid.*, para. 106.

181 Pre-Trial Chamber II, Decision on the Defence's Urgent Request concerning Mr Jean-Pierre Bemba's Attendance of his Father's Funeral, 3 July 2009, ICC-01/05-01/08-437-Red.

182 Trial Chamber III, Decision on the Defence Request for Mr Jean-Pierre Bemba to attend his Stepmother's Funeral, 12 January 2011, ICC-01/05-01/08-1099-Red.

183 Trial Chamber III, Public Redacted Version of the "Decision on Applications for Provisional Release" of 27 June 2011, 16 August 2011, ICC-01/05-01/08-1565-Red, paras. 68-72; Trial Chamber III, Decision on the "Demande de mise en liberté provisoire de M. Jean-Pierre Bemba Gombo afin d'accomplir ses devoirs civiques en République Démocratique du Congo", 2 September 2011, ICC-01/05-01/08-1691.

184 Appeals Chamber, Judgment on the appeal of Mr Jean-Pierre Bemba Gombo against the decision of Trial Chamber III of 27 June 2011 entitled "Decision on Applications for Provisional Release", 19 August 2011, ICC-01/05-01/08-1626-Red (OA7), paras. 84-85.

is fulfilled; any failure to comply with the conditions during those 24 hours does not imply that the Chamber must issue a new warrant of arrest in accordance with rule 119(4) as the original warrant of arrest remains in effect. Rather, it is correct to argue, as Trial Chamber III did in its first decision on the matter, that the exercise of civic rights by *Bemba* does not warrant conditional release for "humanitarian reasons".[185] That said, the Appeals Chamber's approach may be understood as an attempt to restrict the emergence of legal bases granting release outside the ambit of article 60(3). The consequence of this development is, however, that conflicting jurisprudence continues to exist on this matter as conditional release for "humanitarian reasons" is still contemplated by the Court on the basis of inherent powers, while other instances of short-term conditional release are entertained under article 60(3). With a view to providing legal clarity one may envisage adopting a new provision in the Rules regulating conditional release for "humanitarian reasons" which will describe what constitutes "humanitarian reasons" and set out the criteria to be fulfilled.

5. *Release Under Article 60(4) Due to Inexcusable Delay by the Prosecutor*

Distinct and separate from the periodic review of detention under article 60(3) is the Chamber's continuous obligation to assess whether the arrested person must be released so as to avoid that the person is detained for an unreasonable time prior to trial, as enshrined in article 60(4). This provision reads:

> *The Pre-Trial Chamber shall ensure that a person is not detained for an unreasonable period prior to trial due to inexcusable delay by the Prosecutor. If such delay occurs, the Court shall consider releasing the person, with or without conditions.*

It is worth noting that this obligation runs in parallel to the periodic review process under article 60(3) and must be heeded to by the Court at all times, regardless of whether a request was made by the arrested person.[186] The difference between articles 60(3) and (4) lies in the fact that while article 60(3) empowers the Chamber to reconsider specifically the ruling upon an applica-

---

185 "*The Chamber is mindful that participation in the democratic process through the voting in elections or running for public office is a fundamental right, enshrined in key human rights instruments (...). But these instruments, and case law decided pursuant to them, make clear that the right to participation in the democratic process is not absolute and is subject to reasonable restrictions*", Trial Chamber III, Public Redacted Version of the "Decision on Applications for Provisional Release" of 27 June 2011, 16 August 2011, ICC-01/05-01/08-1565-Red, para. 70.

186 Appeals Chamber, Judgment on the appeal of Mr. Thomas Lubanga Dyilo against the decision of Pre-Trial Chamber I entitled "Décision sur la demande de mise en liberté provisoire de Thomas Lubanga Dyilo", 13 February 2007, ICC-01/04-01/06-824 (OA7), para. 98.

tion for interim release, the assessment under article 60(4) extends to the *overall* period of detention. 'Unreasonableness' of the overall period of detention must be assessed based on the specific circumstances of the case.[187] It is therefore only logical that the Court has avoided establishing strict benchmarks in the abstract. However, the Appeals Chamber clarified that prior detention in the custodial State has to be taken into account if this was part of the process of bringing the person to justice for the crimes that form the subject-matter of the proceedings before the Court.[188]

Yet, an "unreasonable period prior to trial" in itself is not sufficient to release someone under article 60(4). Further stringent conditions must be fulfilled: the "unreasonable" length of detention must be occasioned by an "inexcusable delay" attributable to the Prosecutor.[189] "Delay" in this context has been described as a "failure to take timely steps to move the judicial process forward, as the ends of justice may demand".[190] What is considered "inexcusable" will depend to a large extent on the specificities of the case.[191] This statutory requirement establishes a high threshold as the Chamber must clearly attribute such delay to the Prosecutor's conduct which, in addition, is "inexcusable". No detained person has been released to date by the Court on the basis of article 60(4).

---

187 Appeals Chamber, Judgment on the appeals against Pre-Trial Chamber II's decisions regarding interim release in relation to Aimé Kilolo Musamba, Jean-Jacques Mangenda, Fidèle Babala Wandu, and Narcisse Arido and order for reclassification, 29 May 2015, ICC-01/05-01/13-969 (OA5, OA6, OA7, OA8, and OA9), para. 45; see also K Khan, Article 60 MN 17 and 18, in O Triffterer/K Ambos (eds), The Rome Statute of the International Criminal Court – A Commentary (3rd ed, 2015) with further reference to seven factors accepted by the International Criminal Tribunal for the former Yugoslavia (ICTY) as established by the European Commission of Human Rights.

188 Appeals Chamber, Judgment on the appeal of Mr. Thomas Lubanga Dyilo against the decision of Pre-Trial Chamber I entitled "Décision sur la demande de mise en liberté provisoire de Thomas Lubanga Dyilo", 13 February 2007, ICC-01/04-01/06-824 (OA7), para. 121. In other words, if the arrested person was held in detention in the custodial State for conduct other than the one for which he is prosecuted before the ICC, this time period will not be taken into account.

189 See also recently, Appeals Chamber, Judgment on the appeals against Pre-Trial Chamber II's decisions regarding interim release in relation to Aimé Kilolo Musamba, Jean-Jacques Mangenda, Fidèle Babala Wandu, and Narcisse Arido and order for reclassification, 29 May 2015, ICC-01/05-01/13-969 (OA5, OA6, OA7, OA8, and OA9), para. 42. K Khan criticizes that the wording of article 60(4) is unduly limited to delays attributable to the Prosecutor only; rather, "all organs of the Court should be clearly prohibited from unnecessary, never mind inexcusable delays", see K Khan, Article 60 MN 19, in O Triffterer/K Ambos (eds), The Rome Statute of the International Criminal Court – A Commentary (3rd ed, 2015).

190 Appeals Chamber, Judgment in the Appeal by Mathieu Ngudjolo Chui of 27 March 2008 against the Decision of Pre-Trial Chamber I on the Application of the Appellant for Interim Release, 9 June 2008, ICC-01/04-01/07-572 (OA4), para. 14.

191 Examples in K Khan, Article 60 MN 20, in O Triffterer/K Ambos (eds), The Rome Statute of the International Criminal Court – A Commentary (3rd ed, 2015).

VI. Compensation of an Arrested Person

Article 85 addresses the issue of compensation for arrested and convicted persons. Compensation proceedings are civil proceedings in nature and do not form part of the criminal proceedings.[192] Hence, the provisions do not refer to the person making a request as the accused. The first paragraph of article 85 mirrors the wording of article 9(5) of the International Covenant on Civil and Political Rights ("ICCPR") and article 5(5) of the ECHR, while its second paragraph is similar to article 14(6) of the ICCPR. The third paragraph draws upon national legislation and has no equivalent in any of the international instruments.[193] Article 85, which is complemented by rules 173-175, reads:

1. *Anyone who has been the victim of unlawful arrest or detention shall have an enforceable right to compensation.*
2. *When a person has by a final decision been convicted of a criminal offence, and when subsequently his or her conviction has been reversed on the ground that a new or newly discovered fact shows conclusively that there has been a miscarriage of justice, the person who has suffered punishment as a result of such conviction shall be compensated according to law, unless it is proved that the non-disclosure of the unknown fact in time is wholly or partly attributable to him or her.*
3. *In exceptional circumstances, where the Court finds conclusive facts showing that there has been a grave and manifest miscarriage of justice, it may in its discretion award compensation, according to the criteria provided in the Rules of Procedure and Evidence, to a person who has been released from detention following a final decision of acquittal or a termination of the proceedings for that reason.*

This provision is a novelty in international criminal procedural law. Neither the statutes of the *ad hoc* tribunals nor that of the Special Court for Sierra Leone contain a corresponding norm. Although the Presidents of the International Criminal Tribunal for the former Yugoslavia (ICTY) and International Criminal Tribunal for Rwanda (ICTR) requested the Secretary-General of the United Nations to implement a regulation on remedies for violations of the accused's rights, no amendments were made.[194] Notwithstanding the lack of a legal basis, the ICTR Appeals Chamber decided to grant compensation to

192 Trial Chamber II, Decision on the request by Counsel for Mathieu Ngudjolo for one or more hearings to be held and for an order to ensure that Mathieu Ngudjolo attends the hearing or hearings, 30 October 2015, ICC-01/04-02/12-299-tENG, paras 14, relying on the jurisprudence of the ECtHR in footnote 12.

193 For the negotiating history, see G Bitti, Compensation to an Arrested or Convicted Person, in R Lee (ed), The International Criminal Court: Elements of Crimes and Rules of Procedure and Evidence (Transnational Publisher, 2001), p. 623-625.

194 G Bitti, Compensation to an Arrested or Convicted Person, in R Lee (ed), The International Criminal Court: Elements of Crimes and Rules of Procedure and Evidence (Transnational Publisher, 2001), p. 624; Ch Staker/V Nerlich, Article 85 MN 2, in O Triffterer/K Ambos (eds), The Rome Statute of the International Criminal Court – A Commentary (3rd ed, 2015).

persons illegally detained, for example in the *Barayagwiza* and the *Semanza* cases.[195]

Article 85 envisages compensation for violations of rules governing arrest and detention under the Statute and applicable international law.[196] However, an acquittal does not automatically render pre-trial arrest and detention illegal; even if the accused is subsequently found to be innocent, detention remains lawful as long as there were "reasonable grounds to believe" that the person committed the crime.[197]

The statutory provision has been criticized for lacking detail on many crucial points.[198] Indeed, the Statute does not specify how a compensation claim can be made, what criteria are to be applied when deciding upon a request, nor by whom compensation will be paid. The Rules provide some information, but it seems that much will have to be clarified by case law. Article 85 indicates who can make a request for compensation. As explained by *Bitti*, this right can only be exercised by the arrested or convicted person and cannot be transferred to others.[199] According to rule 173(1), the request must be in writing and addressed to the Presidency which, in turn, shall designate a chamber of three judges to consider the request. The designated chamber may be an existing pre-trial or trial chamber[200] composed of judges

---

195 Barayagwiza was compensated for detention in Cameroon without charge or appearance before the ICTR for a 19-months period; ICTR Appeals Chamber, *Jean Bosco Barayagwiza v Prosecutor*, Case No. ICTR-97-19-AR72, Decision on the Prosecutor's Request for Review or Reconsideration, 31 March 2000; *id.* In the case of Semanza, the Appeals Chamber found that his right to be informed promptly of the nature of the charges brought against him was violated since 18 days elapsed between the time he was taken into custody in Cameroon and the time he was informed. Furthermore, his right to challenge the lawfulness of his detention was infringed; *Laurent Semanza v Prosecutor*, Case No. ICTR-97-20-A, Decision, 31 May 2000.

196 Ch Staker/V Nerlich, Article 85 MN 4, in O Triffterer/K Ambos (eds), The Rome Statute of the International Criminal Court – A Commentary (3rd ed, 2015).

197 Trial Chamber II, Décision sur la "Requête en indemnisation en application des disposition de l'article 85(1) et (3) du Statut de Rome", 16 December 2015, ICC-01/04-02/12-301, para. 15; W Schabas, Article 85, in W Schabas (ed), The International Criminal Court – A Commentary on the Rome Statute (OUP, 2010), p. 967 citing M Nowak, U.N. Covenant on Civil and Political Rights CCPR Commentary, (2nd rev. ed., N.P. Engel Publisher, 2005), pp. 238-239.

198 Ch Staker/V Nerlich, Article 85 MN 7, in O Triffterer/K Ambos (eds), The Rome Statute of the International Criminal Court – A Commentary (3rd ed, 2015).

199 G Bitti, Compensation to an Arrested or Convicted Person, in R Lee (ed), The International Criminal Court: Elements of Crimes and Rules of Procedure and Evidence (Transnational Publisher, 2001), p. 626.

200 G Bitti, Compensation to an Arrested or Convicted Person, in R Lee (ed), The International Criminal Court: Elements of Crimes and Rules of Procedure and Evidence (Transnational Publisher, 2001), p. 627. Trial Chamber II was designated in relation to the notice filed by *Ngudjolo* that he would proceed to apply for compensation under article 85. Said Trial Chamber had remained seized of reparation proceedings in the *Lubanga* case and *Katanga* case, Trial Chamber II, Decision on the "Requête de la Défense solicitant des instructions de la Chambre en vue de la soumission de sa requête en indemnisation sur pied de l'article 85", 24 April 2015, ICC-01/04-02/12-285-tENG, para. 1. Equally, a request for compensation lodged by *Mangenda* (*Bemba et al* case) was referred to Trial Chamber

who shall not have participated in any earlier judgment regarding the applicant (rule 173(1), second sentence).[201] This requirement ensures the impartiality of the judges adjudicating the request. To ensure comprehensive impartiality, we suggest that the word "judgment" should include any other decision rendered in the case against the applicant, as the term "judgment" is used specifically in articles 74 or 83.

Rule 173(4) provides that the applicant is entitled (not obliged) to legal assistance throughout the process. As highlighted by *Bitti*, this provision was necessary since article 67 does not apply to compensation proceedings.[202] In light of international human rights standards, this entitlement may include that the Court pays counsel's fee if the applicant is indigent.[203]

Rule 173(2) clarifies that the decision on compensation must be preceded by a "decision" on (i) the unlawfulness of the arrest or detention (at whatever stage of the proceedings); (ii) the reversal of conviction; or (iii) the existence of a grave and manifest miscarriage of justice.[204] As Trial Chamber II explains, such findings must have been made in a previous decision of the Court.[205] Despite its principled view, the Chamber nevertheless accepted, in the interests of justice, to entertain the request for compensation of *Ngudjolo* in the absence of such prior decision.[206]

Within six months from the date when such decision has been notified to the person concerned, he or she may lodge a request for compensation. Pursuant to rule 173(3), the request must contain the grounds and the amount of compensation requested. It is not a statutory obligation to support the request with evidence, as this was considered to be too burdensome for the applicant. However, it has been argued that in case the applicant intends to

---

VI designated to hear this matter, see Presidency, Decision referring the "Request for Compensation for Unlawful Detention" to Trial Chamber VI, 2 October 2015, ICC-01/05-01/13-1329 (with annex).

201 Trial Chamber II emphasised that the Court's instruments do not prevent that the same Chamber, that rendered one of the decisions enumerated under rule 173(2), entertain a request under article 85. This is not contradictory to rule 173(1) as the judges of Trial Chamber II rendering the decisions in the *Ngudjolo* case were all different from those entertaining the article 85 request for *Ngudjolo*. Accordingly, the requirement of impartiality was preserved. Trial Chamber II, Décision sur la "Requête en indemnisation en application des disposition de l'article 85(1) et (3) du Statut de Rome", 16 December 2015, ICC-01/04-02/12-301, para. 16.

202 G Bitti, Compensation to an Arrested or Convicted Person, in R Lee (ed), The International Criminal Court: Elements of Crimes and Rules of Procedure and Evidence (Transnational Publisher, 2001), p. 630.

203 *Ibid.*, pp. 630-631.

204 Sluiter/Friman et al., International Criminal Procedure, p. 367; G Bitti, Compensation to an Arrested or Convicted Person, in R Lee (ed), The International Criminal Court: Elements of Crimes and Rules of Procedure and Evidence (Transnational Publisher, 2001), pp. 627-628.

205 Trial Chamber II, Décision sur la "Requête en indemnisation en application des disposition de l'article 85(1) et (3) du Statut de Rome", 16 December 2015, ICC-01/04-02/12-301, paras 13 and 15.

206 *Ibid.*, para. 16.

seek compensation for salaries lost or specific damages, this claim must be supported by evidence.[207]

The main outline of the procedure leading to the decision on compensation is set out in rule 174. The Prosecutor participates in the compensation proceedings (rule 174(1)). Victims will normally not participate since their personal interests are not affected in this instance.[208] The State on whose territory the arrest took place may be asked to provide observations (rule 103). The judges may adjudge the request for compensation with or without holding a hearing (rule 174(2)). In the latter case, the determination will be based on the request and any other observations received. If, however, the Prosecutor or the person seeking compensation so request, a hearing must be held. The person must not be personally present but may be represented by counsel during the hearing.[209]

The grounds for which the applicant may request compensation are set forth exhaustively in article 85. But the exact prerequisites for compensation remain vague. First interpretative contours on the scope of the different grounds that may be raised by the arrested (or convicted) person can be found in the Court's first decision under article 85, namely in the *Ngudjolo* case. With a request dated 14 August 2015, *Ngudjolo* raised several arguments by way of which he sought to demonstrate that his arrest and detention were unlawful within the meaning of article 85(1), and that he was the victim of a grave and manifest miscarriage of justice within the meaning of article 85(3). He requested (i) to be compensated the sum of 906,346 € for moral damages; and (ii) that outreach activities be undertaken to explain the acquittal of *Ngudjolo* to the population in Ituri.[210]

As regards the first ground, namely the unlawfulness of the arrest or detention, Trial Chamber II held, amongst other, that any arrest and detention at the commencement of ICC proceedings is not rendered unlawful if the person is subsequently acquitted.[211] Also, the fact that at the beginning of the proceedings the accused's role was characterized legally different than ultimately discussed at trial does not render the warrant of arrest unlawful.[212] It also

---

207 G Bitti, Compensation to an Arrested or Convicted Person, in R Lee (ed), The International Criminal Court: Elements of Crimes and Rules of Procedure and Evidence (Transnational Publisher, 2001), p. 629.

208 However, *Bitti* makes the suggestion that the Chamber may nevertheless seek the views of victims under rule 93, *ibid.*, p. 631.

209 Trial Chamber II, Decision on the request by Counsel for Mathieu Ngudjolo for one or more hearings to be held and for an order to ensure that Mathieu Ngudjolo attends the hearing or hearings, 30 October 2015, ICC-01/04-02/12-299-tENG, paras 13-19.

210 *Defence of Mathieu Ngudjolo*, Requête en indemnisation sur pied de l'article 85(1) et (3) du Statut de Rome, 14 August 2015, ICC-01/04-02/12-290 (with annexes); see also his submissions in the hearing held on 23 November 2015, Trial Chamber II, Transcript of Hearing, ICC-01/04-02/12-T-6-ENG, pp. 13-17.

211 Trial Chamber II, Décision sur la "Requête en indemnisation en application des disposition de l'article 85(1) et (3) du Statut de Rome", 16 December 2015, ICC-01/04-02/12-301, para. 18.

212 *Ibid.*, para. 34.

found that failure to question the suspect under article 55(2) in the context of the article 58 application stage did not meet the threshold of article 85(1), as article 55(2) does not impose a positive obligation on the Prosecutor to question suspects.[213] More generally, it espoused that the manner in which the Prosecutor conducts her investigation cannot be made subject of an article 85 request.[214] Having failed to demonstrate that *Ngudjolo* was unlawfully arrested or detained, Trial Chamber II rejected his request under article 85(1).

We would also like to draw attention to one related issue here. The most interesting question in the context of article 85(1) is whether a violation must have been committed by the Court[215] or whether compensation may also be granted on the basis of acts committed by authorities of the custodial State acting upon request of the ICC. In the latter case, the question would arise if the ICC is the right addressee of such claim, as it would have to review the lawfulness of acts of a sovereign State, or whether the Court is prevented from making a finding of any wrongdoing by national authorities. So far, this question has not been addressed by the ICC in the context of article 85[216] nor has it been substantially discussed in academic literature.[217] The idea of attributing wrongful conduct of a State organ to another subject of international law (be it a State or international organization) in order to establish the latter's responsibility is not foreign to international law, as demonstrated by article 7 Draft Articles on the Responsibility of International Organizations for Internationally Wrongful Acts.[218] It is thus not implausible to propose that a violation of a person's rights during detention in the custodial State may be

---

213 *Ibid.*, para. 26. See also the Court's jurisprudence on the *ex parte* nature of the article 58 stage (section III.1. above).

214 *Ibid.*, para. 30.

215 *Mangenda* (*Bemba et al* case) alleges a wrong-doing on the part of the Court and requests to be compensated 3,000 € per day for nine days in prison following a judicial order to release him provisionally, see *Defence of Jean-Jacques Mangenda Kabongo*, Public Redacted Version of Request for Compensation for Unlawful Detention, 1 May 2015, ICC-01/05-01/13-921-Red.

216 *Katanga* had challenged his arrest and detention by the competent authorities of the Democratic Republic of the Congo prior to his surrender to the ICC and requested Trial Chamber II to declare his detention as unlawful. He sought a stay of proceedings or, in the alternative, pecuniary compensation for those breaches or, in case he would be convicted, that his sentence be reduced. However, this request was not addressed on its merits as the Chamber dismissed the request as belated, see Trial Chamber II, Decision on the Motion of the Defence of Germain Katanga for a Declaration on Unlawful Detention and Stay of Proceedings of 20 November 2009 (ICC-01/04-01/07-1666-Conf-Exp), 3 December 2009, ICC-01/04-01/07-1666-Red-tENG. This ruling was upheld by the Appeals Chamber, by majority, in Judgment on the Appeal of Mr Katanga Against the Decision of Trial Chamber II of 20 November 2009 Entitled "Decision on the Motion of the Defence of Germain Katanga for a Declaration on Unlawful Detention and Stay of Proceedings", 12 July 2010, ICC-01/04-01/07-2259 (OA10).

217 Shortly hinted to in Ch Staker/V Nerlich, Article 85 MN 4 and 8, in O Triffterer/K Ambos (eds), Commentary on the Rome Statute of the International Criminal Court – A Commentary (3rd ed, 2015).

218 A/66/10. See also article 6 Draft Articles on the Responsibility of States for Internationally Wrongful Acts, A/56/49.

imputed to the ICC for the purposes of compensation. It is, however, still open to question under what conditions such attribution of State acts to the ICC may be justified.[219]

A look at other international(ized) tribunals may offer some guidance in this respect. The ICTR, for example, established in the *Barayagwiza* case that violations must be of such quality as to constitute an abuse of process (with the consequence that it would be detrimental to the integrity of ICTR proceedings)[220] or be directly attributable to the tribunal. Moreover, the alleged violation must somehow be connected to the international proceedings in order to permit attribution of responsibility for the violation to the international tribunal. In the *Semanza* case, the ICTR was concerned whether the accused's right to be informed promptly of the reasons for his arrest had been violated while he was in national custody before the ICTR Prosecutor requested his arrest and surrender to the ICTR. The relevant Chamber took into account only the period *after* the ICTR Prosecutor had communicated the cooperation request to the national authorities.[221] *Semanza's* detention before that communication was disregarded as it was not linked to the ICTR. Likewise, in the appeal judgment of Case 001 (*Kaing Guek Eav* – alias *Duch*), the Supreme Court Chamber of the Extraordinary Chambers in the Courts of Cambodia ("ECCC"), while referring with approval to the ICTR jurisprudence, confirmed that violations of human rights must "*be attributed to the Tribunal in order to grant the accused a remedy*".[222] It concluded, however, that the prior illegal detention of *Duch* by the Cambodian Military Court – where *Duch* had been incarcerated between 10 May 1999 and 30 July 2007 without facing trial – was not imputable to the ECCC or its organs and that, consequently, no redress was to be provided by the ECCC.[223]

---

219 The attribution of the conduct of a State organ to an international organization requires the organization to exercise "effective control" over the conduct of the organ, Art. 7 Draft Articles on the Responsibility of International Organizations, A/66/10, para. 87. As seen above, it is difficult to argue that, considering the division of responsibilities between the requested State Party and the Court in the execution of warrants of arrest, the ICC exercises "effective control" over the competent authorities of the custodial State with regard to the arrest and detention of the suspect.

220 That would imply an egregious breach of law as determined in the *Barayagwiza* case, where "fundamental rights of the Appellant were repeatedly violated", see ICTR *Jean Bosco Barayagwiza v Prosecutor*, ICTR-97-19-AR72, Appeals Chamber Decision, 31 March 2000, para. 71.

221 ICTR, *Laurent Semanza v Prosecutor*, Appeals Chamber, Decision, Case No. ICTR-97-20-A, 31 May 2000, para. 79.

222 ECCC, *Prosecutor v Kaing Guek Eav*, Appeal Judgment, 3 February 2012, No. 001/18-07-2007-ECCC/SC, para. 398.

223 ECCC, *Prosecutor v Kaing Guek Eav*, Appeal Judgment, 3 February 2012, No. 001/18-07-2007-ECCC/SC, para. 396. In their dissenting opinion, Judge Klonowiecka-Milart and Judge Yasinghe confirm the majority's findings on the legal requirements for granting this remedy but differ insofar as, in their view, the ECCC ought to have taken into account *Duch's* detention by the Cambodian Military Court prior to his transfer to ECCC custody. This is grounded on the belief that the ECCC, as a hybrid court integrated into the national judicial system, should share responsibility and "ought to be accountable for the acts of

It remains to be seen whether the ICC will rely on the same test or establish other criteria. The *Bemba et al.* case (*Mangenda*) could offer, for the first time, an insight as to how the ICC will appreciate the conduct of a State when applying article 85.[224]

Returning to the *Ngudjolo* case, and the Court's first interpretative findings on the law of article 85, we would like to summarize the Trial Chamber's views on the contours of article 85(3). At first, the Chamber underlined the exceptional nature of the ground and highlighted that even if all elements of article 85(3) were to be fulfilled, the Chamber still retained its discretionary powers to accede to the request ("[the Court] may in its discretion award compensation").[225] As to when a "grave and manifest miscarriage of justice" can be assumed, the Chamber sought guidance in the provision's drafting history, national legislation and the practice of other international tribunals. It concluded:

> "*À la lumière de ces considérations, et compte tenu du fait que la présence de « circonstances exceptionnelles » est prévue par l'article 85-3 du Statut, la Chambre est d'avis qu'une erreur judiciaire grave et manifeste au sens de l'article précité est une erreur certaine et incontestable commise dans l'administration de la justice à la suite, par exemple, d'une décision erronée d'une chambre ou de poursuites abusives menées par le Procureur. L'erreur doit avoir engendré une violation Claire des droits fondamentaux du requérant et doit avoir causé un préjudice sérieux au requérant. L'article 85-3 du Statut fixe un seuil élevé pour de telles erreurs et il s'ensuit que toute erreur au cours de la procédure ne constitue pas nécessairement une erreur judiciaire « grave et manifeste »*".[226]

Crucially, it highlighted that an article 85 chamber cannot pass judgment on the propriety of prior decisions in the case.[227] Upon examination of the different arguments, the Chamber held that *Ngudjolo* was not the victim of a

---

the domestic system", see Partially Dissenting Joint Opinion of Judges Agnieszka Klonowiecka-Milart and Chandra Nihal Jayasinghe, paras. 7-8 (annexed to the Appeal Judgment).

224 *Mangenda* (*Bemba et al* case) requests to be compensated 3,000 € per day for nine days in prison following an ICC judicial order to release him provisionally; however, that order could not be enforced immediately as arrangements with the relevant State to which *Mangenda* was supposed to be released had to be finalized, see *Defence of Jean-Jacques Mangenda Kabongo*, Public Redacted Version of Request for Compensation for Unlawful Detention, 1 May 2015, ICC-01/05-01/13-921-Red. As in the *Ngudjolo* case, a rather unusual element in this case is that the request was lodged in the absence of a prior decision, as required by rule 173(2). It appears that *Mangenda* considers the order to release him from detention by the Single Judge on 21 October 2014 as the relevant decision within the meaning of rule 173(2) (see *supra* footnote 166).

225 Trial Chamber II, Décision sur la "Requête en indemnisation en application des disposition de l'article 85(1) et (3) du Statut de Rome", 16 December 2015, ICC-01/04-02/12-301, paras 45 and 46.

226 *Ibid.*, para. 45 (footnote omitted).

227 *Ibid.*, para. 47. This makes it all the more necessary to insist that a decision concerning either of the grounds enumerated in rule 173 is available.

"grave and manifest miscarriage of justice" and denied, accordingly, his request for compensation under article 85(3).

Once the person is found entitled to compensation the question arises which forms of compensation can be considered. While financial compensation will be the rule,[228] the Statute leaves room for other forms of compensation, such as a reduction of sentence. Rule 175 addresses the question how the pecuniary amount is to be calculated and which criteria the Court may take into account. But Rule 175 addresses only the situation of article 85(3). This is striking as it is not apparent at first sight why this rule was designed to be confined to this provision only.[229] However, given the mandate in article 85(3) to award compensation "according to the criteria provided in the Rules of Procedure and Evidence", rule 175 was not extended to article 85 in its entirety. Yet, in spite of the apparently limited reach of rule 175 the Court is likely to award compensation under articles 85(1) and (2) on the basis of similar criteria as provided in rule 175, perhaps adding further criteria as the Court sees fit.

Finally, the decision issued by the Chamber shall be taken by the majority of the Judges, in accordance with rule 174(4). Even without any express mention in the law, it is self-evident that such decision must be sufficiently reasoned in order to comply with international human rights standards (article 21(3)).[230] No mention is made as to the appealability of such a decision.

VII. Conclusion

"When dealing with the right to liberty, one should be mindful of the fundamental principle that deprivation of liberty should be an exception and not a rule".[231] As we have seen in this article, the exception actually became the rule. In most cases, Chambers issued warrants of arrest. Suspects, once transferred into the custody of the Court, remain in detention throughout the entire proceedings before the ICC, as the risk to abscond, interfere with the Court's proceedings or commit further crimes is considered to remain a possibility. Short-term release has been contemplated only in exceptional circumstances for humanitarian reasons. In addition, the legal setting in which the Court has been embedded is such that questions of release and conditions cannot be decided upon independently and unilaterally by the Court. They require a

228 Meester et al., in: Sluiter/Friman et al., International Criminal Procedure, p. 367.

229 Indeed, during the negotiations, some States questioned why this rule should be restricted to article 85(3) only, see G Bitti, Compensation to an Arrested or Convicted Person, in R Lee (ed), The International Criminal Court: Elements of Crimes and Rules of Procedure and Evidence (Transnational Publisher, 2001), p. 635.

230 G Bitti, Compensation to an Arrested or Convicted Person, in R Lee (ed), The International Criminal Court: Elements of Crimes and Rules of Procedure and Evidence (Transnational Publisher, 2001), p. 634.

231 Pre-Trial Chamber II, Decision on Application for Interim Release, 14 April 2009, ICC-01/05-01/08-403, para. 36.

continuous dialogue with States which must show willingness to assist in rendering those rights effective. In this regard, it is a most welcome development that on 10 April 2014 an agreement between Belgium and the Court entered into force by way of which Belgium accepts to provisionally receive detainees from the Court on its territory on a temporary basis and under conditions as imposed by the Chambers.[232] One can only hope that more States will follow this example and thus enable the Court to exercise its discretionary powers on conditional release with ease and in full accord with internationally recognized human rights.

232 See Press Release, Belgium and ICC sign agreement on interim release of detainees, 10 April 2014, ICC-CPI-20140410-PR993 (available on the website of the Court).

Sally Alexandra Longworth[*]

Sentencing at the International Criminal Court

Introduction

The determination of the penalty after a finding of guilt is a fundamental part of any criminal trial. As noted by Trial Chamber II of the International Criminal Tribunal for the former Yugoslavia (ICTY) in the *Furundžija* case "[i]t is the infallibility of punishment, rather than the severity of the sanction which is the tool for retribution, stigmatisation and deterrence. This is particularly the case for the International Tribunal; penalties are made more onerous by its international statute, moral authority and impact upon world public opinion, and this punitive effect must be borne in mind when assessing the suitable length of sentence".[1] For many accused, sentencing is often a key concern throughout the investigatory and trial process, having a profound effect on the conduct of their lives to follow.[2] However, it is an area that has received comparatively less attention than other parts of the trial proceedings.

The role of the defence counsel changes during the sentencing stage of the case. During the trial proceedings, counsel's role involve assisting their client before the court in presenting their version of events and exonerating evidence, challenging the prosecution's evidence, and ensuring the presumption of innocence and other fair trial rights are upheld.[3] In sentencing proceedings, the defence counsel must ensure their client's best interests and rights are upheld so that the sentence passed is fair, proportionate and the least punitive available at law. Counsel must ensure that all relevant factors

* Sally Longworth is a non-practising barrister specialising in international human rights, international humanitarian and international criminal law. She was called to the Bar of England & Wales in July 2010 and holds an LLM in international human rights law from the Raoul Wallenberg Institute of Human Rights and Humanitarian Law. Her previous positions include lecturer and researcher in international law at the Swedish National Defence College, legal assistant for the Sesay Defence Team at the Special Court for Sierra Leone, and for the defence at the Bangladesh International Crimes Tribunal. She has also acted as legal consultant with a number of international and intergovernmental organisations on a broad range of issues, including transitional justice mechanisms, international humanitarian law, international human rights law and procedure and EU law. The views expressed in this commentary are solely those of the author.

1 International Criminal Tribunal for the former Yugoslavia, *Prosecutor v. Furundžija* IT-95-17/1-T-10, Judgement 10 December 1998 para. 290.

2 The relevant provisions in the Rome Statute of the International Criminal Court, 2187 UNTS 90, entered into force 1 July 2002, are Articles 76-80 and 110 (hereinafter "ICC Statute"). See further Rules of Procedure and Evidence of the International Criminal Court, ICC-ASP/1/3, at 10, and Corr. 1 (2002), U.N. Doc. PCNICC/2000/1/Add.1 (2000), Chapter 7 (hereinafter "ICC Rules of Procedure and Evidence").

3 Jarinde Temminck Tuinstra, *Defending the Defenders: The Role of Defence Counsel in International Criminal Trials,* 8 Journal of International Criminal Justice, 463-486, 2010, page 466 (hereinafter "Temminck Tuinstra: Defending the Defenders 2010").

that aid in the determination of the sentence are taken into consideration and no irrelevant or erroneous ones. The factual basis upon which the sentence is imposed must be correct and the personal matters of the client presented so as to aid the court to determine an appropriate sentence in light of the circumstances of the case.

Sentencing in international criminal law is somewhat infamously subject to broad discretion of the Court.[4] No sentencing guidelines exist, in contrast to the practice in many domestic systems, and the sentencing decisions of the *ad hoc* tribunals demonstrates the vast array of different factors taken into account in sentencing and the weight given accordingly in determining sentences. Commentators have highlighted significant areas of inconsistencies in the sentencing practice of the *ad hoc* tribunals.[5] Consistency, both in approach and outcome, is fundamental to the principle of justice and, as such, essential in ensuring a fair outcome to the trial proceedings.[6] Consistency and foreseeability are critical elements in the principle of legality, and ensure that defence counsel can carry out their role sufficiently in advising their clients on what to present in defence and based on this the possible outcomes of the trial.

To date, the ICC Trial Chambers have issued just two sentencing judgements, but these two judgements do provide some guidance for counsel on how the Court goes about determining the sentence in cases before it. This article analyses Trial Chamber I's decision on sentencing in the *Lubanga* case and Trial Chamber II's decision on sentencing in the *Katanga* case to identify key factors taken into account, which may be of assistance for defence counsel in future cases, both in international proceedings and in domestic proceedings, where the Court's practice may be persuasive.

Sentencing powers of the ICC and rules of procedure

After the decision on guilt or innocence of the accused, the trial proceedings move on to sentencing. Except in relation to proceedings on an admission of

4 The *Lubanga* sentencing appeal judgement confirmed that "...the Trial Chamber's determination involves an exercise of discretion with the aim to impose a proportionate sentence that reflects the culpability of the convicted person", based on "its intimate knowledge of the case...balanc[ing] all factors it considers relevant". International Criminal Court, *Prosecutor v. Thomas Lubanga Dyilo,* Situation in the Democratic Republic of the Congo, Judgement on the appeals of the Prosecutor and Mr Thomas Lubanga Dyilo against the "Decision on Sentence pursuant to Article 76 of the Statute, ICC-01/04-01/06 A 4 A 6, Appeals Chamber, 1 December 2014, para. 34 (hereinafter "Lubanga sentencing appeal judgement 2014").

5 See, for example, Kevin Jon Heller, *The Taylor Sentencing Judgement: A Critical Analysis,* Journal of International Criminal Justice 11 (2013), 835-855 (hereinafter "Heller: The Taylor Sentencing Judgement 2013").

6 Dr. Barbara Hola, *Sentencing of International Crimes at the ICTY and ICTR: Consistency of Sentencing Case Law,* Amsterdam Law Forum Vol. 4:4 2012 page 5 (hereinafter "Hola: Consistency of Sentencing Case Law 2012").

guilt, the Trial Chamber may on its own motion hold a further hearing to hear any additional evidence or submissions.[7] If either the Prosecutor or the accused request to hold such a further hearing, the Trial Chamber is obliged to do so.[8] In its sentencing decision, the Trial Chamber shall take into account the evidence presented and submissions made during the trial that are relevant for sentence.[9]

Article 77(1) of the Rome Statute empowers the Court to impose a term of imprisonment for a specified number of years which may not exceed a maximum of 30 years, or a term of life imprisonment when justified by the extreme gravity of the crime and individual circumstances of the convicted person.[10] In addition to imprisonment, the Court may order a fine and forfeiture of proceeds, property and assets derived directly or indirectly from that crime, without prejudice to the rights of bona fide third parties.[11] As is clear from the wording of the provision, fines and forfeiture may only be imposed "in addition" to imprisonment.[12] This taken together with the drafting history of the penalties under the Rome Statute make it clear that imprisonment was envisaged to be the main sentence under the Rome Statute.[13] Under Article 79(2), the Court may (but is not required to) order any money or other property collected in fines or forfeiture to be transferred, by order of the Court, to the Trust Fund. The Trust Fund is established under Article 79(1) for the benefit of the victims of crimes within the jurisdiction of the Court, and of the families of such victims,[14] and is a distinct point of difference between the operations of the ICC and the *ad hoc* tribunals. In accordance with the principle of *nulla poena sine lege* ("no punishment without law") set out in Article 23, the list of penalties available to the Court is exhaustive. Under Article 78, in determining the sentence the Court shall take into account such factors as the gravity of the crime and the individual circumstances of the convicted persons. These factors are elaborated further in Rule 145 of the Rules of Procedure and Evidence.

Both the penalties of the ICTY and the International Criminal Tribunal for Rwanda (ICTR) were limited to imprisonment, although both were empowered to also order the return of property or proceeds acquired by criminal conduct to their rightful owners.[15] Although the Statutes of the ICTY and

7 ICC Statute, *supra* n. 2, Article 76(2).
8 ICC Statute, *supra* n. 2, Article 76(2).
9 ICC Statute, *supra* n. 2, Article 76(1).
10 ICC Statute, *supra* n. 2, Article 77(1)(a) and (b).
11 ICC Statute, *supra* n. 2, Article 77(2)(a) and (b).
12 See further ICC Rules of Procedure and Evidence, *supra* n. 2, Rules 146-148.
13 See William A. Schabas, *Penalties,* in Antonio Cassese, Paola Gaeta and John R.W.D Jones (eds.), The Rome Statute of the International Criminal Court: A Commentary, 2002 (Oxford University Press: Oxford, UK) (hereinafter "Schabas: Penalties, Commentary to the ICC Statute 2002").
14 See further ICC Rules of Procedure and Evidence, *supra* n. 2, Rule 98.
15 Statute of the International Criminal Tribunal for the former Yugoslavia annexed to United Nations Security Council Resolution 827, UN SCOR, 48th sess, 3217th mtg, UN

ICTR do not expressly stipulate that the Tribunals can impose a sentence of life imprisonment,[16] the ICTY and ICTR Rules of Procedure both empower the Tribunals to impose a sentence of imprisonment for the remainder of the convicted person's life.[17] The ICTR has imposed a number of life sentences, all of them following convictions of genocide.[18] The ICTY has also imposed seven life sentences.[19] Article 24(1) of the Statute of the Special Tribunal for Lebanon provides that the Tribunal may impose a life sentence.[20] The Special Court for Sierra Leone (SCSL) differs from the other *ad hoc* tribunals in that neither the Statute nor Rules of Procedure empower the court to impose a life sentence.[21] However, in practice, the SCSL has imposed sentences for very long specified numbers of years.[22]

As with the *ad hoc* tribunals, the ICC is not empowered to impose the death penalty or any other form of corporal punishment.[23] The International Military Tribunal at Nuremberg and the International Military Tribunal for the Far East were empowered to impose the death penalty and did in a number of cases.[24] There was considerable division during the drafting and negotiations of the Rome Statute on how to address penalties.[25] As the President of the Conference noted in connection with the adoption of the Statute on 17 July 1998 "[t]he debate at this Conference on the issue of which penalties should be applied by the Court has shown that there is no international con-

---

Doc. S/RES/827 (1993) Article 24 (hereinafter "ICTY Statute"); Statute of the International Criminal Tribunal for Rwanda annexed to United Nations Security Council Resolution 955, UN SCOR 49th sess., 3453rd mtg, U.N. Doc. S/Res/955 (1994), Article 24 (hereinafter "ICTR Statute"); Statute of the Special Court for Sierra Leone, 2178 UNTS 138, 145, UN Doc. S/2002/246, appendix II Article 19 (hereinafter "SCSL Statute").

16 ICTY Statute, *supra* n. 20, Article 24; ICTR Statute, *supra* n. 20, Article 24.

17 ICTY Rules of Procedure and Evidence, UN Doc. IT/32/Rev.37 (2006), Rule 101(A); ICTR Rules of Procedure and Evidence .N. Doc. ITR/3/REV.1 (1995), Rule 101(A).

18 See for example ICTR, *Prosecutor v. Kambanda,* Judgement and Sentence, ICTR-97-23-S, Trial Chamber, 4 September 1998; ICTY, *Prosecutor v. Akayesu* Sentencing Judgement, ICTR-96-4-S, Trial Chamber I, 2 October 1998; ICTR, *Prosecutor v. Kayishema and Ruzindana* Judgement, ICTR-95-1-T, Trial Chamber II, 21 May 2000; ICTR, *Prosecutor v Rutaganda* Judgement and Sentence, ICTR-96-3-T, Trial Chamber I, 6 December 1999.

19 See http://www.icty.org/sections/TheCases/JudgementList (last accessed 2 July 2015).

20 See Statute of the Special Tribunal for Lebanon, U.N. Doc. S/RES/1757, 30 May 2007, Articles 2, 5 and Article 24 (hereinafter "STL Statute").

21 SCSL Statute, *supra* n. 15, Article 19.

22 Heller: The Taylor Sentencing Judgement 2013, *supra* n. 11.

23 See Schabas: Penalties, Commentary to the ICC Statute 2002, *supra* n. 13, page 1505.

24 The International Military Tribunal at Nuremberg sentenced three offenders to life imprisonment, and 11 persons to death by hanging and the International Military Tribunal for the Far East sentenced 16 offenders to life imprisonment and seven persons to death by hanging. Both tribunals were empowered to impose upon a defendant/accused "on conviction, death, or such other punishment as shall be determined by it to be just." See further Nuremberg Trial Proceedings Vol. 1, Charter of the International Military Tribunal, Article 27 and Charter of the International Military Tribunal for the Far East, Article 16.

25 Schabas: Penalties, Commentary to the ICC Statute 2002, *supra* n. 13, page 1509.

sensus on the inclusion or non-inclusion of the death penalty."[26] Arguments presented in favour of the death penalty included that it would be commensurate with the gravity of the crimes under the Court's jurisdiction and that not including it would reduce the deterrence and credibility of the Court.[27] However, not even all States whose national laws provide for the possibility of the death penalty were in support of its inclusion in the Statute, including the United States of America.[28] Developments in human rights law and state practice are noteworthy in this area.[29] Whereas at the time of the Nuremberg and Tokyo trials the majority of states still included the death penalty in their domestic criminal law,[30] by the mid-1990s when the Rome Statute was drafted and negotiated the number of abolition countries outnumbered states that retained the death penalty, and today 58 countries permit the death penalty.[31] Several delegations also raised concerns regarding the imposition of a life sentence or a long sentence of imprisonment, due to constitutional problems in their domestic systems, as well as potential conflicts with international human rights norms prohibiting cruel, inhuman, and degrading forms

---

26 Quoted in Rolf Einar Fife, *Article 80: Non-prejudice to national application of penalties and national laws,* in Otto Triffterer (ed.), Commentary on the Rome Statute of the International Criminal Court: Observers' Notes, Article by Article, 2nd ed. 2008 (C.H. Beck, Munich/Hart, Portland/Nomos, Baden Baden), page 1443 (hereinafter "Fife: Article 80, Commentary to Rome Statute 2008").

27 Fife: Article 80, Commentary to Rome Statute 2008 *supra* n. 26, page 1445, notes that the proponents in favour for inclusion of the death penalty included Rwanda, Saudi Arabia and other Arab States, Sierra Leone, Singapore, Trinidad and Tobago, Jamaica and other Caribbean States.

28 *Ibid.*

29 See, for example, Second Optional Protocol to the International Covenant on Civil and Political Rights GA res. 44/128, annex, 44 UN GAOR Supp. (No. 49) at 207, UN Doc. A/44/49 (1989); the Protocol to the American Convention on Human Rights to Abolish the Death Penalty Organization of American States Treaty Series 73 1144 UNTS 123 (1979); Protocol number 6 to the European Convention for the Protection of Human Rights and Fundamental Freedoms (ETS No. 114), *entered into force* March 1, 1985; Protocol no. 13 to the European Convention for the Protection of Human Rights and Fundamental Freedoms (ETS No. 187) *entered into force* Jan. 7, 2003. Others treaties include explicit provisions limiting the death penalty, such as the American Convention on Human Rights OEA/ser. K/XVY1.1, Doc. 65, Rev. 1, Corr. 1 OASTS, No. 36 (1970) and the Arab Charter on Human Rights (League of Arab States),22 May, 2004, *reprinted in* 12 Int'l Hum. Rts. Rep. 893 (2005), *entered into force* March 15, 2008).

30 Eric Prokosch, *The Death Penalty versus Human Rights,* in Death Penalty Beyond Abolition (Council of Europe Publishing: Strasbourg, 2004), page 32 notes that at the beginning of the twentieth century Costa Rica, San Marino and Venezuela had permanently abolished the death penalty. Following the loss of life in World War II, numerous other states began to move towards abolition.

31 http://www.amnesty.org/en/death-penalty/abolitionist-and-retentionist-countries (data as of 1 December 2013, last accessed 2 July 2015). Amnesty International recorded executions in 22 countries in 2013. Amnesty International reported that 80% of all known executions were recorded in only three countries: Iran, Iraq and Saudi Arabia. Amnesty International, *Death Sentences and Executions 2013*, Amnesty International Publication 2014, available only at: http://www.amnesty.org/en/library/asset/ACT50/001/2014/ en/652ac5b3-3979-43e2-b1a1-6c4919e7a518/act500012014en.pdf (last accessed 2 July 2015).

of punishments and a neglect for rehabilitation purposes of sentencing.[32] Article 77 of the Rome Statute was therefore a compromise between these extreme positions. The higher end sentence of a specified number of years not exceeding 30 years or a term of life imprisonment included in the final draft was the compromise for not including the death penalty, whereas the requirement under Article 110(3) for review of sentence after two thirds of the sentence or 25 years in the case of life imprisonment was driven by constitutional and human rights considerations.[33]

No set time was discussed as to the meaning of "life imprisonment", so it may be assumed that "life imprisonment" means imprisonment for the remainder of the life of the convicted person.[34] This interpretation is supported by the distinction made in Article 77(1) between the specified period of time and "life imprisonment". In effect, the operation of the mandatory review of the sentence by the Court after 25 years under Article 110(3) means that "life imprisonment" is a minimum of 25 years. The European Court of Human Rights (ECtHR) case of *Vinter and Others v United Kingdom* provided an in-depth assessment of the current state practice in relation to life imprisonment.[35] At paragraph 68 the European Court noted that there are nine countries where life imprisonment does not exist (namely Andorra, Bosnia and Herzegovina, Croatia, Montenegro, Norway, Portugal, San Marino, Serbia and Spain).[36] The maximum term of imprisonment in these countries ranged from 21 years in Norway to 45 years in Bosnia and Herzegovina, and 50 years for cumulative sentences in Croatia.

The ECtHR noted that in the majority of countries where a sentence of life imprisonment may be imposed, there exists a dedicated mechanism for review of the sentence after the prisoner has served a certain minimum period fixed by law. As noted above, such a mandatory mechanism is included in Article 110(3of the Rome Statute. [37] The practice of the *ad hoc* tribunals

---

32 UN Doc. A/AC.249/1997/WG.6/CRP.2/Rev. 1 (10 December 1997). See Schabas: Penalties, Commentary to the ICC Statute 2002, *supra* n. 18, page 1509.

33 Schabas: Penalties, Commentary to the ICC Statute 2002, *supra* n. 13, page 1510. Schabas notes Venezuela, El Salvador, Nicaragua and Colombia in this regard. Note further the decision of the European Court of Human Rights, *Vinter and others v. The United Kingdom* [GC], nos. 66069/09, 130/10 and 3896/10), Judgement of 9 July 2013 (hereinafter "*Vinter and others v. The United Kingdom*").

34 Several options presented during the drafting including in square brackets (indicating a lack of consensus as to inclusion in the instrument): imprisonment for a specified number of years; imprisonment for a maximum (thirty years was suggested); a definitive term of imprisonment (twenty to forty years was suggested), subject to a reduction in accordance with other provisions of the Statute. Also included in square brackets that the Court could specify a minimum period to be served without eligibility for provisional release or parole. See further UN Doc. A/AC.249/1997/WG.6/CRP.2 and Schabas: Penalties, Commentary to the ICC Statute 2002, *supra* n. 18, page 1508.

35 *Vinter and others v. The United Kingdom*, *supra* n. 33.

36 *bid*, para. 68.

37 See further ICC Statute, *supra* n. 2, Article 110(4) and (5) and ICC Rules of Procedure and Evidence, *supra* n. 2 Rules 223 and 224.

differed from the ICC in this respect, as sentences of imprisonment were carried out in accordance with the applicable law of the state designated by the Tribunal for sentence to be served and subject to the supervision of the Tribunal. Any decision on commutation or pardon in accordance with the applicable law of the state concerned remained to be ultimately decided by the relevant Tribunal.[38]

Whilst Article 77(1)(a) provides that a specified period of time to be served "may" not exceed 30 years imprisonment, it is argued here that it is not within the discretion of the Court to provide a sentence above this limit. The drafting history of the Rome Statute indicates the concerns expressed by several delegations at very lengthy sentences and considerable debate on the point of sentencing by the Court. As such, the use of the word "may" is not indicative that it is open to the Court to impose sentences above this limit. Rather, this provision imposes an upper limit to which the Court may sentence an individual.[39] This interpretation is supported by Article 78(3), which provides that the total period of imprisonment for concurrent offences "*shall* not exceed 30 years imprisonment or a sentence of life imprisonment in conformity with article 77, paragraph 1 (b)" (emphasis added).

The sentence imposed by the ICC must be pronounced in public and, wherever possible, in the presence of the accused.[40] If a person is convicted of more than one crime, the Court must pronounce a sentence for each crime and a joint sentence specifying the total period of imprisonment. [41] This total period shall be no less than the highest individual sentence and shall not exceed 30 years or a sentence of life imprisonment.[42] Any time spent in pre-trial detention shall be deducted from the final sentence and the Court may deduct time otherwise spent in detention in connection with the conduct underlying the crime.[43]

In determining the sentence, Article 78(1) provides that the Court shall take into the gravity of the crime and the individual circumstances of the convicted person. Under Rule 145(1) of the Rules of Procedure and Evidence, the Court must bear in mind that the totality of any sentence imposed under Article 77 must reflect the culpability of the convicted person and balance all the relevant factors, including any mitigating and aggravating factors and consider the circumstances both of the convicted person and of

---

38 ICTY Statute, *supra* n. 15, Articles 27 and 28; ICTR Statute, *supra* n. 15, Articles 26 and 27; SCSL Statute, *supra* n. 15, Articles 22 and 23; STL Statute, *supra* n. 20, Articles 29 and 30.

39 C.f. Jamil Ddamulira Mujuzi, *(Mis)interpreting the Statute? The International Criminal Court, the Sentence of Life Imprisonment and Other Emerging Sentencing Issues: A Comment on the Trial Chamber I Decision on the Sentence in Prosecutor v. Thomas Lubanga Dyilo,* International Criminal Law Review 13 (2013) 1037-1045, pages 1043-1044.

40 ICC Statute, *supra* n. 2, Article 76(4).

41 ICC Statute, *supra* n. 2, Article 78(3).

42 *Ibid.*

43 ICC Statute, *supra* n. 2, Article 78(2).

the crime.[44] Rule 145(2) of the Rules of Procedure and Evidence lists mitigating circumstances and aggravating factors the Court "*shall* take into account" (emphasis added). In the Lubanga sentencing appeals decision, it was confirmed that a Trial Chamber's failure to consider one of the mandatory factors listed in Rule 145(1)(b) can amount to a legal error in the determination of sentence.[45] Although non-exhaustive, only two mitigating circumstances are listed, compared with five aggravating factors. All the aggravating and mitigating factors listed in Rule 145(2) have also been identified by the ICTY and ICTR.[46] The *ad hoc* tribunals identified a vast array of aggravating factors and mitigating circumstances in their sentencing practice[47] and it seems likely that in its practice the ICC could do likewise. Factors suggested by delegates in the drafting of the Rome Statute may also be relevant.[48] In addition, in determining the sentence the Court must give consideration, "*inter alia*, to the extent of the damage caused, in particular the harm caused to the victims and their families, the nature of the unlawful behaviour and the means employed to execute the crime; the degree of participation of the convicted person; the degree of intent; the circumstances of manner, time and location; and the age, education, social and economic condition of the convicted person."[49]

There is nothing in the Statute to indicate that the different crimes under the jurisdiction of the Court should be treated differently for the purposes of sentencing.[50] There was also resistance to formal ranking of crimes by the ICTY and ICTR[51] and there is nothing to indicate that the ICC will not do likewise.

When considering a term of life imprisonment, no further guidance is provided in the Statute as to what factors are relevant for assessing the "extreme gravity of the crime" or what individual circumstances are relevant for the assessment of whether a term of life imprisonment should be imposed. This is elaborated on in Rule 145(3) which states that these factors are "evidenced by the existence of one or more aggravating circumstances". As noted above, it is likely that the Court will make reference to the practice of the *ad*

44 ICC Rules of Procedure and Evidence, *supra* n. 2, Rule 145(1)(a) and (b).

45 *Lubanga* sentencing appeal judgement, *supra* n. 4, para. 42.

46 For a list of authorities relating to these points see Schabas: Penalties, Commentary to the ICC Statute 2002, *supra* n. 13, pages 1524-1528.

47 Hola: Consistency of Sentencing Case Law 2012, *supra* n. 6, pages 11-22; Schabas: Penalties, Commentary to the ICC Statute 2002, *supra* n. 13, pages 1524-1525.

48 Schabas: Penalties, Commentary to the ICC Statute 2002, *supra* n. 13, page 1521.

49 ICC Rules of Procedure and Evidence, *supra* n. 2, Rule 145(1)(c). For an overview of all the relevant legal rules relating to sentencing see Lubanga sentencing appeal judgement *supra* n. 4, paras. 31-35.

50 Note, however, the operation of ICC Statute, *supra* n. 2, Articles 31(1)(c) and 124.

51 See, for example, ICTR, *Prosecutor v. Serushago,* Sentence, ICTR-98-39-S, Trial Chamber I, 2 February 1999, para 13. C.f. ICTR, *Prosecutor v Rutaganda,* Judgement and Sentence, ICTR-96-3-T, Trial Chamber I, 6 December 1999, para 451, in which genocide was described as "the crime of crimes".

hoc tribunals elaborating on the interpretation of the listed factors in Rule 145(2)(b) and in identifying further aggravating factors.

The sentencing decisions of the ICC

On 14 March 2012, Trial Chamber I convicted Thomas Lubanga Dyilo as co-perpetrator for "conscripting and enlisting children under the age of fifteen years into the UPC/FPLC and using them to participate actively in hostilities in the Ituri region of the Democratic Republic of Congo…".[52] On 10 July 2012, the Trial Chamber sentenced him to an effective term of 14 years imprisonment. Broken down by charge, the Court sentenced Lubanga to 13 years' imprisonment for the crime of conscripting children under the age of 15 years into the UPC; 12 years' imprisonment for the crime of enlisting children under the age of 15 years into the UPC; and to 14 years' imprisonment for the crime of using children under the age of 15 to participate actively in hostilities. Pursuant to Article 78(3) of the Statute, the Court ordered that the sentences should run concurrently i.e. at the same time.[53] The judgement and appeal, the first of their kind at the ICC, provides some clarification of the Court's interpretation of Article 77 of the Rome Statute.[54]

On 7 March 2014, Germain Katanga was found guilty as an accessory of one count of crimes against humanity (murder) and four counts of war crimes (murder, attacking a civilian population, destruction of property and pillaging) committed on 24 February 2003 during the attack on the village of Bogoro, in the Ituri district of the Democratic Republic of the Congo (DRC). The Trial Chamber acquitted Katanga of other charges of two counts of crimes against humanity (rape and sexual slavery) and one count of war

52 ICC, *Prosecutor v. Thomas Lubanga Dyilo,* Situation in the Democratic Republic of the Congo, Decision on Sentence pursuant to Article 76 of the Statute, ICC-01/04-01/06, Trial Chamber 1, 10 July 2012, para. 1 (hereinafter "Lubanga sentencing decision 2012").

53 *Ibid,* paras. 98 and 99. No explicit reasons as to why the sentences should run concurrently are given in the judgement. Rather, the factors taken into consideration in determining the length of the sentence are outlined at para. 97. At para. 14, the Court also references the practice of the SCSL ordering sentences to run concurrently for similar crimes.

54 See Lubanga sentencing appeal judgement 2014, *supra* n. 4. At the time of writing, the Appeals Chamber was considering a review of Lubanga's sentence under Article 110 and a hearing had been scheduled for 16 July 2015: ICC, *Prosecutor v. Thomas Lubanga Dyilo,* Situation in the Democratic Republic of the Congo, Scheduling order for review concerning reduction of sentence of Mr Thomas Lubanga Dyilo, ICC-01/04-01/06, Appeals Chamber, 15 June 2015. Reparations had already been considered and ordered by both Trial Chamber I and the Appeals Chamber. See ICC, *Prosecutor v. Thomas Lubanga Dyilo*, Situation in Democratic Republic of the Congo, Decision establishing the principles and procedures to be applied to reparations, ICC-01/04-01/06, Trial Chamber I, 7 August 2012; and ICC, *Prosecutor v. Thomas Lubanga Dyilo*, Situation in the Democratic Republic of the Congo, Judgment on the appeals against the "Decision establishing the principles and procedures to be applied to reparations" of 7 August 2012 with AMENDED order for reparations (Annex A) and public annexes 1 and 2, ICC-01/04-01/06, Appeals Chamber, 3 March 2015.

crimes (using children under 15 to participate actively in hostilities).[55] Whilst both the Prosecution and Defence indicated their intent to appeal the decision, both parties discontinued their appeals.[56] On 23 May 2014, Trial Chamber II handed down a sentence of 12 years imprisonment, with time deducted for time spent in detention between 18 September 2007 and 23 May 2014. Judge Christine Van den Wyngaert appended a dissenting opinion to the decision. In this, she noted that as she disagreed with the conviction of Katanga, both on procedural and substantive points of view. She also distanced herself from the sentence imposed and therefore took no position as to the appropriateness of the reasoning adopted by the Majority.[57]

Purpose of punishment

As Ralph Henham highlighted, it is in sentencing "where the aims of punishment are given concrete and public expression in specific cases."[58] Both decisions gave consideration to the purpose of the punishment in determining sentence. In paragraph 16 of the *Lubanga* sentencing judgement, Trial Chamber I states it took note of the preamble of the Statute in considering the purposes of the sentence, which provides that "the most serious crimes of concern to the international community as a whole must not go unpunished".[59] This implies that the key motivation in the punishment of Lubanga was firstly punishment for the wrongful act or retribution. The inclusion of this sentence in the preamble was in part in recognition that the crimes included in the Rome Statute were those that threaten to violate international peace and security for which there should be no impunity.[60] The Chamber further noted preamble paragraphs 5 and 9 which provide that the States

55 ICC, *Prosecutor v. Germain Katanga,* Situation in the Democratic Republic of the Congo, Décision relative à la peine (article 76 du Statut), ICC-01/04-01/07, Trial Chamber II, 23 May 2014, para. 1 (hereinafter "Katanga sentencing decision 2014").

56 See ICC-01/04-01/07, *Defence Notice of Discontinuance of Appeal against the 'Jugement rendu en application de l'article 74 du Statut' rendered by Trial Chamber II on 7 April 2014* ICC-01/04-01/07-3497, 25 June 2014 and ICC-01/04-01/07, *Notice of Discontinuance of the Prosecution's Appeal against the Article 74 Judgment of Conviction of Trial Chamber II dated 7 March 2014 in relation to Germain Katanga*, ICC-01/04-01/07-3498, 25 June 2014.

57 Dissenting Opinion of Judge Christine Van den Wyngaert to *Prosecutor v. Germain Katanga,* Situation in the Democratic Republic of the Congo, Décision relative à la peine (article 76 du Statut), ICC-01/04-01/07, Trial Chamber II, 23 May 2014, para. 1 (hereinafter Dissenting Opinion of Judge Christine Van den Wyngaert to Katanga sentencing decision"). Judge Van den Wyngaert did express a view as to the Majority's decision on the deduction of time spent in detention, which is considered at footnote 157.

58 Ralph Henham, Sentencing and the Legitimacy of Trial Justice, 2012 (Routledge: UK), page 1.

59 ICC Statute, *supra* n. 2, preamble para. 4.

60 Morten Bergsmo/Otto Triffterer, *Premable,* in Otto Triffterer (ed.), Commentary on the Rome Statute of the International Criminal Court: Observers' Notes, Article by Article, 2nd ed. 2008 (C.H. Beck, Munich/Hart, Portland/Nomos, Baden Baden), page 9.

Parties are "[d]etermined to put an end to impunity for the perpetrators of these crimes and thus to contribute to the prevention of such crimes" and that the ICC was established "to these ends and for the sake of present and future generations".[61] It may be inferred from this that the second purpose in the sentence was deterrence. No further elaboration is given as to the purposes of the punishment in the case.

Deterrence and retribution have been identified in cases before the ICTY and ICTR as primary purposes of imposing penalties. [62] This may be contrasted with provisions in human rights law and state practice which emphasis rehabilitation as an essential component in sentencing, whilst also recognising the important function of deterrence and public protection.[63] Article 10(3) of the International Covenant on Civil and Political Rights provides that the penitentiary system shall comprise of treatment of prisoners the essential aim of which shall be their reformation and social rehabilitation.[64] In its General Comment on this provision, the Human Rights Committee stated *inter alia* that no penitentiary system should be only retributory, it should essentially seek the reformation and social rehabilitation of the prisoner.[65] In *Vinter and Others v the United Kingdom,* the European Court of Human Rights noted that there is now clear support in European and international law for the principle that all prisoners, including those serving life sentences, be offered the possibility of rehabilitation.[66] Whilst rehabilitation has been noted in the practice of the *ad hoc* tribunals, [67] it has received limited weight,[68] and was not discussed at the Rome Conference in relation to the provisions of the ICC Statute. [69] This is an area for potential development in the practice of the ICC, particularly as under Article 21(3) the Court must interpret and apply the applicable law consistent with internationally recognised human rights.

---

61 Lubanga sentencing decision 2012, *supra* n. 52, para. 16.

62 See ICTY, *Prosecutor v Delalić et al,* Judgement, IT-96-21-T, 16 November 1998, paras 1231 and 1234; ICTR, *Prosecutor v Rutaganda,* Judgement and Sentence, ICTR-96-3-T, Trial Chamber I, 6 December 1999 para. 456; ICTR, *Prosecutor v Serushago,* Sentence, ICTR-98-39-S, Trial Chamber I, 2 February 1999, para. 20.

63 See, for example, United Nations Standard Minimum Rules for the Treatment of Prisoners (the Mandela Rules) UN Doc. E/CN.15/2015/L.6/Rev.1, Annex, Rule 4.

64 See also American Convention on Human Rights, *supra* n. 29, Article 5(6) and *Vinter and others v the United Kingdom, supra* n. 33, paras. 111-115.

65 UN Human Rights Committee General Comment No. 21 on Article 10 (Forty-fourth session, 1992), Compilation of General Comments and General Recommendations Adopted by Human Rights Treaty Bodies, U.N. Doc. HRI/GEN/1/Rev.6 at 153 (2003), para. 10.

66 *Vinter and others v. United Kingdom, supra* n. 33, para. 115.

67 See, for example, ICTY, *Prosecutor v Delalić et al,* Judgement, IT-96-21-T, Trial Chamber II, 16 November 1998, para. 1233. See also ICTR, *Prosecutor v Serushago,* Sentence, ICTR-98-39-S, Trial Chamber I, 2 February 1999, para. 39.

68 Hola: Consistency of Sentencing Case Law 2012, *supra* n. 6, page 7.

69 Schabas: Penalties, Commentary to the ICC Statute 2002, *supra* n. 13, page 1520, noting that whilst not discussed directly, philosophies of sentencing were revealed indirectly on such questions as life imprisonment, mandatory review and capital punishment.

Trial Chamber II gave more elaboration as to the purpose of the sentence in the *Katanga* case. As with the *Lubanga* case, the Chamber noted the preamble to the Statute, which emphasises punishment of crimes that threaten international peace and security and deterrence. [70] The Court held that in determining the sentence it must meet the legitimate need for truth and justice voiced by the victims and their families.[71] The Trial Chamber considered that the sentence has two important functions: first, as the expression of the social stigma surrounding the crime and its perpetrator, and as a way to recognise the harm and suffering caused to the victims; and second, as deterrence, the aim of which is to dissuade others from committing similar crimes.[72] To what extent sentences have a deterrent effect in reality is very much debated and is inherently difficult to measure in determining what has not happened as a result of a potential punishment. As William Schabas has highlighted, while it is much easier to identify those that have not been deterred, "it is nearly impossible to identify those who are".[73] The Chamber emphasised the need to impose a proportionate sentence as required under Rule 145(1) of the Rules of Procedure and Evidence, so as to ensure that it contributes to the restoration of peace and reconciliation of the people concerned.[74] In contrast to the *Lubanga* sentencing decision, the Court emphasised the need to promote the reintegration of the offender in sentencing, although noted that this goal cannot be regarded as the main purpose of sentencing.

"Life imprisonment" under Article 77

In both the *Lubanga* case and the *Katanga* case, although the Prosecutor had not requested a sentence of life imprisonment,[75] the Trial Chambers gave consideration as to the suitability of life imprisonment in the cases before them. In the *Lubanga* case, the Trial Chamber stated that such a sentence would be inappropriate as the Chamber had not found any aggravating factors in the case.[76] Trial Chamber II similarly considered the imposition of a life sentence totally inappropriate in the *Katanga* case.[77] Consideration of life imprisonment in the judgements thereby highlights the broad stance the Court

---

70 Katanga sentencing decision 2014, *supra* n. 56, paras. 37-38.

71 *Ibid*, para. 38. While the sentencing is without doubt an essential part of achieving justice for victims, it seems curious of the Court to suggest that the act of determining a sentence should somehow also contribute to satisfying their need for truth.

72 *Ibid*, para. 8.

73 William A. Schabas, An Introduction to the International Criminal Court, 4th ed. 2011 (Cambridge University Press: Cambridge, UK) page 61.

74 Katanga sentencing decision 2014, *supra* n. 56, para. 8.

75 Lubanga sentencing decision 2012, *supra* n. 52, para. 94 in which the Trial Chamber noted the Prosecutor requested a sentence of 30 years imprisonment; Katanga sentencing decision 2014, *supra* n. 59, para. 141, in which the Prosecutor had requested 22-25 years.

76 Lubanga sentencing decision 2012, *supra* n. 52, para. 95.

77 Katanga sentencing decision 2014, *supra* n. 56, para. 144.

has taken to the wide discretion open to it in determining sentences under the Rome Statute. There is nothing in the Statute or Rules of Procedure and Evidence which confines the Court to consideration only of such sentences as requested by the Prosecution or other parties. As such, these judgements imply that where the Court considers it appropriate to impose a term of life imprisonment, it will do so even when this is not requested by the Prosecutor.

Determining the sentence

Both decisions highlight the principles' given weight by the ICC in determining the sentence. A more expansive explanation of this is given in the *Katanga* decision by Trial Chamber II. In its decision, the Chamber emphasised the principles which needed to be followed in imposing a sentence, namely the principle of legality as required by Articles 23 and 77 of the Statute, which prevent arbitrariness in the imposition of crimination sanction and thus ensures legal certainty; the principle of proportionality set out in Article 78 and Rule 145, which requires the sentence to be adapted to the gravity of the offence; and finally the principle of individual punishment under Rule 145, further to which the sentence must reflect the individual circumstances of the convicted person and the overall context within which guilt was determined.[78]

In the Lubanga decision, Trial Chamber I also emphasised the need for sentences to be proportionate to the crime, further to Article 81(2)(a). As such, it considered that any automatic starting point for sentencing all offences – as proposed by the Prosecution in this case – would tend to undermine that fundamental principle.[79] The Prosecution had proposed that the Court use a minimum starting point of 24 years. This may be contrasted with the practice in many domestic jurisdictions in which a minimum and maximum sentence are often established in the legislation on which the courts should determine a given case.[80] While the ICC Statute established clear maximum penalties that the Court may impose, the ICC's approach in this regard makes it difficult to predict the minimum level that the Court will begin its consideration of the sentence.

78 *Ibid*, para. 39.

79 Lubanga sentencing decision 2012, *supra* n. 52, para. 93. Note *Vinter and others v. United Kingdom, supra* n. 33, para. 102 which noted that grossly disproportionate sentences would violate the prohibition inhuman or degrading treatment or punishment under Article 3 of the European Convention of Human Rights, noting that this would be rare.

80 See, for example, Swedish legislation implementing the Rome Statute, Lag (2014:406) om straff för folkmord, brott mot mänskligheten och krigsförbrytelser §§ 4, 5, 6, 7, 8, 9, 10, and 11 (available at: https://lagen.nu/2014:406) (last accessed 2 July 2015). Ashely Joy Stein, *Reforming the Sentencing Regime for the Most Serious Crimes of Concern: The International Criminal Court Through the Lens of the Lubanga Trial,* 39 Brooklyn Journal of International Law 521, 2014, pages 558-559 cites some further examples of domestic legislation ratifying the provisions of the Rome Statute.

Gravity of the crime

As noted above, the Court must consider the gravity of the crime in determining the sentence,[81] and any aggravating and mitigating factors under Rule 145(2). In the *Lubanga* sentencing decision, Trial Chamber I confirmed that "[a]ny factors that are taken into account when assessing the gravity of the crime will not additionally be taken into account as aggravating circumstances, and vice versa."[82] This point was confirmed by Trial Chamber II in the *Katanga* case[83] and prevents double counting of factors in the determination of sentencing. As such, factors such as the particular vulnerability or traumatic effects on the victims or discriminatory nature in which the crimes were committed that are taken into account again in assessing the gravity of the crime cannot be considered as aggravating factors in the case at hand. This is a useful point for defence counsel to note when assessing other parties submissions.

Trial Chamber II made a number of clear statements regarding the gravity of crimes under the ICC's jurisdiction which are noteworthy for future cases. Firstly, the Court noted that defendants should be aware that the crimes for which they have to answer before the ICC are the most serious crimes of concern to the international community and hence heavier sentences will be imposed.[84] In light of this, it is noteworthy that the average trial sentences at the ICTY were 18 years and at the ICTR 44.8 years[85] and the SCSL handed down sentences for 50 years and 35 years in the RUF case for similar offences.[86] The Prosecutor highlighted this difference in the appeal of the *Lubanga* sentencing decision, where it was argued the sentence was manifestly disproportionate in comparison to the sentence by the SCSL for similar crimes.[87] The Appeals Chamber dismissed this argument, holding that the Prosecutor had not identified any error in the Trial Chamber's approach to Lubanga's sentence.[88] The Appeals Chamber found the ICTY's approach to previous sentences for the same offence as persuasive, which held that whilst

81 ICC Statute, *supra* n. 2, Article 78(1).

82 Lubanga sentencing decision 2012, *supra* n. 52, para. 35.

83 Katanga sentencing decision 2014, *supra* n. 56, paras. 34-35.

84 *Ibid*, para. 42.

85 The average final sentence after appeal at the ICTY was 18 years and at the ICTR 46.9 years: Silvia D'Ascoli, *Sentencing in International Criminal Law,* 2011 (Hart Publishing: Oxford, UK), page 1870. Following the determination of sentence in *Katanga*, there were mixed reactions as to whether the sentence was too low. See, for example, Olivia Bueno, *Reactions to the Sentencing of Germain Katanga: Some Comfort, Some Frustration*, in *Commentary from Germain Katanga and Mathieu Ngudjolo Chui at the International Criminal Court,* International Justice Monitor, 11 June 2014 available online at: http://www.ijmonitor.org/2014/06/reactions-to-the-sentencing-of-germain-katanga-some-comfort-some-frustration/ (last accessed 2 July 2015).

86 SCSL, *Prosecutor v. Issa Hassan Sesay, Morris Kallon, and Augustine Gbao,* SCSL-04-15-T, Trial Chamber I, 8 April 2009, pages 94 and 96.

87 Lubanga sentencing appeal judgement 2014, *supra* n. 4, para, 74.

88 Lubanga sentencing appeal judgement 2014, *supra* n. 4, para, 77.

this may provide guidance, the court was under an obligation to individualise sentences, meaning previous sentencing practice is but one factor among a host of others which must be taken into account in determining the sentence.[89]

In the Katanga decision, the Trial Chamber noted that in considering that the different crimes for which Katanga was convicted were not necessarily of the same gravity, it is for the Court to determine the exact nature of each offence.[90] The specific circumstances of the case and the form and degree of participation are relevant in the determination of this.[91] Determining the gravity also involves an evaluation of qualitative as well as quantitative factors.[92] The Chamber distinguished in its analysis of gravity between physical attacks against persons and the effects of this, and those committed against objects, such as buildings and other property, the former warranting more severe punishment.[93]

In the *Katanga* sentencing decision, Trial Chamber II considered the scale and discriminatory nature of attacks of crimes amounting to murder as a war crime and crime against humanity, attacks against civilians, looting and destruction as war crimes, and Katanga's role in this.[94] The Court went on to highlight facts relating to the violence and scope of the crimes committed, noting in this regard the number of victims of the crimes charged.[95] The mode of attack and weapons used were also particularly highlighted. The Chamber highlighted the discriminatory nature of the attacks, targeting the Hema population in the attack on Bogoro.[96] In the final part of the analysis of gravity of the crime, the Court considered the current situation in Bogoro and harm to the victims and their families, noting the widespread impact on the community as a whole and the long term impacts of the crimes committed on the population and infrastructure of Bogoro.[97]

In determining the gravity of crimes committed in the *Lubanga* decision, Trial Chamber I made clear that decisions of the *ad hoc* tribunals, although not part of the directly applicable law under Article 21 of the Statute, were nevertheless in a comparable position to the ICC in the context of sentencing, and went on to analyse the jurisprudence of the SCSL in relation to sentencing convictions of the recruitment of children soldiers. As such, whilst

---

89 Lubanga sentencing appeal judgement 2014, *supra* n. 4, para, 76, quoting: ICTY, *Prosecutor v. Furundžija*, Judgement, IT-95-17/1-A 21, Appeals Chamber, July 2000, para. 25; ICTY, *Prosecutor v. Delalić et al.,* Judgement, IT-96-21-A, Appeals Chamber, 20 February 2001, para. 719; ICTY, *Prosecutor v. Strugar,* Judgement, IT-01-42-A, Appeals Chamber, 17 July 2008, paras. 348-349.

90 Katanga sentencing decision 2014, *supra n.* 56, para. 43.

91 *Ibid.*

92 *Ibid.*

93 *Ibid,* paras. 51 and 145.

94 *Ibid,* paras. 44-45.

95 *Ibid,* paras. 46-50.

96 *Ibid,* paras. 53-54.

97 *Ibid,* paras. 55-60.

not binding on the Court, as in other areas it may be concluded that the ICC will take into consideration the practice of the *ad hoc* tribunal sentencing practice in future cases.

The Trial Chamber took note of the factors the SCSL considered in addressing the gravity of the crime, namely the large scale on which the offence was committed and significant degree of brutality.[98] The Court also noted that the SCSL took into account the contribution of the defendant to establishing peace in Sierra Leone in mitigation .[99] The Trial Chamber outlined a number of general factors considered in assessing the gravity of the crimes and the factors listed in Rule 145(1)(c) to the extent of the damage caused. The points highlighted by the Court are of interest for future cases relating to the recruitment, enlistment and conscription of child soldiers. Firstly, it noted the crimes involved to be "undoubtedly very serious crimes that affect the international community as a whole".[100] In addition, the Chamber noted the distinguishing element of compulsion in the crime of conscription.[101] The Court highlighted the real danger in exposing children as potential targets in the crime and the particular vulnerability of children which has been recognised in international treaties as affording them particular protection that does not apply to the general population.[102] The Court gave particular attention to the effect on the victims, setting out consideration to expert evidence on the particular effect of post-traumatic stress disorder on children and psychological and behavioural impacts on the former child soldiers.[103] In this assessment, the Court went on to hold that the age of the children did not both define the gravity of the crime and act as an aggravating factor, however.[104] Accordingly, the age of the children did not constitute an aggravating factor, but was considered in the gravity of the crime.

Both Trial Chamber I and Trial Chamber II gave considerable weight to the participation and intent of the defendants in the respective sentencing

---

98 Lubanga sentencing decision 2012, *supra* n. 52, para. 13. See further paras. 14-15. On appeal, Lubanga raised the argument that the Trial Chamber had erred in fact in taking into account findings made in the Conviction Decision that related to children both over and under the age of fifteen in its assessment of the widespread nature of the crimes for purposes of sentencing. This was rejected by the Appeals Chamber, which held that it was clear from the relevant parts of the Sentencing Decision when read in the content of the Conviction Decision that the finding on "widespread recruitment" pertained to individuals under the age of fifteen. Lubanga sentencing appeal judgement 2014, *supra* n. 4 paras. 99-104.

99 Lubanga sentencing decision 2012, *supra* n. 52, para. 15 noting the SCSL's decision in *Prosecutor v. Fofana and Kondewa*, Sentencing Judgment, SCSL-04-14-A, Trial Chamber I, 9 October 2007, para. 94.

100 Lubanga sentencing decision 2012, *supra* n. 52, para. 37.

101 *Ibid.*

102 *Ibid.* Both the ICC and the SCSL focused on the internationally recognised protection of children and did not consider cultural norms or local traditions in their determination of crimes relating to children.

103 *Ibid*, paras. 30-41.

104 *Ibid*, para. 78.

decisions.[105] Both decisions indicate that the role of the convicted person in the crime is one of the factors at the forefront of consideration by the Court in determining sentencing, particularly in relation to the knowledge of the defendant. This follows the practice of the *ad hoc* tribunals.[106]

Interestingly, in assessing the individual circumstances of Lubanga, Trial Chamber I noted his intelligence and education as contributing to a "marked level of awareness on his part" as a relevant factor in determining the sentence.[107] In its summary of the points borne in mind in determining the sentence, the Court mentions the position of authority held by Lubanga within the UPC/FPLC.[108] No further elaboration is made on the evidence relied on for this particular point. A superior position of responsibility has been identified as an aggravating factor by the *ad hoc* tribunals.[109] In the Lubanga case, this factor appears to have been given greater weight than the defendant's intelligence and education.[110] Trial Chamber II likewise gave consideration to the position of authority held by Katanga in its sentencing decision. The Court held in considering this factor that it needed to be established that the offender not only had authority, and more importantly that they abused that authority.[111] In the *Katanga* case, Trial Chamber II considered that it had not been established that Katanga abused his authority as president of the armed group that committed the attack or used his position to influence the commission of the crimes. As such, this was not taken into consideration by the Court. This approach was confirmed by the Appeals Chamber in the *Lubanga* case. The Appeals Chamber endorsed the approach of the Appeals Chamber of the ICTY and ICTR in this regard which held that what mattered was "not the position of authority taken along, but that position coupled with the manner which the authority is exercised" wrongly or in abuse of that power.[112]

The Trial Chamber's assessment of the gravity of the crime was subject to appeal by the Prosecutor in the *Lubanga* case. The Prosecutor argued that the Trial Chamber did not adequately consider all mandatory factors in its decision. The Appeals Chamber noted that, while the Trial Chamber elaborated on aspects of some of the mandatory factors, it did not explain the weight given to the other mandatory factors considered, or indicate which evidence it relied on for its assessment.[113] The Trial Chamber did, however, state that it had considered the gravity of the crimes and enumerated the factors of Rule 145(1)(c) which it had given "regard" to in making its assess-

105 *Ibid*, para. 53. Katanga sentencing decision 2014, *supra* n. 56, paras. 61-65.

106 Hola: Consistency of Sentencing Case Law 2012, *supra* n. 6, pages 13-14.

107 Lubanga sentencing decision 2012, *supra* n. 52, para. 56.

108 *Ibid*, para. 97.

109 ICTR, *Prosecutor v. Karemera & Ngirumpates,* Judgement, ICTR-98-44-T, Trial Chamber II, 2 February 2012. Para. 1758.

110 Lubanga sentencing decision 2012, *supra* n. 52, para. 97.

111 Katanga sentencing decision 2014, *supra* n. 56, para. 75.

112 *Ibid.*

113 *Ibid,* para. 69.

ment.[114] In analysing the approach taken by the Trial Chamber, the Appeals Chamber held that the fact that *certain aspects* of the relevant evidence were not expressly addressed indicated that they were not considered to be of particular significant to the assessment of the relevant factor.[115] Thus, the Appeals Chamber found that despite not explicitly referring in the Sentencing Decision to the evidence pointed to by the Prosecutor, the Trial Chamber did not err in the weight given to these factors.[116]

Aggravating factors

In the Lubanga case, the Court identified a number of aggravating factors it took into consideration in determining the sentence, but ultimately held that none were present in the given case.[117] An important point in the decision is that the Chamber established the standard of proof for the purposes of sentencing for establishing aggravating factors. The Chamber held that given the potentially significant effect on the overall length of the sentence, it is necessary that any aggravating factors are established to the criminal standard of proof i.e. beyond a reasonable doubt.[118] Given the potential effect on the sentence, this is an important decision in ensuring fairness in the procedure of sentencing. This determination clearly impacted considerably in the deliberations of Trial Chamber I in considering aggravating factors in Lubanga's case, requiring this higher standard of proof of the Prosecution.

---

114 *Ibid,* para. 68.

115 *Ibid,* para. 72.

116 *Ibid,* para. 73. The Appeal Chamber also gave consideration on the potential interaction between the factors of Article 78(1) of the Statute and those of Rule 145(1)(c) of the Rules of Procedure and evidence. It gave two different possible interpretations of this, but ultimately did not determine which of the possible approaches is correct. See Lubanga sentencing appeal judgement, *supra* n. 4, paras. 61-66. Judge Sang-Hyun Song issued a dissenting opinion on this point, arguing that the Appeals Chamber should have provided further guidance on how a Trial Chamber should take these factors into account when determining the sentence. In his view, the Trial Chamber should take into account three overall factors when determining a sentence: a) the gravity of the crime pursuant to article 78 (1) of the Statute as informed by the extent of the damage caused, in particular the harm caused to the victims and their families, the nature of the unlawful behaviour and the means employed to execute the crime; the degree of participation of the convicted person; the degree of intent; and the circumstances of manner, time and location as set out in rule 145 (1) (c) of the Rules of Procedure and Evidence; b) Aggravating and mitigating circumstances pursuant to rule 145 (2) of the Rules of Procedure and Evidence; and c) the individual circumstances of the convicted person pursuant to article 78 (1) of the Statute as informed by the age, education, social and economic condition of the convicted person should be considered in the context of the individual circumstances of the convicted person as set out in rule 145 (1) (c) of the Rules of Procedure and Evidence. See Partly Dissenting Opinion of Judge Sang-Hyun Song, ICC-01/04-01/06-3122-Anx1, 1 December 2014, paras. 1-4.

117 Lubanga sentencing decision 2012, *supra* n. 52, para. 97.

118 *Ibid*, para. 33.

The decision is notable for the number of areas highlighted by the Court as not being taken into consideration in the case at hand and that the Court was unable to reach consensus on many of these factors. For example, whilst the Court noted the conditions endured by the children at the UPC/FPLC training camps,[119] the Majority of the Chamber decided it had not been demonstrated that the individual punishments referred to by the Chamber were the responsibility of Lubanga. In any event, this was not taken into account as an aggravating factor, but was in relation to the gravity of the crime. [120] Similarly, whilst the Chamber considered that it was entitled to consider evidence of sexual violence submitted during the proceedings in determining the sentence, notwithstanding that it did not form part of the Confirmation Decision and Lubanga was not ultimately charged with any crimes of sexual violence,[121] the Majority were ultimately not satisfied upon a review of the evidence presented that the sexual violence against the children who were recruited was sufficiently widespread that it could be characterised as occurring in the ordinary course of the implementation of the common plan for which Lubanga is responsible.[122] Similarly, the Majority were not satisfied that there was sufficient evidence that Lubanga deliberately discriminated against women in committing the offences and as such, motives involving discrimination were not considered as an aggravating factor.[123] The hesitation in taking these factors into consideration is telling of the Court's approach. A clear link between the defendant's conduct and the aggravating factor is therefore fundamental for them to be taken into consideration at this stage, rather than in relation to determining the gravity of the crime/s. It can also be deduced that although these points were determined not to be applicable in the present case (and also are very reflective of the specific events that took place during Lubanga's trial), it is noteworthy for future cases that the Court considered these as relevant factors. The Prosecutor raised in the appeal of the sentencing decision the Trial Chamber's dismissal of these factors, arguing the Chamber erred in law in doing so.[124] The Appeals Chamber was not persuaded by the Prosecutor's argument, noting particularly the Trial Chamber considered not only if the alleged aggravating circumstances occurred in the ordinary course of the crimes for which Lubanga was convicted, but also if they could otherwise be attributable to him in a way that reflects his culpability.[125] Therefore, absent of proof of intent or knowledge, the Trial Chamber would still have had a basis for attributing the aggravating factors to Lubanga had *any* element of culpability, covering a broad range of possibili-

---

119 *Ibid*, para. 57.
120 *Ibid*, paras. 59 and 97.
121 *Ibid*, para. 68.
122 *Ibid*, paras. 69-73.
123 *Ibid*, para. 79. See further ICC Rules of Procedure and Evidence, *supra* n. 2, Rule 145(2)(b)(v).
124 Lubanga sentencing appeal judgement 2014, *supra* n. 4, para. 86.
125 *Ibid*, paras. 88-90.

ties from objective foreseeability to intent, been established beyond reasonable doubt.[126]

Trial Chamber II also held that there were no aggravating circumstances identified in the *Katanga* sentencing decision.[127] As noted above, the Chamber considered the cruelty of the crimes committed and discriminatory nature of the crimes in determining the gravity of the crimes, and so did not consider these again as aggravating circumstances.[128]

Mitigating circumstances

In considering mitigating circumstances, Trial Chamber I in the *Lubanga* sentencing decision explained that it was not restricted to considering only facts and circumstances described in the Confirmation Decision, highlighting Rule 145(2)(a)(ii) which refers to "the convicted person's conduct after the act".[129] The Chamber held that the standard of proof for establishing any mitigating circumstances is on a balance of probabilities i.e. to the standard that the Court is satisfied that more evidence supports the finding than not.[130] These standards for burden of proof established by the Court for aggravating factors and mitigating circumstances are consistent with the standards of proof in international criminal law.

In relation to the specific facts of Lubanga's case, the Chamber gave little weight to Lubanga's statement at sentencing that he hoped for peace in the Ituri region, determining it to be of limited relevance given the persistent recruitment of child soldiers during the period covered by the charges.[131] This is an interesting point to consider for future cases and in potentially presenting aims, motivations and ideology for sentencing purposes.[132] The Court made no comment other than to note that the defence submitted Lubanga had no prior convictions.[133] A lack of criminal record, whilst often cited in the

126 *Ibid*, para. 90 (emphasis of judgement). In the appeal against the sentencing, Lubanga submitted that the Trial Chamber had erred in law by holding that it could consider sexual violence and harsh treatment for the purposes of the sentence despite the fact that they did not form part of the Decision on the Confirmation of Charges, arguing that the Defence reserved the right to raise this error in response to "any ground of appeal which may be submitted by the Prosecutor in response to the Chamber's factual findings in this regard" (para. 117). However, the Appeals Chamber considered that this had not been properly raised as a ground of appeal and rejected the "reservation" as not existing in the Court's legal texts (para. 118).

127 Katanga sentencing decision 2014, *supra* n. 56, para. 144.

128 *Ibid*, para. 71.

129 Lubanga sentencing decision 2012, *supra* n. 52, para. 34.

130 *Ibid.*

131 *Ibid*, para. 87.

132 Temminck Tuinstra: *Defending the Defenders* 2010, *supra* n. 3, page 471.

133 *Ibid*, para. 88.

sentencing practice of the *ad hoc* tribunals, has not been afforded significant weight.[134]

Trial Chamber II gave more consideration to mitigating factors raised in the *Katanga* decision. Its first observation is noteworthy as to the overall weight of mitigating factors in comparison to the gravity of the crimes committed. In its analysis the Court staed that any mitigating factors were relevant only for "easing the pain" and do not take away from the seriousness of the crimes.[135] Trial Chamber II also held that it could consider circumstances in mitigation that are not directly related to alleged offenses, such as having cooperated with the Prosecutor, the expression of sincere remorse or a guilty plea.[136] This is significant for future cases in considering what elements to present to the ICC in mitigation.

The defence had highlighted a number of mitigating factors for the Court to consider in determining the sentence, including Katanga's young age at the time the crimes were committed, the nature of his role, the exceptional circumstances of the case, his ability to change,[137] his cooperation with the Court and the effect of a long separation in relation to his family life.[138] The Court did take into consideration the age of the defender and statements made by the defendant as to his level of maturity and constraints from his the community.[139] The Court gave attention to the fact that Katanga was married with three children, some of whom were young and the effects of separation on them.[140] In stating that these were all relevant factors to take into account in sentencing, the Court again stressed that the nature of the crimes Katanga was convicted of meant that they carried relatively little weight in the determination of the sentence.[141] These observations as to the relative weight afforded to the different factors in determining the sentence is useful guidance for cases in the future.

As in the *Lubanga* case, the defence highlighted Katanga's role in the peace process and demobilisation and reconciliation as a mitigating factor for the Court to consider.[142] Trial Chamber II held that it considered these facts should be taken into account as mitigating factors. However, it noted that such efforts should be real and sincere without any need to demand results.[143] The Court gave considerable analysis to facts put forward by the defence to establish this, highlighting those it considered demonstrated Katanga's will-

134 Schabas: Penalties, Commentary to the ICC Statute 2002, *supra* n. 13, page 1526. See for example ICTY, *Prosecutor v. Furundžija,* Judgement, IT-95-17/1-T-10, Trial Chamber II, 10 December 1998 para. 284.

135 Katanga sentencing decision 2014, *supra* n. 56, para. 76.

136 *Ibid*, para. 32.

137 *Ibid,* "*le fait qu'il soit réellement capable de changer*".

138 *Ibid,* paras. 77, 78 and 79.

139 *Ibid,* paras. 82-83.

140 *Ibid*, paras. 84-85.

141 *Ibid*, para. 88.

142 *Ibid*, paras. 89-90.

143 *Ibid*, para. 91.

ingness and ability to engage in reconciliation processes and participation with the work of the ICC, and evidence that the Court considered indicated his lack of commitment in this regard.[144] The Court detailed the evidence of Katanga's involvement in demobilisation processes,[145] concluding that the positive role he played in demobilisation processes, and particularly the process of disarmament and demobilisation of child soldiers, should be taken into account in determining the sentence.[146] In considering the young age of Katanga and his family situation, the Court considered these two factors likely to promote rehabilitating and reintegration, but were afforded relatively little weight.[147] More weight was given to the active role Katanga took in the disarmament and demobilisation of child soldiers.[148]

Trial Chamber II held that expressions of remorse and sympathy for the victims may be taken into account as mitigating factors. However, it stressed that only sincere expressions of remorse constitute such a relevant factor. The Court also considered that such a factor carried relatively little weight in considering the sentence.[149] In relation to the case at hand, the Court considered that Katanga had had difficulty recognising the crimes committed and did not consider the statements by Katanga in the trial to have been sincere expressions of remorse.[150]

In considering cooperation with the Court as a relevant mitigating factor, Trial Chamber II noted that unlike the *ad hoc* tribunals, Rule 145 does not include this in the list of mitigating factors. The Court took consideration of the approach of the *ad hoc* tribunals, concluding that in its view it was an accepted mitigating factor. It was not necessary for such cooperation to be substantial, but it must go beyond good behaviour, which cannot by itself constitute a circumstance likely to mitigate the sentence.[151] In this regard, the fact that Katanga attended the hearings and behaved well during hearings was not considered as relevant.[152] The Court did note that Katanga had testified at length and answered all questions put to him and also had volunteered information himself.[153] It also noted his good behaviour in custody,[154] but did not rule on whether this could be accepted as a mitigating factor.[155]

The defence in both the *Lubanga* and *Katanga* cases raised violations of the defendant's rights as factors to be taken into consideration by the Court in mitigation. In the *Lubanga* case, although Trial Chamber I rejected the argu-

144 *Ibid*, paras. 92-106.
145 *Ibid*, paras. 107-113.
146 *Ibid*, paras. 114-115.
147 *Ibid*, para. 144.
148 *Ibid*.
149 *Ibid*, para. 117.
150 *Ibid*, paras. 118-121.
151 *Ibid*, paras. 126-127.
152 *Ibid*, para. 128.
153 *Ibid*.
154 *Ibid*, para. 129.
155 *Ibid*, para. 129.

ments submitted by the defence that Lubanga's sentence should be reduced due to alleged violations of his rights to adequate time and facilities for preparation of defence,[156] the Court ultimately did list some of these points as being taken into account when noting that Lubanga was "was respectful and cooperative throughout the proceedings, notwithstanding some particularly onerous circumstances".[157] This list included: the prosecution's failure to disclose exculpatory material, which resulted in a stay of proceedings and a provisional orer to release Lubanga; the prosecution's failure to comply with the Chamber's disclosure orders, leading to a second stay of proceedings and a second provisional order releasing Lubanga; and the prosecution's use of a public interview to make misleading and inaccurate statements to the press about the evidence in the case and Lubanga's conduct during the proceedings.[158] Lubanga challenged the Trial Chamber's determination on appeal, arguing that the Trial Chamber erred in law in finding that he was not entitled to a reduction of his sentence as reparation for violations of his fundamental rights.[159] He relied on case-law from the ICTR to establish his points. The Appeals Chamber followed the Prosecutor's argument that this jurisprudence was not applicable in Lubanga's case, as no comparable violations had occurred in his case as had been found in the case-law he relied on.[160] Examples of such violations included a person not being promptly informed of the nature of the changes against them for a significant period of time[161] and a person being held in provisional detention for more than three years.[162] The allegations of breaches of fundamental rights in Lubanga's case had already been considered as part of the trial proceedings.[163] Despite this being one of the most controversial elements in the whole proceedings, the Appeals Chambers judgement does imply that for the purposes of sentencing where such violations are established the approach in the case-law from the ICTR that an effective remedy (i.e. reduction in sentence) should automatically be available should be followed by the ICC. Furthermore, it can also be seen in these judgements that the examples of serious violations of a person's fundamental rights as highlighted in the Appeals Chamber's judgement should result in an automatic reduction of sentence for the accused, whereas procedural errors such as those listed in the Trial Chambers judgement not amounting to a serious violation of the person's fundamental rights should be considered in mitigation.

156 *Ibid*, paras. 89-90.
157 *Ibid*, para. 91.
158 *Ibid*, para. 91.
159 Lubanga sentencing appeal judgement 2014, *supra* n. 4 para. 105.
160 *Ibid,* para. 109.
161 *Ibid,* para. 109, referencing ICTR, *Jean-Bosco Barayagwiza v. The Prosecutor*, Decision, Appeals Chamber, ICTR-97-19-AR72, dated 3 November 1999, registered on 4 November 1999, paras. 84-85.
162 *Ibid.*
163 *Ibid.*

The defence in the Katanga case also raised violations of the rights of the defence, which taken as a whole it contended should be considered in mitigation of the sentence.[164] These related to the conditions and procedural guarantees of detention in Kinshasa between 10 March 2005 and 18 October 2007. The Court held that if violations of the fundamental rights of the convicted were established it would be appropriate to consider this in mitigation of the sentence to be imposed.[165] However, in relation to the specific facts highlighted by the defence, there was nothing in the Court's Statute that authorised the Court to determine the legality of the detention procedures in the DRC. As such, violations that occurred before the defendant was held on behalf of the ICC could not be considered.[166] The violations must concern the proceedings before the Court for them to be attributable to the Court.[167] This is potentially significant in relation to future cases with similar situations of periods of detention prior to surrender to the Court and how proceedings before this time will be considered by the Court. Trial Chamber II took the date from which Katanga was held on behalf of the Court from 18 September 2007. The Court considered the facts relating to the interrogation on 17 October 2007, noting there was a short period when he did not have the assistance of a lawyer, but that one was appointed later that day and assisted him to the point he was brought to the Hague. The Court held that the defence had not demonstrated that the detention of Katanga was marred by violation of his rights, as at the time of his arrest and surrender to the Court he was assisted by a lawyer.[168]

Deduction for time spent in detention

As noted above, it is within the discretion of the Court to deduct any time spent in detention other than by order of the Court in connection with the conduct underlying the crime. Trial Chamber I did not take into account time spent detained under house arrest in DRC between 2003-2006 by Lubanga, as it considered there was insufficient evidence on a balance of probabilities that he was detained in the DRC for the same conduct which made up the crimes for which he was convicted at the ICC, as set out in Article 78(2).[169] Again, the point to note in this regard is the exercise of the standard of proof required by the Court, but also an important reminder that not all time spent in detention prior to conviction will be taken into consideration – it must be for the conduct underlying the crimes for which the person is ultimately convicted. Lubanga challenged this finding on appeal, arguing that the Trial

164 Katanga sentencing decision 2014, *supra* n. 56, paras. 130-135.
165 *Ibid*, para. 136.
166 *Ibid.*
167 *Ibid*, para. 137.
168 *Ibid*, para. 140.
169 Lubanga sentencing decision 2012, *supra* n. 52, para. 102.

Chamber erred in fact in holding this, highlighting that he was detained by the DRC authorities for his activities as President of the UPC/RP and that the Trial Chamber's findings regarding his "essential contribution" were based on his role as President of the UPC/RP, not on the fact that he intended to conscript, enlist, or use child soldiers.[170] As such, he argued that this was the same conduct for which he was detained in the DRC.[171] The Appeals Chamber rejected this argument, holding that such an interpretation would overly broaden the meaning of "conduct" in that any action taken by an elected official for which they were domestically detained could be considered the same "conduct" in respect of crimes prosecuted under the Statute.[172]

In the Katanga decision, Trial Chamber II followed a similar approach to Trial Chamber I in considering time spent in prison by Katanga in the DRC. The Chamber held it was for the Court to determine first that the defendant had spent time in custody on the Court's order and to then consider whether it was appropriate in the case to deduce time spent pursuant to Article 78(2).[173] The Chamber held that in the case at hand the Congolese authorities were notified of the warrant of arrest against Katanga from 18 September 2007. The time after this notification to the transfer of the defendant to the Court was considered by the Court to have been part of the process in bringing Katanga to justice before the Court.[174] The Court noted that time could be deducted for detention based on the same acts constituting crimes for which the accused is convicted.[175] However, the Court did not consider that this had been established in the present case based on the documentary evidence submitted.[176] As such, time spent in detention between February 2005 and September 2007 was not considered in reducing the sentence.[177]

In both cases, brief reasons for why it was not considered appropriate to impose a fine in addition to the prison terms were given.[178] In the *Katanga* case, Trial Chamber II gave a summary of the information held by the Registry relating to Katanga's financial position and held it would not impose a fine in the absence of any factors that might call into question his financial situation.[179] In the *Lubanga* case, Trial Chamber I simply stated that

170 Lubanga sentencing appeal judgement 2014, *supra* n. 4, para. 113.
171 *Ibid*, para. 113.
172 *Ibid*, para. 116.
173 Katanga sentencing decision 2014, *supra* n. 56, para. 154.
174 *Ibid*, para. 158.
175 *Ibid*.
176 *Ibid*, paras. 159-168.
177 It was on this specific point that Judge Van den Wyngaert disagreed with the Majority's decision. She considered that the evidence before the Court was far from clear that Katanga was not detained between 2005 and 2007 for the crimes committed in Bogoro on 24 February 2003 and that it was unfair to hold this ambiguity against the defendant. See Dissenting Opinion of Judge Christine Van den Wyngaert to Katanga sentencing decision 2014, *supra* n. 57.
178 Lubanga sentencing decision 2012, *supra* n. 52, para. 106; Katanga sentencing decision 2014, *supra* n. 56, para. 169.
179 Katanga sentencing decision 2014, *supra* n. 56, para. 169.

"[d]espite extensive enquiries by the Court, no relevant funds have been identified.[180]

The standard of review on appeal

As noted above, the *Lubanga* sentencing decision was subject to appeal by both the Prosecutor and the Defence. This being the first review of a sentencing decision conducted by the Appeals Decision, the Appeals Chamber had to consider the standard of review for appeals against sentencing decisions. The Chamber held this standard was the same as it has previously determined in respect to discretionary decisions, namely that the Appeals Chamber will not interfere with the exercise of discretion by a Trial Chamber merely because the Appeals Chamber, if it had the power, might have made a different ruling.[181] The Appeals Chamber will interfere with the exercise of discretion in determining the sentence only if: (i) the Trial Chamber's exercise of discretion is based on an erroneous interpretation of law; (ii) the discretion was exercised based on an incorrect conclusion of fact; or (iii) as a result of the Trial Chamber's weighing and balancing of the relevant factors, the imposed sentence is so unreasonable as to constitute an abuse of discretion.[182] Finally, the Appeals Chamber will only interference if the error materially affected the determination of the sentence in accordance with Article 83(2) of the Statute, which the Chamber considered would only be established if the Trial Chamber's exercise of discretion led to a disproportionate sentence.[183]

Conclusion

The sentencing decisions in the *Lubanga* and *Katanga* cases have shed some light on how the ICC approaches sentencing, notably in establishing the standard of proof for aggravating and mitigating factors, identifying the principles to take into consideration in sentencing and that no base line will be used in considering the sentence. Clearly, the Court will reserve higher end sentences for extremely serious cases. Both cases followed the same approach also in confirming that factors taken into account for gravity of the crime will not be considered as aggravating factors and vice versa, and the potential wider scope of mitigating circumstances the Court will consider.[184] Trial Chamber II also gave clear indications as to the weight different factors will be given and expanded on how the Court will go about determining whether

180 Lubanga sentencing decision 2012, *supra* n. 52, para. 106.
181 Lubanga sentencing appeal judgement 2014, *supra* n. 4, paras. 41-42.
182 *Ibid,* para, 44.
183 *Ibid,* para, 45.
184 Lubanga sentencing decision 2012, *supra* n. 52, para. 34.

or not certain factors are present, such as abuse of authority and expression of sincere remorse. All these points will assist defence counsel in considering their strategy in relation to sentencing. The factors taken into consideration and dismissed in the cases provide a point of comparison for defence counsel in considering likely sentences, such as the determination of fines, time deducted from the final sentence and the Court's consideration of procedural discrepancies that are detrimental to the defence. Details for how the figure for the joint concurrent sentence was reached would have been welcomed, as well as detailed reasons why concurrent rather than consecutive sentencing was ordered, but further cases may provide clarify on this point.

It must be borne in mind that although a permanent court, unlike the *ad hoc* tribunals, the exercise of the principle of complementarity[185] means there are likely to be a limited number of cases that go to trial before the ICC. Of these, not all will result in pleadings or findings of guilt and determination of sentence.[186] It is follows from this that establishing a clear framework on which sentences can be determined is unlikely to happen quickly. Nevertheless, in determining their sentencing strategy and advising their clients on likely sentences, defence counsels will find that some important principles have been established in these early cases. Building on this work will be important in ensuring consistency in approach and outcome and to ensure that the overriding principles of legality and justice are maintained until the end in the Court's procedure. This is an area that warrants greater attention. Any other approach by the Court would undermine the whole process at the last hurdle and thus risk undermining the system of international criminal justice.

185 ICC Statute, *supra* n. 2, preamble paragraph 10. See further ICC Statute, *supra* n. 2, Articles 12, 17 and 19.

186 To date, of the 39 people the ICC has publicly indicted three people have died before trial, four have had the charges against them dismissed, two have had charges against them withdrawn, one has been acquitted and one case has been declared inadmissible before the Court. See http://www.icc-cpi.int/en_menus/icc/situations%20and%20cases/ Pages/ situations%20and%20cases.aspx (last accessed 2 July 2015).

Isabel Düsterhöft and Dominic Kennedy[*]

How to Manage the Defence – Experiences from the ADC-ICTY

1. Introduction

In domestic criminal law, it is common knowledge that the Defence plays a crucial part in the process of any trial and that it is an equal player to the Prosecution, vigorously defending the rights of the accused. This is, or in theory should be, the case at the international criminal courts and tribunals. Defence counsel at these courts are actively engaged in defending individuals accused of the most serious crimes of concern to the international community. They ensure on a daily basis that their clients' rights are protected and that they are provided with the best possible defence. In doing so, there are a few internationally recognised standards that apply to any accused in (international) criminal proceedings: 1) the presumption of innocence; 2) the right to a fair trial without undue delay; 3) the right to the assistance of counsel; 4) adequate time and facilities to prepare the defence.[1] All of these have been enshrined in the statutes of the various international criminal tribunals and courts[2] since the establishment of the Nuremberg International Military Tribunal in 1945.[3]

---

* Isabel Düsterhöft, BA, BA (Hons.), LL.M, MA, former Head of Office for the Association of Defence Counsel Practicing Before the ICTY and Representing Counsel Before the MICT, and Lecturer in European Studies at The Hague University of Applied Sciences. Dominic Kennedy, JP, LL.B (Hons), LL.M, Magistrate in England and Wales, former Administrator at the Permanent Court of Arbitration and Head of Office for the Association of Defence Counsel Practicing Before the ICTY. The authors would like to thank ADC-ICTY interns Benjamin Schaefer and Fábio Correia Kanagaratnam for their invaluable contributions to this chapter.

1 Article 12, *International Covenant of Civil and Political Rights*, December 16, 1966, UNTS, Vol. 999, p. 171; Article 6, *European Convention for the Protection of Human Rights and Fundamental Freedoms*, as amended by Protocols Nos. 11 and 14, November 4, 1950, ETS 5; Article 8, *American Convention on Human Rights, "Pact of San Jose,"* Costa Rica, November 22, 1969; Article 21, *Updated Statute of the International Criminal Tribunal for the Former Yugoslavia*, as amended on July 7, 2009 by Resolution 1877; Article 20, *Amended Statute of the International Criminal Tribunal for Rwanda*, as amended on December 16, 2009, by Resolution 1901; Article 17, *Statute of the Special Court for Sierra Leone*, annexed to the Agreement between the United Nations and the Government of Sierra Leone, January 16, 2002; Article 67, *Rome Statute of the International Criminal Court*, entered into force on July 1, 2002; Article 16, *Statute of the Special Tribunal for Lebanon*, S/RES/1757 (2007).

2 The International Criminal Tribunal for the Former Yugoslavia was established by UN Security Council Resolution 827, 25 May 1993, S/RES/827 (1993); the International Criminal Tribunal for Rwanda was established by UN Security Council Resolution 922 on November 8, 1994, S/RES/922 (1994); the Special Court for Sierra Leone was established

However, it is apparent that the various international courts and tribunals organise their defence section in vastly different manners. The International Criminal Tribunal for the Former Yugoslavia (ICTY) and the International Criminal Tribunal for Rwanda (ICTR) do not have defence organs or offices in their internal structure and rely on the work of two professional associations. These are the Association of Defence Counsel Practicing Before the ICTY (ADC-ICTY)[4] and the Association des Avocats de la Défense (ADAD). The Special Court for Sierra Leone (SCSL), the Extraordinary Chambers in the Courts of Cambodia (ECCC) and the International Criminal Court (ICC) have an integrated defence office as part of the Registry. It is only the latest addition to the field of international criminal law, the Special Tribunal for Lebanon (STL) that has given the weight that is due to the Defence and created a separate defence organ within the official structure.

This apparent lack of providing a crucial "fourth organ" in the majority of international courts and tribunals undermines the importance of Defence in international justice. This is interesting and worrying at the same time. The imbalance between the Prosecution's resources and acknowledgment, and the lack of support and recognition of the Defence is troublesome in the context of judging some the most serious cases of international concern. This lack of importance for the defence function has been heavily criticised, such as by Rupert Skilbeck, who noted that:

> *"[I]t has to be acknowledged that it is absolutely essential for the defence to be considered on an equal basis to the prosecution from the very start, in terms of legal capacity, administrative support, investigations, public relations, media coverage and outreach. Without this, there cannot be a fair trial".*[5]

In the same vein, Michaïl Wladimiroff stated that "the principle of the rule of law within the criminal justice system does not only depend on the way in which investigative, prosecutorial and adjudicatory institutions fulfil their

---

by *Agreement Between the United Nations and the Government of Sierra Leone on the Establishment of a Special Court for Sierra Leone*, January 16, 2002, available at: http://www.rscsl.org/documents.html, last visited: September 2, 2014; the Extraordinary Chambers in the Courts of Cambodia were established by an *Agreement Between the United Nations and the Royal government of Cambodia Concerning the Prosecution und Cambodian Law of Crimes Committed during the Period of Democratic Kampuchea*, June 6, 2003, available at: http://www.eccc.gov.kh/en/documents/legal/agreement-between-united-nations-and-royal-government-cambodia-concerning-prosecutio, last visited: September 2, 2014; the Special Tribunal for Lebanon was established by UN Security Council Resolution 1757 (2007), *S*/RES/1757 (2007), May 30, 2007.

3 *Charter of the International Military Tribunal – Annex to the Agreement for the prosecution and punishment of the major war criminals of the European Axis*, August 8, 1945; *International Military Tribunal for the Far East Charter, January 19, 1946*.

4 In light of the official widening of the mandate of the ADC-ICTY to the Mechanism for International Criminal Tribunals (MICT) in August 2015, the full name of the association now reads: Association of Defence Counsel Practicing Before the Interantional Criminal Tribunal for the Former Yugoslavia – And Representing Counsel Before the MICT.

5 *Skilbeck, Rupert* (2004): Building the Fourth Pillar: Defence Rights at the Special Court for Sierra Leone, in Essex Human Rights Review, Vol. 1/No.1, p. 85.

duties, but also on the proper fulfilment by the defence counsel of his duties".[6] It is in this context that the recent discussions at the ICC to possibly eliminate the only defence office of the Court, the Office for Public Counsel of the Defence (OPCD),[7] are more than worrisome and raise serious questions with regard to whether there have been any lessons learned from the previous courts and tribunals. It appears that this is a step back from the STL's structure and it is the authors' view that this development deserves utmost attention.

However, it is not the purpose of this chapter to examine the advantages and disadvantages of the different manners in which the defence is organised. It is taken for granted that any organisation of the Defence at these courts needs to be given sufficient weight and importance to allow for a fair and just trial. In another publication the authors have argued that any international court or tribunal should have a defence organ that actively supports the defence teams in their daily work, supplemented by a defence office as part of the Registry that administers the assignments and payment of counsel and a defence counsel association, which represents the interests of its membership. This proposal thus draws on the structure in place at the STL and supplements this with the benefits of having an association of counsel as for example the ADC-ICTY.[8]

The aim of this chapter is to provide the reader with an insight into the importance of managing the Defence at an international court or tribunal. To facilitate the practical nature of this chapter, it will look in detail at the ADC-ICTY, as an example of an association that has successfully and effectively managed the Defence at an international criminal tribunal. This chapter will therefore examine the role of the ADC-ICTY in managing the daily functions of the Defence and will provide an overview of advantages and disadvantages associated with such an organisational structure. Finally, the chapter will conclude with an outlook into the future and lessons learned from the ADC-ICTY, in the hope that future international criminal courts and tribunals will be able to provide for an effective management of the essential "fourth organ" to any international trial, the Defence.

---

6 *Wladimiroff, Michaïl* (1999): The Assignment of Defence Counsel Before the International Criminal Tribunal for Rwanda, in Leiden Journal of International Law 12, p. 958.

7 This is part of the ICC *Re*Vision project aimed at reforming and restructuring the entire Registry. How and to what extent the Defence's institutional importance would be recognised within the reformed structures is to date not yet determined.

8 *Kennedy, Dominic and Düsterhöft, Isabel* (forthcoming): The Proper Role for International Defense Counsel Organizations, in Rohan, Colleen and Zyberi, Gentian (eds.), Defense Perspectives on International Criminal Justice, Cambridge University Press.

2. The ADC-ICTY[9]

The ICTY was the first international criminal tribunal of its kind after the Nuremberg and Tokyo trials and it is interesting to note that the Defence did not receive any official status within this Tribunal. In fact, it was largely excluded from the work and structure of the ICTY. Apart from having defence counsel practice before the Tribunal to prepare individual cases, the Defence was not involved in any internal processes, such as the development of the Rules of Procedure and Evidence.

The Defence was initially denied the opportunity to effectively exercise its important function. A particular example of this is that defence counsel were not allowed general access to the ICTY building, except for the lobby, one defence room for all teams and the courtroom. Generally, while the Prosecution had lawyers permanently present at the ICTY, defence counsel did not have an established law office throughout proceedings. They could not rely on the abundance of assistance provided to the Prosecution in the form of a number of experienced trial and appellate lawyers and support staff permanently present at the Tribunal.

The Defence had no collective voice that would represent the interests of all defence counsel and staff. Each defence team had to liaise and negotiate individually with the Registry regarding its resources and finances. This led to an unbeneficial position for the Defence, being clearly the "weaker" actor in terms of resources and constituted an obvious inequality of arms in comparison to the Prosecution.

2.1. Establishment

Due to these insufficient and unsatisfactory defence structures within the Tribunal, in 2002, at the initiative of the Judges at the ICTY, the ADC-ICTY was created. The Judges deemed it necessary to have an association that could manage and collectively represent a group of highly qualified defence counsel. Moreover, such an association proved to be of importance in light of the Code of Professional Conduct for Counsel Appearing before International Tribunal and possibly related disciplinary proceedings. This initiative lead to a rule change by the ICTY Judges, requiring all defence counsel wishing to practice before the Tribunal to be part of an officially recognised association

9 A detailed chapter on the ADC-ICTY has been written by the author *Kennedy, Dominic* (2011): The Association of Defence Counsel practising before the ICTY, in Manual on International Criminal Defence – ADC-ICTY Developed Practices, prepared within the War Crimes Justice Project (UNICRI, ADC-ICTY, ODIHR OSCE), pp: 203 - 217, available at: http://wcjp.unicri.it/deliverables/manual.php, last visited: September 2, 2014.

of counsel;[10] the ADC-ICTY remains the only recognised association until today.

Therefore, the ADC-ICTY was officially established in October 2002, after a decision made at the 27th plenary session of the Judges in July that year, and was recognised by the Registrar in December. Its first Constitution was drafted by a working group consisting of four defence counsel, a member of the Dutch Bar and a representative from the Registry in January 2002.[11] The ADC-ICTY was established as an independent bar association under Dutch law and is registered with the Dutch authorities. Hence, the ADC-ICTY is wholly independent from the ICTY and not part of its internal structure. Membership of the ADC-ICTY is required to be able to practise as Defence Counsel before the Tribunal and members have to be in good standing under the terms of the ADC-ICTY's Constitution. This set-up remains the same at present and the following sub-chapters provide a short overview of the objectives and the internal structure of the ADC-ICTY, as the only association of its kind in international criminal legal institutions.

2.2. Objectives

The ADC-ICTY's objectives are outlined in Article 2 of its Constitution and encompass the following:[12]

- Supporting the function, efficiency and independence of Defence Counsel practising before the ICTY;
- Promoting and ensuring proficiency and competence of Defence Counsel in the fields of advocacy, substantive international criminal law and information technology systems relevant to representing accused before the ICTY;
- Offering advice to the President, Chambers and the Registrar of the ICTY in relation to the right of the accused to a fair trial and the Rules, as well as Regulations, Practice Directives and Policies related to the Defence;
- Overseeing the performance and professional conduct of Defence Counsel in relation to their duties, responsibilities and obligations pursuant to the Statute, Rules, the Code of Professional Conduct, the

10 *See* Tenth Annual Report of the ICTY, UN Doc. A/58/297-S/2003/829, Annex, para. 11; now Rule 44 (A) (iii) of the ICTY Rules of Procedure and Evidence, IT/32/Rev. 43, 24 July 2009.

11 Constitution of the ADC-ICTY, amended on 23 October 2004, available at: http://adc-icty.org/Documents/adcicty_constitution.pdf, last visited September 12, 2014; an earlier proposal for a Statute was submitted by an *Ad-Hoc* Working group composed of the ICTY President, Judge Jorda, Judges Hunt and Orie, the then Deputy Registrar, Mr. Christian Rohode, and Tomislav Visnjic on behalf of the Defence.

12 Constitution of the ADC-ICTY.

Directive on Assignment of Counsel and the Detention Rules and Regulations of the ICTY.

In fulfilling these objectives, the ADC-ICTY has continuously worked on "building bridges"[13] between the Defence and the Tribunal. It has also aimed at breaking down perceived barriers between the Defence and the ICTY's organs,[14] allowing for increased participation of the Defence with the other organs. In this context, the ADC-ICTY has been involved in tribunal-wide projects, working groups and committees, including consultations prior to the adoption of new legal aid policies and in the review of the Directive of Assignment of Defence Counsel. In addition to fulfilling these objectives, the ADC-ICTY is also dedicated to keeping all of its members informed and up-to-date regarding any substantive, procedural and practical developments at the ICTY and any issues that may affect the work of the Defence.

In December 2012, the objectives and role of the ADC-ICTY expanded when the Registrar of the Mechanism for International Criminal Tribunals (MICT or Mechanism) provisionally recognised the ADC-ICTY also as the association for the Mechanism.[15] Subsequently, the ADC-ICTY received its official and full recognition as the association of counsel for the MICT by the Registrar in August 2015.[16] The MICT is the institution following the ICTY and ICTR and was established by the United Nations Security Council to carry out and take over a number of crucial functions of the two tribunals after the end of their respective mandates.[17] The Mechanism started its work in 2012 in Arusha and in 2013 in The Hague. It is noticeable that the requirement for defence counsel practicing before the MICT to be a member in good standing of an association of counsel was also included in the MICT Rules of Procedure and Evidence, just as in the ICTY Rules.[18] This was not the case in the original draft rules and only included upon the ADC-ICTY having made submissions to the President of the MICT, requesting that this requirement be inserted. This most certainly shows the importance attached to the ADC-ICTY and the essential role of such an association in the framework of an international criminal justice institution.

---

13 *Kennedy, Dominic:* The Association of Defence Counsel practising before the ICTY, p. 205.

14 *Kennedy, Dominic:* The Association of Defence Counsel practising before the ICTY, p. 205, i.e. Chambers, Registry and Prosecution.

15 This provisional recognition was also affirmed by the President of the MICT in his 26 February 2014 decision in the case *Augustin Ngirabatware v. The Prosecutor,* Public Redacted Version, *Decision on Motion to Quash and Revise a Decision of the Registrar on Level of Complexity and Seeking Further Relief,* MICT-12-29-A, February 26, 2014.

16 MICT, Decision Recognising the ADC-ICTY as an Association of Defence Counsel Practicing at the Mechanism, 24 August 2015.

17 UN Security Council Resolution 1966 (2010), December 22, 2010, S/Res/1966 (2010).

18 Rule 42 (A) (iii), *Rules of Procedure and Evidence for the Mechanism for International Criminal Tribunals*, June 8, 2012.

2.3. *Organisation and Structure*

As a bar association registered in the Netherlands, the ADC-ICTY is entirely independent and has an autonomous, fully functional internal structure with a number of constitutional committees. It is governed by an Executive Committee,[19] comprising of one President and four Vice-Presidents. This Committee is responsible for the administration, finances, policy and representation of the Association. The day-to-day functions are carried out by a paid employee, a Head of Office, serving on behalf of the Executive Committee. In addition to these, the ADC-ICTY also has a number of other committees that are elected on an annual basis at the General Assembly and that are staffed with members of the association.

The Membership Committee's role is to review applications for membership and to admit counsel to the association so that they are eligible to practice before the Tribunal.[20] The Training Committee is responsible for legal, trial advocacy and case management training for defence counsel and ADC-ICTY members.[21] Its main task is the annual training for counsel, which is organised in conjunction with the General Assembly and focuses on various pertinent issues every year.

The Disciplinary Council[22] is an independent organ of the ADC-ICTY, responsible to the General Assembly and carries out the following tasks: 1) monitoring the conduct of members of the ADC-ICTY in the representation of a suspect or accused; 2) adjudicating on complaints received against members of the ADC-ICTY for alleged misconduct; 3) providing advisory opinions on matters relating to the Code of Conduct, the Directive on the Assignment of Counsel and the interpretation of the Constitution.[23] Each of these committees play an invaluable role in the effective operation of the ADC-ICTY.

3. *Experiences in Managing the Defence from the ADC-ICTY*

This section will provide a more detailed and practical overview of what it actually means "to manage the Defence" at an international tribunal. Keeping the organisational structures of the ADC-ICTY and the ICTY in mind, this section will address the management of the association, defence counsel, support staff and interns separately, as well as provide an overview of the ADC-ICTY's relationship with organs of the Tribunal. To underline the prac-

19 Articles 7 - 10, Constitution of the ADC-ICTY.
20 Article 4, Constitution of the ADC-ICTY.
21 Articles 20 - 21, Constitution of the ADC-ICTY.
22 Articles 15 - 19, Constitution of the ADC-ICTY.
23 Article 16, Constitution of the ADC-ICTY. Further information regarding the Disciplinary Council and all other committees can be found in *Kennedy, Dominic:* The Association of Defence Counsel practising before the ICTY, p. 207.

tical nature, examples may be provided, which have been drawn upon from the authors' personal experiences.

3.1. Managing the Association

3.1.1. Committees and Head Office

The Head of Office of the Association is responsible for the day-to-day operations in close consultation with the President and Vice-Presidents. It is vital that the members of the Executive Committee are active and committed to dealing with the many issues which arise involving the Association. As members of all Committees are elected on a voluntary basis, it is the Head of Office's function to coordinate between the Committees and ensure that all issues are attended to in an efficient and timely manner. This can prove difficult in practice, as members frequently work on multiple complex cases at a time and can be located in different time zones around the world.

It is furthermore the Head of Office's responsibility to mediate between the different committees and the Tribunal and to ensure that all communication is successful and effective. From time to time, the Head of Office will attend meetings with Tribunal representatives on behalf of a committee when no members are available. The Head of Office is also responsible for keeping accurate minutes and records of all meetings, tasks and decisions. Therefore, the institutional knowledge lies not only with the membership of the Association but also with the Head of Office, who is the only person who has regular access to the complete institutional archive of the ADC-ICTY.

3.1.2. Finances and Membership

As has been previously mentioned, the ADC-ICTY was established as an independent bar association under Dutch law. This entails managing the Association and ensuring the Dutch rules and regulations are complied with. The finances must be kept up to date, reviewed by the internal auditors[24] and discussed and approved annually by the General Assembly.[25] The Association is liable to pay income tax and social security payments for all staff of the Association but is not liable to tax on other income as it is registered as a non-profit organisation. This is in contrast to all other defence staff who are paid directly by the UN and therefore their income is tax exempt. It is the Head of Office's responsibility to communicate with tax advisors, the tax authorities, banks and the Chamber of Commerce, depending on what is necessary to ensure that the association meets all its requirements under Dutch law.

---

24 Two full members of the ADC-ICTY are appointed as internal auditors according to Article 10(2) of the ADC-ICTY Constitution.

25 Article 11(3), ADC-ICTY Constitution.

All members of the ADC-ICTY are required to pay an annual fee for membership and those members who are assigned to a case must pay monthly fees for the services of the ADC-ICTY.[26] The issue of the level of fees payable has in the past been controversial, especially when fees need to be increased to ensure the Association and its staff is sustainable. The Head of Office, as part of his/her duties, has the unenviable task of ensuring that all members pay their fees to keep the Association financially viable. If a member is not in good standing this can lead to termination of their membership which can have the consequence of barring an individual from appearing in court, as the ICTY requires all counsel appearing before the Tribunal to be in good standing with the ADC-ICTY.[27] This requirement ultimately entrusts in the Association the power to control who can and cannot appear as counsel before the Tribunal, thus giving a self regulating function.

It is the Head of Office who keeps an accurate overview of the ADC-ICTY's membership. He/she also assists Counsel in applying for the lists of counsel at the ICTY and MICT and coordinates with the respective parts of the Registry to facilitate the admission procedure. Any questions which relate to past or current ADC-ICTY membership are channelled through the Head Office.

3.1.3. External Relations and Media

The Head of Office and the Executive Committee are also responsible for external representation of the Association. This includes attending a wide variety of events to ensure that the members of the ADC-ICTY are represented and seen to be active in the international community. This is a vital public relations function, as to many, Defence are perceived to be the "under dogs" of international justice and it is an opportunity to show that there are two sides, just as in any domestic jurisdiction. Moreover, the ADC-ICTY organises frequent events for counsel, support staff and interns, as well as external participants, to show the Association's active involvement in the international criminal sphere. Special attention is paid to transferring its institutional knowledge to the younger generations.

The Association also engages in external media work, including press releases concerning issues of importance to the function of the Defence, publishing a newsletter which is sent to more than 1,000 readers worldwide, as well as keeping an up-to-date website. All media requests for interviews with counsel come through the ADC-ICTY Head Office. The Head Office also gives interviews on topics that lie within its expertise and has participated in many research projects from universities.

An important work done by the Association was the *Manual on International Criminal Defence: ADC-ICTY Developed Practices*, published in 2011

26 Article 5, ADC-ICTY Constitution.
27 Rule 44(A)(iii), ICTY RPE.

together with the United Nations Interregional Crime and Justice Research Institute (UNICRI) and the OSCE Office for Democratic Institutions and Human Rights (ODIHR). A large number of defence counsel contributed chapters to this Manual and it has not only been heavily used in the region of the Former Yugoslavia, but also at other international courts and tribunals. It summarises the institutional knowledge of the ADC-ICTY in an accessible book, which is one of the greatest achievements of the ADC-ICTY, especially in view of preserving its legacy. It is currently envisaged to update the Manual and translate it into French to make it more widely accessible.

In terms of legacy efforts, in November 2013, the ADC-ICTY organised a Legacy Conference with more than three hundred people attending. The conference featured a keynote address from ICTY President, Theodor Meron, Judges from the ICTY and renowned defence counsel. The Conference addressed a number of topics essential to the legacy of the ADC-ICTY and the ICTY, many of which are also addressed in this collected volume. The Conference was hailed as a success by many of those attending. This was the Association's response to a series of legacy events organised by the ICTY, to which the Defence was not invited. The conference proceedings and a series of accompanying articles were made publicly available in November 2014, as a one-year anniversary of this event.

3.1.4. Management of the Daily Tasks

The day-to-day tasks which need to be fulfilled on behalf of the Association can be as mundane as ensuring that waste is removed, or that there is adequate office equipment for defence staff, to representing the interests of defence counsel at meetings with the ICTY President or Registrar. There is a wide spectrum of tasks, each with the end result of maintaining a high level of defence representation before the Tribunal and the best possible working conditions. It is almost impossible to enumerate the many tasks that the Head Office is engaged in. It is not uncommon that the Head of Office is approached regularly with problematic and time-sensitive issues as the Head Office is the primary point of contact place for all staff and interns.

The Head of Office is supported by one or two interns at a time to assist with certain administrative and organisational tasks. Managing the ADC-ICTY is a very labour intensive task and is achieved with the very little staff and resources available. The Association has never received any direct funding from the Tribunal towards the operating costs of the association, and has so far successfully managed to remain a self-sufficient and well-working organisation.

3.2 Managing Defence Counsel

Over the twelve years of the ICTY there have been over 450 full members of the ADC-ICTY. Over 220 of these have been actively involved as defence counsel in proceedings before the Tribunal. The needs of defence counsel vary depending on the magnitude of the case at hand and the size of the teams. Usually, two defence counsel are assigned to each accused at the ICTY, a lead counsel and a co-counsel. Each lead counsel appointed to a case is free to create the kind of legal team which best fits the circumstances of his client's case.

A vital element to ensure a competent and professional body of lawyers is to facilitate regular procedural and substantive training to keep all counsel up-to-date with changes to the Rules of Procedure and Evidence and jurisprudence. In addition, the cases occurring before the ICTY require that defence counsel acquire a complete understanding of military, cultural and political issues relevant at the time of the conflict in the former Yugoslavia. As adequately described by Mark Ellis:

> *"The repertoire of skills used in a 'domestic' criminal case, while extremely relevant, does not necessarily include the legal background required in an international war crimes case. The average attorney simply is not schooled in this practice. In effect, the attorney who undertakes to defend an alleged war criminal must be multi-talented".*[28]

The ADC-ICTY is offered a limited biennial budget from the UN to provide training to defence counsel but must organise the training independently. In recent years this has been done on an annual basis. The ADC-ICTY has a Training Committee which is elected by the General Assembly and is responsible for developing the annual training events in conjunction with the Head of Office.[29] These trainings are popular amongst counsel and are, in exceptional circumstances, also open to staff and external participants.

An additional function which is provided by the ADC-ICTY for defence counsel is access to a Disciplinary Council.[30] The Disciplinary Council is responsible for maintaining professional standards for lawyers practicing before the ICTY. The members are elected by the ADC-ICTY General Assembly and members are wholly independent of other committees of the Association. The Council may receive complaints regarding misconduct of counsel from any full member of the association, any accused person of other staff members of the ICTY.[31] The Council can also be approached by any member of the Association for an advisory opinion if they are faced with an

28 *Ellis, Mark S.* (1997): Achieving Justice Before the International War Crimes Tribunal: Challenging for the Defence Counsel, in Duke Journal of Comparative & International Law Vol. 7, No. 2, p. 523.

29 Part VI, ADC-ICTY Constitution.

30 The Disciplinary Council is provided for in Part V of the ADC-ICTY Constitution.

31 Article 18, ADC-ICTY Constitution.

ethical or moral dilemma during proceedings.[32] Any decision by the Disciplinary Council remains confidential unless all parties involved request for it to become public. The Council holds the important position of safe-guarding professional standards which in turn results in the accused receiving the best possible legal representation. In addition, two of the ADC-ICTY's members are representing the Defence on the ICTY's Disciplinary Panel and Board, which are the ICTY's official disciplinary mechanisms. Having the Defence's view represented on these is essential and it is not uncommon that the Defence representatives' views diverge from those of the rest.[33] It is crucial that the Defence's view is also heard in relation to disciplinary proceedings and that critical opinions are made public so as to allow for a fair system.

Another important function which the ADC-ICTY offers for all defence counsel is the filing of *amicus curiae* briefs on pertinent issues which affect the right to fair trial or the efficient functioning of the defence teams. Issues in which the Association has intervened in during proceedings have ranged from payment issues for defence staff to substantive jurisprudence issues which could affect the Defence as a whole.[34] The Association has also intervened as *amicus curiae* at other courts and tribunals and receives numerous requests on an annual basis.[35] While not all requests are in fact taken on, it is important for counsel to know that there is an Association of Defence Counsel in existence that will consider their concerns and possibly support their position when such support is most needed. This function of the ADC-ICTY has been highly appreciated by many defence teams.

The ADC-ICTY also has a Rules Committee, which is elected annually at the General Assembly and which represents the interest of all practising

---

32 Article 19, ADC-ICTY Constitution.

33 Such as in the Disciplinary Board's decision in the case of Toma Fila, where ADC-ICTY members Colleen Rohan and Karim Khan QC appended powerful dissenting opinions, see *ICTY Disciplinary Board in the Matter of Mr. Toma Fila*, IT-13-93-Misc.1, Decision on Appeals to the Disciplinary Board (public), 8 July 2013.

34 See e.g. *Prosecutor v. Brdjanin*, IT-99-36-A, Amicus Brief of Association of Defence Counsel - ICTY, 5 July 2005; *Prosecutor v. Stanišić and Simatović*, IT-03-69-T, Association of Defence Counsel (ADC-ICTY) Motion for Leave to Appear as Amicus Curiae, 21 February 2011; *Prosecutor v. Prlić et al.*, IT-04-74-T, Association of Defence Counsel (ADC-ICTY) Motion for Leave to Appear as Amicus Curiae, 10 December 2010; *Prosecutor v. Kamuhanda*, MICT-13-33, ADC-ICTY *Amicus Curiae* Observations, 10 September 2015.

35 See e.g. ICTR, *Prosecutor v. Gaspard Kanyarukiga*, ICTR-02-78-A, Association of Defence Counsel (ADC-ICTY) Motion for Leave to Appear as Amicus Curiae, 8 April 2011; ICC, *Prosecutor v. Abdallah Banda Abakaer Nourain and Saleh Mohammed Jerbo Jamus*, ICC-02/05-03/09, Amicus Curiae Brief of the Association of Defence Counsel Practicing Before the International Criminal Tribunal for the Former Yugoslavia On Defence Request for a Temporary Stay of Proceedings (public), 20 February 2012; ICC, *The Prosecutor v. Jean-Pierre Bemba Gombo, Aimé Kilolo Musamba, Jean-Jacques Mangenda Kabongo, Fidèle Babala Wandu and Narcisse Arido,* ICC-01/05-01/13, Application of The ADC-ICTY to File and *Amicus Curiae* Brief on The Motion on the Inadmissibility of Material Obtained in Violation of the Statutory Guarantee that Accused and Counsel be Able to Communicate Freely and in Confidence, 16 September 2015.

defence counsel before the ICTY and its Rules Committee meetings, along with at least three permanent judges and non-voting representatives from the Prosecution and Registry. The ICTY Rules Committee must submit a report on proposed amendments to the last plenary session of each calendar year for consideration by all judges of the ICTY. The ADC-ICTY Rules Committee members are permitted to submit proposals for amendments to the ICTY RPE and to present the views of the Defence on proposed amendments. Ensuring that the Defence is able to weigh in on rule amendments is essential to guaranteeing a balanced set of rules. As these Rules are at the core of every defence counsel's role before the Tribunal, this Committee has an essential responsibility to fulfil. This participation is a noticeable improvement from the early years at the ICTY when the ICTY Committee on Rules of Procedure and Evidence was comprised solely of the Judges of the Tribunal and did not have a mechanism which permitted any input from defence counsel.

Managing defence counsel also entails mundane tasks, such as ensuring that adequate resources and facilities are provided, delivering mail, assisting with IT issues, facilitating between teams and the Tribunal, and representing their interests on a daily basis in all negotiations and communication with the Tribunal. This is certainly not an elaborate list and it tends to be longer when counsel are not present in The Hague.

3.3. Managing Support Staff

In order to adequately prepare and present the defence in complex cases each lead defence counsel needs to create a competent team of support staff which includes legal assistants, case manager and investigators. A team is necessary to divide up the myriad tasks associated with the pre-trial, trial and appeal proceedings. A well balanced and qualified team is also imperative to ensure that a variety of skills are available to adequately represent the accused. The ADC-ICTY receives all the applications for positions of support staff and the Head of Office provides an initial filter, sending the suitable candidates to the defence team for consideration. The ADC-ICTY keeps a list of applications for legal assistant, case manager and investigator positions that counsel may draw upon when required. Positions to work for Defence are highly sought after and a large number of applications are received by the Head Office. In reality, support staff is often hired from within existing defence teams and are frequently former interns or staff that worked with counsel on other cases.

All support staff are required to sign a confidentiality agreement when they commence employment with a defence team. This imposes a high level of obligations on support staff, some of whom are not trained lawyers. To ensure that all staff understands what their duties are they are given legal ethics training on arrival. The consequences of breaching the confidentiality undertaking can be serious, including contempt of court proceedings before the Tribunal.

The ADC-ICTY offers assistance to support staff to ensure that they can carry out their work in the most efficient manner. This support includes providing logistical arrangements and ensuring all staff are trained to use the range of legal computer tools necessary. Regular IT trainings are offered, as well as lectures and trainings on ethics, legal writing and military structure. As counsel are frequently absent from the Tribunal, the ADC-ICTY often times coordinates directly with support staff for daily requests.

Over the past years, the ADC-ICTY has also organised a number of major Mock Trials for support staff, as well as interns and external participants, together with the International Criminal Law Bureau (ICLB). These featured a series of preparatory lectures and performance in-court in front of judges and defence counsel. Moreover, the association has also organised advocacy trainings and Mock Trials together with the Office of the Prosecutor. All of these events have been highly successful and popular among staff and interns and a great amount of resources and time goes into organising these.

3.4 Managing Interns

The defence teams rely heavily on highly skilled interns to complement the team. The ADC-ICTY coordinates the Internship Programme ensuring that a regular stream of highly qualified interns are available for all defence teams at each stage of proceedings. The ADC-ICTY has also a number of internship agreements with universities in the Netherlands and abroad and is committed to establishing a network of young professionals from its large number of interns. During the existence of the Association there have been over 1000 interns from over 60 countries. There are usually between 40 and 60 interns at a time, not all of which work at the Tribunal on an everyday basis.

The tasks of interns vary heavily depending on the stage of the case, the types of crimes charged in the indictment and what counsel or support staff they have been assigned to. The interns come from a number of educational backgrounds, the majority have studied law but other disciplines are also useful for defence teams and the Head Office. The internship offers a unique experience to gain practical experience in international law. Most interns stay for a period of three to six months, and, occasionally, they decide to stay even longer and are promoted to *pro bono* legal assistant or case manager. Unfortunately, due to lack of resources all defence internships are unpaid.

The Association organises a number of events for the interns, among which are monthly field trips to other institutions in The Hague, monthly Defence Symposia with counsel, advocacy trainings, IT trainings and Mock Trials. The Head of Office is the director of the internship programme and interns often consult the Head Office with regard to a variety of problems, such as finding accommodation, obtaining a residence permit or visa and opening a bank account.

After the twelve years of existence of the Association and the numerous individuals who have completed an internship there, the Association has in fact established one of the most far-reaching and competitive networks of young professionals in the field of international criminal law. In an attempt to connect individuals in this network and to facilitate a strong bond with the Association, the ADC-ICTY has established its Affiliate Membership category. This is not a constitutional membership category of the ADC-ICTY, but is aimed at young professionals, students, academics and interns who have an interest in the ADC-ICTY. The Head Office prepares monthly newsletters on jobs and opportunities for this membership category and organises lectures and trainings. The future vision is to establish a profitable network of highly qualified young professionals that may prove mutually beneficial for the Association and its members.

3.5 Managing the Relationships with Other Organs and Other Courts

It is imperative that the ADC-ICTY has a good working relationship with the other organs of the Tribunal. The Office of Legal Aid and Defence Matters (OLAD)[36] is the primary link and mediator between the Defence and the other sections of the ICTY. OLAD is a part of the Registry and is headed by the Head of OLAD who is answerable to the Registrar. OLAD determines whether an accused is indigent, administers payment to the accused's defence team and has financial investigators to ensure that the legal aid system functions effectively. The Registry works to ensure that it provides financial support to those accused who need it.

It is vital that the President and Head of Office of the ADC-ICTY build a good rapport with the staff of OLAD as this ensures a smoother more productive environment which is to the benefit of all defence counsel. In the past there have been tense relationships which made progress much slower because, like in most places of work, there can be personality clashes which are difficult to overcome. OLAD's atypical position within the Registry further contributes to the problem. They are tasked with trying to continuously build bridges between the Defence and the Registry as a whole, while being ultimately responsible to the Registrar.

Regular meetings take place between the President of the Association and the Head of OLAD to ensure that everyone is kept up-to-date on any pending issues. Some issues can take weeks or even months to finalise, largely due to lengthy formalities which can be involved. It requires strong determination and on occasions the need to accept compromises. On the whole, the ADC-ICTY and the Registry find amicable solutions which are acceptable to both sides. There have been rare instances where the Association was not satisfied with a final outcome and there was the need to approach the President of the Tribunal to intervene.

---

36 Formerly known as the Office of Legal Aid and Detention Matters.

In addition to OLAD, the ADC-ICTY is also involved in a number of negotiations with the Immediate Office of the Registrar and other parts of the Registry. Such negotiations usually concern the promulgation of legal aid policies or other policies affecting the daily work of Counsel and the Defence teams, such as e-mail policies and travel and daily subsistence allowance. While many consultations are done via OLAD, the Registry has increasingly directly consulted the ADC-ICTY, most likely due to many issues now pertaining to the MICT. OLAD is not a MICT office and while the Head of OLAD has a "double-hatting" at the ICTY and the MICT, Defence related issues are discussed with the MICT Registry. The Registry section of the MICT responsible for the Defence is headquartered in Arusha and, therefore, increasing contact with the staff in Tanzania has taken place.

Another way in which the Defence cooperates with other officials of the Tribunal is Defence involvement in outreach activities of the ICTY. Although this is limited, there has been involvement in training events in the region of the former Yugoslavia and also presentations to visiting groups to the Tribunal. The ADC-ICTY has recently established a very favourable relationship with the Tribunal's media and outreach offices and is frequently invited to participate in events and contribute to the work of these sections. This relationship has not always been as positive and the Defence was often times excluded from many important events, such as the Legacy Conferences of the ICTY.

With regards to the Chambers[37] and the Prosecution, interaction with these parts of the Tribunal usually occurs during training events. Moreover, the Head of Office is part of the ICTY's Training Advisory Committee and has been involved in discussions relating to professional development and career transition at the ICTY. The ADC-ICTY has opened most of its monthly lectures and trainings to participants from all sections of the Tribunal and also to participants from outside the ICTY. The aim of such inclusive events is to further a better cooperation between all sections of the Tribunal regarding issues relating to training and professional development.

While the ADC-ICTY's first and most frequent point of contact is most certainly the Registry and OLAD, the Association has tried to establish mutually beneficial relationships with other parts of the Tribunal. However, due to the fact of not being an official organ of the Tribunal, there is always a limit to these professional interactions. Often, valuable ideas and proposals are hindered from being implemented due to internal concerns within the other organs of the Tribunal. While there should naturally be a certain distance between the Defence, the OTP and Chambers, this should not be the case on concerning issues such as career development and training opportunities. The Defence's general role as "under dog" of the Tribunal continues to pose an obstacle in successfully cooperating with all organs and it is ordinarily up to

37 As mentioned, members of the Association are also involved in the ICTY Committee on Rules of Procedure and Evidence.

individuals, who have sufficient influence, to ensure that the cooperation continues to be mutually beneficial.

4. Conclusion

The Defence at an international court is an integral part to all proceedings and managing it effectively is paramount to guaranteeing a successful functioning of the defence teams and a fair representation of the accused. There are many different structures in place between the different international courts and tribunals and the foregoing has provided an overview of one such structure, organising the Defence by the means of an association of counsel.

While subsequent tribunals and courts have opted for different ways of organising the Defence, such as including a defence office in the Registry (ICC, ECCC, SCSL) or creating a separate defence organ (STL), the history of the ADC-ICTY and its achievements have shown that it is a highly effective manner of ensuring a successful defence function. In fact, at the First Meeting of the Defence Offices of International Criminal Tribunals in Paris on 4 and 5 December 2013, the ADC-ICTY was suggested to have the ideal structure for a creation of an independent organisation of lawyers appearing before the international criminal tribunals.[38] Its highly effective internal functioning was commended and following this meeting, there have been a number of proposals to create a similar association for the ICC, with a Constitution largely modelled upon the one of the ADC-ICTY.

While this is most certainly a very welcome step forward and hopefully one that will be realised as part of the ICC Registry's *Re*Vision Project, it would also be crucial to establish a separate defence office, much like at the STL. As former UN Secretary-General, Kofi Annan, noted: the "[...] need for a defence office to protect the rights of suspects and accused has evolved in the practice of the United Nations-based tribunals as part of the need to ensure 'equality of arms'".[39] Having a defence organ within the structure of the ICC and any new international (*ad hoc*) tribunal, would in fact make the "overall structure of the Court much fairer", as noted by Ken Gallant.[40]

38 The Final Conclusion of this meeting was sent to the authors in December 2013. Another International Meeting of the Defence Offices took place in The Hague in December 2014 and focused more specifically on the protection of Defence lawyers and the importance of a separate Defence organ/office in international criminal courts and tribunals. It was concluded that the members of the profession expressed their wish that "in all current and future international criminal courts the establishment of a Defence office, as an independent organ, on par with the Office of the Prosecutor, following the example of the STL", be established. The Third Meeting will take place in October 2015 in Geneva.

39 *UN Security Council*, Report of the Secretary-General on the Establishment of a Special Tribunal for Lebanon, U.N. Doc., S/2006/893, (Nov. 15, 2006), para. 30.

40 *Gallant, Kenneth S.* (2014): Addressing the Democratic Deficit in International Criminal Law and Procedure: Defense Participation in Lawmaking, in Jalloh, Charles Chernor (ed.), The Sierra Leone Special Court and its Legacy, Cambridge University Press, p. 584.

Therefore, it is the authors' opinion that recognising the importance of managing the Defence and giving it the voice it deserves is paramount to any fair trial. However, the amount of resources, work and dedication required for managing the Defence, especially in the form of an independent association should not be underestimated. Hopefully, the ICC and tribunals to come are going to find an effective mechanism for structuring the Defence in a manner that ensures a successful and diligent representation of the accused.

Philipp Müller[*]

Promoting Justice between Independence and Institutional Constraints: The Role of the Office of the Public Counsel of the Defence at the ICC

1. Introduction

When the International Criminal Court (ICC) was created by the Rome Statute in July 1998, and when it commenced its operations four years later, it radically altered international criminal justice in several ways. In contrast to the ad-hoc and hybrid tribunals, which had generally been part of a mechanism of post-conflict justice and reconciliation, the ICC was the first court whose jurisdiction was confined to crimes committed after its establishment. This expressed a new aim at the ongoing delivery of international justice in all parts of the world rather than being a targeted, one-off effort like its predecessors. Moreover, the ICC was the first international tribunal which at the same time is an international organisation and whose governing body, the Assembly of States Parties (ASP), is composed of Member State representatives.[1] The Member States may even refer a situation, including one in their own country, to the ICC, thereby requesting the Prosecutor to determine whether crimes within the Court's jurisdiction have been committed.[2] Accordingly, the Rome Statute regime has radically altered the mechanisms of international criminal justice and has broadened the field of actors involved by prominently featuring participation by States parties. By contrast, the drafters of the Rome Statute appear to have been more cautious towards responding to the often-voiced calls for a more solid institutional representation of the Defence. Indeed, many academics and legal practitioners had criticised a lack of equality of arms and an institutional bias in favour of the Prosecution before the ad-hoc tribunals, up to allegations that the judicial proceedings merely acted as a fig leaf for an otherwise politically motivated decision to convict or acquit a given accused. Thus, increased Defence participation and representation would have been crucial to underline the legitimacy and credibility of the court as well as to actually reinforce the integrity of the legal process.

---

* LPC Candidate, The University of Law, Guildford, UK; LLM, Leiden University, The Netherlands.

1 The powers of the ASP are set out in Rome Statute of the International Criminal Court, 2187 UNTS 90, Art. 112, 121; the Court has international legal personality by virtue of Article 4 and its relationship to the UN is governed by a bilateral agreement concluded pursuant to Article 2, see *Negotiated Agreement between the International Criminal Court and the United Nations*, ICC-ASP/3/Res.1, 4 October 2004.

2 *Ibid.*, Art. 13, 14.

Nonetheless, it was only after the Court had been constituted that the first judges, who drafted the Regulations of the Court, addressed these concerns by creating a new Office of the Public Counsel for the Defence (OPCD) as an independent bureau representing the interests of the Defence at the Court. Comprised of independent counsel, yet enjoying the practical and logistical advantages of being integrated into the Court's structure, it was intended to provide assistance to Defence teams as well as temporary representation of suspects or accused persons. Throughout the years, the focus of the Office's work has undergone a significant change; while it started off assisting one team in the pre-trial phase of its case, the range of its activities has grown with the increasing involvement of the Court in new situations and cases. Since, it has been assigned to represent the interests of the Defence during investigations into various situations, has offered *ad-hoc* representation to several suspects, has taken up the permanent direct representation of one client, and is, as of today, assisting 19 Defence teams at the Court with words and actions, making an important contribution to the equality of arms between the Defence and the Prosecution at the ICC and improving the effectiveness of Defence work through unification of research and the provision of swift practical advice. At the same time, insufficient funding, particularly in terms of staffing, has prevented it from performing in full all aspects of its mandate, and it struggles to retain its institutional independence and assistance capacities in the light of further budgetary cuts and proposals to restructure the ICC Registry.

This article will briefly outline the mandate of the OPCD, the key considerations which have led to its establishment, and the delineation of its mandate. It will then analyse in more detail how the OPCD has performed this mandate and how it has been involved in the day-to-day business of Defence counsel before the ICC. At the same time, it will consider criticism brought forth with respect to its range of activities, institutional structure, and involvement in situations and cases with a view to making suggestions on how the functioning and the quality of services offered by the OPCD can be improved. Subsequently, it will outline and respond to the proposals made by the ICC Registrar in the context of his *Re*Vision Project to restructure the Court's Registry, showing how they impact upon the mandate and activities of the OPCD and examining whether the proposed arrangements will be able to safeguard the interests of the Defence, promote equality of arms, and contribute to the efficiency and quality of Defence work in the same way as the existing structures.

2. Establishment and Mandate of the OPCD

The legal framework for the establishment of an Office of the Public Counsel for the Defence (OPCD) is provided for in Regulation 77 of the Regulations of the Court, as adopted by the plenary session of Judges at the International Criminal Court (ICC) held from 17 to 28 May 2004.[3] The OPCD commenced its operations in April 2006 and with the arrival of its first Principal Counsel in the following year, it became fully functional and capable of carrying out all aspects of its mandate to represent and protect the rights of the Defence during the initial stage of an investigation and to provide legal and practical support to Defence counsel, suspects, and defendants before the Court.[4] Though it forms part of the Registry for administrative purposes, the Regulations foresaw from the beginning that the OPCD shall function as an entirely independent organ in all aspects of its work, providing independent legal advice and not being answerable to any other organ inside the Registry while performing its tasks.[5] This is reinforced by Regulation 144(1) of the Regulations of the Registry, according to which "[t]he members of the Office shall not receive any instructions from the Registrar in relation to the discharge of their tasks as referred to in regulations 76 and 77". In the course of the 2011 review of the Regulations of the Court, the mandate of the OPCD was significantly expanded. The amended Regulation 77 contains new tasks to advance submissions on behalf of a suspect or accused who has not yet secured legal assistance, or where the mandate of temporary counsel is limited to other issues, as well as assisting or representing Defence counsel or Defence witnesses subject to proceedings under Article 70 of the Rome Statute.[6] Furthermore, the new Regulation 77 expressly permits counsel from the OPCD to be appointed as counsel, duty counsel, or standby counsel for an accused under Regulations 73 and 76 of the Regulations of the Court, while provisions to the same effect have been included in Regulations 73(4) and 76(2). Another aspect of the OPCD's mandate is that it may be asked by the Registrar to act as a mediator in a conflict between a suspect or accused and their Defence counsel.[7]

The reasons for the creation of the OPCD through the Regulations were two-fold: first, the Judges sought to improve the capacities of Defence counsel to represent suspects and accused before the Court with a view to improving the fairness of the proceedings in terms of the equality of arms between Defence and Prosecution. This perceived need to level the playing field between Prosecution and Defence was a result of the situation prevalent before the *ad-hoc* tribunals, where Defence counsel were often considered unequal to the Prosecution in terms of resources, expertise, and time available to

3 International Criminal Court, Report to the Assembly of States Parties on options for ensuring adequate defence counsel for accused persons, Doc No ICC-ASP/3/16, 6-10 September 2004, para. 12.

4 International Criminal Court, *Newsletter #15*, May 2007, available at <http://www.icc-cpi.int/NR/rdonlyres/80C21BC3-8E17-46B0-AA4B-B2B6B7B3CBF1/278452/ICCNL15200705_En.pdf> (accessed 19 November 2014).

5 Regulations of the Court, Regulation 77(2).

6 Regulations of the Curt, Regulation 77(4)(d), (f).

7 Regulations of the Registry, Regulation 119(3).

them.[8] Over the time, a recognition emerged that for trials of such high complexity to operate fairly and effectively, defendants require institutional support to mount a strong Defence,[9] i.e. that the Defence had to be considered on an equal footing to the Prosecution throughout the entirety of the case in terms of legal capacity, administrative support, investigations, public relations, media coverage, and outreach.[10] While the idea of establishing a public defender's office was expressly rejected as entailing too many potential conflicts of interest and as being little cost-effective, it was decided to make in-house counsel available at any stage of the proceedings for advice and effective representation on an *ad-hoc* basis. At the same time, the system employed at the *ad-hoc* tribunals was retained, under which a defendant could freely select their Defence counsel from a list composed of external counsel and members of a Defence team would be assigned on an *ad-hoc* basis as external consultants.[11]

The second goal the Judges sought to achieve through the creation of the OPCD was to provide for more efficient Defence work so that the strengthening of Defence capabilities would go along with a minimum of additional expenses. As expressed by former Judge Adrian Fulford, the Office was intended to lower costs by increasing the efficiency of Defence work and significantly reducing the size of individual Defence teams.[12] This was, for instance, to be achieved by avoiding reduplications in research and work efforts and by providing the Defence with an 'institutional memory' and a 'knowledge base' consisting of an extensive body of general research and draft motions, allowing Defence teams to operate in a focused manner while at the same time minimising the time they require to familiarise themselves with the law and procedure of the Court.[13]

The significance of such an institutional memory must be appreciated in the light of the traditional lack of continuity in international Defence work: attorneys and barristers practicing before international tribunals tend to be based in their home countries and many of them prefer to return there after the completion of their case rather than remaining at the court and practicing on other cases or situations, which means that little knowledge is being

---

8 Y McDermott, "General Duty to Ensure the Right to a Fair and Expeditious Trial", in G Sluiter *et al.* (*eds.*), *International Criminal Procedure: Principles and Rules* (Oxford: Oxford University Press, 2013): 798.

9 Human Rights Watch, *Courting History: The Landmark International Criminal Court's First Years*, July 2008, 76.

10 R Skilbeck, "Building the Fourth Pillar: Defence Rights at the Special Court for Sierra Leone", *Essex Human Rights Review*, 1 (2004): 86; see *Infra* 89, 2.

11 T Gut *et al.*, "Defence Issues", in G Sluiter *et al.* (eds.), International Criminal Procedure: Principles and Rules (Oxford: Oxford University Press, 2013): 1229.

12 Sir Adrian Fulford LJ, "Reflections of the Trial Judge", *Criminal Law Forum*, 22 (2011): 222.

13 Cf. G Mettraux and A Cengic, "The Role of a Defence Office - Some Lessons from Recent and not so Recent War Crimes Precedents", in M Bohlander (*ed.*), *International Criminal Justice: A Critical Analysis of Institutions and Procedures* (London: Cameron May, 2007): 399-400.

passed on to pupils or junior counsel. Furthermore, the communication between Defence teams is often limited. Thus, there is a real risk, which is reflected by the experience at the *ad-hoc* tribunals, that knowledge is lost when a case is concluded since it is not passed on from one generation of Defence counsel to the next. This transition is managed more effectively at international Prosecution departments, where professionals work under temporary or permanent contracts rather than retainers and communication is ensured by a strict hierarchy and organisational structure. By setting up the OPCD, the judges hoped to facilitate the transition process on the Defence side and prevent the loss of knowledge when an experienced professional retires from international practice.

In a similar way, assignment of the OPCD to represent Defence interests in the early stages of an investigation enables to Office itself to build up a body of experience, which provides for more efficient work than if new counsel was appointed every time on an *ad-hoc* basis. The promotion of efficiency and synergies in Defence work at the ICC does not only benefit the Registry through a reduction in spending, but also strengthens Defence capacities by allowing Defence counsel to make more of their, in comparison with the Office of the Prosecutor (OTP), highly limited resources. Accordingly, increased efficiency, as provided by the OPCD, is less an aim in itself than another component by which the OPCD contributes to the promotion of the equality of arms between the parties at the ICC.

3. Overview of the Office's Work

3.1. Assistance to Defence Teams

Directly assisting Defence counsel in the performance of their mandate remains the most important aspect of the OPCD's work. Pursuant to Regulation 77(4)(b) of the Regulations of the Court, the OPCD shall '[provide] general support and assistance to Defence counsel and the person entitled to legal assistance, including legal research and advice and, on the instruction or with the leave of the Chamber, advising on and assisting with the detailed factual circumstances of the case.' In accordance with this provision, OPCD provides legal and practical support and assistance to all Defence teams without prioritisation or discrimination, including *ad-hoc* Defence counsel and counsel assisting clients suspected or accused of violations of Article 70 of the Rome Statute, whether or not they are entitled to legal aid from the Court.[14] This assistance is, at least to a certain extent, capable of counterbalancing the vast resources and structural support available to Prosecution counsel. It has further been suggested such assistance could be rendered to a suspect or accused who chooses to defend himself since a self-representing accused is particu-

14 Cf. *Infra* 89, 3.

larly unlikely to have the legal skills, let alone the knowledge of international criminal law and procedure, required to build up an effective Defence without outside support.[15] Currently, OPCD is assisting 19 Defence teams operating at the tribunal with five permanent members of staff, including its Principal Counsel, one legal adviser, one associate legal adviser, one case manager, and one legal assistant.[16]

The OPCD is capable of significantly facilitating the commencement of new Defence counsel's work at the ICC through the provision of manuals dealing with practical and legal matters, draft motions, as well as hands-on personal assistance.[17] It has prepared short step-by-step guidelines on topics relevant to any new counsel arriving at the Court.[18] Though the majority of Defence counsel who take up work at the ICC are experienced litigators in their own country, only very few of them have previously appeared before an international criminal tribunal, and even those who have practiced before other international courts may not be familiar with the special procedures before the ICC. More generally, counsel with a civil law background may require some assistance with the largely common law-influenced procedure.[19] The OPCD's assistance is therefore capable of ensuring a better representation of suspects from the earliest stages of the proceedings onward by minimising the time counsel need to familiarise themselves with the rules and procedure of the Court. Furthermore, it provides for a better accessibility of the ICC for advocates who have not previously practiced before international tribunals, thereby acknowledging the increasing interest among lawyers in developing nations, particularly situation countries, in practicing as counsel before the ICC. This, in turn, augments the range of choice for suspects and accused in the exercise of their right to freely choose legal representation as prior experience in international criminal practice becomes less important for a lawyer's ability to mount a good Defence for his client.

Moreover, Defence counsel may, subsequently to their appointment, at any time, request the OPCD to conduct research into legal and procedural issues arising in their case. Though emphasis is put on issues which are potentially of common concern to all Defence teams,[20] the OPCD aims to assist

---

15 *Supra* 12, 1252; *Supra* 14, 418.

16 International Criminal Court, *Proposed Programme Budget for 2015 of the International Criminal Court*, ICC-ASP/13/10, 18 September 2014, 116.

17 X-J Keïta and M Taylor, "Office of the Public Counsel for the Defence", *Behind the Scenes: The Registry of the International Criminal Court*, 69; *Supra* 10, 79.

18 Examples are manuals on how a motion is filed, what the applicable time limits are, and how the interlocutory appeals procedure works at the ICC.

19 The American Non-Governmental Organizations Coalition for the International Criminal Court, *Defending Atrocity Crimes – The Requirements of Defence Counsel before the ICC*, 21, available at http://www.amicc.org/docs/Necessary%20Requirements%20for%20Defense.pdf.

20 International Bar Association, Counsel Matters at the International Criminal Court: a Review of Key Developments Impacting Lawyers before the ICC, November 2012, 4-5; *Supra* 10, 79.

counsel with any legal or practical problem of difficulty they encounter; in any event, extensive practical assistance to one Defence team, as it has been provided in the past *inter alia* by the assignment of five staff members from the OPCD to assist in the review of thousands of documents potentially subject to professional privilege in the *Mbarushimana* case, is unlikely to be provided at present considering the current staffing level in the Office.[21] Next to one-off assistance following requests by individual teams, the Office also maintains ongoing research projects, such as a list of oral decisions and issues relevant for cases in the pre-trial stage. Its ongoing legal research upon request by Defence teams contributes to the 'institutional memory' of the Defence, using the experience made by individual Defence teams in order to share the knowledge thus gained with other counsel and ensuring that every Defence team practicing before the tribunal can achieve their full potential.[22] This is intended to counterbalance the benefit for Prosecution counsel provided by a separate Appellate and Legal Advisory Section (LAS) within the OTP; though the LAS still has almost the same staffing as the OPCD while its considerably narrower mandate permits it to better concentrate on rendering legal assistance to Prosecution teams,[23] this represents a major step forward from the *ad-hoc* tribunals, where solely the OTP was able to benefit from the services of a permanent office offering legal advice.[24] By providing a similar service to the Defence, the OPCD is capable of streamlining and facilitating a broad range of work processes on the Defence side, thereby improving the efficiency of Defence work and the overall quality of legal service Defence counsel can offer to their clients.

Last, staff members of the OPCD, insofar as they fulfil the criteria for admission to the Registrar's list of counsel, can render practical assistance to Defence counsel by appearing before the tribunal pursuant to Regulation 77(4)(c) of the Regulations of the Court. During the pre-trial phase of the *Lubanga* case, counsel from the OPCD have regularly appeared before the Chamber alongside Defence counsel to present research made by the OPCD to the Chamber,[25] and on one occasion even on behalf of the absent defendant and his counsel.[26] More recently, the OPCD's Principal Counsel was present

---

21 See *Prosecutor v Callixte Mbarushimana*, Decision on the "Defence Request for OPCD Support, ICC-01/04-01/10-115, 21 April 2011.

22 *Supra* 18, 70.

23 Currently, the LAS of the ICC OTP consists of four permanent members of staff including one Senior Legal Advisor (P-5); see *Supra* 17, para. 156.

24 Cf. G Townsend, "Structure and Management", in L Reydams, J Vouters, and C Ryngaert, *International Prosecutors* (Oxford: Oxford University Press, 2012): 231-33, 246-50.

25 *Prosecutor v Thomas Lubanga Dyilo*, Transcript 24 April 2006, ICC-01/04-01/06-T-4-EN; *Prosecutor v Thomas Lubanga Dyilo* Transcript 29 January 2007, ICC-01/04-01/06-T-48-EN; *Prosecutor v Thomas Lubanga Dyilo* Transcript 5 September 2006, ICC-01/04-01/06-T-17-EN; *Prosecutor v Thomas Lubanga Dyilo*, Transcript 24 August 2006, ICC-01/04-01/06-T-13-EN.

26 *Prosecutor v Thomas Lubanga Dyilo*, Transcript 26 October 2006, ICC-01/04-01/06-T-26-EN.

at initial appearance hearings in the cases of *Bemba et al.* and Charles Blé Goudé, on an exceptional basis and upon express request of Defence counsel.[27] In contrast, in the later stages of the *Lubanga* pre-trial case, it has refused to carry out an assignment by the Chamber to temporarily replace the suspect's counsel, emphasising it was not among its tasks to temporarily step in for counsel, join a Defence team or to function as counsel where the suspect has previously chosen to be represented by another lawyer.[28] It emerges that presently, the OPCD does not consider it part of its mandate to appear before a Chamber in support of Defence counsel unless expressly requested by the latter due to exceptional circumstances.

The OPCD's ability to respond to all requests by Defence teams equally and on time has been impaired by inadequate level of staffing. In order to maintain its ability to have a meaningful impact on the fairness of the proceedings before the Court, it is therefore crucial that the permanent staff is assisted by legal interns assigned on a temporary basis. Furthermore, the OPCD has entered into agreements with universities and research institutes to receive legal research on non-confidential issues.[29] The Office also maintains contact with Defence office counterparts at other international courts and tribunals with a view to exchanging expertise and research in common areas and has endeavoured to facilitate the exchange of experience and expertise between different Defence teams by convening informal Defence seminars on issues of common concern.[30] By these means, the OPCD has managed to maximise its capacities even though its low budget and broad mandate still negatively impact its ability to effectively discharge its mission, including its readiness to provide all assistance required by defendants and their legal teams.[31]

Nonetheless, the establishment of the OPCD as an entity providing practical and legal assistance to Defence teams throughout the entirety of their case has led to key improvements in terms of equality of arms between Defence and Prosecution before the ICC. The support of a permanent body, particularly in the early stages of a case, lowers the bar for lawyers who wish to become involved in practicing before the ICC and creates a more level

---

27 *Prosecutor v Jean-Pierre Bemba Gombo et al.*, Transcript 27 November 2013, ICC-01/05-01/13-T-1-ENG; *Prosecutor v. Charles Blé Goudé*, Transcript 27 March 2014, ICC-02/11-02/11-T-3-Red-ENG, p. 2.

28 *Prosecutor v Thomas Lubanga Dyilo*, Observations of the Office of the Public Counsel for the Defence on the Decision of Pre-Trial Chamber I entitled "Decision on the defence request for extension of time", ICC-01/04-01/06-823-tENG, 12 February 2007, paras. 8-16; see also *Prosecutor v Thomas Lubanga Dyilo*, Corrigendum to Decision on the Defence request for extension of time limit, ICC-01/04-01/06-815-Corr, 12 February 2007; also J P W Temminck Tuinstra, *Defence Counsel in International Criminal Law* (The Hague: T M C Asser, 2009): 82-83.

29 *Supra* 18, 70.

30 *Ibid.*

31 *Supra* 10, 84; see also International Criminal Court, *Proposed Programme Budget for 2014 of the International Criminal Court*, ICC-ASP/12/20, 29 July 2013, para. 584.

playing field between counsel from different backgrounds. This may, in turn, contravene perceptions of a predominance of Western lawyers and legal colonialism before international criminal tribunals and give local lawyers and communities a larger sense of ownership in the judicial process before the Court.[32] Moreover, it generally augments the quality of Defence work by ensuring that counsel are adequately equipped with knowledge of international criminal law and procedure to effectively defend their clients,[33] which does not only ensure a fairer trial for the defendant, but also generally improves the quality of legal discourse at the ICC.

3.2. Direct Representation of Defence Interests

The second key aspect of the OPCD's mandate, as outlined in Regulation 77, is to appear directly before the tribunal and make submissions, either on behalf a suspect or accused who has not yet secured legal assistance or whose temporary counsel's mandate is limited to other issues, or in order to represent and protect the rights of the Defence during the initial stages of an investigation.[34] Due to its physical presence at the seat of the Court, assistance to a suspect or accused may commence directly after their transfer to The Hague, and the OPCD has prepared a manual outlining the rights of suspects which is provided to them immediately upon arrival.[35] In particular with regard to responding to applications of prospective victims in the situation stage and the *ad-hoc* representation of suspects in immediate need for assistance, the OPCD's permanent presence at the Court and its continuity in terms of staffing allow it to offer swift legal advice, effectively safeguard the rights of persons during an investigation under Article 55 of the Rome Statute, and build up a degree of experience which could not have been achieved if a new duty counsel had been assigned in each individual situation.

Pursuant to Regulation 77(4)(a), it is part of the OPCD's mandate to represent and protect the interests of the Defence during the initial stages of an investigation, particularly before individual suspects have been named; this notably includes responding to victims' applications to participate in the proceedings arising out of an investigation into a situation. In the situation in the Democratic Republic of the Congo (DRC), Pre-Trial Chamber I initially assigned this task to an external counsel; however, on 23 May 2007, it changed its approach and mandated the OPCD to respond to the applications which had been brought.[36] Since, the OPCD has filed observations to a num-

---

32 *Supra* 14, 414-15.

33 *Ibid.*, 416.

34 Regulations of the Court, Regulation 77(4)(a) and (d).

35 *Supra* 10, 79.

36 International Criminal Court, *Situation in the Democratic Republic of the Congo*, Decision authorising the filing of observations for participation in the proceedings, 23 May 2007, ICC-01/03-329-tEN; See also American University Washington College of Law, War Crimes Research Office, *Protecting the Rights of Future Accused During the Investigation*

ber of victims' applications and has made submissions regarding the scope of the victims' right to participate and the information to which the Office was entitled for the purpose of submitting its responses.[37] Furthermore, it has successfully argued on the scope of victim participation during the investigation stage, which has led, *inter alia*, to the Appeals Chamber's clarification that victims have no general right to participate in the situation stage outside the scope of judicial proceedings.[38] The OPCD has further been authorised to respond to victims' applications to participate in the proceedings in the situation in Darfur, Sudan,[39] where the Office's work has largely paralleled its submissions in the DRC situation.[40] In other cases, it has made submissions on proposed activities of the Trust Fund for Victims,[41] requested the Chamber to consider disclosure of a Registry report on received applications for participation by victims,[42] and has called upon the Prosecutor to respect the principle of presumption of innocence before individual arrest warrants had

---

Stage of International Criminal Court Operations, 2008, 37, where it is suggested that the reason for this change in the approach taken by the court was that OPCD only became fully functional by January 2007.

37 E.g. *Situation in the Democratic Republic of the Congo*, Public Redacted Version of Response to 'Demande du représentant légal des victimes (expurgé)', ICC-01/04-364, 26 July 2007; Situation in the Democratic Republic of the Congo, Request for access to previous filings, and an extension of the page limit and time limit, ICC-01/04-379, 29 August 2007; Situation in the Democratic Republic of the Congo, Version publique expurgée, Observations du Bureau du Conseil Public pour la Défense sur les 13 demandes de participation en tant que victime dans la situation en République Démocratique du Congo, ICC-01/04-586-Red, 16 December 2010; also *Supra* 37, 37.

38 Situation in the Democratic Republic of the Congo, Judgment on Victim Participation in the Investigation Stage of the Proceedings in the Appeal of the OPCD against the Decision of Pre-Trial Chamber I of 7 December 2007 and in the Appeals of the OPCD and the Prosecutor against the Decision of Pre-Trial Chamber I of 24 December 2007, ICC-01/01-556, 19 December 2008, para. 56; cf. also C. Van den Wyngaert, "Victims before international criminal courts", in G. Vermeulen (ed.), *Defence Rights: International and European Developments* (Antwerp: Maklu, 2012): 60-61.

39 *Situation in Darfur, Sudan*, Decision authorising the filing of observations on applications a/0021/07, a/0023/07 to a/0033/07 and a/0035/07 to a/0038/07 for participation in the proceedings, ICC-02/05-85, 23 July 2007, 3-4.

40 E.g. *Situation in Darfur, Sudan*, Public Redacted Version of Request for the Single Judge to order the production of relevant supporting documentation pursuant to Regulation 86(2)(e), ICC-02/05/95, 21 August 2007; *Situation in Darfur, Sudan*, Request for the Single Judge to order the Prosecutor to disclose exculpatory materials, ICC-02/05-97, 24 August 2007; *Situation in Darfur, Sudan*, OPCD's Response to the 24 June 2008 Consolidated Statement of Views and Concerns of the Legal Representatives of the Participating Victims (a/0011/06 to a/0013/06, a/0015/06, a/0023/07, a/0024/07, a/0026/07, a/0029/07, a/0036/07 to a/0038/07), ICC-02/05-147, 3 July 2008; see also *Supra* 37, 44.

41 *Situation in Uganda*, OPCD Observations on the Notification under Regulation 50 of the Regulations of the Trust Fund for Victims, ICC-02/04-122, 12 March 2008; *Situation in the Central African Republic*, Requête aux fins d'autorisation de soumettre des observations sur la notification du conseil des directeurs du fonds au profit des victimes du 11 octobre 2012 et aux fins de communication d'informations additionnelles sur les activités spécifiques proposé, ICC-01/05-40, 10 October 2012.

42 *Situation in the Republic of Kenya*, Response of the Office of the Public Counsel for the Defence to the "Prosecutor's Request for Reclassification", ICC-01/09-52, 16 March 2011.

been issued.[43] In contrast, a request by the OPCD to be provided with an opportunity to present legal submissions on the issue of jurisdiction and admissibility has been rejected; according to the Single Judge, Article 19 of the Rome Statute does not permit the OPCD to file observations on or challenge the Court's jurisdiction.[44] Last, in the Situation in Sudan, the Pre-Trial Chamber alluded that the OPCD may have the right to participate in proceedings conducted by the OTP in a situation state when it rejected the application of *ad-hoc* counsel for the Defence to be present at interviews conducted by the OTP with individuals arrested in Sudan for violations of international humanitarian law and human rights with reference to the competence of the OPCD;[45] however, there is no indication that counsel from the Office has ever been invited to such proceedings during subsequent investigations.[46]

On occasion, the OPCD has also been appointed to protect and represent the interests of a particular suspect before the Court. Most importantly, on 6 December 2011, Pre-Trial Chamber I authorised the OPCD in accordance with Regulation 77 to 'represent the interests of the Defence in all instances related to the proceedings against Saif al-Islam Gaddafi in the present case until otherwise decided by this Chamber.'[47] Though the Registrar had suggested external counsel to be appointed for the suspect,[48] the Chamber declined appointment of counsel before confirmation was received that the defendant had given a power of attorney.[49] When a delegation comprising, among others, members of the OPCD visited the suspect in Libya in Spring 2012, he expressed the wish that the Office assist him in the selection of counsel and continue to represent him before the Court until permanent counsel would be appointed.[50] Though the Chamber recognised that Gaddafi's declaration did not amount to a formal power of attorney, it considered it sufficient evidence that he wished OPCD to fully represent him until regular counsel could be obtained; as a consequence, the Chamber appointed two

---

43 *Situation in the Libyan Arab Jamahiriya*, Application concerning public statements made by the Prosecutor and respect for the presumption of innocence principle, ICC-01/11-5-tENG, 25 May 2011.

44 *Situation in Darfur,* Sudan, Corrigendum to Decision on the Applications for Participation in the Proceedings of Applicants a/0011/06 to a/0015/06, a/0021/07 to a/0023/07 and a/0035/07 to a/0038/07, ICC-02/05-111-Corr, 14 December 2007, para. 25; *Supra* 37, 43-44.

45 *Situation in Darfur, Sudan*, Decision on the Ad hoc Counsel for the Defence's Request for leave to Appeal the Decision of 2 February 2007, ICC-02/05-52, 21 February 2007, 7.

46 *Supra* 37, 32.

47 *Prosecutor v Saif al-Islam Gaddafi and Abdullah al-Senussi*, Public Redacted Version of Decision Requesting Libya to file Observations Regarding the Arrest of Saif al-Islam Gaddafi, ICC-01/11-01/11-39-Red, 6 December 2011.

48 *Prosecutor v Saif al-Islam Gaddafi and Abdullah al-Senussi,* Public Redacted Version of ICC-01/11-01/11-35-Conf-Exp "Observations of the Registrar pursuant to communication received on the 27 November 2011", ICC-01/11-01/11-35-Red, 30 November 2011.

49 *Supra* 48, para. 6.

50 *Prosecutor v Saif al-Islam Gaddafi and Abdullah al-Senussi*, Decision Appointing Counsel from OPCD as Counsel for Saif Al-Islam Gaddafi, 17 April 2012, ICC-01/11-01/11-113, para. 3.

lawyers from OPCD as Defence counsel for the suspect.[51] The case made the headlines when in June 2012, a delegation comprising of OPCD counsel Melinda Taylor, two staff members of the Registry, and one translator, while on a mission to visit Gaddafi in Zintan, Libya, were arrested by the local militia. Though most commentators were sympathetic to the position of the OPCD and Ms Taylor, there was sporadic criticism, notably by Prosecutor Luis Moreno Ocampo.[52] Following prolonged international tension between the ICC, other members of the international community, and the Libyan authorities, the delegates were eventually released on 2 July and returned to the Hague.[53] In spite of the incident, the OPCD continued its mandate to represent Saif al-Islam Gaddafi for another eight months, when it requested to withdraw from the case on due to an 'imminent depletion in staffing', which was deemed likely to significantly affect its ability to fulfil its mandate. New counsel was appointed by a decision of the Pre-Trial Chamber on 17 April 2013.[54]

Next to its appointment in the Gaddafi case, the OPCD has only been sporadically appointed as duty counsel to assist during the initial appearance of a suspect who had not yet been able to obtain Defence counsel. Such assignment was made for the first time for the initial appearance hearing of Germain Katanga;[55] after the hearing, the Pre-Trial Chamber asked the Registrar to appoint new duty counsel in consultation with the suspect, emphasising that the OPCD had only accepted nomination for the initial appearance and that it had explicitly asked not to be further designated as the OTP was about to disclose confidential material and the OPCD feared a conflict of interest with respect to its assistance to other suspects.[56] By contrast, Pre-Trial Chamber II went beyond this highly narrow scope of appointment in the context of the OPCD's appointment as duty counsel for Narcisse Arido, one of the accused in the *Bemba et al.* case, when it appointed Principal Counsel from the OPCD as duty counsel 'to assist and represent the interests of [the suspect] immediately before, during and immediately after his first appearance before the Chamber.'[57] During the initial appearance, the Single Judge, following a proposal from the OPCD, ordered that the OTP should disclose

---

51 *Ibid.*, para. 5.

52 M. Kersten, "Justice after the War: The International Criminal Court and post-Gaddafi Libya", in K. J. Fisher, and R. Stewart (*eds.*), *Transnational Justice and the Arab Spring* (Abingdon: Routledge, 2014): 198.

53 *Ibid.*, 195-98; M. C. Bassiouni, *Libya: From Repression to Revolution, A Record of Armed Conflict and International Law Violations* (Leiden: Brill, 2013): 379-80.

54 *Prosecutor v Saif al-Islam Gaddafi and Abdullah al-Senussi*, Decision on the "Request to Withdraw", ICC-01/11-01/11-311-Red, 17 April 2013, paras 4, 7.

55 *Prosecutor v Germain* Katanga, Désignation de Conseil de Permanence, 19 October 2007, ICC-01/04-01/07-39-Anx1; *Prosecutor v Germain Katanga*, Déclaration d'Acceptation de Désignation, 19 October 2007, ICC-01/04-01/07-39-Anx2; see also *Infra* 57, 2-3.

56 Pre-Trial Chamber 1, Decision on the appointment of duty counsel, 5 November 2007, ICC-01/04-01/07-52, 3-5.

57 Pre-Trial Chamber II, Notification of the appointment of duty counsel for Mr. Narcisse Arido, ICC-01/05-01/13-268, 18 March 2014.

certain material to the OPCD to keep it and pass it on as soon as new counsel would be appointed.[58] Accordingly, this time the Chamber decided not to appoint new duty counsel to retain the disclosure until permanent Defence counsel was appointed but to assign this task to the OPCD.

The aforementioned amendments made in 2011 to Regulation 77 and the subsequent appointment of the OPCD as counsel for Saif al-Islam Gaddafi appear to suggest that at the time, the Judges indeed wanted the OPCD to be more ready for appointment to assist individual defendants. Only little earlier, Judge Adrian Fulford, in a speech to the Assembly of States Parties, had criticised the OPCD of having failed to live up to its envisaged purpose of increasing efficiency of defence work and reducing legal aid costs due to a lack of 'hands-on, case-focused help to individual defendants and to the Court'. He complained that since the end of the pre-trial phase in *Lubanga*, the OPCD had not been in court for a long time, and proposed to 'investigate carefully whether it provides sufficient practical assistance to justify the considerable costs that are involved.' However, it may be doubted that the OPCD is, at present, capable of representing individual defendants beyond sporadic assignments for simple tasks and short periods of time. Whereas in general, counsel from the Office enjoy the same degree of professional independence and are subject to the same qualification requirements as external counsel,[59] it must be born in mind that the size and staffing of the OPCD is not considerably higher, if at all, than that of an individual Defence team. Taking into account that the OPCD must not neglect the other tasks which form part of its mandate, it is clear that it would be impossible to expect the OPCD to be able to represent a suspect or accused to the same extent as a Defence team with no other obligations.

Moreover, prolonged representation of a defendant by the OPCD is likely to raise issues of conflict of interest as it may receive information from other Defence teams potentially revealing confidential information or their case strategy and would therefore have to terminate its assistance to certain teams with which such a conflict could arise. In addition, the considerable amount of work involved in managing a whole Defence case would unavoidably distract resources required to assist Defence counsel so that even counsel with whom no direct conflict of interest could arise would be prejudiced. It has been suggested that due to this risk of conflicts of interest, the idea of a public defender's office at the ICC, like it exists at the SCSL, was rejected in favour of an advisory organ such as the OPCD.[60] Last, it is unclear whether appearance before the court would indeed increase the quality of assistance the OPCD may offer to individual Defence teams; in contrast, it may be ar-

58 Pre-Trial Chamber II, Transcript, ICC-01/05-01/13-T-4-Red2-ENG, 20 March 2014, 10-12; see also Pre-Trial Chamber II, Notification of Disclosure & Transfer of Materials to Permanent Counsel, ICC-01/05-01/13-322, 8 April 2014.

59 Cf. *Supra* 21, 12.

60 *Supra* 14, 410; *Supra* 4, para. 9.

gued that an OPCD counsel who appears alongside a regular Defence counsel would be largely redundant and an inefficient use of the Office's time. As the OPCD is able, where it has been permitted by counsel, to follow the transcripts of ongoing proceedings in 'real time' from its offices, it may still render immediate assistance via electronic communication where required by counsel during court proceedings.[61] As a consequence of these needs to remain efficient in the performance of its mandate, to avoid conflicts of interest, and to have regard for the considerable workload involved, the OPCD is hardly capable of performing more than a 'backup' function, taking up the representation of individuals only if absolutely necessary and explicitly requested by the suspect or accused.[62]

3.3. External Representation of the Defence

Though not expressly mentioned in Regulation 77, the OPCD has, on occasion, assumed the task of representing the rights of the Defence both inside and outside the ICC. It has provided substantive input on Defence issues in relation to the proposed amendments to the Regulations of the Court and strategic plans of the Court for victims, intermediaries, and counsel.[63] Furthermore, it has given advice and made recommendations with respect to software and IT protocol for the distribution of evidence in court as part of a working group comprising of representatives of the different organs of the court with a mandate to discuss, research, and make recommendations regarding issues concerning the Court's e-court system.[64] It has repeatedly been involved in consultations regarding the Court's legal aid scheme, amongst others with the Registrar, the Counsel Support Section (CSS), and the Hague Working Group of the Bureau of the Assembly of States Parties.[65] Moreover, it has been representing the interests of the Defence in the context of the planning of the Court's new permanent premises.[66] In contrast, at the Advisory Committee on Legal Texts, which considers and reports on proposals for amendments to the Rules of Procedure and Evidence, the Elements of Crimes, and the Regulations of the Court, Defence interests are not repre-

---

61 Cf. *Supra* 18, 70.

62 *Infra* 89, 4; *Supra* 21, 12; Cf. *Supra* 14, 418; a situation where the timely assignment of counsel could be necessary in a sense as to temporarily override the concerns expressed could be where a suspect or accused requires legal assistance while their eligibility for legal aid is disputed by the Registry similar to the situation in *Prosecutor v Prlic et al.* before the ICTY, where an accused was without legal assistance and expected to 'participate in the proceedings, file responses, file a pretrial brief and address the pretrial judge'; counsel from the OPCD could step in where neither the accused nor the court are willing or able to pay for external counsel.

63 *Supra* 18, 70.

64 K A A Khan, and A A Shah, "Defensive Practices: Representing Clients before the International Criminal Court", *Law and Contemporary Problems*, 76 (2013): 217-18.

65 E.g. International Criminal Court, Report of the Bureau on legal aid, ICC-ASP/12/29, 15 October 2013.

66 *Supra* 18, 70; *Supra* 10, 82.

sented by the OPCD but by an independently elected representative of counsel included in the list of counsel.[67]

Moreover, the OPCD has represented the interests of the Defence externally towards NGOs, States, and affected communities,[68] and has participated in information conferences and training courses in The Hague and elsewhere.[69] It has often been tasked with representing Defence issues in general ICC outreach activities, ostensibly as a counterpart to the omnipresent representatives of the OTP. At the same time, the Office does not currently have the capacity in terms of time and resources to function as a permanent external representative of the Defence at symposia, press conferences, and other outreach activities of the Court,[70] and announcements that representatives of the OPCD will feature in 'new audiovisual programming explaining the ICC's role and activities before the Court' do not appear to have been realised so far.[71] Instead, the OPCD focuses on sporadic participation at information events and smaller-scale outreach efforts directly directed at lawyers involved in international criminal Defence work. Though effective coordination between the OPCD and the Court's Public Information and Documentation Section (PIDS) could improve the institutional presence of the Defence and in particular ensure that Defence issues are conveyed to the general public at ICC outreach events,[72] it would be unrealistic to expect that the interests of the Defence could be adequately represented by a neutral organ instead of a representative of Defence counsel or the OPCD.

Accordingly, though the OPCD is able to perform outreach activities on behalf of the Defence, it can hardly be asserted that there is equality of arms with the OTP in this field. The OTP has its own Public Information Unit

---

67 Regulations of the Court, Regulation 4(1); see also e.g. International Criminal Court, Annual Report of the Advisory Committee on Legal Texts issued pursuant to rule 16 of the Rules of Procedure of the Advisory Committee on Legal Texts, 27 September 2012; cf. also W Schabas, *An Introduction to the International Criminal Court* (Cambridge: Cambridge University Press: 2011): 384.

68 *Supra* 18, 71.

69 International Criminal Court, *What is the mandate of the OPCD*, available online at <http://www.icc- cpi.int/en_menus/icc/structure%20of%20the%20court/defence/office%20of%20public%20counsel%20for %20the%20defence/frequently%20asked%20 questions/Pages/what%20is%20the%20mandate%20of%20the %20opcd_.aspx>; Counsel from the OPCD has been speaking, for instance, at the Africa Legal Aid Conference in Johannesburg in September 2014; a German Lawyer's Conference in June 2013 in Düsseldorf; at an International Criminal Law seminar in Lisbon in November 2013; at an International Conference on 'Building a Legacy' in November in November 2013; at a Conference on Legal Aid in Criminal Proceedings in the European Union in Warsaw in December 2011, at the T.M.C. Asser Institute in the Hague in November 2011; at a Conference of the Conférance Internationale des Barreaux in Lomé in December 2009; at a visit to the ICC organised by the International Bar Association in May 2008; and at the General Assembly of the French Conseil National des Barreaux in May 2008.

70 Cf. e.g. in *Supra* 10, 82-83; *Infra* 72, para. 13.

71 International Criminal Court, *Report of the Court on the public information strategy 2011-2013*, ICC-ASP/9/29, 22 November 2010, para. 43.

72 *Supra* 10, 82-83.

(PIU), which performs outreach activities 'driven by the Prosecutorial Strategy [and] the specific mandate of the Office'.[73] Though it receives the support of the PIDS for this purpose, the PIU has recognised that the Registry is unable to perform such activities on its behalf because of the latter's neutrality.[74] In the past, the OTP has released a vast body of press releases, some of which include audio-visual content, has called press conferences,[75] has organised regular lectures by distinguished professors, publicists, and practitioners of international criminal law and related disciplines,[76] and has been maintaining a 'network of relationships' with States, international organisations, and NGOs with a view to obtaining assistance and practical resources in their investigatory activities.[77] This stands in stark contrast to the OPCD, whose staffing levels do not permit extensive outreach activities, and which has been subject to consistent budgetary restraints in this area. In 2007, the Office began to use most of its outreach budget to fund a case manager position, which was considered indispensable in light of the increasing caseload at the Court,[78] and since, it has consistently used only a small share of its approved budget for travel and outreach.[79] This is reflected in the OPCD's 2015 proposed budget, in which the funds available for such activities have been cut by 85%, enabling the Principal Counsel from OPCD to participate at one key conference concerning the rights of the Defence before the Court.[80] Though overall this significant cut in the external representation budget has been offset by increases, or lesser cuts, on staff expenses, this development reflects and evinces the inability of the OPCD to perform adequate outreach activities on behalf of the Defence as well as the fact that its priorities are shifting away from this field of activity.

4. *The Future Role of the OPCD and the Proposals made under the Registry ReVision Project*

The Registry *Re*Vision Project has been initiated by ICC Registrar Herman van Hebel subsequent to authorisation by the Assembly of States Parties at its

73 International Bar Association, *ICC External Communications: Delivering Information and Fairness*, June 2011, 12.

74 *Supra* 17, para. 147.

75 Including on the Uganda arrest warrants on 14 October 2004, on the situation in Kenya on 25 November 2009 and on 1 April 2010, and on the situation in Libya on 16 May 2011.

76 International Criminal Court, *Guest Lectures*, available at <http://www.icc-cpi.int/en_menus/icc/structure%20of%20the%20court/office%20of%20the%20prosecutor/network%20with%20partners/guest%20lectures/Pages/guest%20lectures.aspx>.

77 N Jurdi, *The International Criminal Court and National Courts: A Contentious Relationship* (Farnham: Ashgate, 2011): 191.

78 *Supra* 10, 84.

79 Since 2008, the amount of money used for travel activities has varied between €1,100 and 6,600 (with the exception of 2012, where more funds were used); this stands in stark contrast to 2007, when €14,800 of travel funds were used for a barely operational office.

80 The proposed travel budget for 2015 is €2,600; *Supra* 17, para. 563.

2013 session to 'reorganize and streamline the Registry's organizational structure' with a view to achieving at least three per cent savings in 2014.[81] For this purpose, the Registrar seeks to 'optimize the Registry's performance in terms of efficiency, effectiveness and sustainability' and to 'implement an improved organisational design, as well as measures to improve performance, reduce bureaucracy, and avoid duplication' in a process expected to last until 2015.[82] In an outline dated 15 September 2014, the Registrar has criticised the functioning, support, and administration of Defence work at the tribunal for 'fragmentation, unnecessary bureaucracy, inefficiency, and a lack of clarity in relation to the performance of Defence-related functions.'[83] With respect to the OPCD, the paper notices a lack of cooperation and the presence of conflicts with the CSS because the former has taken up certain functions ordinarily to be performed on behalf of the Registrar under Rule 20 RPE, and generally calls into question the OPCD's ability to represent the general interests of the Defence and counsel practicing before the Court because it is not an executive body of the profession or subject to any democratic oversight by counsel.[84]

4.1. The new Defence Office

As a consequence of the alleged shortcomings, the Registrar has proposed to amend the Regulations of the Court and merge OPCD and CSS into a newly formed 'Defence Office', while concurrently establishing an independent, self-governing 'Association of Defence Counsel'. The Defence Office will retain all staff from OPCD and CSS, but be headed by one manager and form part of the 'Division of Judicial Support' together with, *inter alia* the Detention Section and the Court Management Section.[85] It will take over all responsibilities previously carried out by the CSS as well as certain areas of work previously performed by the OPCD, such as providing information, legal advice, and practical support and assistance to Defence counsel, including on the use of information technology.[86] In contrast, the proposal foresees that all OPCD functions of representing clients and the interests of the Defence in the early stages of an investigation will, in the future, be taken over by duty counsel appointed on an *ad-hoc* basis, while the representation of Defence interests within the Court will be performed by the Association of

---

81 International Criminal Court, *Official Records, Vol. 1,* Assembly of States Parties to the Rome Statute of the International Criminal Court, ICC-ASP/12/20, 20-28 November 2013, 20.

82 *Supra* 17, para. 277.

83 International Criminal Court, *Registry ReVision Project: Basic Outline of Recent Proposals regarding the Defence*, 15 September 2014, available online at <http://michaelgkarnavas.net/files/140954-outline-defence- proposals.pdf>, 1.

84 *Ibid*, 2.

85 See also International Criminal Court, *ICC Registry Organigram*, 15 September 2014, available online at <http://michaelgkarnavas.net/files/organigram-from-registry.pdf>.

86 *Supra* 84, 3-4.

Defence Counsel.[87] The extent of the legal research and assistance to counsel which the new Defence Office will be able to provide remains unclear from the proposals, but the nature of the Office's work and the breadth of its mandate suggests that it will provide more general advice and assistance to Defence teams rather than undertake prolonged, specialised research on key topics which may then become part of the institutional memory of the Defence.

The OPCD has responded to the proposals brought forth by the Registrar in a memorandum sent out to all Defence counsel practicing before the ICC;[88] in addition, Judge Adrian Fulford has criticised the proposed structural changes in a speech held on 29 October 2014 in London.[89] Both responses express deep concern about the disbandment of the OPCD as an independent office assisting the Defence and the complete abolishment of in-house counsel offering swift and focused assistance and representation to suspects in immediate need of legal advice.[90] Similarly, the OPCD emphasises that the Association of Defence Counsel, which would take over the representational tasks currently exercised by the OPCD, is in a weaker position to advance Defence issues due to its position outside the ICC structure.[91] Moreover, Judge Fulford fears that the Defence Office may, in the future, turn out to be the prime target of staffing cuts, with the result that the responsibilities retained from the former OPCD to provide legal and practical assistance to counsel will be gradually disbanded as the Registrar may find that Defence teams should possess the necessary practical skills and be capable of doing their own legal research if they wish to practice before the Court. As a consequence, both responses express a concern that the defendants' rights at the Court are at risk of being undermined, and that the equality of arms between Defence and Prosecution may be negatively affected by the proposed changes.

As recognised by both the OPCD and Judge Fulford, it is particularly worrying that the proposals seek to replace an independent Office assisting Defence counsel at the ICC with one which is essentially integrated into the hierarchy of the Registry. It is of critical importance that any lawyer appearing before a court or tribunal, whether national or international, is independent of any interests or external pressure which may impair their task of adequately advising their client, or which may undermine the value of legal

87 *Ibid.*

88 Reprinted in "ICC-*Re*Vision Project: Memorandum by the OPCD", *ADC-ICTY Newsletter*, 73 (2014), 1.

89 Sir Adrian Fulford LJ, Chatham House Speech at the memorial seminar for Sir Richard May, 29 October 2014; there is no official transcript of the speech currently available but the speech has been reprinted with the judge's permission at <https://www.facebook.com/RozenbergJ/posts/1501437393441890>.

90 *Ibid.*, *Supra* 89, 2-4.

91 *Supra* 89, 7.

advice given;[92] this absolute necessity is also reflected in Article 6 of the Code of Professional Conduct for counsel.[93] However, the nature of its work, including the administration of legal aid and appointment of counsel and their legal assistants, seriously puts into question the independence of the new Defence Office. From a legal perspective, the Office will essentially take over certain functions currently performed by the CSS which are, pursuant to Rule 20 RPE, incumbent upon the Registrar;[94] accordingly, it will be acting on behalf of the Registrar when performing these functions. Hence, the Defence Office will cease to be independent and become part of the hierarchy of the Registry both in legal and practical terms.

Next to the glaring contradiction with Regulation 144 of the Regulations of the Registry, the practical implications of this lack of independence on the ability of the Defence Office to effectively assist Defence counsel are potentially grave. Notably, the task of deciding on legal aid applications requires the Defence Office to weigh the interests of the Court in containing expenses against the interests of Defence counsel to mount the best possible defence for their clients, which can generate tensions and difficult relationships between them. An entity involved in such a task will not be able to provide substantive legal assistance to counsel without encountering conflicts of interest and general mistrust by Defence counsel.[95] Only an office independent from the Registry will be entrusted by counsel with requests for assistance potentially revealing confidential information, impending motions, or aspects of case strategy, or be granted direct access to potentially confidential material, for example when asked to receive disclosure for temporarily absent counsel or assist in the use of the court's IT environment; for the same reason, the OTP entertains its own Legal Advisory Section and does not delegate even the most general requests for legal research and advice to an organ of the Registry.[96] Last, insofar as the OPCD currently requires assistance by Defence teams to carry out its mandate, for instance by allowing it to access life transcripts from the courtroom, such requests are less likely to be granted if the Office loses its independence. As a consequence, without its independ-

92 See e.g. Council of Bars and Societies of Europe, *Charter of Core Principles of the European Legal Profession and Code of Conduct for European Lawyers*, 9, 15; United Nations Congress on the Prevention of Crime and the Treatment of Offenders, *Basic Principles on the Role of Lawyers*, para. 16; J. Flamme, "The fundamental right to a full and fair defence before the ICC: On the confines of common law and Roman-German Law: an analysis", in G. Vermeulen (ed.), *Defence Rights: International and European Developments* (Antwerp: Maklu, 2012): 46.

93 Assembly of State Parties, Code of Professional Conduct for counsel, ICC-ASP/4/Res.1, 2 December 2005, Art. 6.

94 *Supra* 84, 3.

95 Cf. *Supra* 10, 77; see also *Supra* 4, para. 12, where it was expressly stated that the OPCs will not be involved in the administrative and financial management of the legal aid programme; *Supra* 14, 417, 427, where it is stated as a central rule for the establishment of a Defence Office that financial responsibility of dealing with the defence and the substantive assistance which Defence teams must receive are to be disassociated.

96 *Supra* 89, 3.

ence, the OPCD will cease to be able to assist Defence counsel in many of its current areas of work, and its activities are likely to become confined to administrative functions and general research for the benefit of the Defence.[97]

4.2. Creation of an Independent Association of Defence Counsel

Next to the establishment of the Defence Office, the Registrar's restructuration plans in the context of the *Re*Vision project also include the creation of a new, independent, and self-governing Association of Defence Counsel. If created according to the Registrar's proposals, it will take over the OPCD's task to represent Defence interests towards organs and committees of the Court and before Chambers and its position as an interlocutor between Defence counsel and the Registry. Furthermore, it will be involved in assessments of the competence of counsel for admission to the List of Counsel, the training of Defence counsel, the provision of advice on conduct and ethics issues, and the oversight of Defence counsel's performance and adherence to ethical standards.[98]

This creation of an independent bar association for Defence counsel practicing before the ICC is a significant step towards a better promotion of Defence rights at the Court, and it appears that many of its prospective tasks, in particular its disciplinary and oversight functions and its mandate to ensure that Defence counsel adhere to high standards of cthics and conduct, can better be carried out by a body which is not only composed of those whom it regulates, but which is also fully and solely accountable to counsel. Nonetheless, it must be guaranteed that counsel do not abuse this position and impose prohibitively high professional standards, effectively barring lawyers with no prior experience in international criminal practice from representing defendants at the Court.[99] Moreover, an independent bar association may allow for a more effective representation of Defence interests in internal decision-making bodies of the ICC; this is not only because it would abolish the unnecessary fragmentation which currently exists and in which different people represent the Defence in different organs and committees, but it would also counter criticism alleging that the OPCD lacked legitimacy to represent the interests of the Defence towards other organs of the Court. It has been contended that such criticism is mostly voiced from outside the Defence, while Defence counsel themselves have generally maintained a cooperative relationship with the OPCD and have provided an overwhelmingly positive assessment of its services.[100] Nonetheless, an Association of Defence Counsel

---

97 *Ibid.*

98 *Supra* 84, 3-4.

99 Cf. *Supra* 90.

100 International Bar Association, *IBA Comments on draft Registry Revision Project Paper: 'Basic Outline of Proposals to Establish Defence and Victims Offices*, 12 January 2015, available at <http://www.internationallawbureau.com/wp-content/ uploads/2015/01/ here. pdf>, 5.

will likely be able to provide for more legitimacy through representatives who are elected by and accountable to Defence counsel, and may further establish procedures and structures to unify the voice of the Defence towards its partners and to have this unified opinion accepted as a legitimate expression of the concerns and wishes of the Defence.

On the other hand, the creation of an Association of Defence counsel may imply a number of relevant problems which should be addressed before the proposals can be seriously considered. Most importantly, the structures and procedures the Association of Defence Counsel will be operating with have not yet been formulated with sufficient clarity; neither has any decision been made on the issue of financing. Though the Registrar has announced to approach the ASP for approval to subsidise the Association, he has conceded that, in view of the still limited number of cases before the court, obtaining funds from the ASP may be problematic.[101] In fact, it seems highly unlikely that, while all staff members currently employed at the OPCD and CSS are to be retained and the legal aid scheme is to be unaffected by the restructuration,[102] additional funds will be made available for a new entity. Accordingly, recent proposals made by Defence counsel envisage a new 'ICC Bar', which is funded primarily by its members and membership of which is to be compulsory for list counsel.[103] While the imposition of a meaningful membership fee would help fund the organisation, it would also affect counsel and prospective counsel from different parts of the world in an unequal way and would possibly deprive certain lawyers of the benefit of membership, or, particularly in the light of compulsory membership, prohibit them from representing clients at the ICC altogether.[104] Eventually, the lack of both clear rules and structures and a concept for obtaining the necessary funds has the potential to significantly delay the creation of the Association of Defence Counsel, and it remains largely unclear which steps have in fact been taken in this regard. At the same time, the *Re*Vision Project is to be finalised in 2015 and the changes it brings about are likely to be implemented shortly after;[105] as one Defence counsel has phrased it, the disbandment of the OPCD is a 'done deal'.[106] It is crucial that, if the Association of Defence Counsel is supposed to take over a meaningful amount of tasks from the OPCD as proposed

101 *Supra* 84, 4.
102 *Ibid.*
103 M G Karnavas, *Establishment of a Victims and Defence Office at the ICC*, 31 March 2015, available at <http://michaelgkarnavas.net/blog/2015/03/31/icc-victims-and-defence-office/>.
104 For example, the current membership fees of the ADC-ICTY are €250 p.a. to be paid in one instalment, while an additional €80 per month is to be paid by assigned counsel during the pre-trial, trial, and appeals stage of their cases.
105 International Justice Monitor, *ICC Registrar Discusses Restructuring and Need for Larger Budget*, 23 July 2014, available at <http://www.ijmonitor.org/2014/07/icc-registrar-discusses-restructuring-and-need-for-larger-budget/>.
106 M G Karnavas, *ICC Registrar supports establishment of an Association of List Counsel*, 20 September 2014, available at <http://michaelgkarnavas.net/blog/2014/09/20/icc-registrar-supports-association/>.

by the Registrar, there is no gap between the latter ceasing to perform these functions and the former commencing its work; otherwise, there is a risk that these functions, notably the internal representation of Defence interests, will not be meaningfully performed for a potentially prolonged period of time.

4.3. Will the Office persist?

The plans brought forth by the Registrar to restructure the Registry and dissolve the OPCD possibly represent the most significant change to Defence structures and interests at the ICC so far and potentially impact equality and fairness between Defence teams as well as between the Defence as a whole and the OTP. Even if the Association of Defence Counsel will be able to take over all tasks assigned to it, and become operational directly after the OPCD ceases its work, some of its key functions, notably those relating to ongoing legal research and individualised assistance to Defence teams, are unlikely to be retained. This will create a particular burden on lawyers with little experience in international criminal law while those who have previously been practicing before the *ad-hoc* tribunals will have a 'head start' which may give them a meaningful advantage in securing clients. Furthermore, much of the advance made in terms of equality of arms between Prosecution and Defence will be lost with the OPCD; this is particularly worrisome considering that the OTP's budget and staffing level are going to further increase in the coming years while the expenses of the Registry, including legal aid, are being cut by the Registrar for the purpose of assisting the OTP in securing increased funding from the ASP.[107] While it is important that the OTP retains its capabilities to effectively investigate crimes committed in situation countries, the Registrar should remain mindful of his duty under Rule 20(1) to 'organise the staff of the Registry in a manner that promotes the rights of the defence, consistent with the principle of fair trial as defined in the Statute' and to 'carry out [his] functions […], including the financial administration of the Registry, in such a manner as to ensure the professional independence of counsel'. In any event, considering that the ICC has not been free from criticism as to a lack of equality of arms before the *Re*Vision proposals have been made,[108] it is a troubling development that current efforts by the Registrar to improve on alleged redundancies and inefficiencies disproportionately affect Defence interests and capabilities. More generally, placing the OPCD on an equal footing with other administrative sections within the Division of Judi-

---

107 *Supra* 106; see also International Justice Monitor, *Q&A with International Criminal Court Registrar Herman von Hebel: Part I*, 21 August 2013, available at <http://www.ijmonitor.org/2013/08/q-a-with-international-criminal-court-registrar-herman-von-hebel-part-i/>.

108 See e.g. R. Heinsch, "How to achieve fair and expeditious trial proceedings before the ICC: Is it time for a judge-dominated approach?", in C. Stahn and G. Sluiter, *The Emerging Practice of the International Criminal Court* (Leiden: Martinus Nijhoff, 2009): 483; also *Supra* 93, 40 *et seq.*; *Supra* 74, 34-35.

cial Support is likely to be seen as a significant downgrading of the status of the Office, and hence the Defence, within the structure of the Court.[109]

Certainly, it is not only commendable but absolutely necessary to periodically review the structure and routines at the Court with a view to increasing efficiencies and minimising redundancies. In order to gain legitimacy and approval among States parties, the ICC must show that it deals with their contributions responsibly and actively seeks not to create an excessive financial burden. On the other hand, the legitimacy of the Court will eventually not be derived from the money it saves but from the justice it provides to affected communities, victims, and defendants by means of criminal trials, and if the provision of justice ceases to be the paramount consideration of all participants involved in ICC work, the Court will have foregone its purpose. Thus, the proposed restructuration will not improve the legitimacy and efficiency of ICC work unless it has due regard to the principle of equality of arms at all stages of the process. In this regard, the concerns about the dissolution of the OPCD are three-fold: first, it will leave Defence counsel without an independent office embedded into the structures of the Court with secured funding and a physical presence in The Hague; second, it will leave a gap in the performance of tasks of interest to the Defence by removing the provision of certain services formerly provided by the OPCD, notably the maintenance of an 'institutional memory', which is likely to place an additional burden on new counsel and small teams operating under the legal aid scheme; and third, it will leave the representation of Defence interests during an investigation solely to duty counsel and deprive suspects and accused persons of swift *ad-hoc* legal assistance when they so require. Next to the aspect of procedural fairness, the disbandment of the OPCD may have adverse consequences on the efficiency of Defence work; in particular when considering that Regulation 77 had been drafted with the explicit aim to remedy redundancies and inefficiencies in Defence work, it remains likely that, once an extensive body of procedural and substantive law has arisen before the ICC, the services offered by the OPCD may be capable of offsetting the money and efforts invested in it.

5. Conclusion

Since its inception in 2006, the OPCD has provided valuable assistance to Defence teams, suspects, and accused persons through legal and practical assistance, appearance before Chambers, and representation of Defence interests inside and outside the Court. Though the legal representation of individual defendants has been the most visible aspect of its operations, the more important parts of its mandate are to provide ongoing assistance to counsel, during which it remains largely outside the view of the public, the Registrar,

109 *Supra* 101, 5.

and even the Judges. Nonetheless, its impact on the capacities of the Defence and the equality of arms before the Tribunal remains undisputed, and is perhaps best evinced by the steady reliance by Defence lawyers on the services of the Office. Nevertheless, the Office has found it very difficult from the very beginning to secure sufficient funds and achieve adequate recognition of its achievements by other stakeholders at the Court; as a result, it was hardly ever able to fulfil its entire mandate, which in turn has led to discontent with its work and doubts whether funds granted to the Office are well-invested and has prevented the OPCD from successfully lobbying for more staffing and a higher budget. Consequently, it was essential that the Registrar, together with the Principal Counsel and staff members from the OPCD, attempt to reformulate its mandate and either provide for an independent and strongly staffed Defence Office as a fourth pillar before the Court, which would, however, have required an amendment to the Rome Statute, or streamline the Office's activities and shift the focus to hands-on provision of legal and practical assistance to the Defence and the maintenance of an 'institutional memory', possibly modelled after the OTP-LAS.

Unfortunately, the Registrar's proposals in the context of the *Re*Vision project have led to essentially the opposite situation. Though certain functions have been delegated in a way which alleviates the OPCD from tasks which can also be adequately performed by other entities, notably an independent Association of Defence Counsel, the OPCD's core competence, namely the provision of in-depth assistance to Defence teams, may be bound to disappear without replacement. Thereby, meaningful advances made by the OPCD in contributing to the functioning and effectiveness of the Defence at the Court and promoting the equality of arms with the Prosecution are in danger of being lost, and Defence counsel are likely to encounter a *déjà vu* of the situation at the *ad-hoc* tribunals, which has often been described as insufficiently balanced and evincing an institutional bias in favour of the Prosecution. Whereas the proposed Defence Office will lack the independence required to effectively assist Defence teams on many issues of significance and will have a mandate too broad to allow the provision of in-depth legal assistance to Defence teams, the proposed Association of Defence Counsel may only be able to take over certain tasks once the many open questions, from its internal rules to funding, are cleared up and it becomes operational. In any event, it remains unlikely that even a functioning Association will be able to offset the lack of an independent Defence Office or to conceal the reality that no changes in the court structure will do justice to the principle of equality of arms without a meaningful addition of funds to the Defence both in terms of professional support and legal aid.

*Mayeul Hiéramente / Patricia Schneider**

Kein faires Verfahren ohne effektive Verteidigung

Zusammenfassende Bemerkungen zu einem vergessenen Akteur der internationalen Strafjustiz und Ausblick

Internationale Strafgerichte sind im 21. Jahrhundert als Akteure der Weltpolitik nicht mehr wegzudenken. Die Tribunale für Ruanda (ICTR) und das ehemalige Jugoslawien (ICTY) schließen ihre Tore, der Internationale Strafgerichtshof (ICC/IStGH) ist etabliert und wächst aus den Kinderschuhen heraus. Politiker und Medien fordern die Einschaltung des IStGH zur Aufarbeitung der in Syrien begangenen Verbrechen, die Afrikanische Union und der UN-Sicherheitsrat beschäftigen sich mit Strafverfahren gegen zwei amtierende Staatsoberhäupter und selbst der Palästinakonflikt gerät in den Fokus des Weltstrafgerichts.[1] ICTR, ICTY und IStGH eint dabei eine gemeinsame Zielsetzung: Die strafrechtliche Aufarbeitung begangenen Unrechts und Gerechtigkeit für die Opfer. Damit verbunden ist die Hoffnung auf Versöhnung von Opfer- und Tätergruppen sowie die Verhinderung von Revisionismus und Märtyrertum durch Etablierung von Fakten. In der politischen sowie wissenschaftlichen Betrachtung der internationalen Strafjustiz wird ein *Akteur indes weitgehend ausgeblendet* bzw. nicht als eigener Akteur wahrgenommen: Die Verteidigung (der Angeklagte und sein Verteidigungsteam).

Dabei nimmt die *Verteidigung beziehungsweise das Auftreten der Angeklagten oftmals eine zentrale Rolle sowohl im Strafverfahren als auch im gesamten Aufarbeitungsprozess* ein. Die Verfahren gegen Milošević, Šešelj, Karadžić, Haradinaj, Gotovina und Mladić (am ICTY) zeigen dies ebenso wie die Verfahren gegen al-Bashir, Saif al-Islam al-Gaddafi, Kenyatta und Ruto[2] (am IStGH). In der öffentlichen Wahrnehmung stehen nicht nur Individuen vor den Richtern, sondern Serben, Kosovaren, Kroaten, Kalenjin oder Kikuyu

* Mayeul Hiéramente, Dr. iur., Rechtsanwalt in der Kanzlei Wessing & Partner Rechtsanwälte mbB in Düsseldorf sowie Alumnus der International Max Planck Research School on Retaliation, Mediation and Punishment (IMPRS-REMEP) in Freiburg. Er lehrt Völkerstrafrecht im Masterprogramm „Peace and Security Studies“ der Universität Hamburg, Kontakt: mayeulhieramente@gmail.com.
Patricia Schneider, Dr. phil., Promotion über „Internationale Gerichtsbarkeit als Instrument friedlicher Streitbeilegung“ (2003), wissenschaftliche Referentin am Institut für Friedensforschung und Sicherheitspolitik an der Universität Hamburg (IFSH), Akademische Koordinatorin und Dozentin im Masterprogramm „Peace and Security Studies“, Chefredakteurin und Mitherausgeberin der sicherheitspolitischen Fachzeitschrift „S+F. Sicherheit und Frieden – Security and Peace“, Kontakt: schneider@ifsh.de.

1 Siehe z.B. R. Frau, *Die Situation in Palästina vor dem IStGH – Überweisung durch die UN-Generalversammlung*, S+F (2013), 221.

2 Dazu M. Hiéramente, *Wahlen in Zeiten der Strafverfolgung. Die Situation in Kenia und der Internationale Strafgerichtshof, Die* Friedens-Warte (2013), 187.

(oder gar Afrikaner[3]). Ob die internationale Strafjustiz die in sie gesetzten Ziele verwirklichen kann, hängt auch von der Perzeption der betroffenen Bevölkerung ab.[4] Der Angeklagte und sein Verteidiger können Einfluss auf diese Wahrnehmung nehmen. Koskenniemi hat das Dilemma der internationalen Strafjustiz im Verfahren gegen Slobodan Milošević treffend auf den Punkt gebracht:

> *„The Milošević trial – like international criminal law generally –oscillates ambivalently between the wish to punish those individually responsible for large humanitarian disasters and the danger of becoming a show trial."*[5]

So wirkt die Erwartungshaltung der medialen Öffentlichkeit sowie der nationalen und internationalen Politik auf die Verfahrensführung ein. Da die internationale Strafjustiz – sowohl Anklage als auch Verteidigung – auf Finanzierung, Kooperation und „moral support" angewiesen ist, spielt das Bild, welches vom Angeklagten gezeichnet wird eine zentrale Rolle. Dies führt zu den *wesentlichen Fragen*, der im Rahmen des Sammelbands nachgegangen wurde:

- *Was ist die Rolle der Verteidigung im internationalen Strafverfahren in der praktischen Realität?*
- *Ist der Angeklagte ein Akteur des historischen Aufarbeitungsprozesses oder ist er reines Objekt des Prozesses?*
- *Welche praktischen und organisatorischen Hürden bestehen bei der Gewährung eines fairen Verfahrens?*

Diese und weitere Fragen werden in diesem Sammelband anhand praktisch relevanter Fallkonstellationen diskutiert. Im Einzelnen:

In „The Defence in International Criminal Trials: Important Actor or Necessary Evil?" gewährt *Colleen Rohan* praktische Einblicke in die Welt der internationalen Strafverteidigung, die alltäglichen Hürden im Umgang mit Gerichten, Anklage und der Staatengemeinschaft sowie die *raison d'etre* der Verfahrensgarantien für (mutmaßliche) Kriegsverbrecher und Völkermörder. Die Autorin konstatiert und exemplifiziert, dass die Leine, an der die Verteidigung gehalten wird, vergleichsweise kurz ist. Ein Abweichen von der „Kernaufgabe" der prozessualen Beweisführung wird auf Verteidigerseite nicht selten als sanktionswürdig eingestuft, ja, die Verteidigung von in der Öffentlichkeit oftmals vorverurteilten Angeklagten als illegitim hingestellt.

---

3 Siehe z.B. Resolution der Afrikanischen Union v. 12. Oktober 2013, Ext/Assembly/AU/Dec.1(Oct. 2013).

4 Lesenswert sind die Ausführungen bei S. Ford, *A Social Psychology Model of the Perceived Legitimacy of International Criminal Courts*, Vanderbilt Journal of Transnational Law (2012), 405 sowie die ausführlichen Betrachtungen bei L. Fletcher und H. Weinstein, *Violence and Social Repair: Rethinking the Contribution of Justice to Reconciliation*, Human Rights Quarterly (2002), 573.

5 M. Koskenniemi, *Between Impunity and Show Trials*, Max Planck Yearbook of United Nations Law (2002), 1.

Der Anklagebehörde und den jeweiligen Chefanklägern wird im Gegensatz dazu ein breiter Raum für eine Teilnahme am politischen Diskurs gelassen. Dieses Ungleichgewicht schlägt sich nach Ansicht der Autorin auch in der weiteren Praxis nieder und stelle die Verteidigung vor die wiederholte Herausforderung für die Ideale und damit für die Glaubwürdigkeit der internationalen Strafjustiz einzutreten.

Mayeul Hiéramente befasst sich in seinem Beitrag „Die Deutungshoheit im Gerichtssaal oder ‚Die Bändigung des Ungeheuers'" mit dem sich selbst vor Gericht verteidigenden Angeklagten sowie den Implikationen einer solchen „Selbst"-Verteidigung. Entscheidet sich ein Angeklagter für das ihm nach den relevanten Statuten grundsätzlich zustehende Recht, seine Verteidigung in die eigenen Hände zu nehmen, sieht er sich zahlreichen praktischen Herausforderungen und – nicht selten – dem Misstrauen der Öffentlichkeit sowie der Anklage ausgesetzt. Der Grat zwischen effektiver Verteidigung in der Sache und der Mitwirkung an der Geschichtsschreibung seiner Heimat ist für den Angeklagten äußerst schmal. Ihn zu beschreiten wird für alle Verfahrensbeteiligten zu einem diffizilen Unterfangen. Der Beitrag betrachtet die Motivationen von Anklage, Richtern und Angeklagten diesen Weg einzuschlagen oder zu versperren.

Philipp Graebkes Aufsatz über „Die Verteidigung im Verfahren gegen Adolf Eichmann" präsentiert eine Chronologie der Ereignisse des Verfahrens, mit besonderer Aufmerksamkeit auf Eichmanns Strafverteidiger Robert Servatius. An diesem Beispiel zeigt der Autor, welch großes öffentliches Interesse zur damaligen Zeit bestand. Der Fall Eichmann steht als Beispiel für die „versuchte oder erreichte Politisierung" von großen, völkerstrafrechtlichen Verfahren. Angefangen mit den Anstrengungen Servatius' als Verteidiger ausgewählt zu werden, erzählt Graebke die Geschichte des Verfahrens bis zur Urteilsverkündung und Servatius' Abreise aus Israel. Mit Anekdoten und großer Aufmerksamkeit für Details legt der Autor dar, wie die Politik sich am Verfahren beteiligte: sei es durch eine Gesetzesänderung, die die Ernennung Servatius als Strafverteidiger durch den Justizminister überhaupt erst möglich machte, oder durch die Tatsache, dass die Parteilichkeit des Staates Israel früh anerkannt wurde. Zudem legt Graebke genaues Augenmerk auf die Beweisführung während des Verfahrens sowie der eigentlichen Strategie von Servatius' Verteidigung: Eichmann wurde als kleines Rädchen dargestellt, der weder eigenmächtig handelte, noch die Befehle seiner Vorgesetzen verweigern konnte; Gastötungen und die Beschaffung von Skeletten verharmloste sein Verteidiger gar als „medizinische Angelegenheiten". Diese Linie konnte bei offensichtlich rechtswidrigen Befehlen nicht überzeugen. Vielmehr konnte er direkt in Verbindung mit der Einweisung von Juden in Ghettos und Lager, der Planung der sog. Endlösung und deren Umsetzung gebracht werden. Eichmann wurde in allen Punkten schuldig gesprochen und zum Tode verurteilt.

Julia Gebhard analysiert in ihrem Aufsatz „Arguing Human Rights from the Bench?" die Berücksichtigung von Menschenrechtsnormen in der praktischen Anwendung durch IStGH-Richter. Dabei konzentriert sie sich auf die Frage, inwieweit bei der Interpretation des materiellen Völkerstrafrechts auf Menschenrechte Bezug genommen wird. Gebhard untersucht durch Befragungen, wie Richter am IStGH menschenrechtliche Argumentationsmuster in ihre Entscheidungen einfließen lassen und unter welchen Voraussetzungen eine richterliche Bereitschaft besteht, auf externe Rechtsquellen und Rechtsprechung zurückzugreifen. Gebhard analysiert zudem mögliche Einflussfaktoren wie die Herkunft der Richter und den normativen Rahmen, in dem sie handeln, um ihre Positionen bezüglich der Rolle menschenrechtlicher Regime am IStGH zu erklären. Die Autorin prognostiziert, dass das beträchtliche Ausmaß der bestehenden Divergenzen hinsichtlich der Wahrnehmung der Bedeutung von Menschenrechten in Zukunft geringer wird, da die Richter in künftigen Fällen auf eine größere Bandbreite von Präzedenzfällen zurückgreifen können und somit weniger eigenständig interpretieren und entscheiden müssen. Der Beitrag liefert einen seltenen Einblick hinter die Kulissen der Rechtsfindung und ermöglicht auf diese Weise ein besseres Verständnis für die Entscheidungsfindung der internationalen Richter.

Marie O'Leary untersucht in „Compelling Fair Trials" die Möglichkeiten des IStGH Zeugen zu einer Aussage in Den Haag vorzuladen, sowie die weiteren Optionen, sie zur Aussage in Verfahren anzuhalten. Bis zu einer Entscheidung der Berufungskammer im Fall Ruto & Sang im Jahr 2014 war nicht geklärt, ob das Römische Statut des IStGH erlaubt, Zeugen zwangsweise vorzuladen, oder ob das Gericht – Anklage und Verteidigung – auf eine freiwillige Kooperation hoffen mussten. Insbesondere für die Verteidigung, die über nur begrenzte Ressourcen und Kontakte zu den staatlichen Institutionen verfügt, ist ohne die Möglichkeit der zwangsweisen Vorführung von Zeugen die Beweisgewinnung und Wahrheitsfindung deutlich erschwert. O'Leary fasst zuerst die aktuelle Sachlage zusammen und greift die grundsätzliche Problematik auf, dass Vorladungen außerhalb des eigenen Staatsgebiets regelmäßig nicht erzwungen werden können. Befragungen und Aussagen per Videoübertragung zuzulassen, wird als pragmatischer Kompromiss dargestellt. Da die Gerichte solche Aussagen jedoch als weniger verlässlich bewerten, stellt dies laut der Autorin nicht die ideale Lösung dar. Letztlich kommt die Autorin zu dem Schluss, dass der IStGH nur dann effektiv und fair arbeiten kann, wenn zwischen der Verteidigung und der Strafverfolgung Chancengleichheit herrscht. Dazu gehört, dass Zeugen beider Seiten aussagen können, belastende und entlastende Aussagen gesammelt und Wahrheitsfindung unter Waffengleichheit von Verteidigung und Anklage stattfinden kann.

Dem Gericht fehlen bisher die Sanktionsmittel, unwillige Zeugen zur Aussage anzuhalten und Staaten zur Kooperation dabei zu zwingen.

Masha Fedorova untersucht in „Disclosure of Information as an Instrument Ensuring Equality of Arms in International Criminal Proceedings" die Offenlegung von Beweisen im Kontext von internationalen Strafverfahren. Zentrale Schwierigkeit ist, dass die Anklage nicht zur Offenlegung des gesamten Akteninhalts verpflichtet ist. Fedorova argumentiert, dass die Verpflichtung zur Offenlegung von Dokumenten zwar dem Grunde nach besteht, die vage Formulierung der Verpflichtung und die tatsächliche Praxis indes zu großen Herausforderungen für die Verteidigung führen. Die Verteidigung kann sich in vielen Fällen nicht ausreichend auf Verfahren vorbereiten, da viele Dokumente nur kurz vor oder nach den Offenlegungsfristen bei der Verteidigung eingehen. Sanktionen im Falle verspäteter Offenlegung werden selten beziehungsweise gar nicht ausgesprochen. Darüber hinaus können der Schutz von Opfern sowie mögliche Risiken für die nationale Sicherheit ein Offenlegen der Dokumente verhindern. Fedorova vergleicht die Praxis der Offenlegung von Beweisen von ICTY/R sowie IStGH und moniert die regelmäßig verspäteten Offenlegungen auf der einen sowie die Bereitstellung von unsortierten Dokumentenmassen auf der anderen Seite, was die Arbeit der Verteidigung behindert und zum Ungleichgewicht zwischen den beiden Lagern beiträgt. Fedorova hält es in der Konsequenz für unverzichtbar, langfristig zu einem gemeinsamen Dossier-System (case file) überzugehen und auch Strafverfolger im Fall eines Fehlverhaltens persönlich zur Verantwortung zu ziehen.

Eleni Chaitidou und *Elisa Hoven* analysieren in ihrem Aufsatz „The Person's Liberty at stake" den praktischen Umgang mit Haftbefehlen und Vorladungen am Internationalen Strafgerichtshof (IStGH). Das von Chaitidou und Hoven identifizierte Kernproblem ist, dass Verhaftung und Arrest von Verdächtigen die Regel anstatt der eigentlich zu fordernden Ausnahme sind. Theoretische Abhandlungen zum Recht auf persönliche Freiheit werden der Praxis des IStGH gegenübergestellt, Verdächtige wegen Fluchtgefahr oder drohender Beeinflussung des laufenden Verfahrens festzunehmen. Die unzureichende Begründung zahlreicher Haftentscheidungen zeigt, dass ein stärkerer Dialog zwischen Theorie und Praxis nötig ist; dies ist in Anbetracht der Beschneidung elementarer Menschenrechte wie dem Freiheitsrecht des von der Unschuldsvermutung profitierenden Angeklagten besonders relevant.

Die Festlegung der Strafe ist ein zentraler Teil jedes Strafprozesses. In ihrem Artikel „Sentencing at the International Criminal Court" untersucht *Sally Alexandra Longworth* die Entscheidungsprozesse bei der Festsetzung des Strafmaßes am IStGH in den Fällen Lubanga und Katanga. Sie analysiert die strafmildernden und strafschärfenden Aspekte, die vom Gericht bei der Urteilsfindung in Betracht gezogen wurden und vollzieht die Entscheidungsfindungen am IStGH sowie anderer internationaler Straftribunale nach. Sie moniert, dass es an klaren Richtlinien zur Festlegung des Strafmaßes fehlt. Dass dies eine Strafzumessungsverteidigung deutlich erschwert, ist evident. Eine bessere Nachvollziehbarkeit der Strafzumessungsentscheidung wäre in jedem Falle wünschenswert.

Isabel Düsterhöft und *Dominic Kennedy* analysieren in ihrem Artikel „How to Manage the Defence" die „Association of Defence Counsel practicing before the ICTY" (ADC-ICTY) als möglichen Idealtypus einer Verteidigungsvereinigung. Im Fall des Internationalen Strafgerichtshof für das ehemalige Jugoslawien (ICTY) wurde der Verteidigung stets weniger Aufmerksamkeit zuteil als der Strafverfolgung. Die Ankläger verfügten über mehr Ressourcen und größere Anerkennung während der Verteidigung teilweise sogar der Zugang zum Gebäude verwehrt blieb. Die Verteidigung hatte keine permanente Repräsentanz im Gerichtsgebäude und keine gemeinsame Vertretung – alle Verteidigungsteams mussten ihre Ressourcen und Finanzen individuell aushandeln. Die Gründung der ADC-ICTY sollte die Position der Verteidigung im Gesamtgefüge des ICTY stärken. Die Autoren illustrieren, mit einem „Insider"-Blick auf die praktischen Hürden, die Bemühungen der ADC-ICTY, der Verteidigung eine einheitliche Stimme zu verleihen und die Organisation der Verteidigung durch Schulungen etc. zu optimieren, Resümierend wird die ADC-ICTY als eine ideale Struktur für eine unabhängige Organisation von Anwälten vor internationalen Tribunalen gelobt. Der Aufsatz kann daher als Leitfaden für den Aufbau einer erfolgreichen Verteidigervereinigung verstanden werden.

In „Promoting Justice between Independence and Institutional Constraints: The Role of the Office of the Public Counsel of the Defence at the ICC" beschreibt *Philipp Müller* die Einrichtung des Office of the Public Counsel for the Defence (OPCD) am IStGH und dessen Leistungen. Die momentanen Entwicklungen drohen, nach Ansicht des Autors, die bisherige Arbeit zunichte zu machen. Der Autor analysiert die Performanz des OPCD in Verbindung mit seiner Struktur und seiner Beteiligung an Fällen und Prozessen sowie aktuelle Reformbemühungen (ReVision). Der Autor führt dabei drei Gründe an, aus denen das OPCD erschaffen wurde: Zum einen sollte das OPCD die Nachteile kleiner Verteidigungsteams kompensieren, indem es die Arbeit der Verteidigung unterstützt, die Koordination zwischen Verteidigern erhöht und redundanten Tätigkeiten vorbeugt. Zweitens sollte das OPCD die Interessen der Verteidigung vor und während der Verfahren vertreten. Hinzu kommt, dass das OPCD Öffentlichkeitsarbeit/Aufklärungsarbeit gegenüber Nichtregierungsorganisationen, Zivilgesellschaft und Regierungen betreiben sollte, was in den letzten Jahren aus Budgetgründen indes kaum mehr möglich war. Insgesamt wird das OPCD von dem Autor in ein positives Licht gerückt. Dennoch soll ein Teil der Aufgaben in Zukunft von einer Ständigen Unabhängigen Vereinigung von Verteidigern (Permanent Association of Defence Counsel) übernommen werden, deren Einrichtung Müller im Prinzip positiv bewertet. Veränderungen an der momentanen Struktur sieht er indes kritisch: Durch den Wegfall von Kapazitäten für spezielle Recherchen würde das „institutionelle Gedächtnis" entfallen. Zusätzlich würde das Budget der Strafverfolgung auf Kosten des ohnehin geringeren Verteidigungsbudgets anwachsen, was sowohl der Verteidigung als auch der Legitimität des IStGH schaden würde.

Die Facette an Themen, die durch die Beiträge in diesem Sammelband behandelt werden, zeigt, dass ein Verständnis für das Wirken internationaler Strafgerichte – Richterschaft, Anklage und Verteidigung – nur mittels eines *disziplinübergreifenden Dialogs* erreicht werden kann.[6] Internationales Strafrecht ist mehr als nur die Anwendung von Strafgesetzen. Politische Rahmenbedingungen und Zielsetzungen prägen die internationale Rechtsanwendung ebenso wie die – oft vernachlässigten – Anforderungen an Budgetierung, Organisation und mediale Selbstdarstellung. Das Handeln der „Verteidigung in internationalen Strafverfahren" und die zu überwindenden Hürden stehen geradezu sinnbildlich für das Zusammenspiel zwischen rechtlichen, politischen und wirtschaftlichen Einflüssen und eignen sich daher für einen ersten tieferen Einblick in die Materie. Eine Materie, die aufgrund der Zielsetzung internationaler Strafjustiz und der nunmehr auf Dauer angelegten Etablierung des Den Haager Strafgerichtshofs, auch in Friedensforschung und Sicherheitspolitik von Bedeutung ist und noch weiter gewinnen wird.

Teil des Leitbilds des Instituts für Friedensforschung und Sicherheitspolitik an der Universität Hamburg (IFSH) ist es Strategien zur Vermeidung und Minderung kollektiver Gewalt zu analysieren und zu entwickeln. Im Arbeitsprogramm des IFSH werden u.a. folgende Fragen formuliert: „Inwieweit müssen die etablierten Friedenstheorien und -strategien sowie Agenden und Instrumente insbesondere deutscher und europäischer Friedens- und Sicherheitspolitik angesichts der gewandelten Rahmenbedingungen verändert oder angepasst werden? Inwieweit haben traditionelle deutsche und europäische Agenden der Herstellung und Sicherung des Friedens mit ihren konstitutiven Prinzipien – Verrechtlichung und Transnationalisierung, Demokratisierung und Menschenrechtsförderung, Marktwirtschaft und freier Handel – noch Aussicht auf Erfolg?[7] In diesem Kontext kann auch die Betrachtung des Instruments der *internationalen Strafgerichtsbarkeit* betrachtet werden. Sie steht *stellvertretend für die institutionalisierte Verrechtlichung als Voraussetzung für die Beendigung von Gewalt und Friedenskonsolidierung*. Die

6 Vgl. bereits M. Hiéramente, *It's about politics, stupid! Warum das internationale Strafrecht die Friedensforschung braucht*, ZeFKo (2012), S. 173.

7 Institut für Friedensforschung und Sicherheitspolitik an der Universität Hamburg (IFSH), *Mittelfristiges Arbeitsprogramm 2013-2018 „Friedensstrategien heute – Friedens- und Sicherheitspolitik an Bruchstellen der Globalisierung*"; http://ifsh.de/file-IFSH/IFSH/pdf/Publikationen/MAP%202013-2018.pdf, S. 12.

internationalen Strafgerichte stehen geradezu symbolhaft für die Prinzipien Frieden, Gerechtigkeit und Versöhnung; so dass es kaum eine Rolle spielt, dass nur über eine verhältnismäßig geringe Anzahl von Straftätern tatsächlich verhandelt wird.[8]

Wie das Jugoslawien-Tribunal soll der IStGH *zum ersten* insbesondere Kriegsverbrecher bestrafen. Seine Zuständigkeit ist aber nicht auf einen bestimmten Schauplatz und einen begrenzten Zeitraum beschränkt. Wie schon das Internationale Militärtribunal in Nürnberg konzentriert sich der IStGH dabei auf zentrale Verbrechen mit politischem Gehalt: Völkermord, Verbrechen gegen die Menschlichkeit, Kriegsverbrechen und – möglicherweise in Zukunft[9] – Verbrechen gegen den Frieden bzw. der Aggression. *Zum zweiten* sollen unkooperative Regierungen international politisch isoliert (selbst wenn die Festnahme der Akteure nicht durchgesetzt werden kann, sehen sich diese damit immerhin ihrer Bewegungsfreiheit und ihrer politischen Wirkung beraubt) und der internen Opposition gleichzeitig Auftrieb verliehen werden. *Drittens* soll auf diese Weise anderen Regierungen ein erhöhter Rechtfertigungsdruck auferlegt werden, wenn sie mit „Unrechtsstaaten" verkehren, ohne ihren Worten politische Taten folgen zu lassen. *Viertens* sollen Einzelstaaten verstärkt dazu bewegt werden, die oben genannten Kernverbrechen auf nationaler Ebene zu verfolgen, um das Tätigwerden des IStGH zu erübrigen oder sogar zu verhindern. *Fünftens* wird der Gerichtshof als ein weiteres Zeichen der abnehmenden Bedeutung von Nationalstaaten und als ein Schritt in Richtung des Entstehens globaler supranationaler Strukturen gewertet, weg von bloßer Koordination souveräner Einheiten hin zu einer stärker hierarchisierten Weltordnung.[10] Die Einsetzung von internationalen Straftribunalen berührt dabei den harten Kern nationaler Interessen, da sie einerseits die Drohung einschließt, auch höchste Entscheidungsträger strafrechtlich zur Verantwortung zu ziehen, und andererseits Strafrecht als Kernbereich staatlicher Souveränität betrachtet wird.[11]

Fest steht, dass die internationalen Strafgerichte einen signifikanten Beitrag zur Rechtsentwicklung geleistet haben – dies hat sich auch in diesem Band anhand der Untersuchung der Rolle der Verteidigung in den verschiedenen Gerichten gezeigt. Diese Entwicklung ist indes noch nicht abgeschlossen und es zeigen sich weiterhin Aushandlungsprozesse und Verbesserungspotenzial im Bereich der Verteidigung und darüber hinaus. Ebenso wird aufgrund fehlender Vollstreckungsorgane der Gerichte eine hohe Abhängigkeit von der Zusammenarbeit und Kooperationsbereitschaft der beteiligten Staaten deutlich, beispielsweise bei der Einbestellung von Zeugen. Der IStGH steht dabei vor der schwierigen Herausforderung, Frieden und Gerechtigkeit in Einklang zu bringen und für das jeweilige Ansinnen zu werben. Die

8 P. Schneider, *Internationale Gerichtsbarkeit als Instrument friedlicher Streitbeilegung. Von einer empirisch fundierten Theorie zu einem innovativen Konzept* (2003), S. 139.
9 Kreß/von Holtzendorff, *Durchbruch in Kampala*, VN (2010), S. 260.
10 Schneider, supra Fn. 8, S. 131-138.
11 Schneider, supra Fn. 8, S. 123.

Verfolgung von Verletzungen des Völkerrechts in Ländern, in denen Konflikte erst vor Kurzem beigelegt wurden oder sogar noch andauern, kann schließlich die Gefahr bergen, Friedensprozesse zu gefährden. Die Debatte um das Verfahren des IStGH im Sudan zeigt im Grunde eine klare Spaltung in der Weltgemeinschaft. Während westliche Staaten und Nichtregierungsorganisationen das Verfahren des IStGH oftmals als eine Voraussetzung für die Beendigung der Gewalt und einen Erfolg des Friedensprozesses hervorgehoben haben, befürchteten insbesondere einige afrikanische Staaten negative Auswirkungen und sahen im IStGH ein neokolonialistisches Machtinstrument des Westens.

Dies *unterstreicht die Wichtigkeit, die Legitimität der Verfahren nicht zu gefährden*. Wenn (berechtigte) Vorwürfe unfairer Verfahren erhoben werden, erschwert dies zwangsläufig, dass internationaler Strafgerichte ihre Ziele erreichen. Dadurch kann die Logik ausgehebelt werden, dass die Straftribunale individuelle Verantwortlichkeiten feststellen und ahnden, die Aufklärung von Schuld und der Zwang zur Sühne zu Gerechtigkeit führen, um damit schließlich zur Konsolidierung von Frieden beizutragen sowie generalpräventiv weiteren Menschenrechtsverletzungen entgegenzuwirken.[12] Die Wichtigkeit fairer Verfahren liegt auch angesichts einer potenziell destabilisierenden Funktion von Strafprozessen auf der Hand, wie sich beispielsweise auf dem Balkan zeigte, als Forderungen des ICTY nach Auslieferung für politische Unruhe sorgten und Massendemonstrationen und Regierungskrisen zur Folge hatten.[13] Kurzum: Die Herausforderungen der internationalen Strafjustiz sind enorm. Umso wichtiger erscheint es mit Verve für die Durchführung, gerechter, fairer und transparenter Verfahren einzutreten, (auch) um weitere Angriffspunkte für die ohnehin oft kritisch gesehenen internationalen Strafgerichte zu vermeiden.

Zusammenfassend können *vier wesentliche Herausforderungen* für die internationale Strafjustiz identifiziert werden, für die keine Patentlösungen zur Verfügung stehen: (1) Ausgleich zwischen Frieden und Gerechtigkeit in Krisenregionen, (2) Einbeziehung der Bevölkerung und nationaler Gerichte, (3) effektive Staatenkooperation und Stärkung einer gemeinsamen Weltordnung und (4) Vermeidung parteilicher Strafverfolgung der Anklage unterstützt durch faire Verfahren und effektive Verteidigung.[14] Vor allem der gerade in die neuen, auf Dauer angelegten Räumlichkeiten umgezogene IStGH wird sich in den nächsten Jahren und Jahrzehnten diesen vier Herausforderungen zu stellen haben.

Auch in Zukunft werden die Bestrebungen nach Frieden und Gerechtigkeit nicht immer miteinander in Einklang stehen und strafrechtliche Ermittlungen unter die *Bedingungen der politischen Machbarkeit* gestellt werden.

---

12 P. Schneider, *Menschenrechtsschutz durch Internationale Strafgerichte: Nützlich oder schädlich? Wirksam oder ineffektiv?* (2008), S. 81, 85, 93-97.

13 Schneider, supra Fn. 12, S. 89.

14 Schneider, supra Fn. 12, S. 95.

Mag der IStGH zwar selbst wiederholt seine vermeintlich unpolitische Haltung betonen; ohne politische Unterstützung sind indes auch der Anklagebehörde um die Chefanklägerin Fatou Bensouda – jedenfalls rein faktisch – die Hände gebunden. Die Tatsache, dass zahlreiche Ermittlungsverfahren – z.B. im Kongo, in Libyen, im Sudan und in der Zentralafrikanischen Republik – sowie Vorermittlungen – z.B. im Irak, in Palästina, in Afghanistan und in der Ukraine – zentrale Krisenregionen dieser Welt betreffen, lässt vermuten, dass die Debatte „*Peace through Justice*" oder „*Peace versus Justice*" auch in Zukunft wiederholt aufflammen wird. Die politische Natur der angeklagten Taten und die Rolle der Angeklagten als (ehemalige) Staatsoberhäupter, Regierungschefs oder Minister wird es – gerade aufgrund des Fokus des IStGH auf die Verfolgung der „most responsibles" – mit sich bringen, dass eine Entkopplung von den Realitäten der Weltpolitik nicht möglich sein wird und dass das Den Haager Gericht noch häufig dem Vorwurf der Instrumentalisierung wird ausgesetzt sein.

Eine Herausforderung wird es auch sein, die *betroffene Bevölkerung* effektiv an den Verfahren und der Aufarbeitung der Vergangenheit zu *beteiligen*. Als Zeugen und Opfer werden einige Betroffene den Weg in die Niederlande auf sich nehmen können/müssen. Weitere werden über die Outreach-Programme bzw. die Öffentlichkeitsarbeit des Gerichts direkt vor Ort über das Werken und Wirken des IStGH informiert werden. Eine effektive Aufarbeitung erfordert allerdings eine stärkere Einbindung der nationalen und lokalen Institutionen, die örtlich, sprachlich und personell näher an der Bevölkerung agieren und sich den unmittelbaren Konflikten und Straftaten zuwenden können, anstatt, wie in den IStGH-Verfahren, die Verantwortlichkeit der Führungsspitze zu analysieren. Eine Aufarbeitung vor Ort erlaubt zudem pragmatische Ansätze, die über den engen Fokus des Strafrechts hinausgehen oder diesen sogar – etwa im Rahmen von Wahrheits-und Versöhnungs- oder Historikerkommissionen – ersetzen.

Eine Konfliktbewältigung oder gar Befriedung kann einem internationalen Strafgericht allein nicht abverlangt werden. Damit ein Gericht die diesem zukommende Rolle auch erfüllen kann, bedarf es zudem einer *stärkeren Unterstützung des gesamten Gerichtshofs*. Richter, Anklage und Verteidigung – mithilfe der für den praktischen Ablauf notwendigen aber in der medialen Wahrnehmung unbeachteten Kanzlei – sind auf eine umfangreiche Staatenkooperation angewiesen. Beweise müssen gesammelt werden, Zeugen gefunden und eine Reise nach Den Haag ermöglicht werden, per Haftbefehl gesuchte Beschuldigte festgesetzt und eine Aufnahme des Verurteilten – und auch des Freigesprochenen – nach Abschluss des Verfahrens garantiert werden. Mangels umfassender Ermittlungsbefugnisse des IStGH-Personals und aufgrund der stets bestehenden Ressourcenknappheit wird ein internationales Strafgericht nur so gut sein, wie es die Mitgliedstaaten erlauben. Eine umfassende Staatenkooperation ist unerlässlich. Doch darf eine solche keinesfalls in Form eines blinden Gehorsams oder gar einseitig mit der Anklagebehörde erfolgen. Es gehört auch zur Aufgabe der heute 123 Mitgliedstaaten, die Wahrung elementarer Verfahrensfairness zu gewährleisten und vom Gericht einzufordern. Dies impliziert, dass Kooperationsanfragen des Gerichts nur im Rahmen des Status beantwortet und gegebenenfalls verweigert werden müssen.

Zu einer umfassenden Kooperation gehört ebenfalls, dass auch *Anfragen der Verteidigung* – gegebenenfalls vermittelt über die Organe des Gerichts – *umfassend und zeitnah beantwortet* und den Verteidigungsteams Ermittlungen in Tatortnähe, die Kontaktaufnahme mit Zeugen und – man erinnere an den Fall der in Libyen in Haft genommenen Verteidiger – persönliche Sicherheit garantiert werden. Die Möglichkeit, die rechtlichen Interessen der Beschuldigten durch *professionelle Verteidiger* (zumeist ein Team von drei bis fünf Personen) wahrnehmen zu lassen, ist im Rahmen von rechtlich und tatsächlich zutiefst komplexen Verfahren eine *Grundvoraussetzung für ein faires Verfahren.* Das Gericht und die Mitgliedstaaten der „Versammlung der Vertragsstaaten" haben dafür Sorge zu tragen, dass auch in der Praxis den prozessualen Rechten der Verteidigung ausreichend Rechnung getragen wird. Es reicht dabei nicht aus, wenn seitens der Richter auf die Einhaltung der Prozessregeln im Gerichtssaal geachtet wird. *Um ein faires Verfahren zu gewährleisten und dem Eindruck von „show trials" entgegenzusteuern, bedarf es einer ausreichenden Finanzierung, öffentlicher Unterstützung im Rahmen der Sachverhaltsermittlung sowie der Möglichkeit an der Fortgestaltung des Projekts „Internationaler Strafgerichtshof" aktiv mitzuwirken.* Der Angeklagte ist als Paria der Weltgemeinschaft kein prädestiniertes Objekt für politische und mediale Unterstützung. Umso mehr bedarf es einer aktiven Auseinandersetzung mit der Frage, *wie in derart politisch, medial und emotional aufgeladenen Verfahren eine effektive Verteidigung gewährleistet* werden kann. Als Verfechter des Rechtsstaats schulden wir dies; dieser Sammelband soll einen kleinen Beitrag dazu leisten.